WORLD MARKETS OF TOMORROW

WORLD MARKETS OF TOMORROW

Economic Growth; Population Trends
Electricity and Energy; Quality of Life

By
FREMONT FELIX

HARPER & ROW, PUBLISHERS

LONDON, NEW YORK, EVANSTON, SAN FRANCISCO

Copyright © 1972 by Fremont Felix
All Rights Reserved
No part of this book may be used or reproduced in any manner whatsoever without written permission except in the case of brief quotations embodied in critical articles and reviews

First published 1972
Published by Harper & Row Ltd
28 Tavistock Street, London WC2E 7PN

Standard Book Number 06-318003-0

Printed in Great Britain by
William Clowes & Sons Limited
London, Colchester and Beccles

Preface

In presenting this '186 Countries Review', we feel in a position akin to that of a theatre producer who has assembled an extraordinary cast of international stars, all of whom would deserve individual billing but can only be given brief appearances, to present, each time, a different facet of their personalities.

We hope that the reader, when he occasionally picks up this volume from his reference shelf, will feel, with Richmond in *Richard II*, that:

The weary sun has made a golden set
And by the bright track of his fiery car
Gives token of a goodly day tomorrow.

(Act V, Scene III)

Acknowledgement

The bibliography, which follows the 'Areas and Countries Profiles of Growth', includes the specific United Nations Statistical Publications from which we have drawn practically all our basic data, but we would like specially to acknowledge here, the constant contribution to world knowledge and progress thus provided by the United Nations.

Contents

Preface	v
Acknowledgement	vi
List of Tables	xiii
List of Charts	xv
Alphabetical List of 186 Countries	xvii

PART ONE

CHAPTER ONE Prologue 3
   Our Aims 3
   With What Degree of Credibility Can 153 Country Forecasts be Regarded? 5
   In the Present Time of Uncertainty and Unrest, Why Make Projections? 6
   Why Carry Projections to the Year 2020? 6

CHAPTER TWO Introducing 186 Countries 8
   Alphabetical List of Countries, Respective Profile Pages . . 8
   Total and Arable Areas 8
   Population 13
   Population Density 13
   Increase in Population 13
   Per Capita GNP in 1967 18
   Can *Per Capita* Averages be Regarded as Meaningful . . 18
   Conversion of Currencies into U.S.$ at the Official Rate of Exchange   20

CHAPTER THREE Aspects of Life 21
   Number of Students in Institutions of Higher Learning . . 21
   Charts can be Fun 22

Forecasting Increase in College Attendance	25
Hospital Beds	26
Daily Newspapers Circulation	29
Telephones in Use	30
Television Receivers per 1,000 Inhabitants	32
Tourist Receipts	35
Passenger Automobiles in Use	36
Crude Steel Consumption	38

CHAPTER FOUR Economic Growth 41

Gross National Product	42
Gross National Product *Per Capita*	42
Per Capita Economic Growth	42
How is Economic Growth Projected?	43
Patterns of *Per Capita* Economic Growth and Energy Consumption	43
Patterns of Growth: How Were these Patterns Obtained?	44
Justification of the Validity of the Approach Used: World Median Pattern	48
Family of Growth Patterns	49
Are these Patterns Empirical or Theoretical?	49
Per Capita GNP Values which would Correspond to more than 10,000 KEC	51
Justification of the Patterns	51
Global Chart of Patterns of Growth	52
Patterns of Growth for All Countries	52
Pattern Indexes of Growth for All Countries	54
Are Pattern Indexes of Growth Comparable to Percentage Growth Rates?	56
How Sensitive is the Selection of the Appropriate Pattern?	56
Which are the Economically Fastest Growing Countries?	57
Why Cannot Constant Growth Rates be Maintained Indefinitely?	57
Tapered Character of the Pattern	58
Comparison of Projections of GNP *Per Capita* in the Year 2000	59
Are Growth Patterns Restrictive?	60
Any Course of Economic Growth Can be Dissected into Segments of Patterns	60
Why Introduce so Complex a Pattern Notion?	62

CHAPTER FIVE Factors of Growth 64

Why do Growth Rates Differ?	64
Sources of Growth	65

Contents

Index of Growth *v.* Investment Ratio	67
Do High Rates of Population Increase Slow Down *Per Capita* Economic Growth?	70
Natural Resources as a Stimulus to Growth	72
Exports Stimulate Growth Through Industrialization Strategy	73
How Wide is the Range which, at a given stage of Development Encompasses Manageable Rates of Growth?	75
What is Par for the Course?	75
Growth Rates which are quite Desirable for Industrialized Countries may be totally Inadequate for Developing Countries	77
What is the Most Desirable Rate of Growth?	77
Can, or Should, Individuals, Groups, Contribute to Improved Nature Growth?	78
Per Capita GNP	79
How are Different Degrees of Inflation Accounted for?	80
GNP Deflator	80
Continuous Records of GNP Deflators for 65 Countries of the World	82
How have Countries Rated in terms of Inflation, from 1958 to 1967?	83
GNP and GNP *Per Capita* Series from 1948 to 1967 for each Country	84
Establishing the Growth Pattern for each Country	84
Contribution of the Analyses of Energy Use to the Forecasting of Economic Growth	84
Steps in the Process of Determining the Pattern Index of Growth of GNP, also of Energy	86
How can a GNP Forecast in terms of Constant 1967 U.S.$ be Converted in Constant 1971 Francs?	87
Many Limitations have Prevented us from Describing the Method used in still greater detail	87
Comparison of *Per Capita* GNP in 1967 and in 1990	87
Lower and Upper Boundaries of *Per Capita* GNP in 1990	89
Countries which Will Achieve the Greatest Gains in Rank of *Per Capita* GNP	90
Countries which Will Achieve the Greatest Gains in Percentage Points?	91

CHAPTER SIX **'Have' and 'Have Not' Countries** . . . 92

Can the Gap between the Highly-Industrialized and the Developing Countries be Minimized? 92

First and Second United Nations Development Decades . . 94
How Can the Industrialized Nations Speed-Up the Growth of the
    Developing Countries? 96
'Have' and 'Have Not' Countries 97

CHAPTER SEVEN Population Stabilization 99

Why Make Assumptions as to the Course of the Population Growth
    Rate for Each Country? 99
Net Per Cent Increase in Population for Each Country . . 99
Selection of a Reducer of the Rate of Population Increase . . 100
Where would Population Stabilize in this Assumption? . . 101
A Graduated Reduction of the Rate of Population Increase Must be
    Achieved 106

CHAPTER EIGHT Gross National Product 109

Where Can GNP Projections for any Country be found in this
    Volume? 109
All GNP Data is on the Basis of 1967 U.S.$ 109
Comparison of the Forecasted Growth of the GNP for All Countries . 111
Recapitulation of GNP and Population Tables and Charts . . 111
GNP in 1990 125
Gains in Ranking of their GNP 125
GNP Gains in Billion U.S.$ 127

CHAPTER NINE Gross Area Product and Gross World Product . 128

Determination of Gross World Product 128
What will be the Changes in the Major Areas' Share of the Gross
    World Product in the Next 20 Years? 129
Which of the Major World Markets, in Terms of Economic Areas, Will
    Have the Most Dynamic Growth in the Next 20 Years? . . 131
Which World Markets Will be the Largest Gainers in Absolute Terms? 133
Profiles of Growth for 150 Countries 134
All the World Markets of the Future 136

CHAPTER TEN Energy, Electricity and the Environment . . 139

World Growth Projections of Consumption of Energy, etc. . . 139
Control of the Environment 143

Contents   xi

    Total Use of Energy for All Countries of the World . . . 143
    Per Capita Use of Energy for All Countries of the World . . 146
    What is the Cost of Energy? 148
    How does the Amount of Energy Used for the Production of $1 of GNP Vary Throughout All Countries of the World? . . . 148
    Comparisons of Growth Trends of GNP and Energy . . . 152
    Use of Electricity 157
    Installed Electric Capacity in All Countries of the World . . 157
    Electricity and the Environment 157
    At its *Per Capita* GNP Level, the United States is a Minimum User of Electricity and of Energy in Relation to the GNP these Contribute to Generate 167
    Optimum Use of Energy Resources 173

CHAPTER ELEVEN **Quality of Life** 174

    Zero Economic Growth 174
    No Industrialized Nation has the Option to Retire into Pastoral Utopia 175
    Restraint in future Growth is Implicit in our Pattern . . . 175
    Technology and Environmental Disruption 176
    Economic Density 178
    Energy's Contribution to the Quality of Life 178
    Recycling 178
    Will Anti-Pollution Expenditures Lower the Productivity or Prove Inflationary? 180
    What is the Full Cost to Society of Energy? 181
    Our Challenge 182
    Creation of New Communities 184
    A Global Development Strategy is Needed 185
    The Greening of the World 185
    How Will These Increased Incomes that we have been Projecting be Used? 186

PART TWO

CHAPTER TWELVE **Individual Country Profiles** . . . 191

CHAPTER THIRTEEN **Maps** 353

CHAPTER FOURTEEN **Complementary Notes** . . . 359
    Use of SemiLogarithmic and Log-Log Scale Paper for Charts . . 359
    Use of Exchange Rates to Derive GNP *Per Capita* in U.S.$ Equivalents 359
    Gross Domestic Products and Other Aggregates Related to Gross National Product 360

CHAPTER FIFTEEN **Bibliography** 363

List of Tables

Table
I Alphabetical list of 186 countries *Profile Page*
II Areas in square kilometers
IIIa Arable land and land under permanent crops—square kilometers
IIIb Summary of arable and other land uses for major areas of the world
IV Populations—1969
V Population density—inhabitants per square kilometer—1967
VI Births and deaths per 100 population—1969
VII Average annual population growth rate: 1961-1967
VIII 1967 Gross national product *per capita* in U.S.$
IX Number of third-level students per 100,000 population
X Hospital beds per 1,000 population
XI Daily newspapers circulation per 1,000 inhabitants
XII Telephones in use—1968
XIII Television receivers—1968
XIVa Tourist receipts—1968 (in U.S.$ at exchange rate)
XIVb Tourist receipts as percent of gross national product
XV Passenger automobiles in use—1968
XVI Crude steel consumption in kilograms per inhabitant—1968
XVII GNP *per capita* growth pattern and recorded 6-year annual increase
XVIII Investment ratio: gives domestic capital formation as a percentage of GNP
XIX Reciprocal of GNP deflator for 65 countries, referred to 1967 as 1.00
XIXa GNP *per capita* in 1990 compared to 1967

List of Tables

XIXb	Range of 1990 GNP/capita (in 1967 U.S. $) and of percent yearly increases (1967-1990)
XX	Alphabetical listing showing GNP ranking in 1967
XXI	GNP *per capita*, population, GNP, in 1967-1980-2000-2020
XXIIa	GNP in 1990 compared to 1967
XXIIb	GAP in 1967 and 1990 compared for 11 major areas of the world
XXIIc	World growth projections: use of energy including electricity, hydro and nuclear
XXIII	Total use of energy-billion kilograms energy equivalent coal—1968
XXIV	Kilograms of energy equivalent coal *per capita*—1968
XXV	GNP U.S. $ kilogram of energy equivalent coal and reciprocal—1967
XXVI	Coefficient of elasticity—GNP pattern: energy pattern—1967
XXVII	Installed electric capacity kilowatts—1968
XXVIII	Use of electricity—billion killowatt-hours—1968
XXIX	Use of electricity—kilowatt-hour *per capita*—1968
XXX	Kilowatt-hours per U.S. $ of gross national product—1967
XXXI	Economic density: 1967 GNP U.S. $ per square kilometer

List of Charts

Chart	
1	Number of students per 100,000 population in 1967
2	Number of hospital beds
3	Daily newspapers circulation
4	Number of telephones in use
5	Number of television receivers
6	Automobiles in use
7	Crude steel consumption
8	Annual percent increase *v.* stage of growth
9	Doubling time in years in term of annual rate of increase
10	Growth curve in term of years, derived from basic pattern
11	Patterns of growth
12	Growth patterns for all countries
13	Illustration of economic growth according to different patterns
14	Investment ratio
15	GNP *per capita* in 1990
16a	$100 to $1200 *per capita* range—Selected countries in Group A
16b	$100 to $1200 *per capita* range—Selected countries in Group B
16c	$1200 to $14000 *per capita* range—Selected countries in Group A
16d	$1200 to $14000 *per capita* range—Selected countries in Group B
17	Population growth curves
18	World population from A.D. 800 and projection to the year 2020
19	World population from 1940 and projection to the year 2125

List of Charts

20	Population for the 50 most important countries projected to the year 2020
21a	0.06 to 12.5 billion $ GNP range—Selected countries in Group A
21b	0.06 to 12.5 billion $ GNP range—Selected countries in Group B
21c	12.5 to 4500 billion $ GNP range—Selected countries in Group A
21d	12.5 to 4500 billion $ GNP range—Selected countries in Group B
22	Gross world product and world population projected to 2020
23	Contribution of the primary sources in meeting world's energy needs
24	Percentage share of primary sources in meeting world's energy needs
25	Elasticity ratio: growth of GNP related to growth of energy
26	Growth in *per capita* use of electricity in Norway, U.S.A. and France
27	Growth of use of electricity in the U.S.A. projected to 2250
28	Yearly increase in the use of electricity in the U.S.A.
29	Growth of *per capita* electricity, energy and GNP in the U.S.A. projected to 2080
30	Contents of electricity per $ of GNP v. kilowatt-hours *per capita*
31	Contents of electricity per $ of GNP, v. GNP *per capita*
32	Contents of energy per $ of GNP, v. GNP *per capita*
33	Future trend, for the U.S.A. of contents of energy and electricity per $ of GNP

Foreword

An enormous amount of work has gone into this book, which offers a wide spectrum of usefulness and a variety of attractions.

In the first place, merely glancing through the pages shows that here is a most convenient guide to the current basic economic features of the many countries of the world, a well-organized reference book which one wants to have on one's desk. Furthermore, the comparative tables which are one form of the presentation are accompanied by enlightening remarks. Let me give just one example.

Table XXIV ranks the countries according to the consumption of energy *per capita*. Now, facing this table, the author mentions that adequate nourishment of the body requires, per head, an intake equivalent to the burning of 130 kgs of coal per year. This 'fuelling' of the body is, of course, not included in the figures relative to the fuelling of the economy and, as is well known, adequate intake of food is in most cases not attained and, in some cases, exceeded. But, by spelling out, in this place, standard requirements for 'the fuelling of the body', the author suggests that here is a meaningful yardstick for assessing the fuelling of the economy, and the reader is impelled to take his pencil and work out that, in the case of the United States, the fuelling of the economy absorbs 79 times as much energy as is required for the fuelling of bodies, while, in the case of both China and Brazil, the ratio is 3.5 times. It is less than that in the case of as many as 82 countries; indeed, in the case of 39 countries the fuelling of the economy is less than the equivalent of what is required for proper nourishment.

It is an appealing characteristic of the author that he thus stimulates the reader into following up hints. He guides with a delicate touch; thus, after we have been astonished to find, in the same Table XXIV, that consumption of energy *per capita* is as high in the Bulgarian economy as in the French, we are prepared for the following table which brings out the wide spread of countries in terms of the ratio between energy consumption and GNP, and we are then eager for his commentaries which are concise and loaded with substance. Fremont Felix makes an important contribution to our grasp of the present, which would, by itself, make his book valuable.

But his purpose is far more ambitious: it is to present long-range estimates of economic growth for all the various countries and areas. I happen to be distrustful of long-range estimates and dissatisfied with the GNP concept; that I should nonetheless preface this book testifies to the keen interest aroused by the originality of Fremont Felix's treatment.

This volume offers to the reader tables and charts, data and forecasts; but above all it offers the excitement of following the workings of a bold and stimulating mind.

BERTRAND DE JOUVENEL

To Alice, whose constant inspiration has created this book.

Author's Notes

Short as the passage of time has been since the manuscript of this book was handed to the printers, momentous political developments have occurred, new perspectives have been opened in world economy, renewed emphasis has been placed on potential perils to the environment.

Reassuring as it was to a punctilious author to see that the building blocks detailed throughout the text provide the desired framework for appraising new trends and for quantifying their impact, it was deemed worthwhile to present in these 'stop-press' notes an immediate introduction to our method of grading the markets of tomorrow and to its applicability under changing conditions, also some comments on recent 'survival' scares.

PER CAPITA RATING OF ECONOMIC GROWTH

Table 00 updates Table XVII (on page 55) and ranks all countries in dynamism of *per capita* economic growth as measured by our pattern index of economic growth which is likely to vary but little over long periods. At this time, we shall mention, only, that the conventional measure of growth, percent increase from one year to the next, shown in the column at the right as annual increase from 1970 to 1975, cannot achieve comparable validity, neither for comparison between countries, nor for the assessment of a country's growth at various stages of its development. The ranking in Table 00 calls attention to a number of 'growth countries' such as Zambia, Ivory Coast, Surinam, U.S. Virgin Islands, Reunion, Brazil, Gabon, Greece, Hong Kong, Iran, Singapore, Taiwan; etc. Supplementing our references in the Bibliography and in the text, we are making added mention here of the unparalleled contribution of the World Bank to the correction of economic imbalances throughout the world.

1970 TO 1975 INCREASE IN YEARLY GNP

Table 0 combines market size and dynamism of growth into one yardstick, GNP in 1975 less GNP in 1970, giving a direct comparison of market growth over a 5-year period.

For the 153 countries rated in descending order, the top places are well-known but, further down the line, a number of challenging market implications will appear.

For *Mainland China*, the economic potential of which has been the subject of greatly increased speculation since President Nixon's visit, the growth pattern we have presented on page 217 should remain valid until revisions prove advisable on the basis of the new economic data which will become increasingly available. We forecast that Mainland China, in sixth position, just ahead of the United Kingdom, will represent 3.25% of the total world market.

In addition to individual countries' market assessments, Table 0 makes it easy to evaluate, in a matter of seconds, the total growth potential of any economic or geographic group:

For the *Europe of Ten*, we total 134.14, as we go down, starting with West Germany (36.8) continuing with France (34.0), the United Kingdom (24.4), Italy (22.0), the Netherlands (6.36), Belgium and Luxembourg (4.40), Denmark (3.40), Norway (2.08) and concluding with Ireland (0.70). This places the Europe of Ten three-quarters of the way from the U.S.A. to the U.S.S.R.

USE OF ENERGY AND QUALITY OF LIFE

In recent months, there has probably been no area of public interest where misinformation has run as wild as in the forecasting of the growth of energy use throughout the world. 'Exponential growth', meaning that the current rates, expressed in yearly percent increase, would be maintained, decade after decade, has been blithely invoked *and* computerized to prove that within the next hundred years, unless radically drastic steps of incalculable consequences are taken, civilisation and life on earth are doomed.

In Chapter Ten, the growth in energy use as related to economic growth is discussed in great detail but, because of the apocalyptic implications of the exponential growth syndrome, we have added, on page 188, Table XXXII which gives for each country the energy growth pattern index, comparable to the economic growth pattern index shown in Table 00 and in Table XVII.

Author's Notes xxi

The reader who has familiarized himself with the pattern approach developed in Chapters Four and Five will be able, in a few minutes, by using the applicable curve of Chart 12, to obtain energy use figures, paralleling the GNP values in the profile page, for any one of 153 countries.

IGNORING THE CORRECTIVE AND CREATIVE POTENTIAL OF NEW TECHNOLOGIES

The prophets of exponential doom compound the errors in their argumentation by ignoring that technology grows in inventiveness and innovation at rates which defy imagination.

To assume that the impact of pollution and that the exhaustion of earth's resources will continue to amplify at rates overshadowing today's pace is to overlook that, in the less than three quarters of a century that has elapsed since the Wright brothers' first flight, technology has literally lifted man to the moon.

A new dimension has indeed been added to man's thinking. In *World Markets of Tomorrow* we hope to have included ample material and data to help arrive at the right answers to the questions that man's new sense of responsibility for the quality of life on earth will raise.

London, April 1972 FREMONT FELIX

Errata

Page 4—Fourteenth line: Read 'plans' not 'plants'.

Page 54—(A) and (B) table: For production reasons, the colour scheme had to be changed: Countries in Africa are white not grey. In Charts 16 and 21 the Western European countries are yellow not purple.

Page 55—In Table XVII, the first column of figures is superseded by those in Table 00. The second column: Recorded 6-year increases in % may be compared with the second column of Table 00: Forecasted 5-year increases in %.

Page 60—Second small print paragraph: Read $300 not $267. Third small print paragraph: Read $375 not $300.

Page 62—Ninth line from the bottom: After 'records' insert 'that'.

Page 68—Chart 14: Delete 'Swaziland' in top center square.

Page 76—Chart 15: Brazil shown in the vertical of $309 in 1967 should be moved up to $1056 in 1990.

Page 82—Sixth line: Read 'deflator' not 'deflector'.

Page 88—Table XIXa: Change Brazil from Position 90 to 70; the five figures in its row to read 1,056   309   79   +9   5.45%.

Page 91—Insert Brazil between Gabon and French Oceania: 5.45%.

Page 104—Chart 18: In the caption, read 2200 not 2020.

Page 106—Sixth line: Read 2200 not 2300.

Pages 112 and 113—For Brazil, in 1980, 2000 and 2020, change the figures to those in Profile Page 203.

Page 126—Table XXIIa: Change Brazil from position 13 to 9; the figures are to read:
    155   26.8   11   +3.

Page 127—Change Brazil figures to: 128 Billion $ and 7.9%.

Page 132—Table: Change Caribbean & Other America from 5.15 to 5.95%.

Page 133—Table: Change Caribbean & Other America: in first column from 347 to 412. In second column from 238 to 303.

World Markets of Tomorrow   xxiii

TABLE 00—Country index of 'per capita' economic growth pattern and equivalent average annual increase 1970-1975

Growth Pattern Index %		1970-75 Annual Increase %	Growth Pattern Index %		1970-75 Annual Increase %	Growth Pattern Index %		1970-75 Annual Increase %
187.50	Japan	7.8		Norway	4.0		El Salvador	6.7
	Romania	7.5		South Africa	6.5		India	5.2
	Libya	13.5	112.50	Sweden	4.0	62.50	Pakistan	5.0
	Trucial Oman	9.5		Trinidad & Tobago	5.9		Peru	5.5
				United Kingdom	3.7		Syria	6.0
181.25	Bulgaria	6.5						
				Cyprus	5.7		Brunei	6.2
168.75	U S S R	6.9	106.25	Netherlands	4.4		Guam	7.7
				Panama Republic	8.1		Guatemala	5.8
162.50	Zambia	10.8		Portuguese Guinea	6.5	56.25	Guinea	6.0
	Qatar	11.7					Philippines	5.7
				Austria	3.9		Sierra Leone	5.0
156.25	Ivory Coast	14.6	100.00	France	4.7		U A R Egypt	5.2
				Ireland	3.7		Uganda	9.2
150.00	Muscat & Oman	9.3						
				Algeria	8.0		Morocco	5.1
	Korea Republic	9.3		Australia	4.3		Nigeria	5.2
143.75	Ryukyu Islands	8.5		Bermuda	4.4	50.00	Tanzania	4.1
	Surinam	7.2	93.75	Iraq	7.2		Togo	5.4
	Yugoslavia	7.0		Liberia	6.4			
				New Caledonia	4.8		Afghanistan	4.8
137.50	Bahama Islands	7.0		Turkey	7.1		Guadeloupe	4.3
	Hungary	5.0				43.75	Niger	7.2
				Communist Asia:			Paraguay	5.5
	East Germany	3.6		Mainland China	5.9			
	West Germany	4.8		North Korea	7.0		Burma	4.5
131.25	Poland	5.1		North Vietnam	7.7		Cameroun	4.3
	Saudi Arabia	8.5	87.50	Mongolia	7.6		Chad	6.6
	Spain	6.8		Congo Brazzaville	6.0		Colombia	5.8
	US Virgin Islands	10.7		French Guyana	8.5		Congo-Kinshasa	5.4
				New Zealand	4.8		Cuba	3.9
130.00	Iceland	5.7		Panama Canal Zone	6.6		Dominican Republic	5.1
				Thailand	7.0		Ecuador	4.9
	Denmark	4.6				37.50	Ghana	3.8
	Finland	4.9		Bolivia	3.3		Honduras	5.4
125.00	French Oceania	8.5		Ceylon	6.8		Indonesia	4.1
	Portugal	6.9		Kuwait	7.4		Kenya	4.9
	Reunion	9.6	81.25	Mexico	7.4		Laos	6.7
	United States	4.3		Mozambique	6.0		Mali	5.2
				Tunisia	6.5		Ruanda	7.1
	Brazil	8.8		Vietnam - South	6.5		Senegal	5.5
	Gabon	7.0					Yemen	6.5
	Greece	6.3	78.75	Ethiopia	7.9			
	Hong Kong	9.0				31.25	Nepal	5.0
118.75	Iran	8.4		Cambodia	6.7		Sudan	4.3
	Italy	5.1	75.00	Malawi	6.8			
	Mauritania	8.8		Malaysia	6.3	28.13	Madagascar	4.0
	Puerto Rico	5.8		Switzerland	4.5			
	Singapore	8.3				25.00	Upper Volta	4.7
	Taiwan	8.2		Angola	5.1		Uruguay	2.6
				Chile	4.7			
	Albania	8.3		Jamaica	5.1		Burundi	4.4
	Bahrain	6.8	68.75	Lebanon	6.5	18.75	Central African Rep	3.6
	Belgium/Luxembourg	3.6		Martinique	5.6			
	Canada	4.3		Nicaragua	6.8		Dahomey	4.3
112.50	Czechoslovakia	3.5		Venezuela	5.5	12.50	Mauritius	2.9
	Israel	6.9						
	Jordan	9.7		Argentina	4.1	9.38	Somalia	4.8
	Malta	5.0	62.50	Barbados	4.0			
				Costa Rica	7.3	6.25	Haiti	2.9

TABLE 0   Increase in yearly GNP between 1970 and 1975 (In billion 1967 U.S $)

United States	210.00	Ivory Coast	1.560	Iceland	0.207		
U S S R	107.50	Saudi Arabia	1.510	Honduras	0.201		
Japan	64.30	Malaysia	1.500	Papua & New Guinea	0.198		
West Germany	36.80	Puerto Rico	1.460	Paraguay	0.176		
France	34.00	North Korea	1.430	Reunion	0.174		
Mainland China	25.20	Peru	1.270	Madagascar	0.168		
United Kingdom	24.40	North Vietnam	1.130	Yemen	0.166		
Italy	22.00	Ethiopia	1.110	Cyprus	0.157		
Brazil	17.10	Zambia	1.070	Uruguay	0.138		
India	16.00	Iraq	1.000	Guinea	0.136		
Canada	15.30	Kuwait	0.990	Mali	0.129		
Mexico	13.20	Morocco	0.900	Niger	0.128		
Spain	12.50	Ceylon	0.860	Bahama Islands	0.115		
Poland	8.30	South Vietnam	0.840	Guadeloupe	0.115		
Roumania	7.58	Singapore	0.780	Liberia	0.113		
Australia	7.20	Syria	0.710	Sierra Leone	0.111		
Netherlands	6.36	Ireland	0.700	Chad	0.109		
Sweden	5.94	Cuba	0.620	Malawi	0.103		
South Africa	5.92	Ghana	0.590	Mauritania	0.101		
Turkey	5.81	Lebanon	0.525	Ruanda	0.101		
Yugoslavia	5.30	Burma	0.500	US Virgin Islands	0.101		
Pakistan	5.05	Guatemala	0.487	Guyana	0.100		
Iran	4.82	Mozambique	0.480	Gabon	0.096		
East Germany	4.80	Cambodia	0.458	Togo	0.087		
Switzerland	4.43	Panama Republic	0.458	French Oceania	0.084		
Belgium & Luxembourg	4.40	Sudan	0.440	Guam	0.083		
Korea Republic	3.90	El Salvador	0.415	Swaziland	0.079		
Philippines	3.80	Nicaragua	0.402	Surinam	0.078		
Argentina	3.70	Albania	0.401	Upper Volta	0.076		
Denmark	3.40	Ecuador	0.400	Muscat & Oman	0.068		
Czechoslovakia	3.27	Southern Rhodesia	0.380	Congo-Brazzaville	0.067		
Venezuela	3.19	Kenya	0.367	Martinique	0.065		
Hungary	2.98	Dominican Republic	0.365	Malta	0.061		
Greece	2.95	Tunisia	0.360	Haiti	0.056		
Indonesia	2.94	Jordan	0.351	Laos	0.054		
Finland	2.80	Nepal	0.350	Portuguese Guinea	0.050		
Thailand	2.61	Afghanistan	0.343	New Caledonia	0.046		
Bulgaria	2.56	Angola	0.328	Panama Canal Zone	0.046		
Austria	2.54	Ryukyu Islands	0.328	Burundi	0.044		
Colombia	2.35	Jamaica	0.322	Somalia	0.040		
Israel	2.33	Tanzania	0.317	Central African Rep	0.038		
Libya	2.32	Trinidad & Tobago	0.310	Dahomey	0.038		
Portugal	2.28	Costa Rica	0.307	Bahrain	0.037		
Tawain	2.26	Uganda	0.278	Windward Islands	0.037		
Norway	2.08	Bolivia	0.268	Bermuda	0.035		
U A R Egypt	2.04	Qatar	0.266	South Yemen	0.034		
Algeria	1.85	Mongolia	0.258	Mauritius	0.031		
New Zealand	1.80	Trucial Oman	0.252	Channel Islands	0.030		
Chile	1.70	Congo-Kinshasa	0.235	Barbados	0.029		
Nigeria	1.68	Cameroun	0.213	Netherlands Antilles	0.027		
Hong Kong	1.63	Senegal	0.211	Brunei	0.024		

Alphabetical List of 186 Countries

TABLE I

Country	Page	Country	Page	Country	Page
Afghanistan	192	*Gibraltar	345	Pakistan	290
Albania	193	*Gilbert & Ellice Isl.	345	Panama	291
Algeria	194	Greece	239	*Panama Canal Zone	292
*American Samoa	340	*Greenland	345	*Papua & NewGuinea	348
*Angola	195	*Guadeloupe	240	Paraguay	293
Argentina	196	*Guam	241	Peru	294
Australia	197	Guatemala	242	Philippines	295
Austria	198	Guinea	243	Poland	296
*Bahama Islands	199	Guyana	244	Portugal	297
Bahrein	200	Haiti	245	*Portuguese Guinea	298
Barbados	201	Honduras	246	*Portuguese Timor	349
Belgium & Lux.	202	*Hong Kong	247	*Puerto Rico	299
*Bermuda	203	Hungary	248	Qatar	300
Bhutan	340	Iceland	249	Reunion	301
Bolivia	204	Ifni	346	Romania	302
Botswana	340	India	250	Ruanda	303
Brazil	205	Indonesia	251	*Ryukyu Islands	304
*British Honduras	341	Iran	252	*SaoTome & Principe	349
*Brit. Solomon Isl.	341	Iraq	253	Saudi Arabia	305
*Brunei	206	Ireland	254	Senegal	306
Bulgaria	207	Isle of Man	346	*Seychelles Isl.	349
Burma	208	Israel	255	Sierra Leone	307
Burundi	209	Italy	256	Sikkim	350
Cambodia	210	Ivory Coast	257	Singapore	308
Cameroun	211	Jamaica	258	Somalia	309
Canada	212	Japan	259	South Africa	310
*Cape Verde Isl.	341	Jordan	260	Southern Rhodesia	312
Centr. Afric. Rep.	213	Kenya	261	Southern Yemen	350
Ceuta & Melilla	342	Korea - North	262	Spain	311
Ceylon	214	Korea - Republic	263	*Spanish Sahara	350
Chad	215	Kuwait	264	Sudan	313
*Channel Islands	342	Laos	265	*Surinam	314
Chile	216	Lebanon	266	Swaziland	351
China - Mainland	217	*Leeward Islands	346	Sweden	315
China - Taiwan	218	Lesotho	347	Switzerland	316
Colombia	219	Liberia	267	Syria	317
*Comoro Islands	342	Libya	268	Tanzania	318
Congo Brazzaville	220	*Macao	347	Thailand	319
Congo Kinshasa	221	Madagascar	269	Togo	320
Costa Rica	222	Malawi	270	Tonga	351
Cuba	223	Malaysia	271	Trinidad & Tobago	321
Cyprus	224	Mali	272	Trucial Oman	322
Czechoslovakia	225	Maldive Islands	347	*Trust Ter.Pacif. Isl.	351
Dahomey	226	Malta	273	Tunisia	323
Denmark	227	*Martinique	274	Turkey	324
Dominican Rep.	228	Mauritania	275	U.A.R. Egypt	325
Ecuador	229	Mauritius	276	Uganda	326
El Salvador	230	Mexico	277	United Kingdom	327
Equatorial Guinea	343	Mongolia	278	United States	328
Ethiopia	231	Morocco	279	Upper Volta	331
*Faeroe Islands	343	Mozambique	280	Uruguay	332
Fiji Islands	343	Muscat & Oman	281	U.S.S.R.	330
Finland	232	Nepal	282	*US Virgin Islands	329
France	233	Netherlands	283	Venezuela	333
*French Guyana	344	*Netherl. Antilles	348	Vietnam - North	334
*French Oceania	234	*New Caledonia	284	Vietnam - South	335
*Fr.T.Afars & Issas	344	*New Hebrides	348	Western Samoa	352
Gabon	235	New Zealand	285	West Irian	352
Gambia	344	Nicaragua	286	*Windward Islands	336
Germany - East	236	Niger	287	Yemen	337
Germany - West	237	Nigeria	288	Yugoslavia	338
Ghana	238	Norway	289	Zambia	339

Dependencies or Juridically Associated Territories

PART ONE

CHAPTER ONE

Prologue

OUR AIMS

We should like this volume to be of interest to a wide range of readers. Although Economic Growth is the central theme, we shall be discussing other aspects of National Growth:

(i) Population increase, for which we shall propose manageable ceilings.
(ii) Use of energy which, together with the use of electricity, we regard as a valid indicator of the stage of economic growth.
(iii) The reciprocal impact, sometimes regarded as conflicting, of Growth and of Quality of Life, and the extent to which both may not only coexist but mutually flourish.

In this first part, a number of global tables, occasionally supplemented by charts, will show how the world's 186 countries compare in many well-known aspects, as well as in some which may be less familiar.

They may better acquaint the reader with all the countries which, together with his own, form what may be the only particle of the universe where beings are striving to make their world a still better 'spaceship' on which to journey into the future.

In the pages facing these tables attention has been drawn to those aspects which might be of special interest. As a rule the sequence of countries has been so arranged that the relevant data is in descending order of magnitude.

Should the reader have difficulty locating a specific country in any table, we suggest that he look up that country in the second (alphabetically arranged) part of the book. This will quickly show the corresponding figure (area, population, etc) and help to place the country in the respective global table.

The second part of the volume is a new kind of reference book: reference for the present and 'reference' for the future for each of 153 countries.

Because even the smallest countries present unusual aspects whether one is interested in potential markets or in remote areas where the quality of life has not been tampered with, we have analysed the potential for growth for many of them. These are presented, the same as the Big-Leaguers, in uniform, alphabetic sequence, from Afghanistan through Zambia.

Since no economic growth data was available for the 33 smallest countries, 1968 profiles for these have been grouped, three to a page, in a separate alphabetical sequence. These are a continuation of the pages which, for the 153 largest countries in terms of GNP, show, in addition to their 1968 profile, growth forecasts at 5-year intervals up to the year 2020.

Demographic and economic growth data, directly applicable to national development plants at Governmental level, as well as to market evaluations, is thus provided for each of the 186 countries for which we have let the record—and also the hopes—speak.

With a complete presentation of the range of *per capita* growth rates which each country is expected to achieve, we hope to show that 3½% real growth in GNP *per capita* for the world as a whole can be substantially exceeded by many of the developing countries.

This should encourage those with low records of growth to date to raise their sights realistically on the basis of the proved achievements of countries with comparable resources in the same geographical areas and at the same present stage of development.

In addition to the extrapolations of economic growth, this volume may show that the same approach can be used to evaluate prospective needs and growth in various aspects of life: university attendance, number of hospital beds, newspaper circulation, use of telephones, television sets, steel, automobiles, estimates of labor force, mile-lanes of highways, hotel rooms, etc.

Judicious extrapolation can similarly be applied to any of the growth areas such as space exploration, scientific and sociological research, etc., which will unfold as our civilization continues to expand in ever-widening fields of human and technological progress.

Obviously, such a method of extrapolation requires that abundant and valid data of a quality comparable to that used here be available. The 'quantum jump' advances being achieved in data-storage and memory systems ensure that this will be achieved.

We should like this volume to bring to many the confidence that the world economy can grow and flourish in a balanced 'synergistic' alliance with an improved quality of life.

The steadily widening investigations of man's impact on nature

Prologue 5

and the environment attest to this problem having become one of the most important issues in the years lying ahead of us.

From the chapters on economic growth and on energy use we shall derive evidence of the range of solutions available to correct those evils against which mankind is rebelling.

In many instances, the analyses and the world-wide comparisons of a broad range of human and economic aspects will restore in true perspective the constructiveness of the relation between man and technology which misinformed concern has distorted. We shall show that, through the full use of resources which continued economic growth—and *only* continued economic growth will make available—solutions will be found not only to prevent further damage to the environment but in many cases to correct past excesses and restore beauty where it has been defaced.

At the end of the volume, grouped under 'Complementary Notes', additional comments are provided for those who may wish a fuller definition or exposé of some of the terms or aspects which may not be of interest to the general reader.

WITH WHAT DEGREE OF CREDIBILITY CAN 153 COUNTRY FORECASTS BE REGARDED?

We would like to answer, in advance, the question that some may ask: How is it possible for the author to present economic projections for 153 countries at a time, when the elaboration of a valid forecast for a single country requires months of work by local teams of economists who have direct access to all the relevant data, programs, etc?

This is explained, in detail, in Chapter Four: Economic Growth, but we can sum it up in a few words, here: For the past twenty years, we have kept our fingers on the economic pulse of each country of the world for which valid growth data was available. (There were eighty of these, initially.)

Our findings, which were recorded in a number of papers[14,15,20,21,36] have developed a global set of growth patterns, spanning the full range of recorded and potential growth rates, encompassing the most highly industrialized as well as the youngest, emerging countries. The forecasted growth of any one country can, with considerable accuracy and in full recognition of its prospects, be unerringly matched to one, and just one, of these patterns.

It is thanks to the combination of a continuing program of economic analyses of all countries and of an original method, universal in its conception yet specific in its application, that it has proved possible to prepare 153 forecasts, each of a validity not only comparable to that of a single, individually prepared, projection but possibly superior.

We say 'possibly superior' because, as the reader may judge from glancing at the fold-out Chart 12, the forecast for each country is a better one because all countries of the world have helped to develop it.

IN THE PRESENT TIME OF UNCERTAINTY AND UNREST, WHY MAKE PROJECTIONS?

Long-term forecasts and projections are valuable at any time because they provide planning tools for governments and industries to allocate wisely natural, financial and human resources.

Current developments are making it even more desirable that 'blueprints for the future' be available—even if they have to be scrapped often.

Concern over the threat to our environment will lead to the establishment of community, metropolitan, state, national and international organizations charged with making crucial decisions involving considerable expenditures.

Forecasts such as we are presenting here have an urgent importance. The most immediate one relates to definite programs for which advance knowledge is vital. For example, in order to anticipate and prepare community reaction to the siting of new electric power plants, the State of Maryland has requested that each utility file a complete list of proposed sites for all the electric power plants they will need for *the next 30 years,* so that they can be proved environmentally acceptable, etc.

This is just one of the many examples which could be cited whereby by presenting to the individuals, to the groups, to the communities who are likely to be directly affected by both near-term and long-range decisions, an advance plan or program, a more receptive attitude will be engendered, a growing willingness to bear the required burdens will be developed.

WHY CARRY PROJECTIONS TO THE YEAR 2020?

There are considerable differences of opinion as to how far into the future it is reasonable to carry extrapolations and forecasts of economic growth.

Prologue

It is generally agreed that business plans should look at least 10 years ahead, and this sets a first 'terminal date' for forecasting.

In trying to pick the 'winners' and the 'losers' in the world economic 'steeplechase', we have used 20 years as a meaningful span of time. The projections which we regard as the most important, from the point of view of helping to formulate long-range plans on a national basis, are those for 1990 in Table XIX and in Chart 15.

Of course, 30 years ahead brings us to the year 2000 with the magic connotation which is inspiring a number of volumes and essays. Practically all our tables and charts are extended to the year 2020 which, as pointed out in a recent speech[22], is not beyond the time-span with which we should be concerned now.

> 'A little thought on the time scales for engineering development will indicate that it takes from 30 to 50 years to bring a new technology from its initial development phase to the stage of exploitation where that technology is playing a major role in our economy. One need only look at the development of aircraft, automobiles, water-cooled power reactors, and many other engineering developments in our civilization to realize the general validity of this thesis.'

A 50-year lead-time is not excessive for the appraisal of the availability into the next century of the mineral and natural resources on which we have been drawing without too much concern about their eventual exhaustion but which we shall be husbanding in a new perspective of conservation and replenishment.

CHAPTER TWO

Introducing 186 Countries

Because of the global scope of this book, we feel it would be useful to provide the reader with identifying and reference information for all countries.

ALPHABETICAL LIST OF COUNTRIES, RESPECTIVE PROFILE PAGES (TABLE I)

Table I has already been presented. This list introduces the cast of countries to be studied in detail. It will be noted that not all of the 'countries' are independent, and that their total number is much greater than those which are members of the United Nations.

Some of these are dependencies, others are juridically associated with independent countries, and all such territories have been identified with an asterisk. Our reason for treating them separately is that they have an independent economic life of their own.

Conversely, Alaska and Hawaii are non-contiguous parts of the United States with whom they are included.

TOTAL AND ARABLE AREAS

Tables II and III continue this alignment of all countries. In order of descending magnitude they list, respectively, the total areas and the arable areas under permanent cultivation.

It will be noted that, whereas for a few of the countries which have the largest areas, both total as well as arable, their rank changes but little in the descending scales of Tables II and III, the relatively desertic countries show wide losses in rank: Algeria 29 places, Sudan 32, U.A.R. Egypt 38, Upper Volta 40, Mongolia 42, Angola 75, Saudi Arabia 98. On the other hand, some countries of Africa and Asia improve their rank substantially from Table II to Table III: Iraq, seat of the Garden of Eden, gains 19 places, Morocco and Nigeria 20, Pakistan 21, Ivory Coast 33.

Introducing 186 Countries

TABLE II—Areas in square kilometers

	WORLD TOTAL	135,721,000						
1	U.S.S.R.	22,402,200	63	Philippines	300,000	125	Lesotho	30,355
2	Canada	9,976,139	64	Southern Yemen	287,683	126	Brit.Solomon Isl.	29,785
3	Communist China	9,561,000	65	Ecuador	283,561	127	Albania	28,748
4	United States	9,363,353	66	Upper Volta	274,200	128	Equatorial Guinea	28,051
5	Brazil	8,511,965	67	New Zealand	268,675	129	Burundi	27,834
6	Australia	7,686,810	68	Gabon	267,667	130	Haiti	27,750
7	India	3,268,090	69	Spanish Sahara	266,000	131	Ruanda	26,338
8	Argentina	2,808,602	70	Yugoslavia	255,804	132	British Honduras	22,965
9	Sudan	2,505,813	71	West Germany	247,973	133	Qatar	22,014
10	Algeria	2,381,741	72	Guinea	245,857	134	Fr.Ter.Afars & Issas	22,000
11	Congo Kinshasa	2,345,409	73	United Kingdom	244,030	135	El Salvador	21,393
12	Greenland	2,175,600	74	Ghana	238,537	136	Israel	20,700
13	Saudi Arabia	2,149,690	75	Romania	237,500	137	New Caledonia	19,000
14	Mexico	1,972,546	76	Laos	236,800	138	Fiji Islands	18,272
15	Libya	1,759,540	77	Uganda	236,037	139	Swaziland	17,363
16	Iran	1,648,000	78	Guyana	214,969	140	Kuwait	16,000
17	Mongolia	1,565,000	79	Muscat & Oman	212,379	141	Potuguese Timor	14,925
18	Indonesia	1,491,564	80	Malaysia	201,320	142	New Hebrides	14,763
19	Peru	1,285,216	81	Senegal	196,192	143	Bahama Islands	11,405
20	Chad	1,284,000	82	Yemen	195,000	144	Gambia	11,295
21	Niger	1,267,000	83	Uruguay	186,926	145	Jamaica	10,962
22	Angola	1,246,700	84	Syria	185,180	146	Lebanon	10,400
23	Mali	1,240,000	85	Cambodia	181,035	147	Cyprus	9,251
24	Ethiopia	1,221,900	86	South Vietnam	173,809	148	Puerto Rico	8,897
25	South Africa	1,221,037	87	Tunisia	164,150	149	Sikkim	7,107
26	Colombia	1,138,914	88	Surinam	163,265	150	Brunei	5,765
27	Bolivia	1,098,580	89	North Vietnam	158,750	151	Trinidad & Tobago	5,128
28	Mauritania	1,030,700	90	Nepal	140,797	152	Cape Verde Isl.	4,033
29	U.A.R. Egypt	1,001,449	91	Greece	131,944	153	French Oceania	4,000
30	Pakistan	946,716	92	Nicaragua	130,000	154	Western Samoa	2,842
31	Tanzania	939,702	93	Czechoslovakia	127,869	155	Reunion	2,510
32	Nigeria	923,773	94	North Korea	120,538	156	Ryukyu Islands	2,196
33	Venezuela	912,050	95	Malawi	117,800	157	Comoro Islands	2,171
34	Mozambique	783,030	96	Cuba	114,524	158	Windward Islands	2,071
35	Turkey	780,576	97	Dahomey	112,622	159	Mauritius	2,045
36	Chile	756,945	98	Honduras	112,088	160	Guadeloupe	1,779
37	Zambia	752,614	99	Liberia	111,369	161	Trust Ter.Pacif.Isl.	1,779
38	Burma	678,033	100	Bulgaria	110,912	162	Ifni	1,500
39	Afghanistan	647,497	101	Guatemala	108,889	163	Panama Canal Zone	1,432
40	Somalia	637,657	102	East Germany	107,901	164	Faeroe Islands	1,399
41	Centr. Afric. Rep.	622,984	103	Iceland	103,000	165	Martinique	1,102
42	Botswana	600,372	104	Korea Republic	98,477	166	Hong Kong	1,034
43	Madagascar	587,041	105	Jordan	97,740	167	Sao Tome & Principe	964
44	Kenya	582,644	106	Hungary	93,030	168	Netherl. Antilles	961
45	France	547,026	107	Portugal	91,971	169	Leeward Islands	907
46	Thailand	514,000	108	French Guyana	91,000	170	Gilbert & Ellice Isl.	886
47	Spain	504,750	109	Austria	83,849	171	Tonga	699
48	Cameroun	475,442	110	Trucial Oman	83,600	172	Bahrain	598
49	Papua & New Guinea	461,691	111	Panama	75,650	173	Isle of Man	588
50	Sweden	449,793	112	Sierra Leone	71,740	174	Singapore	582
51	Morocco	445,050	113	Ireland	70,283	175	Guam	549
52	Iraq	434,924	114	Ceylon	65,610	176	Barbados	430
53	West Irian	412,781	115	Togo	56,000	177	Seychelles Isl.	376
54	Paraguay	406,752	116	Costa Rica	50,700	178	US Virgin Islands	344
55	Southern Rhodesia	389,361	117	Dominican Rep.	48,734	179	Malta	316
56	Japan	369,765	118	Bhutan	47,000	180	Maldive Islands	298
57	Congo Brazzaville	342,000	119	Denmark	43,069	181	American Samoa	197
58	Finland	337,009	120	Switzerland	41,288	182	Channel Islands	195
59	Norway	324,219	121	Portuguese Guinea	36,125	183	Bermuda	53
60	Ivory Coast	322,463	122	Taiwan	35,961	184	Ceuta & Melilla	31
61	Poland	312,520	123	Netherlands	33,612	185	Macao	16
62	Italy	301,225	124	Belgium & Lux.	33,099	186	Gibraltar	6

TABLE IIIa—Arable land and land under permanent crops—square kilometers

#	Country	Area	#	Country	Area	#	Country	Area
1	U.S.S.R.	2,243,000	65	Vietnam Republic	28,370	129	Guyana	1,950
2	United States	1,764,400	66	Ghana	28,350	130	Brit. Solomon Isl.	1,450
3	India	1,637,200	67	U.A.R. Egypt	28,010	131	Trinidad & Tobago	1,390
4	China	1,093,540	68	Finland	27,610	132	Gabon	1,270
5	Canada	434,040	69	Denmark	27,090	133	New Guinea	1,140
6	Australia	414,610	70	Mozambique	26,490	134	Mauritius	1,040
7	Argentina	330,070	71	Peru	26,250	135	Comoro Islands	900
8	Brazil	297,600	72	West Malaysia	26,240	136	Western Samoa	900
9	Pakistan	282,140	73	Ecuador	25,960	137	New Caledonia	800
10	Turkey	266,010	74	Libya	25,110	138	New Hebrides	700
11	Mexico	238,170	75	Korea Republic	23,190	139	Luxembourg	680
12	Nigeria	217,950	76	Nepal	22,660	140	Brunei	660
13	Spain	204,820	77	Togo	21,600	141	French Polynésia	640
14	France	198,160	78	Cuba	20,440	142	Reunion	620
15	Poland	154,940	79	Vietnam North	20,180	143	Tonga	550
16	Burma	160,870	80	Ceylon	19,800	144	Pacific Islands	530
17	Italy	151,950	81	Uruguay	19,570	145	Ryukyu Islands	510
18	Indonesia	126,970	82	Korea North	18,940	146	Guadeloupe	490
19	Ethiopia	125,250	83	Rhodesia	18,370	147	British Honduras	470
20	South Africa	120,580	84	Austria	16,720	148	Surinam	450
21	Tanzania	117,020	85	Kenya	16,700	149	Gilbert & Ellice Isl.	410
22	Iran	115,930	86	Dahomey	15,460	150	Papua	320
23	Niger	115,010	87	Guatemala	14,980	151	Martinique	320
24	Thailand	114,150	88	Ireland	11,940	152	Cape Verde Isl.	300
25	Romania	105,600	89	Jordan	11,400	153	Soa Tome & Principe	300
26	Upper Volta	96,640	90	Dominican Rep.	10,670	154	Barbados	260
27	Ivory Coast	88,590	91	Burundi	10,080	155	Antigua	260
28	Philippines	85,460	92	Ruanda	9,950	156	Isle of Man	230
29	Yugoslavia	82,460	93	Somalia	9,570	157	St. Lucia	210
30	Germany Fed. Rep.	81,790	94	Paraguay	9,470	158	Niue Islands	200
31	Morocco	79,000	95	Netherlands	9,130	159	St. Vincent	180
32	Afghanistan	78,440	96	China Taiwan	9,000	160	Dominica	170
33	Iraq	74,960	97	Angola	9,000	161	Seychelles Islands	170
34	United Kingdom	73,820	98	Belgium	8,860	162	Grenada	160
35	Mali	72,000	99	Nicaragua	8,730	163	St.Kitts Nevis Anguilla	160
36	Congo Kinshasa	72,000	100	Norway	8,430	164	Malta	160
37	Sudan	71,000	101	Honduras	8,230	165	West Berlin	140
38	Chad	70,000	102	Laos	8,000	166	Hong Kong	130
39	Algeria	67,870	103	New Zealand	7,820	167	Singapore	130
40	Centr. Afric. Rep.	59,000	104	Sarawak	7,000	168	Bahamas	130
41	Syria	58,610	105	El Salvador	6,480	169	Guam	120
42	Senegal	57,220	106	Namibia	6,420	170	East Berlin	110
43	Japan	56,840	107	Congo Brazzaville	6,300	171	Cook Islands	100
44	Hungary	56,130	108	Costa Rica	6,220	172	American Samoa	80
45	Czechoslovakia	53,530	109	Panama	5,640	173	Channel Islands	60
46	Venezuela	52,140	110	Albania	5,010	174	US Virgin Islands	60
47	Colombia	50,470	111	Saudi Arabia	4,620	175	Netherl. Antilles	50
48	East Germany	49,740	112	Cyprus	4,320	176	Faeroe Islands	30
49	Uganda	48,880	113	Botswana	4,280	177	St.Pierre & Miquelon	30
50	Zambia	48,000	114	Israel	4,110	178	Lichtenstein	20
51	Bulgaria	45,580	115	Switzerland	4,040	179	French Guyana	20
52	Chile	45,110	116	Haiti	3,700	180	St. Helena	20
53	Tunisia	45,100	117	Lesotho	3,530	181	UK Virgin Islands	20
54	Portugal	43,700	118	Lebanon	3,160	182	Montserrat	20
55	Cameroon	43,000	119	Mauritania	2,630	183	Turks & Caicos Isl.	10
56	Greece	38,510	120	Portuguese Guinea	2,630	184	Afars & Issas	10
57	Liberia	38,500	121	Swaziland	2,540	185	Panama Canal Zone	10
58	Sierra Leone	36,640	122	Southern Yemen	2,520	186	Iceland	10
59	Mongolia	35,000	123	Puerto Rico	2,440	187	Cayman Islands	5
60	Bolivia	30,910	124	Sabah	2,440	188	Nauru	3
61	Sweden	30,310	125	Jamaica	2,410	189	Kuwait	3
62	Cambodia	29,840	126	Fiji Islands	2,250	190	Norfolk Islands	2
63	Malawi	29,270	127	Equatorial Guinea	2,210	191	Bermuda	2
64	Madagascar	28,560	128	Gambia	2,000	192	Spanish Sahara	2

Introducing 186 Countries 11

Increasing the quantity of land under cultivation, one of the factors of growth enumerated in Chapter Five is undoubtedly the most ancient method practiced for achieving economic growth. We can expect that uninterrupted progress in this direction will be further aided by the large-scale use of water desalting in nuclear plants, which will be discussed later.

TABLE IIIb—Summary of arable and other land uses for major areas of the world

AREAS IN SQ. KM.

TOTAL AREA	Arable land and land under permanent crops	Permanent meadows & pastures	Forested lands	Other Areas		
				Unused but potentially productive	Built-on areas, wasteland & other	
4,930,000 (100%)	1,490,000 (30.3%)	910,000 (18.4%)	1,400,000 (28.4%)	1,130,000 (22.9%)		Europe
19,680,000 (100%)	2,200,000 (11.2%)	2,800,000 (14.2%)	7,390,000 (37.5%)	7,290,000 (37.1%)		North America
20,570,000 (100%)	1,220,000 (5.9%)	5,020,000 (24.4%)	10,030,000 (48.8%)	4,300,000 (20.9%)		Latin America
12,070,000 (100%)	750,000 (6.2%)	1,870,000 (15.5%)	1,310,000 (10.9%)	8,140,000 (67.4%)		Near East
11,170,000 (100%)	2,720,000 (24.4%)	1,090,000 (9.8%)	4,490,000 (40.2%)	2,870,000 (25.6%)		Far East
25,030,000 (100%)	1,920,000 (7.7%)	8,180,000 (32.6%)	5,370,000 (21.5%)	9,560,000 (38.2%)		Africa
8,510,000 (100%)	430,000 (5.1%)	4,620,000 (54.2%)	820,000 (9.7%)	2,640,000 (31.0%)		Oceania
101,960,000 (100%)	10,730,000 (10.5%)	24,490,000 (24.0%)	30,810,000 (30.2%)	35,930,000 (35.3%)		

Table IIIa shows for 7 areas of the world the percentages of areas in all classifications, from arable land under permanent crops to unused and wasteland.

We note that the Near East is the only area having 67.5% unused and desertic land, nearly twice the world average. At the present, and for years to come, oil more than makes up for this shortage of arable land but, as we shall discuss in Chapter Eleven, at some future date several of these deserts in coastal areas will be irrigated by

TABLE IV—Populations—1969

World Total : 3,552,000,000

Country	Population	Country	Population	Country	Population
Communist China	740,000,000	Austria	7,371,000	Congo Brazzaville	880,000
India	536,983,000	Saudi Arabia	7,230,000	Bhutan	825,000
U.S.S.R.	240,571,000	Cambodia	6,701,000	West Irian	815,000
United States	203,216,000	Madagascar	6,643,000	Mauritius	799,000
Pakistan	126,000,000	Switzerland	6,230,000	Guyana	742,000
Indonesia	116,000,000	Ecuador	5,890,000	Cyprus	630,000
Japan	102,322,000	Syria	5,866,000	Botswana	629,000
Brazil	90,840,000	Cameroon	5,680,000	Portuguese Timor	590,000
Nigeria	63,870,000	Angola	5,430,000	Kuwait	570,000
West Germany	60,842,000	Upper Volta	5,278,000	Muscat & Oman	565,000
United Kingdom	55,534,000	Southern Rhodesia	5,090,000	Portuguese Guinea	530,000
Italy	53,170,000	Tunisia	5,027,000	Fiji Islands	519,000
France	50,320,000	Guatemala	5,014,000	Gabon	485,000
Mexico	48,933,000	Yemen	5,000,000	Reunion	436,000
Philippines	37,178,000	Denmark	4,910,000	Swaziland	410,000
Thailand	34,738,000	Mali	4,881,000	Surinam	389,000
Turkey	34,375,000	Bolivia	4,804,000	Windward Islands	388,000
Spain	32,949,000	Haiti	4,768,000	Gambia	357,000
Poland	32,555,000	Finland	4,703,000	Martinique	332,000
U.A.R. Egypt	32,501,000	Malawi	4,398,000	Malta	323,000
Korea Republic	31,130,000	Zambia	4,208,000	Guadeloupe	323,000
Iran	27,892,000	Ivory Coast	4,195,000	Equatorial Guinea	286,000
Burma	26,980,000	Dominican Rep.	4,174,000	Comoro Islands	270,000
Ethiopia	24,769,000	Hong Kong	3,990,000	Macau	260,000
Argentina	23,983,000	Niger	3,909,000	Barbados	254,000
North Vietnam	21,340,000	Guinea	3,890,000	Cape Verde Isl.	250,000
Canada	21,089,000	Norway	3,851,000	Netherl. Antilles	218,000
Colombia	20,463,000	Senegal	3,780,000	Iceland	203,000
Yugoslavia	20,351,000	Chad	3,510,000	Bahrain	207,000
Romania	20,010,000	Ruanda	3,500,000	Bahama Islands	195,000
South Africa	19,618,000	Burundi	3,475,000	Sikkim	191,000
South Vietnam	17,867,000	El Salvador	3,390,000	Ceuta & Melilla	163,000
Congo Kinshasa	17,100,000	Ireland	2,921,000	Brit.Solomon Isl.	150,000
East Germany	17,096,000	Laos	2,893,000	Leeward Islands	143,000
Afghanistan	16,516,000	Uruguay	2,852,000	Western Samoa	141,000
Sudan	15,186,000	Israel	2,822,000	Trucial Oman	135,000
Morocco	15,050,000	New Zealand	2,777,000	British Honduras	120,000
Czechoslovakia	14,418,000	Puerto Rico	2,754,000	Channel Islands	117,000
Taiwan	13,800,000	Somalia	2,730,000	Brunei	116,000
Algeria	13,349,000	Lebanon	2,645,000	Maldive Islands	108,000
North Korea	13,300,000	Dahomey	2,640,000	French Oceania	105,000
Peru	13,172,000	Sierra Leone	2,512,000	Guam	102,000
Tanzania	12,926,000	Honduras	2,495,000	Qatar	100,000
Netherlands	12,873,000	Papua & NewGuinea	2,315,000	New Caledonia	98,000
Australia	12,296,000	Paraguay	2,303,000	Trust Ter.Pacif; Isl.	95,000
Ceylon	12,240,000	Jordan	2,160,000	Fr.Ter.Afars & Issas	85,000
Nepal	10,845,000	Albania	2,075,000	Tonga	83,000
Malaysia	10,583,000	Singapore	2,017,000	New Hebrides	80,000
Kenya	10,506,000	Jamaica	1,959,000	SaoTome & Principe	66,000
Hungary	10,295,000	Nicaragua	1,915,000	Panama Canal Zone	62,000
Venezuela	10,035,000	Libya	1,869,000	US Virgin Islands	56,000
Belgium & Luxem.	9,983,000	Togo	1,815,000	Ifni	56,000
Chile	9,566,000	Costa Rica	1,695,000	Gilbert & Ellice Isl.	54,000
Portugal	9,560,000	Centr. Afric. Rep.	1,518,000	Bermuda	52,000
Uganda	9,500,000	Panama	1,417,000	Seuchelles Isl.	51,000
Iraq	9,350,000	Mongolia	1,240,000	Isle of Man	50,000
Greece	8,835,000	Southern Yemen	1,220,000	Spanish Sahara	48,000
Ghana	8,600,000	Liberia	1,150,000	Greenland	47,000
Bulgaria	8,436,000	Mauritania	1,140,000	French Guyana	40,000
Cuba	8,250,000	Trinidad & Tobago	1,040,000	Faeroe Islands	38,000
Sweden	7,978,000	Ryukyu Islands	982,000	American Samoa	32,000
Mozambique	7,376,000	Lesotho	930,000	Gibraltar	27,000

Introducing 186 Countries 13

nuclear-desalted water and will contribute to the added greening of the world

POPULATION

Population figures are the basis for many of the considerations developed throughout this volume and the recapitulation in Table IV gives a comprehensive image of the numbers involved.

It will also prove convenient in showing immediately how the population of any particular country, as read from its own page in Part Two, compares with that of the other countries.

Of the world total of 3,552,000,000, one notes that for every 100 persons on the face of the earth, 21 are in Mainland China, 15 in India, nearly 7 in the U.S.S.R., 6 in the U.S.A. and altogether 10 in Pakistan, Indonesia and Japan. In these seven countries, we have accounted for nearly 60% of the world population!

POPULATION DENSITY

Continuing our presentation of tables which make it easier to compare the relative status of all countries of the world, Table V shows population density in sequence of decreasing magnitude.

Note that the population density for the United States is very near that of the average for the world: one human being in an area equal to that of a city block, *if* they were all equally spread out. As a matter of 'scale', major urbanized areas (defined as having a population of 100,000 or more) have a population density of the order of 1,500 per square kilometer.

Eliminating the small islands and territories in the top 15, we note the familiar high density in the Netherlands, in Belgium and Luxembourg, in Japan.

To find that India is more densely populated than East Germany and that Communist China and Bulgaria have the same population density is somewhat surprising.

At the low end of the scale, immediately following the U.S.S.R. and Brazil, a large number of African countries range from 10 to 1 inhabitants per sq. km.

INCREASE IN POPULATION

Due to the complexity of this 'explosive' question, two tables were deemed necessary.

TABLE V—Population density—inhabitants per square kilometer—1967

#	Country	Density	#	Country	Density	#	Country	Density
1	Macao	16,750	63	Communist China	75	125	Guinea	15.10
2	Ceuta & Melilla	5,200	64	Bulgaria	75	126	Uruguay	14.92
3	Gibraltar	4,167	65	Nepal	75	127	Portuguese Guinea	14.70
4	Hong Kong	3,708	66	Indonesia	74	128	Finland	13.80
5	Singapore	3,366	67	Cuba	69	129	Nicaragua	13.70
6	Malta	1,800	68	Albania	68	130	Tanzania	12.97
7	Bermuda	953	69	Nigeria	67	131	Bahama Islands	12.62
8	Channel Islands	595	70	Greece	66	132	Ivory Coast	12.45
9	Barbados	580	71	Cyprus	66	133	Chile	11.90
10	Ryukyu Islands	435	72	Spain	64	134	Norway	11.65
11	Mauritius	389	73	Thailand	64	135	Southern Rhodesia	11.62
12	Netherlands	375	74	Gilbert & Ellice Isl.	62	136	Laos	11.58
13	Taiwan	365	75	Sao Tome & Principe	62	137	Cameroun	11.50
14	Maldive Islands	348	76	Cape Verde Isl.	58	138	Madagascar	10.82
15	Bahrain	323	77	Trust Ter. Pacif. Isl.	52	139	U.S.S.R.	10.50
16	Puerto Rico	303	78	Western Samoa	47	140	Venezuela	10.27
17	Korea Republic	302	79	Guatemala	43	141	Brazil	10.19
18	Martinique	299	80	Turkey	42	142	New Zealand	10.15
19	Belgium & Lux.	298	81	Ireland	41	143	Liberia	9.97
20	Japan	270	82	Panama Canal Zone	39	144	Equatorial Guinea	9.87
21	Lebanon	242	83	Burma	38	145	Peru	9.63
22	West Germany	233	84	Portuguese Timor	38	146	Mozambique	9.12
23	United Kingdom	226	85	Cambodia	35	147	Argentina	8.39
24	Netherl. Antilles	220	86	Malawi	35	148	Malaysia	7.42
25	Trinidad & Tobago	197	87	Ifni	35	149	Congo Kinshasa	6.97
26	Guadeloupe	180	88	Ghana	34	150	Sudan	5.73
27	Windward Islands	179	89	Sierra Leone	34	151	Paraguay	5.33
28	Ceylon	178	90	Uganda	34	152	Algeria	5.27
29	Italy	174	91	Kuwait	33	153	Zambia	5.25
30	Jamaica	171	92	Morocco	32	154	New Hebrides	5.22
31	Guam	171	93	U.A.R. Egypt	31	155	New Caledonia	4.95
32	Haiti	165	94	Costa Rica	31	156	British Honduras	4.94
33	Reunion	165	95	Togo	31	157	Brit. Solomon Isl.	4.92
34	US Virgin Islands	163	96	Syria	30	158	Papua & New Guinea	4.88
35	India	156	97	Gambia	30	159	Angola	4.24
36	Leeward Islands	154	98	Lesotho	29	160	Somalia	4.17
37	East Germany	148	99	Tunisia	28	161	Southern Yemen	4.07
38	Switzerland	147	100	Faeroe Islands	27	162	Mali	3.79
39	El Salvador	147	101	Fiji Islands	27	163	Fr. Ter. Afars & Issas	3.77
40	American Samoa	146	102	Yemen	26	164	Bolivia	3.47
41	Seychelles Isl.	130	103	Sikkim	26	165	Qatar	3.40
42	Israel	129	104	Afghanistan	24	166	Saudi Arabia	3.24
43	North Vietnam	127	105	French Oceania	24	167	Cuyana	3.16
44	Ruanda	126	106	Mexico	23	168	Niger	2.80
45	Burundi	120	107	Honduras	22	169	Chad	2.66
46	Philippines	116	108	Dahomey	22	170	Muscat & Oman	2.66
47	Comoro Islands	115	109	Swaziland	22	171	Congo Brazzaville	2.52
48	Tonga	113	110	United States	21	172	Centr. Afric. Rep.	2.34
49	Pakistan	113	111	Jordan	21	173	Surinam	2.22
50	Czechoslovakia	112	112	Iraq	19	174	Trucial Oman	2.15
51	Denmark	112	113	Ethiopia	19	175	West Irian	2.12
52	Hungary	110	114	Ecuador	19	176	Canada	2.05
53	North Korea	105	115	Senegal	19	177	Iceland	1.93
54	Portugal	103	116	Brunei	19	178	Gabon	1.77
55	Poland	102	117	Panama	18	179	Australia	1.54
56	South Vietnam	98	118	Upper Volta	18	180	Mauritania	1.06
57	France	91	119	Sweden	17	181	Libya	0.99
58	Austria	87	120	Colombia	17	182	Botswana	0.98
59	Isle of Man	85	121	Kenya	17	183	Mongolia	0.74
60	Romania	81	122	Iran	16	184	French Guyana	0.42
61	Dominican Rep.	80	123	Bhutan	16	185	Spanish Sahara	0.17
62	Yugoslavia	78	124	South Africa	15	186	Greenland	0.02

WORLD AVERAGE 25

Introducing 186 Countries 15

TABLE VI—Births and deaths per 100 population—1969

	Birth	Death		Birth	Death		Birth	Death
WORLD	3.4	1.4	Jordan	4.7	1.6	Bolivia	4.40	2.00
AFRICA	4.7	2.0	Kuwait	4.7	0.6	Brazil	3.90	1.10
NORTHERN AFRICA	4.7	1.6	Syria	4.7	1.5	Colombia	4.40	1.10
Algeria	4.4	1.4	Turkey	4.3	1.6	Ecuador	4.70	1.30
Morocco	4.6	1.5	MIDDLE SOUTH ASIA	4.4	1.6	Guyana	4.00	1.00
Sudan	5.2	1.8	Ceylon	3.2	0.8	Peru	4.40	1.20
Tunisia	4.5	1.6	India	4.2	1.7	Venezuela	4.60	1.00
U.A.R. Egypt	4.3	1.5	Iran	4.8	1.8	TEMPERATE SOUTH		
WESTERN AFRICA	4.9	2.3	Nepal	4.1	2.1	AMERICA	2.60	0.90
Dahomey	5.4	2.6	Pakistan	5.0	1.8	Argentina	2.20	0.80
Gambia	3.9	2.1	SOUTHEAST ASIA	4.3	1.5	Chile	3.40	1.10
Ghana	4.7	2.0	Cambodia	5.0	2.0	Paraguay	4.50	1.20
Guinea	4.9	2.6	Indonesia	4.9	2.1	Uruguay	2.40	0.90
Ivory Coast	5.0	2.5	Laos	4.2	1.7	EUROPE	1.80	1.00
Liberia	4.4	2.5	Malaysia	3.5	0.8	NORTHERN EUROPE	1.80	1.10
Mali	5.0	2.5	Singapore	2.5	0.6	Denmark	1.68	0.97
Mauritania	4.5	2.5	Thailand	4.6	1.3	Finland	1.60	0.96
Niger	5.2	2.5	EAST ASIA	3.0	1.3	Iceland	2.09	0.69
Nigeria	5.0	2.5	China Mainland	3.4	1.5	Ireland	2.09	1.13
Senegal	4.6	2.2	China Taiwan	2.9	0.6	Norway	1.76	0.97
Sierra Leone	4.4	2.2	Hong Kong	2.1	0.5	Sweden	1.43	1.04
Togo	5.0	2.4	Japan	1.9	0.7	United Kingdom	1.71	1.19
Upper Volta	4.9	2.8	North Korea	3.9	1.1	WESTERN EUROPE	1.70	1.10
EASTERN AFRICA	4.7	2.1	South Korea	3.6	1.1	Austria	1.72	1.31
Burundi	4.6	2.6	Mongolia	4.0	1.0	Belgium	1.48	1.28
Kenya	5.0	2.0	Ryukyu Islands	2.2	0.5	France	1.68	1.10
Madagascar	4.6	2.2	NORTHERN AMERICA	1.8	0.9	West Germany	1.97	1.19
Mauritius	3.1	0.9	Canada	1.77	0.74	Luxembourg	1.42	1.23
Reunion	3.7	0.4	United States	1.76	0.96	Netherlands	1.86	0.82
Ruanda	5.2	2.2	LATIN AMERICA	3.8	0.9	Switzerland	1.71	0.93
Southern Rhodesia	4.8	1.4	MIDDLE AMERICA	4.3	0.9	EASTERN EUROPE	1.70	1.00
Tanzania	4.7	2.2	Costa Rica	4.5	0.8	Bulgaria	1.69	0.86
Uganda	4.3	1.8	El Salvador	4.8	1.3	Czechoslovakia	1.49	1.07
Zambia	5.1	2.0	Guatemala	4.6	1.6	East Germany	1.43	1.43
MIDDLE AFRICA	4.6	2.3	Honduras	4.9	1.6	Hungary	1.51	1.12
Cameroon	5.0	2.6	Mexico	4.4	1.0	Poland	1.62	0.76
Centr. Afric. Rep.	4.8	2.5	Nicaragua	4.7	1.6	Romania	2.63	0.96
Chad	4.5	2.3	Panama	4.2	1.0	SOUTHERN EUROPE	1.90	0.90
Congo Brazzaville	4.1	2.4	CARIBBEAN	3.5	1.1	Albania	3.56	0.80
Congo Dem. Rep.	4.3	2.0	Barbados	2.9	0.9	Greece	1.82	0.83
Gabon	3.5	2.5	Cuba	2.8	0.8	Italy	1.76	1.01
SOUTHERN AFRICA	4.1	1.7	Dominican Rep.	4.8	1.5	Malta	1.61	0.90
Lesotho	4.0	2.3	Guadeloupe	3.2	0.8	Portugal	2.05	1.00
South Africa	4.0	1.6	Haïti	4.5	2.0	Spain	2.05	0.87
ASIA	3.8	1.5	Jamaica	3.9	0.8	Yugoslavia	1.89	0.86
SOUTHWEST ASIA	4.4	1.5	Martinique	3.0	0.7	U.S.S.R.	1.79	0.77
Cyprus	2.5	0.7	Puerto Rico	2.5	0.6	OCEANIA	2.50	1.00
Iraq	4.8	1.5	Trinidad & Tobago	3.0	0.8	Australia	2.00	0.91
Israel	2.6	0.7	TROP. SOUTH AMERICA	3.9	0.9	New Zealand	2.26	0.89

Table VI records only birth and death rates as of 1969, with countries grouped by geographical area.

Table VII shows the net population increase, which includes births and immigration as well as deaths and emigration. It shows the average yearly population increase registered between 1961 and 1967.

As can be seen, there is a wide span in population growth

TABLE VII—Average annual population growth rate: 1961-1967

#	Country	Rate	#	Country	Rate	#	Country	Rate
	WORLD AVERAGE	1.90 %	63	South Vietnam	2.70 %	125	Mauritania	1.90 %
1	Kuwait	9.40 %	64	Trinidad & Tobago	2.70	126	Sikkim	1.90
2	Trucial Oman	9.10	65	Guinea	2.70	127	Switzerland	1.88
3	US Virgin Islands	8.20	66	Guyana	2.70	128	Iceland	1.80
4	Qatar	6.90	67	New Caledonia	2.70	129	Bermuda	1.80
5	Macao	6.80	68	Trust Ter. Pacif. Isl.	2.70	130	Equatorial Guinea	1.80
6	American Samoa	5.40	69	Western Samoa	2.70	131	Maldive Islands	1.80
7	Guam	5.10	70	Ghana	2.70	132	Canada	1.72
8	Panama Canal Zone	4.60	71	South Africa	2.62	133	Puerto Rico	1.72
9	Somalia	4.10	72	North Korea	2.60	134	Saudi Arabia	1.70
10	Mexico	3.93	73	Lebanon	2.60	135	Liberia	1.70
11	Greenland	3.90	74	Singapore	2.60	136	Argentina	1.60
12	Libya	3.70	75	Togo	2.60	137	Faeroe Islands	1.60
13	Brunei	3.70	76	Mauritius	2.60	138	Portuguese Timor	1.50
14	Bahrain	3.70	77	West Irian	2.60	139	Fr. Ter. Afars & Issas	1.50
15	Comoro Islands	3.60	78	Gilbert & Ellice Isl.	2.60	140	Congo Brazzaville	1.50
16	El Salvador	3.60	79	Turkey	2.53	141	Communist China	1.50
17	Dominican Rep.	3.60	80	U.A.R. Egypt	2.53	142	United States	1.47
18	Bahama Islands	3.50	81	Chile	2.50	143	U.S.S.R.	1.42
19	Costa Rica	3.50	82	Tanzania	2.50	144	Angola	1.40
20	Surinam	3.50	83	Uganda	2.50	145	Bolivia	1.40
21	Venezuela	3.44	84	Papua & New Guinea	2.50	146	Netherl. Antilles	1.40
22	Ecuador	3.40	85	Laos	2.50	147	Ifni	1.40
23	Nicaragua	3.40	86	Centr. Afric. Rep.	2.50	148	Netherlands	1.34
24	Honduras	3.40	87	India	2.48	149	Uruguay	1.30
25	Philippines	3.34	88	Ceylon	2.40	150	Ryukyu Islands	1.30
26	Panama	3.30	89	Senegal	2.40	151	Sierra Leone	1.30
27	Tonga	3.30	90	Cambodia	2.40	152	France	1.22
28	Israel	3.27	91	Madagascar	2.40	153	Mozambique	1.20
29	Taiwan	3.26	92	Malawi	2.40	154	Poland	1.17
30	Hong Kong	3.20	93	Cape Verde Isl.	2.40	155	West Germany	1.14
31	North Vietnam	3.20	94	Indonesia	2.34	156	Cyprus	1.00
32	Southern Rhodesia	3.20	95	Nigeria	2.32	157	Barbados	1.00
33	Fiji Islands	3.20	96	Cuba	2.30	158	Japan	0.96
34	Colombia	3.19	97	Tunisia	2.30	159	Yugoslavia	0.93
35	Malaysia	3.10	98	Southern Yemen	2.30	160	Ceuta & Melilla	0.90
36	Guatemala	3.10	99	Guadeloupe	2.30	161	Leeward Islands	0.90
37	Paraguay	3.10	100	Spanish Sahara	2.30	162	Spain	0.88
38	Ruanda	3.10	101	Algeria	2.20	163	Portugal	0.84
39	British Honduras	3.10	102	Cameroun	2.20	164	Bulgaria	0.81
40	Peru	3.06	103	Yemen	2.20	165	Norway	0.80
41	Thailand	3.06	104	Upper Volta	2.20	166	Gabon	0.80
42	Zambia	3.00	105	Windward Islands	2.20	167	Channel Islands	0.80
43	Mongolia	3.00	106	New Hebrides	2.20	168	Denmark	0.78
44	Niger	3.00	107	Seychelles Isl.	2.20	169	Finland	0.77
45	Chad	3.00	108	Pakistan	2.13	170	Greece	0.75
46	Botswana	3.00	109	Burma	2.10	171	Italy	0.74
47	Brazil	2.93	110	Congo Kinshasa	2.10	172	Romania	0.73
48	Korea Republic	2.91	111	Mali	2.10	173	United Kingdom	0.71
49	Syria	2.90	112	Martinique	2.10	174	Sweden	0.71
50	Sudan	2.90	113	Jamaica	2.00	175	Czechoslovakia	0.68
51	Kenya	2.90	114	Haiti	2.00	176	Belgium & Lux.	0.65
52	Albania	2.90	115	Burundi	2.00	177	Isle of Man	0.60
53	Reunion	2.90	116	Bhutan	2.00	178	Gibraltar	0.60
54	Dahomey	2.90	117	Gambia	2.00	179	Austria	0.48
55	Lesotho	2.90	118	French Guyana	2.00	180	Hungary	0.40
56	Swaziland	2.90	119	Brit. Solomon Isl.	2.00	181	Ireland	0.30
57	Iran	2.84	120	New Zealand	1.99	182	Portuguese Guinea	0.20
58	Ivory Coast	2.80	121	Australia	1.90	183	East Germany	0.00
59	Morocco	2.80	122	Ethiopia	1.90	184	Muscat & Oman	0.00
60	Iraq	2.80	123	Afghanistan	1.90	185	Sao Tome & Principe	−0.20
61	French Oceania	2.80	124	Nepal	1.90	186	Malta	−0.40
62	Jordan	2.70						

Introducing 186 Countries 17

throughout the world, ranging from a 10% increase per year to a slight decrease.

In the lead are several small countries which became prosperous quite suddenly, and as a consequence had to draw heavily on imported technical and managerial talent largely from areas with common cultural, social and religious traditions. Kuwait, Trucial Oman and Quatar are in the category. Other small countries in the top bracket have also had growth thrust upon them, requiring additional manpower which has augmented the population.

The growth rate of 1.9% for the world as a whole results from a 3.4% birth rate and a 1.4% death rate.

(i) The African continent has the highest world birth rate, 4.7%.
(ii) Western Africa, whose birth rate is highest, 4.9%, shares with Middle Africa the highest death rate, 2.3%.
(iii) Asia and Latin America follow with a 3.8% increase. However, Asia's death rate is 1.5% while Latin America's is only 0.9%.
(iv) Ranging from Mexico's 3.93% to Brazil's 2.93%, El Salvador, the Dominican Republic, Costa Rica, Venezuela, Equador, Nicaragua, Honduras, Panama, Colombia, Guatemala, Paraguay and Peru form a compact squad in the upper quarter of net population increase ascribable to a common heritage of religious traditions.
(v) Close on their heels, in the upper third, come the Middle East countries: Syria, Sudan, Iran, Morocco, Iraq, Jordan, Lebanon, Turkey and the U.A.R.
(vi) India does not show the extremes of birth or death rates one would expect.
(vii) Western and Eastern Europe share within very close limits the same birth rate, 1.8%, and the same death rate, 1.0%, which figures, incidentally, are close to those for the United States, 1.8% and 0.9%.
(viii) There is not a single European country for which the increase in population is larger than the 1.9% average for the world. Switzerland, nudged by Iceland, comes closest to the average and is trailed by the Netherlands and France.
(ix) Italy ranks fairly low. Ireland, because of its high emigration rate, is even lower—almost at the bottom.
(x) The Eastern bloc, led by Communist China and the U.S.S.R., are in the lowest quarter, while Russia shows the lowest death rate of all, 0.77%. East Germany apparently loses as many people through political emigration as it gains through birth.
(xi) Japan has successfully maintained the low rate of population

increase which has been regarded as one of the contributing factors in its strong economic growth.

'PER CAPITA' GNP IN 1967

Gross National Product (GNP) *per capita* will be discussed in detail, starting in a subsequent chapter, but since its value for each country is shown in several charts which will be discussed in the next Chapter, a complete list is shown now, in Table VIII, in descending sequence.

In so continuous a sequence, it is unnecessary to attempt to draw sharp dividing lines between emerging countries, developing countries, countries in transition, industrialized countries, etc. *Per capita* figures of $100, $300, $1,000, etc, are sometimes mentioned as relevant bench-marks and many more could be used but it is obvious that there cannot be any hard and fast compartmentalization on humanity's road to higher standards of well-being and to greater dignity of life.

The world average GNP *per capita* in 1971 is $780 in terms of 1967 dollars—which is approximately $1,000 in terms of 1971 dollars.

CAN GNP 'PER CAPITA' AVERAGES BE REGARDED AS MEANINGFUL?

Many will question the soundness of using *per capita* income averages in countries where there is a wide disparity in the stage of development of different areas. The same questioning attitude is observed when, as in the case of oil-rich countries with a very small population, the extremes of high and low *per capita* wealth result in a national average enjoyed by few.

Raising such doubts is very legitimate indeed, and the analyses and research preceding the preparation of this volume make it possible to give a very positive answer: Over-simple as the use of averages may appear, numerous checks of the pattern method applicability to out-of-the-way conditions have emphatically confirmed its soundness in that respect.

For instance, we have charted separately the economic growth of the widely differing areas of Brazil and we have obtained practically the same result as if Brazil had been considered as a completely homogenous country, defined by a single average. The pattern curves each for a specific rate of growth and stage of development

TABLE VIII—1967 Gross national product 'per capita' in U.S.$

1	United States	4,040	63	Ryukyu Islands	540	125	Papua & NewGuinea	200
2	Kuwait	3,530	64	Martinique	540	126	Morocco	191
3	Qatar	3,250	65	Jamaica	531	127	Angola	190
4	Sweden	3,041	66	Yugoslavia	530	128	Congo Brazzaville	190
5	Canada	2,805	67	Mexico	528	129	Bolivia	189
6	Iceland	2,780	68	Lebanon	520	130	Mozambique	180
7	Switzerland	2,595	69	Portugal	493	131	Brit.Solomon Isl.	180
8	Denmark	2,497	70	American Samoa	490	132	Korea Republic	162
9	Bermuda	2,410	71	Barbados	478	133	U.A.R. Egypt	160
10	US Virgin Islands	2,380	72	Guadeloupe	470	134	Thailand	155
11	France	2,340	73	Costa Rica	425	135	Ceylon	152
12	Australia	2,250	74	Gabon	418	136	Muscat & Oman	150
13	Norway	2,199	75	Mongolia	410	137	Ifni	150
14	West Germany	2,085	76	Gilbert&ElliceIsl.	380	138	Cambodia	148
15	Belgium & Lux.	2,045	77	Surinam	363	139	Mauritania	147
16	New Zealand	2,000	78	British Honduras	360	140	Cameroun	145
17	United Kingdom	1,975	79	Nicaragua	359	141	South Vietnam	144
18	Finland	1,874	80	Turkey	353	142	Sierra Leone	140
19	Netherlands	1,804	81	Saudi Arabia	350	143	Togo	140
20	Panama Canal Zone	1,720	82	Bahrain	350	144	Southern Yemen	130
21	Faeroe Islands	1,710	83	Malaysia	335	145	Western Samoa	130
22	New Caledonia	1,620	84	Cuba	330	146	Pakistan	129
23	Guam	1,620	85	Guyana	324	147	Centr.Afric.Rep.	120
24	Bahama Islands	1,570	86	Albania	320	148	Kenya	117
25	Israel	1,490	87	Colombia	313	149	Madagascar	116
26	Austria	1,465	88	Tonga	310	150	Comoro Islands	110
27	Puerto Rico	1,387	89	Brazil	309	151	Cape Verde Isl.	110
28	French Oceania	1,340	90	Guatemala	300	152	Indonesia	104
29	East Germany	1,300	91	Zambia	298	153	Nepal	102
30	Italy	1,279	92	Fiji Islands	290	154	North Vietnam	100
31	Isle of Man	1,250	93	Iran	283	155	Uganda	95
32	Netherl. Antilles	1,180	94	Peru	283	156	India	90
33	Japan	1,155	95	El Salvador	280	157	Congo Kinshasa	90
34	Czechoslovakia	1,110	96	Swaziland	280	158	Sudan	90
35	Libya	1,073	97	Ceuta & Melilla	280	159	Guinea	90
36	Ireland	1,067	98	New Hebrides	280	160	Laos	90
37	Trucial Oman	1,050	99	SaoTome & Principe	280	161	Botswana	90
38	Channel Islands	980	100	Philippines	278	162	Gambia	90
39	U.S.S.R.	970	101	Dominican Rep.	275	163	China-Mainland	89
40	Venezuela	911	102	Taiwan	274	164	Haïti	84
41	Hungary	900	103	Jordan	268	165	Nigeria	80
42	Spain	822	104	Ivory Coast	263	166	Tanzania	80
43	Greece	808	105	TrustTer.Pacif.Isl.	260	167	Mali	80
44	Brunei	800	106	Mauritius	257	168	Dahomey	80
45	French Guyana	790	107	Ghana	252	169	Portuguese Timor	80
46	Trinidad & Tobago	783	108	Algeria	250	170	Maldive Islands	80
47	Poland	780	109	Leeward Islands	243	171	Ethiopia	77
48	Greenland	760	110	Equatorial Guinea	240	172	Burma	70
49	Cyprus	750	111	Macao	240	173	Afghanistan	70
50	Romania	720	112	Honduras	236	174	Yemen	70
51	Bulgaria	690	113	Syria	234	175	Niger	70
52	Singapore	646	114	Southern Rhodesia	233	176	Chad	70
53	Argentina	635	115	Ecuador	231	177	Ruanda	60
54	Hong Kong	620	116	North Korea	230	178	Lesotho	60
55	South Africa	619	117	Iraq	230	179	Bhutan	60
56	Gibraltar	610	118	Liberia	230	180	Sikkim	60
57	Malta	587	119	Paraguay	224	181	Seychelles Isl.	60
58	Chile	585	120	Senegal	214	182	Malawi	51
59	Panama	581	121	Tunisia	214	183	Upper Volta	50
60	Fr.Ter.Afars& Issas	580	122	Windward Islands	212	184	Burundi	50
61	**Uruguay**	**577**	123	Portuguese Guinea	210	185	Somalia	50
62	**Reunion**	**560**	124	Spanish Sahara	210	186	West Irian	50

combined their individual 'appraisal' into a valid 'consolidated statement'.

CONVERSION OF CURRENCIES INTO U.S. DOLLARS AT THE OFFICIAL RATE OF EXCHANGE

In the Complementary Notes, at the end of this volume, attention is called to the possible shortcomings inherent to this method.

Generally speaking, it is not inappropriate to state that even where the validity of comparisons may be jeopardized by such flaws, there is far more to be gained by using whatever the best data available is, while recognizing its shortcomings, than by excluding a set of data—and the corresponding country—from a world-wide comparison.

CHAPTER THREE

Aspects of Life

From the many which could have been analysed, eight aspects of life have been selected and reviewed in the following pages, in three-fold presentations for each:
  (i) a table listing the statistical data for each country, in descending order,
  (ii) a chart plotting the same data in terms of GNP
  (iii) a few comments among the many which the study of the data presented might suggest.

The charts offer an additional element of significance as they bring out any relationship which may exist with GNP, at the same time as they give an exact image of the full range spanned by the different countries.

NUMBER OF STUDENTS IN INSTITUTIONS OF HIGHER LEARNING

The data from which Table IX and Chart 1 were prepared are based on UNESCO figures for higher learning institutions, such as universities, teacher training colleges, technical institutes, etc. and include only students working towards a degree. These figures are for either 1965, 1966, 1967 or 1968, whichever were the latest available in January 1971.

Chart 1 shows this attendance, expressed in number of students per 100,000 population, in terms of the GNP *per capita*. The student attendance is read along the vertical scale: a logarithmic, sometimes called proportional, scale which gives as much space between 1 and 10 as it does between 10 and 100, 100 and 1,000, 1,000 and 10,000, etc.

Such a spacing is particularly suitable to comparisons between countries at greatly different stages of development and it will be used in most of the charts.

The same logarithmic scale is used to measure GNP *per capita* along the horizontal axis. Thanks to this double logarithmic scale (called 'log-log' for short) there is no crowding of points anywhere within this chart. Additional comments on the use of logarithmic scales will be found in the Complementary Notes at the end.

CHARTS CAN BE FUN

Charts can be fun: as we delve into this one, let the eye travel upward on either side of the $100 *per capita* mark on the horizontal axis. We pass in succession Dahomey, Togo, Ruanda, Tanzania,

TABLE IX—Number of third-level students per 100,000 population

(67)	United States	3,471	(67)	Korea Republic	574	(66)	Nepal	100
(67)	US Virgin Islands	2,380	(67)	U.A.R. Egypt	565	(66)	Senegal	94
(67)	Panama Canal Zone	2,293	(67)	Hungary	513	(68)	Seychelles Isl.	94
(67)	Canada	2,201	(67)	Spain	491	(66)	Reunion	90
(67)	U.S.S.R.	1,830	(66)	Costa Rica	487	(67)	Guyana	84
(67)	Puerto Rico	1,771	(67)	Cuba	470	(68)	Antigua	82
(67)	New Zealand	1,743	(67)	East Germany	437	(67)	Algeria	78
(67)	Guam	1,736	(67)	Iraq	419	(67)	Ivory Coast	66
(67)	Ukrainian S.S.R.	1,660	(66)	Bolivia	414	(68)	New Caledonia	66
(65)	Philippines	1,605	(67)	Portugal	412	(67)	Morocco	64
(66)	Israel	1,488	(66)	Martinique	405	(66)	Sudan	62
(64)	West Berlin	1,481	(66)	Malta	399	(67)	Ghana	59
(67)	Netherlands	1,445	(67)	Turkey	384	(67)	Cyprus	55
(67)	Byelorussian SSR	1,421	(67)	South Africa	360	(66)	Guadeloupe	55
(67)	Japan	1,398	(67)	Ecuador	356	(67)	Bahrain	55
(67)	Australia	1,296	(67)	Mexico	338	(67)	Madagascar	52
(67)	Sweden	1,250	(67)	Hong Kong	293	(68)	Kenya	49
(67)	France	1,239	(65)	Paraguay	290	(67)	Congo Democr. Rep.	36
(67)	Denmark	1,203	(66)	Pakistan	278	(67)	Cameroun	34
(67)	Lebanon	1,156	(66)	Colombia	268	(68)	Lesotho	34
(67)	Argentina	1,135	(67)	Dominican Rep.	256	(67)	Sierra Leone	34
(67)	Finland	1,110	(67)	Brazil	251	(66)	Haiti	34
(67)	Bulgaria	1,103	(66)	Nicaragua	236	(68)	Sarawak	31
(67)	Scotland	1,058	(65)	India	225	(56)	North Vietnam	29
(67)	Yugoslavia	1,057	(67)	El Salvador	214	(66)	Saudi Arabia	28
(67)	China Taiwan	1,054	(64)	Surinam	206	(67)	Afghanistan	27
(67)	Czechoslovakia	961	(65)	American Samoa	200	(68)	Zambia	23
(67)	Poland	904	(67)	South Vietnam	200	(67)	Uganda	23
(67)	Ireland	799	(67)	Luxembourg	199	(68)	Mauritius	23
(66)	Mongolia	755	(68)	Guatemala	197	(65)	Gabon	22
(66)	Greece	750	(67)	Malaysia	184	(67)	Southern Rhodesia	19
(67)	Ryukyu Islands	736	(67)	Indonesia	175	(68)	Swaziland	18
(67)	Austria	734	(67)	Kuwait	170	(67)	Ethiopia	17
(67)	Romania	734	(67)	Jordan	168	(67)	Malawi	16
(67)	United Kingdom	716	(67)	Tunisia	161	(66)	Western Samoa	16
(67)	Italy	715	(67)	Bahama Islands	155	(66)	Faeroe Islands	16
(67)	Panama	697	(66)	Barbados	151	(66)	Angola	14
(67)	West Germany	695	(67)	Iran	149	(67)	Laos	13
(67)	North Ireland	680	(66)	Ceylon	141	(67)	Nigeria	13
(67)	Peru	674	(67)	Cambodia	139	(65)	Guinea	11
(67)	Singapore	665	(66)	Honduras	133	(66)	Mozambique	10
(67)	Albania	633	(66)	Libya	132	(67)	Tanzania	9
(65)	Uruguay	629	(67)	Congo Brazzaville	129	(67)	Burundi	8
(67)	Venezuela	629	(66)	Burma	127	(67)	Ruanda	7
(67)	Chile	625	(62)	China Mainland	122	(66)	New Guinea	7
(67)	Belgium	618	(67)	Jamaica	119	(67)	Dahomey	5
(66)	Iceland	614	(68)	Liberia	113	(66)	Togo	5
(67)	Syria	593	(67)	Trinidad&Tobago	107	(65)	Somalia	2
(67)	Switzerland	593	(66)	British Honduras	103	(67)	Upper Volta	1,1
(67)	Norway	588	(67)	Thailand	102			

Aspects of Life 23

where we approach 10 students per 100,000. We continue with Nigeria, Guinea, Ethiopia, Uganda, Congo-Kinshasa, Haiti, Kenya, Madagascar, Sudan and Nepal, by which time we have passed the 100 level.

We pursue our travels into Cambodia, Burma, Ceylon, Indonesia,

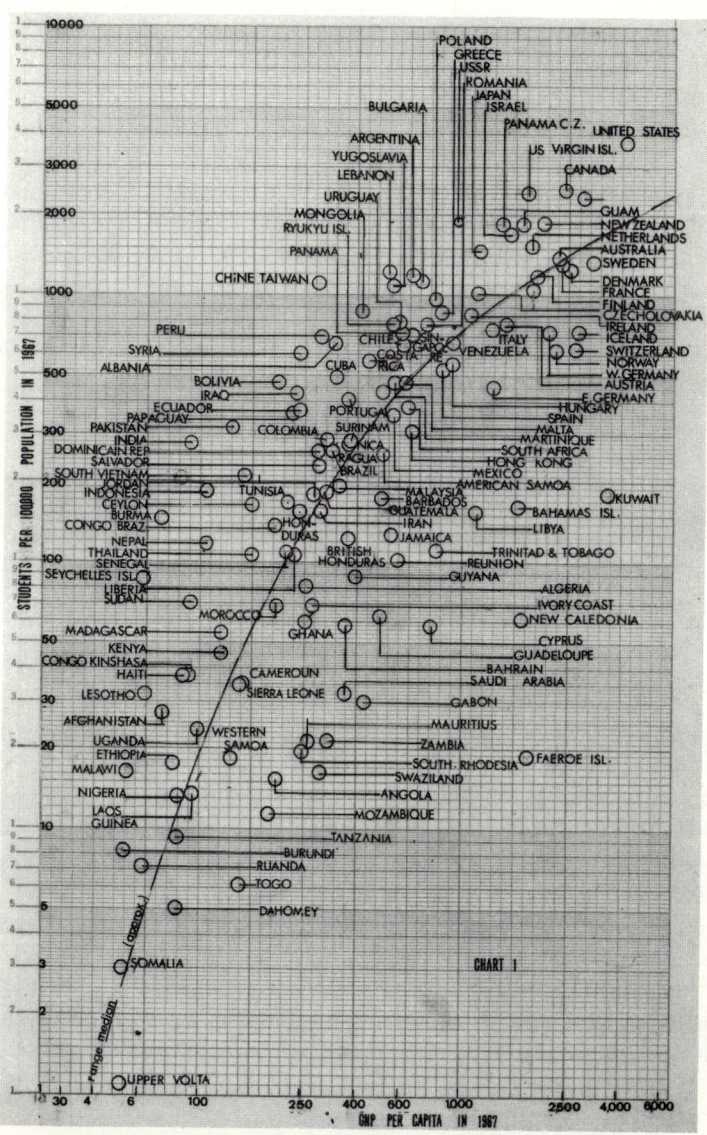

CHART 1—Number of students per 100,000 population in 1967

South Vietnam, India and Pakistan, where we will have reached the term of our journey from the-newly-born African nations to the Asian countries with attendance of 300 students per 100,000 population.

These are the Indies whose fabled wealth lured Christopher Colombus to America. Their GNP *per capita* is still very low, but their centuries-old cultural heritage is reflected in their high status: 40 times that of our starting bench mark.

On an entirely different track we can travel from left to right on this chart at, say, the 150 level on the vertical axis, starting with Burma at the $70 *per capita* level.

We revisit Cambodia and proceed through Congo-Brazzaville, Hondurus and Iran, where we find ourselves on the median line near the $300 *per capita* level.

On the same route, as we proceed, always at the 150 students per 100,000 level, we reach Libya with $1,100, the Bahamas with $1,600 and come very close to Kuwait where the attendance to institutions of higher learning has not yet had the time to catch up with a $3,500 *per capita* wealth which nearly matches that of the United States.

After traveling as we have done: vertically along lines of constant GNP *per capita,* or horizontally along lines of constant student attendance, we can explore Western Europe where we note the influence of common cultural background and traditions, in the fairly close 'bunching' of the points representing its different countries. The similarities of its different people in their economic motivation, their attitude towards work and education is reflected also in other charts of this volume.

With these entirely diverse explorations, we are in a better position to follow the middle of the road as we travel the median line.

Although there is a wide spread between the lowest and the highest GNP *per capita* for the same relative attendance, the median trend—one which leaves as many countries above the line as below—is fairly well defined.

As might be expected, the increase in attendance as *per capita* income rises is particularly pronounced at the lowest levels of *per capita* income.

This can be seen from the figures shown at the top of p. 25, which have been taken from the median line.

For countries in an early stage of development, twice the GNP *per capita* means a seven-fold increase in the number of students. Even at

Aspects of Life 25

GNP 'per capita' in 1967	Higher level students per 100,000 population in 1967
75	7
150	45
300	195
600	400
1,200	850
2,400	1,300
4,800	2,000

the highest *per capita* brackets, further increases in a country's wealth still result in a very substantial increase of attendance.

Because of the considerable spread, widely different conclusions may be reached from the comparisons which this chart suggests but the median trend provides strong evidence that, whether we look at the emerging nations of Africa where it is amplified sevenfold, or at the industrialized Europe where the amplification is only one and a half, greater *per capita* wealth will bring education and culture to vastly increased numbers, which, in turn, will establish a broader base for further economic growth.

FORECASTING INCREASE IN COLLEGE ATTENDANCE

As an example of the applicability of this type of presentation to the forecasting of increase in university attendance, we are quoting from a recent address[30]: 'The number of college students—in the United States—is expected to rise by more than 50% from its present level of 7½ million to about 11½ million in 1985'

Anticipating on some of the suggestions presented in later parts of this volume, let us refer to the Profile for the United States in Chapter Twelve where we note that, in 1985, the *per capita* GNP will be $6,560, and the population 249,000,000.

We return to Chart 1, where we draw, by eye, a trend line which starts from the point plotted for the United States (3,471 students per 100,000 population and $4,040 *per capita* GNP) and which parallels the median trend line shown in broken lines.

According to this U.S.A. trend line, for a *per capita* GNP of $6,560 we would expect about 4,600 students per 100,000 population; this, for a population of 249,000,000 would indicate 11,000,000 students which exactly checks the estimate above.

HOSPITAL BEDS

The same as Chart 1, a median trend can be detected quite clearly in Chart 2.

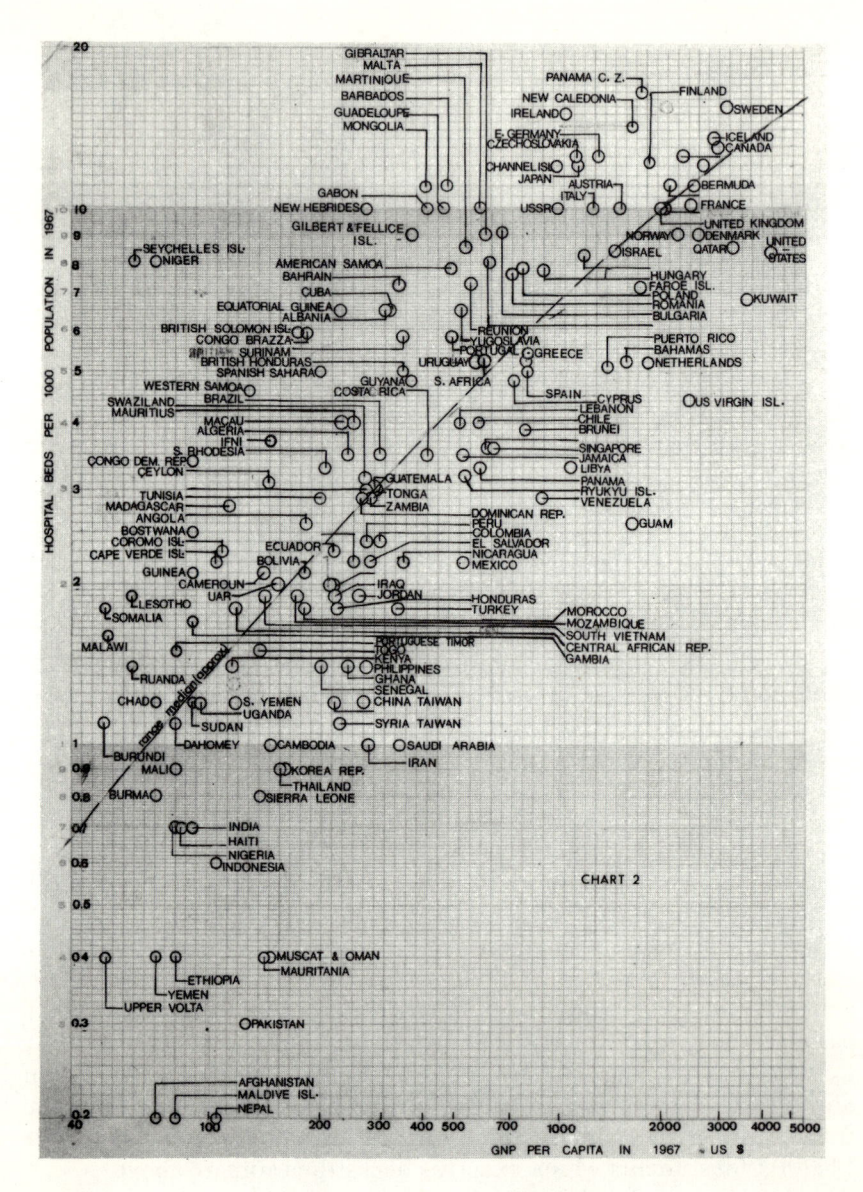

CHART 2—Number of hospital beds

TABLE X—Hospital beds per 1,000 population

(66)	SoaTome&Principe	33.3	(65/66)	Faeroe Islands	6.7	(66)	East Malays.-Sabah	2.4
(66)	Nauru	33.3	(64)	Granada	6.7	(67)	Colombia	2.4
(66)	Greenland	16.7	(65)	Argentina	6.7	(67)	Peru	2.4
(67)	Panama Canal Zone	16.7	(67)	Congo Brazzaville	5.9	(65)	Nicaragua	2.4
(66)	St.Pierre&Miquelon	16.7	(66)	Equatorial Guinea	5.9	(67)	Comoro Islands	2.3
(67)	Wallis Futuna Isl.	16.7	(66)	Albania	5.9	(67)	Ecuador	2.3
(66)	St. Helena	14.3	(68)	Greece	5.9	(67)	Bolivia	2.2
(66)	Falkland Islands	14.3	(67)	Portugal	5.9	(67/68)	U.A.R. Egypt	2.2
(65)	French Guyana	14.3	(66)	Yugoslavia	5.9	(67)	El Salvador	2.2
(66)	Ireland	14.3	(67)	Brit. Solomon Isl.	5.9	(67)	Cameroun	2.1
(67)	Isle of Man	14.3	(67/68)	Nire Islands	5.9	(66)	Cape Verde Isl.	2.0
(66)	Sweden	14.3	(66)	Cuba	5.9	(67)	Liberia	2.0
(66)	New Caledonia	14.3	(62)	South Africa	5.3	(66)	Mexico	2.0
(67)	Czechoslovakia	12.5	(67)	Bahamas	5.3	(67)	Paraguay	2.0
(67)	East Germany	12.5	(66)	Surinam	5.3	(66)	Ivory Coast	2.0
(67)	Luxembourg	12.5	(67)	Netherlands	5.3	(67)	Lesotho	1.9
(67)	Monaco	12.5	(67)	Spanish Sahara	5.0	(66)	Guinea	1.9
(67)	Scotland	12.5	(67)	British Honduras	5.0	(67)	Mozambique	1.9
(67)	Australia	12.5	(63)	Dominica	5.0	(67)	Tanganyika	1.9
(67)	Barbados	11.1	(66)	Montserrat	5.0	(67)	Iraq	1.9
(67)	Bermuda	11.1	(63)	Spain	5.0	(67)	Centr. Afric. Rep.	1.8
(66)	Canada	11.1	(67)	Pacific Islands	5.0	(64)	Somalia	1.8
(66)	Japan	11.1	(67)	St. Lucia	4.8	(67)	Turkey	1.8
(66)	Finland	11.1	(66)	Turks & Caicos Isl.	4.8	(67)	Honduras	1.8
(67)	West Germany	11.1	(67)	Guyana	4.8	(66)	Jordan	1.7
(65)	Iceland	11.1	(66)	Uruguay	4.8	(66)	South Vietnam	1.7
(66)	Switzerland	11.1	(67)	Cyprus	4.8	(66)	Portuguese Guinea	1.6
(67)	North Ireland	11.1	(66/67)	Puerto Rico	4.6	(65)	Morocco	1.5
(66)	Fr. Ter.Afars & Issas	10.0	(62)	St. Vincent	4.6	(66)	Gambia	1.5
(67)	Gabon	10.0	(65)	Trinidad & Tobago	4.4	(67)	Portuguese Timor	1.5
(67)	Guadeloupe	10.0	(67)	US Virgin Islands	4.4	(67)	Senegal	1.4
(67)	Austria	10.0	(66)	Western Samoa	4.2	(67)	Philippines	1.4
(65)	Channel Islands	10.0	(67)	Mauritius	4.0	(67)	Kenya	1.4
(67)	Italy	10.0	(67)	Chile	4.0	(66)	Togo	1.4
(65)	Malta	10.0	(67)	Lebanon	4.0	(66)	Ruanda	1.3
(67)	U.K (England/Wales)	10.0	(67)	St.Kitts Nevis Ang.	4.0	(66)	Ghana	1.3
(66)	Cook Islands	10.0	(67)	Macau	4.0	(65)	Malawi	1.3
(63)	New Hebrides	10.0	(66)	West Malaysia	4.0	(66/67)	Uganda	1.1
(67)	New Zealand	10.0	(67)	Brunei	3.9	(67)	Burundi	1.1
(67)	U.S.S.R.	10.0	(68)	Congo Dem. Rep.	3.7	(66)	Chad	1.1
(65)	Mongolia	9.1	(67)	Ifni	3.7	(67)	Syria	1.1
(67)	Bulgaria	9.1	(67)	Hong Kong	3.7	(62)	Dahomey	1.1
(66/67)	Denmark	9.1	(67)	Singapore	3.6	(67)	Iran	1.0
(67)	Gibraltar	9.1	(63)	Algeria	3.5	(65)	Sudan	1.0
(66)	Norway	9.1	(68)	Swaziland	3.5	(66)	China Taiwan	1.0
(67)	Gilbert & Ellice Isl.	9.1	(67)	Costa Rica	3.5	(66)	Southern Yemen	1.0
(66)	Papua	9.1	(67)	Jamaica	3.5	(66)	Saudi Arabia	0.9
(67)	Martinique	8.4	(67)	Brazil	3.5	(67)	Thailand	0.9
(67)	Netherl. Antilles	8.4	(65)	Ryukyu Islands	3.5	(67)	Burma	0.8
(67)	United States	8.4	(67)	Libya	3.3	(63)	Sierra Leone	0.8
(67)	Israel	8.4	(67)	Southern Rhodesia	3.3	(66)	Korea Republic	0.8
(65)	France	8.4	(67)	Panama	3.3	(65)	Cambodia	0.8
(66)	French Polynesia	8.4	(68)	Venezuela	3.2	(66)	Mali	0.8
(66)	New Guinea	8.4	(67)	Guatemala	3.1	(67)	Haiti	0.7
(66)	Qatar	7.7	(67)	Ceylon	3.1	(68)	Indonesia	0.7
(68)	Belgium	7.7	(67)	Fiji	3.1	(65)	India	0.6
(67)	Hungary	7.7	(67)	Dominican Rep.	2.9	(66)	Nigeria	0.5
(67)	Poland	7.7	(67)	Tonga	2.9	(64)	Yemen	0.4
(67)	Romania	7.7	(67)	Madagascar	2.8	(67)	Upper Volta	0.4
(67)	Bahrain	7.4	(66)	Zambia	2.6	(66)	Ethiopia	0.4
(66)	Niger	7.2	(67)	Guam	2.6	(66)	Muscat & Oman	0.4
(66)	Seychelles Islands	7.2	(66)	Tunisia	2.6	(67)	Pakistan	0.3
(64)	Antigua	7.2	(67)	Botswana	2.5	(65)	Mauritania	0.3
(66)	American Samoa	7.2	(67)	Zanzibar	2.5	(66)	Maldive Islands	0.2
(66)	Reunion	6.7	(67)	East Mal.-Sarawak	2.5	(67)	Nepal	0.2
(67)	Kuwait	6.7	(66)	Angola	2.4	(66)	Afghanistan	0.2

28   World Markets of Tomorrow

Every time the GNP *per capita* doubles, the number of hospital beds is increased by approximately 65%. Here again, increased *per capita* wealth means better social services.

This is one of the few charts where the United States is below the median. The availability of ampler resources for access to private nursing homes and other facilities accounts for this.

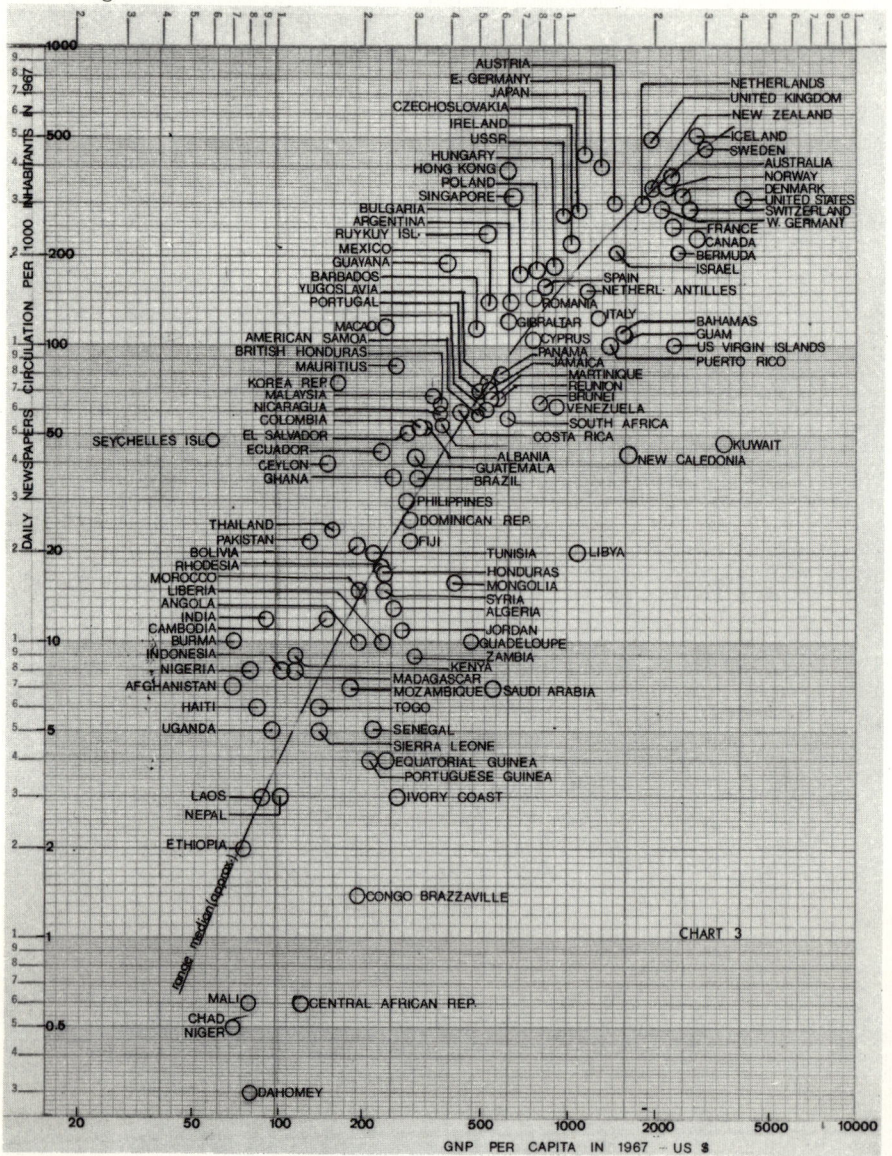

CHART 3—Daily newspapers circulation

Aspects of Life

DAILY NEWSPAPERS CIRCULATION

The facing Chart 3 of daily newspapers circulation per 1,000 inhabitants in terms of the GNP *per capita,* does not point to as clearly defined a trend as some of the other charts. Yet, the upper boundary is of interest with Hong Kong, Japan, the United Kingdom and Iceland leading.

This is another of the few charts where the United States is below the median trend line.

For an approximation of the total amount of exposure to news, one might add the number of television sets:

TABLE XI — Daily newspapers circulation per 1,000 inhabitants

(68)	Sweden	518	(68)	Mauritius	96	(65)	Pakistan	18
(69)	Hong Kong	493	(61)	Cuba	88	(67)	Honduras	17
(68)	Japan	492	(68)	Yugoslavia	83	(67)	Mongolia	16
(67)	United Kingdom	488	(67)	Panama	81	(61)	Iran	15
(65)	Luxembourg	477	(67)	Korea Republic	75	(67)	Syria	15
(68)	East Germany	445	(68)	Malaysia	75	(65)	Southern Rhodesia	15
(65)	Iceland	435	(68)	Brunei	71	(66)	Morocco	14
(68)	Norway	383	(67)	Jamaica	71	(68)	Algeria	14
(68)	New Zealand	373	(67)	Portugal	71	(68)	India	13
(69)	Switzerland	368	(68)	Vietnam Rep.	70	(63)	Iraq	12
(67)	Australia	363	(67)	French Polynesia	68	(68)	Jordan	12
(68)	Denmark	356	(67)	Martinique	67	(64)	Namibia	12
(68)	West Germany	328	(67)	Reunion	66	(66)	Cambodia	11
(67)	Singapore	325	(68)	American Samoa	65	(67)	Angola	10
(63)	Uruguay	314	(63)	Taiwan	64	(66)	Burma	9
(67)	United States	309	(67)	Venezuela	62	(66)	Guadeloupe	9
(68)	U.S.S.R.	305	(67)	Costa Rica	60	(67)	Kenya	9
(67)	Netherlands	301	(61)	South Africa	57	(66)	Liberia	9
(65)	Belgium	285	(66)	British Honduras	55	(67)	Zambia	9
(67)	Czechoslovakia	283	(67)	Albania	53	(67)	Madagascar	8
(68)	Ryukyu Islands	269	(67)	Colombia	53	(67)	Afghanistan	7
(67)	France	251	(68)	Kuwait	52	(65)	Indonesia	7
(65)	Austria	249	(67)	El Salvador	51	(67)	Mozambique	7
(68)	Ireland	242	(65)	Nicaragua	49	(66)	Nigeria	7
(68)	Bermuda	228	(66)	Surinam	49	(67)	Saudi Arabia	7
(66)	Canada	212	(67)	Seychelles Isl.	48	(67)	Togo	6
(68)	Hungary	205	(59)	Peru	47	(68)	Uganda	6
(68)	Poland	199	(61)	Turkey	45	(67)	Sierra Leone	5
(68)	Bulgaria	195	(67)	Ecuador	44	(67)	Senegal	5
(67)	Guyana	191	(68)	Ceylon	44	(65)	Haiti	5
(66)	Israel	188	(67)	New Caledonia	43	(59)	Gambia	5
(68)	Spain	176	(66)	Guatemala	38	(64)	Cameroun	4
(68)	Romania	158	(67)	Cook Islands	37	(67)	Equatorial Guinea	4
(66)	Netherl. Antilles	138	(67)	Brazil	36	(67)	Portuguese Guinea	4
(66)	Argentina	128	(67)	Ghana	36	(62)	Tanzania	3
(68)	Bahamas	122	(69)	French Guyana	34	(66)	Ivory Coast	3
(67)	Gibraltar	120	(66)	St.Kitts Nevis Anguil	30	(67)	Laos	3
(68)	Guam	120	(66)	Philippines	27	(66)	Nepal	3
(64)	Chile	118	(67)	Granada	26	(65)	Ethiopia	2
(65)	Mexico	116	(67)	Dominican Rep.	26	(64)	Somalia	2
(67)	Barbados	115	(68)	Bolivia	23	(66)	Congo Brazzaville	1.3
(67)	Macau	114	(64)	Antigua	22	(67)	Centr. Afric. Rep.	0.6
(66)	Italy	112	(66)	Thailand	22	(66)	Mali	0.5
(68)	US Virgin Islands	112	(68)	Tunisia	22	(65)	Chad	0.4
(67)	Cyprus	103	(66)	Fiji	20	(65)	Niger	0.4
(67)	Puerto Rico	102	(67)	Libya	20	(67)	Dahomey	0.3
(65)	Trinidad	102	(55)	China Mainland	19			

30   World Markets of Tomorrow

The comparable totals (newspapers plus TV sets) would then be, per thousand inhabitants, 309 plus 400 = 709 in the U.S.A. compared with 305 plus 114 = 419 in the U.S.S.R. for instance.

TELEPHONES IN USE

Of all the similar Charts presented here, the facing Chart 4 shows most nearly over the entire range a straight line relationship with the GNP.

The median line trend points to the number of telephones increasing on the average somewhat faster than the GNP.

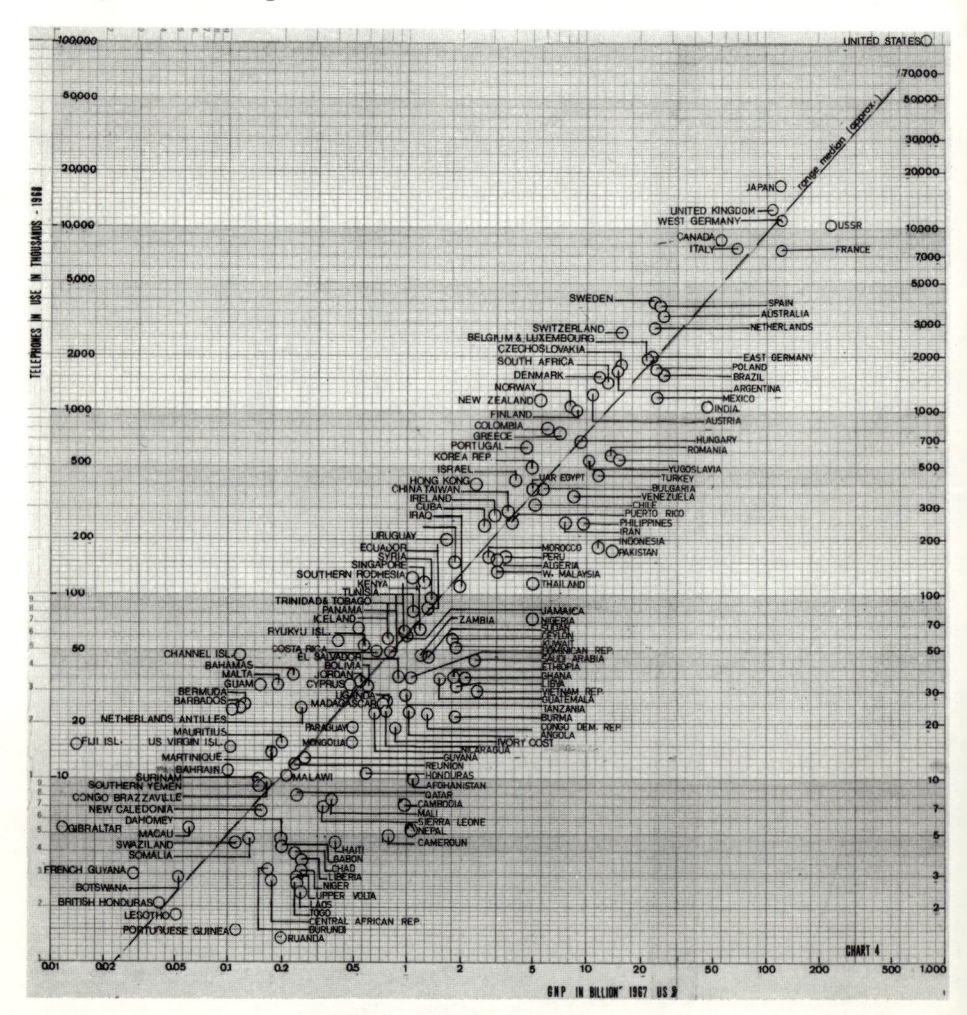

CHART 4—Number of telephones in use

TABLE XII—Telephones in use—1968

Country	Number	Country	Number	Country	Number
United States	109,255,000	Liban	150,370	Mongolia	16,220
Japan	17,330,791	West Malaysia	135,927	Mauritius	15,966
United Kingdom	12,799,000	Southern Rhodesia	125,844	US Virgin Islands	14,984
Germany Fed.Rep.	11,248,979	Singapore	119,184	Fiji Islands	14,507
U.S.S.R.	10,800,000	Thailand	114,419	Martinique	14,130
Canada	8,821,000	Iraq	113,388	Guyana	12,815
Italy	7,752,024	Luxembourg	97,978	Reunion	12,431
France	7,503,491	Syria	96,613	Honduras	11,150
Sweden	3,934,694	Ecuador	88,000	Sarawak	10,789
Spain	3,702,244	Nigeria	75,900	Panama Canal Zone	10,619
Australia	3,392,436	Iceland	66,267	Sp.Possess.N.Afric.	10,543
Netherlands	2,912,384	Kenya	65,445	Bahrain	10,236
Switzerland	2,685,800	Tunisia	61,923	Malawi	10,174
Germany East	1,896,151	Jamaica	61,012	Afghanistan	10,000
Belgium	1,839,457	Panama	58,608	Guadeloupe	9,662
Czechoslovakia	1,789,373	Ceylon	57,598	Sabah	9,638
Poland	1,650,896	Ryukyu Islands	54,762	Surinam	9,600
Argentina	1,599,861	Kuwait	51,168	Congo Brazzaville	9,287
Brazil	1,560,701	Costa Rica	50,093	Southern Yemen	9,110
Denmark	1,516,802	Trinidad & Tobago	49,030	Lichtenstein	8,571
South Africa	1,397,725	Channel Islands	47,609	Qatar	8,237
Austria	1,242,785	Zambia	47,735	Mali	7,800
Mexico	1,174,885	Sudan	45,086	Cambodia	7,315
New Zealand	1,155,465	Saudi Arabia	44,250	Sierra Leone	7,000
India	1,057,193	El Salvador	36,842	Guinea	6,600
Norway	1,036,027	Bahamas	36,513	New Caledonia	6,573
Finland	1,009,336	Guatemala	36,165	Gibraltar	5,444
Colombia	817,423	Ethiopia	36,034	French Polynesia	5,403
Greece	761,550	Ghana	35,950	Nepal	5,400
Hungary	684,389	Dominican Rep.	35,735	Macau	5,319
Portugal	653,407	Jordan	34,500	Cameroon	5,000
Romania	568,588	Cyprus	33,396	Dahomey	4,800
Yugoslavia	549,019	Malta	33,092	Somalia	4,800
Korea Republic	489,912	Guam	33,000	Swaziland	4,461
Turkey	450,485	Bolivia	32,300	Haiti	4,450
Hong Kong	426,540	Libya	31,700	Gabon	4,300
Israel	419,118	Vietnam Republic	30,964	Chad	3,953
Bulgaria	378,152	Namibia	30,813	Liberia	3,600
U.A.R. Egypt	365,000	Tanzania	29,348	Burundi	3,200
Venezuela	345,704	Bermuda	26,436	Niger	3,172
Chile	312,042	Senegal	26,244	Upper Volta	2,999
China Taiwan	280,192	Uganda	25,874	French Guyana	2,990
Ireland	274,134	Netherl. Antilles	24,920	Botswana	2,966
Iran	250,300	Barbados	24,834	Togo	2,800
Puerto Rico	248,415	Ivory Coast	24,390	Centr. Afric. Rep.	2,800
Cuba	242,000	Madagascar	23,993	Brunei	2,681
Philippines	241,496	Congo Dem. Rep.	23,919	Laos	2,454
Uruguay	205,174	Nicaragua	23,484	British Honduras	2,111
Indonesia	181,377	Angola	22,978	San Marina	2,022
Pakistan	176,807	Mozambique	22,636	Lesotho	1,844
Peru	165,121	Burma	22,080	Portuguese Guinea	1,517
Morocco	160,326	Paraguay	19,128	Ruanda	1,389
Algeria	156,038	Papua	16,312		

As a convenient figure to remember, and if we assume that a country's GNP increases by 6% every year, we could expect the number of telephones to increase by 7%, which means that it would double in 10 years.

In the many countries where inadequate telephone service is sometimes a source of irritation to the visitor, this points to what should be a minimum rate expansion of the number of telephones available, this of course to be accompanied by correspondingly higher standards of service.

TELEVISION RECEIVERS PER 1,000 INHABITANTS

Table XIII and Chart 5, showing television receivers in use per 1,000 inhabitants, spread over a wide range: from 0.01 in India to 400 in the United States.

TABLE XIII—Television receivers per 1,000 inhabitants—1968

Country	Value	Country	Value	Country	Value
United States	400	Venezuela	75.0	Southern Rhodesia	9.9
Canada	299	Cuba	72.0	El Salvador	9.0
Sweden	298	Paraguay	70.0	Jordan	8.4
US Virgin Islands	286	Yugoslavia	66.0	Tunisia	8.1
United Kingdom	280	Malta	65.0	Iran	7.6
Bermuda	260	Barbados	60.0	Morocco	7.1
Germany Fed.Rep.	259	Brazil	60.0	Thailand	6.5
Denmark	250	Romania	58.0	Saudi Arabia	5.7
Germany East	245	Singapore	55.0	Guadeloupe	5.5
Gibraltar	240	Cyprus	52.0	Philippines	5.5
Australia	230	Costa Rica	47.0	Greece	4.6
New Zealand	221	Mexico	47.0	Zambia	4.3
Netherlands	211	Honduras	45.0	Liberia	3.6
Japan	210	Chile	44.0	Korea Republic	3.2
Finland	198	Guam	43.5	Haiti	2.4
Kuwait	193	Hong Kong	43.0	Gabon	2.1
Norway	191	Trinidad & Tobago	40.5	Ivory Coast	1.7
Belgium & Lux.	191	Reunion	34.0	Kenya	1.5
Czechoslovakia	190	Jamaica	29.8	Sierra Leone	1.2
France	187	Portugal	29.6	Cambodia	1.1
Puerto Rico	175	Colombia	25.0	Uganda	1.1
Switzerland	167	Peru	24.2	Sudan	1.0
Spain	165	Iraq	20.8	Upper Volta	0.9
Italy	155	Nicaragua	19.6	Ghana	0.7
Austria	154	Dominican Rep.	19.3	Indonesia	0.7
Ireland	152	Martinique	18.2	Surinam	0.7
Lebanon	149	Mauritius	16.8	Congo Brazzaville	0.6
Hungary	137	China Taiwan	14.7	Congo Leopoldville	0.6
Iceland	126	U.A.R. Egypt	14.0	Nigeria	0.6
U.S.S.R.	114	Guatemala	13.8	Albania	0.5
Bahrain	109	Syria	12.6	Ethiopia	0.3
Argentina	107	Algeria	12.1	Pakistan	0.3
Poland	106	Malaysia	12.0	Senegal	0.3
Panama	81	Ecuador	11.8	Turkey	0.2
Uruguay	77	Israel	11.2	India	0.01
Bulgaria	75				

Aspects of Life

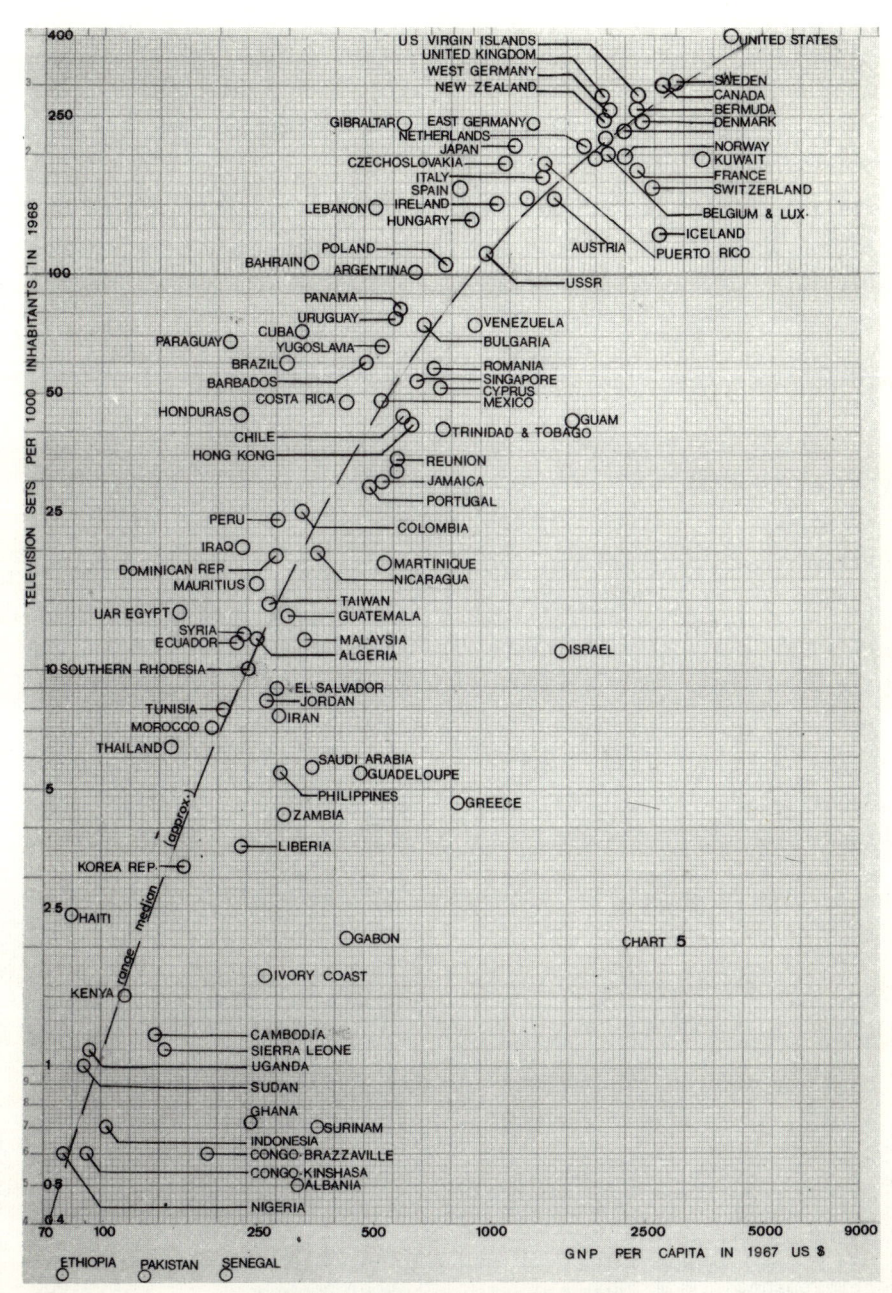

CHART 5—Number of television receivers

In Chart 5, near the upper and lower boundaries we note respectively Haiti, Paraguay, Gibraltar, as having relatively a large number of sets in use and Albania, Gabon, Greece, Israel, Iceland and

TABLE XIVa—Tourist receipts—1968 (in U.S.$ at exchange rate)

United States	1,770,000,000	Iraq	47,000,000
Italy	1,476,000,000	Kenya	46,000,000
Spain	1,213,000,000	Tunisia	45,000,000
Mexico	1,137,000,000	Colombia	43,000,000
France	954,000,000	Iran	42,000,000
Canada	918,000,000	India	35,000,000
Germany Fed.Rep.	906,000,000	Peru	22,000,000
Austria	687,000,000	Trinidad & Tobago	22,000,000
United Kingdom	677,000,000	New Zealand	22,000,000
Scandinavia	512,000,000	Brazil	21,000,000
Netherlands	342,000,000	Malta	19,000,000
Belgium	288,000,000	Poland	18,000,000
Portugal	214,000,000	Korea Republic	17,000,000
Argentina	175,000,000	Malaysia	15,000,000
Hong Kong	160,000,000	Libya	15,000,000
Japan	126,000,000	Cyprus	14,000,000
Greece	120,000,000	Jordan	13,000,000
Australia	113,000,000	Dominican Rep.	10,000,000
Lebanon	110,000,000	Ecuador	8,000,000
Israel	97,000,000	Guatemala	7,000,000
Morocco	84,000,000	Pakistan	6,000,000
Jamaica	80,000,000	Bolivia	3,000,000
South Africa	77,000,000	Iceland	3,000,000
China Taiwan	65,000,000	Mauritius	3,000,000
Bermuda	63,000,000	Nigeria	3,000,000
Czechoslovakia	61,000,000	Vietnam Republic	2,000,000
Thailand	58,000,000	Haiti	2,000,000
Singapore	49,000,000	Indonesia	2,000,000
Philippines	48,000,000	Sudan	1,000,000
Hungary	48,000,000	Nepal	800,000

Aspects of Life

Kuwait as having a small number of sets in relation to their *per capita* GNP.

From a potential market point of view, the latter group of countries and, for that matter, all those which are below the median could be regarded as indicative of a market which could be substantially developed.

In Chapter Nine under 'All the World Markets of the Future' we have developed, based on Chart 5, an example of market forecasting for a specific country: the United Kingdom, for a specific product: television sets to which the reader may wish to turn, now.

TOURIST RECEIPTS

Whereas the world receipts total in 1966 was 14% higher than in 1965, the figure for 1967, because of the 6-day war, was only 7% higher than in 1966. In 1968, as a result of student unrest in France etc. the receipts were actually 9% lower than in 1967.

The totals for 1968, in Table XIVa, become more pertinent from

TABLE XIVb—Tourist receipts as percent of gross national product.

Bermuda	43.00 %	Lybia	0.81 %
Malta	10.06	India	0.76
Lebanon	8.35	West Germany	0.76
Jamaica	8.08	Colombia	0.72
Hong Kong	6.76	Ecuador	0.63
Austria	6.40	Peru	0.63
Mexico	4.72	United Kingdom	0.62
Portugal	4.64	South Africa	0.59
Spain	4.60	Iran	0.56
Tunisia	4.60	Iceland	0.55
Kenya	4.00	Haiti	0.52
Morocco	3.11	Hungary	0.52
Cyprus	3.05	Guatemala	0.50
Trinidad & Tobago	2.79	Philippines	0.50
Singapore	2.58	Malaysia	0.45
Israel	2.44	Australia	0.42
Iraq	2.42	New Zealand	0.40
Jordan	2.38	Czechoslovakia	0.38
Italy	2.25	Korea Rep.	0.36
China Taiwan	1.80	United States	0.22
Greece	1.71	Brazil	0.08
Canada	1.61	Nepal	0.08
Mauritius	1.51	Sudan	0.08
Netherlands	1.50	Vietnam Rep.	0.08
Argentina	1.19	Poland	0.07
Thailand	1.14	Nigeria	0.06
Dominican Rep.	0.95	Pakistan	0.04
Japan	0.83	Indonesia	0.02
France	0.82		

an economic standpoint, when converted into percentages of the total country GNP, as shown in Table XIVb.

There are a number of tourist-favored countries which rank between Bermuda and Mali as far as the percentages shown are concerned, but data for these was lacking.

PASSENGER AUTOMOBILES IN USE

Chart 6, which shows the number of automobiles in terms of the country GNP, is the only chart in this group which points to a use which increases faster than the GNP: Reading from the median trend

TABLE XV—Passenger automobiles in use—1968

World Total	170,090,000				
United States	83,281,300	Turkey	112,600	Jordan	20,400
France	11,500,000	Israel	112,600	Panama Canal Zone	17,800
Germany Fed.Rep.	11,322,400	Southern Rhodesia	108,800	Sierra Leone	16,000
United Kingdom	10,949,000	Kuwait	92,500	Malaysia - Sabah	15,900
Italy	8,178,500	Ceylon	84,700	Bolivia	14,500
Canada	6,159,600	Kenya	80,600	Guyana	14,200
Japan	5,209,000	Luxembourg	78,000	Sarawak	13,600
Australia	3,444,800	Libya	77,300	Liberia	13,400
Sweden	2,072,200	Hong Kong	73,000	Mauritius	12,300
Netherlands	1,950,000	Trinidad & Tobago	67,600	French Polynesia	12,100
Belgium	1,813,100	Angola	64,400	Honduras	12,000
Spain	1,577,200	Nigeria	63,000	Surinam	10,900
Brazil	1,537,000	Iraq	61,500	Laos	10,600
South Africa	1,405,000	Tunisia	60,600	Dahomey	9,900
Switzerland	1,180,500	Jamaica	60,000	Bermuda	9,800
Argentina	1,152,300	Canary Islands	56,800	Fiji Islands	9,300
Austria	1,056,300	Zambia	48,200	Southern Yemen	9,000
Mexico	1,000,000	Congo Dem. Rep.	46,100	Malawi	8,800
Denmark	954,700	Cyprus	42,400	Somalia	8,200
East Germany	920,200	Madagascar	41,600	Brunei	7,800
New Zealand	829,900	Ivory Coast	40,600	Guinea	7,600
Norway	619,000	Panama	40,400	Haiti	7,300
Czechoslovakia	598,600	Ryukyu Islands	38,300	Afars & Issas	7,000
Finland	580,700	Iceland	37,000	Paraguay	6,900
Indonesia	505,200	Sao Tome & Principe	34,300	New Guinea	6,500
Venezuela	482,000	Vietnam Republic	34,100	Papua	6,500
Yugoslavia	439,000	Costa Rica	33,700	Gabon	6,300
Puerto Rico	383,300	Dominican Rep.	33,300	Togo	5,800
Poland	373,900	Korea Republic	33,100	Upper Volta	5,200
Ireland	340,900	Uganda	32,800	Mali	4,800
Ireland Northern	263,000	Bahamas	32,400	Gibraltar	4,500
Philippines	232,700	Ghana	32,200	Centr. Afric. Rep.	4,300
West Malaysia	200,500	Malta	31,500	French Guyana	4,300
Morocco	189,500	El Salvador	31,300	Nepal	4,000
Iran	180,400	China Taiwan	30,700	Mauritania	3,700
Greece	169,100	Ethiopia	29,500	Chad	3,700
Hungary	163,600	Afghanistan	29,200	Burundi	3,200
Uruguay	142,000	Netherl. Antilles	29,100	British Honduras	3,000
Colombia	141,100	Syria	29,000	Ruanda	2,900
Pakistan	139,400	Burma	28,900	Gambia	2,300
Chile	130,200	Sudan	27,400	Botswana	2,200
Thailand	129,500	Cameroon	26,900	Spanish Sahara	2,200
Singapore	126,500	Martinique	25,200	St.Kitts Nevis Anguil.	1,800
Lebanon	123,900	Cambodia	23,100	New Hebrides	1,200
Algeria	117,000	Reunion	22,300	Seychelles Islands	1,000
U.A.R. Egypt	115,900	Ecuador	22,000		

Aspects of Life

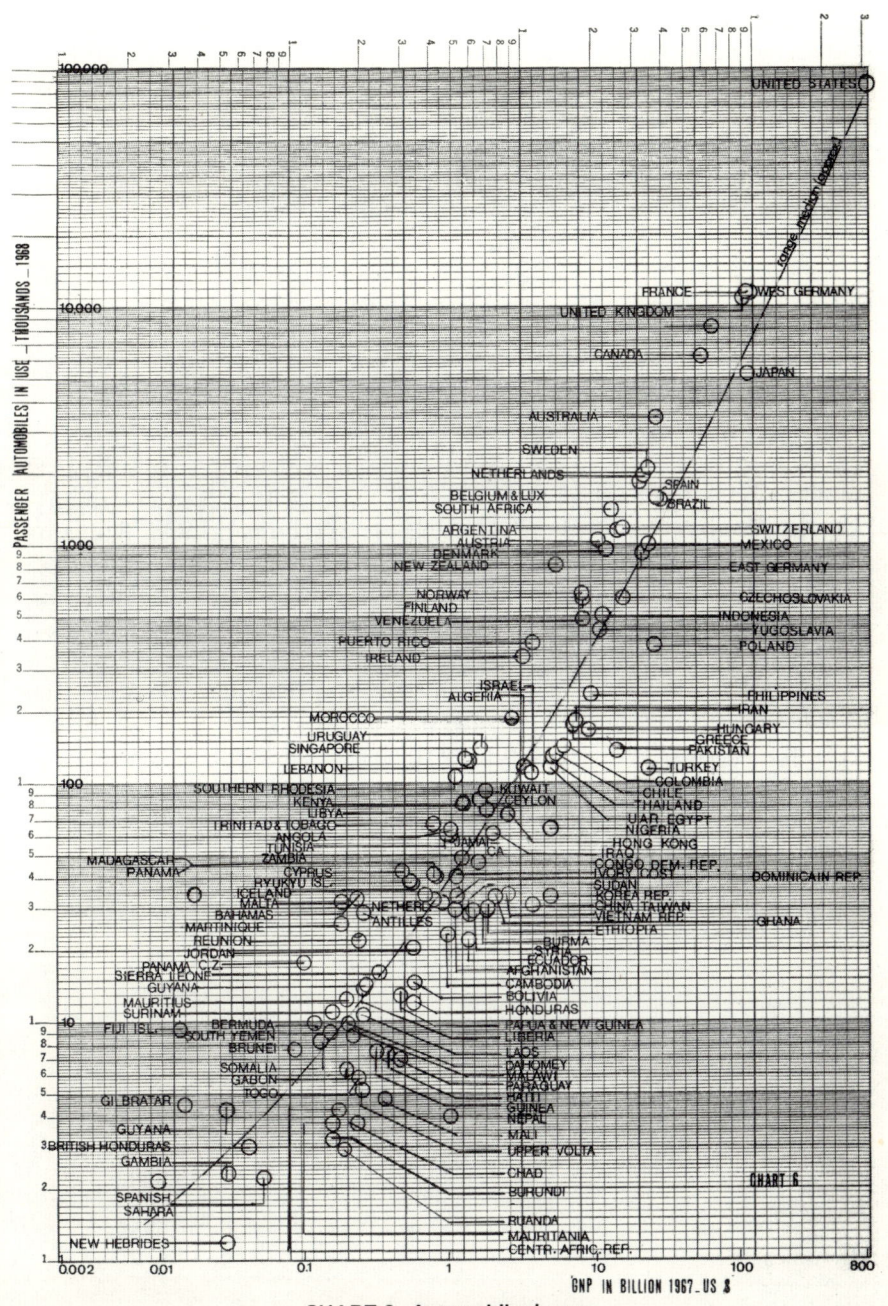

CHART 6—Automobiles in use

and comparing two countries, one with a GNP of $10 billion, the other with a GNP of $100 billion, it appears that a 10 to 1 ratio of GNP corresponds to a 20 to 1 ratio of passenger automobiles in use.

This is not surprising. Had we included more products the demand for which increases with the availability of disposable income, we would have also encountered similar trends.

We note from Table XV that one-half of the automobiles of the world are in the United States.

CRUDE STEEL CONSUMPTION

The correlation between steel consumption and GNP shown in Chart 7 has been mentioned very often.

In addition to Japan, Sweden and the United States that one expects to find close to the upper range, it is of interest to note that practically all of the Eastern bloc countries: East Germany, Czechoslovakia, U.S.S.R., Poland, Hungary, Bulgaria and Rumania are all quite high.

This reflects the emphasis on heavy industry in these countries, accompanied by curtailment of consumer-oriented expenditures, which are held to the minimum.

By holding down the level of consumption and devoting the remainder of the output to investment, so as to increase future output, fast rates of industrial growth can be achieved, at a price!

At the lower boundary, we note the countries where agricultural production contributes essentially to the overall economy: Greece, Ireland, Israel, Denmark, Switzerland.

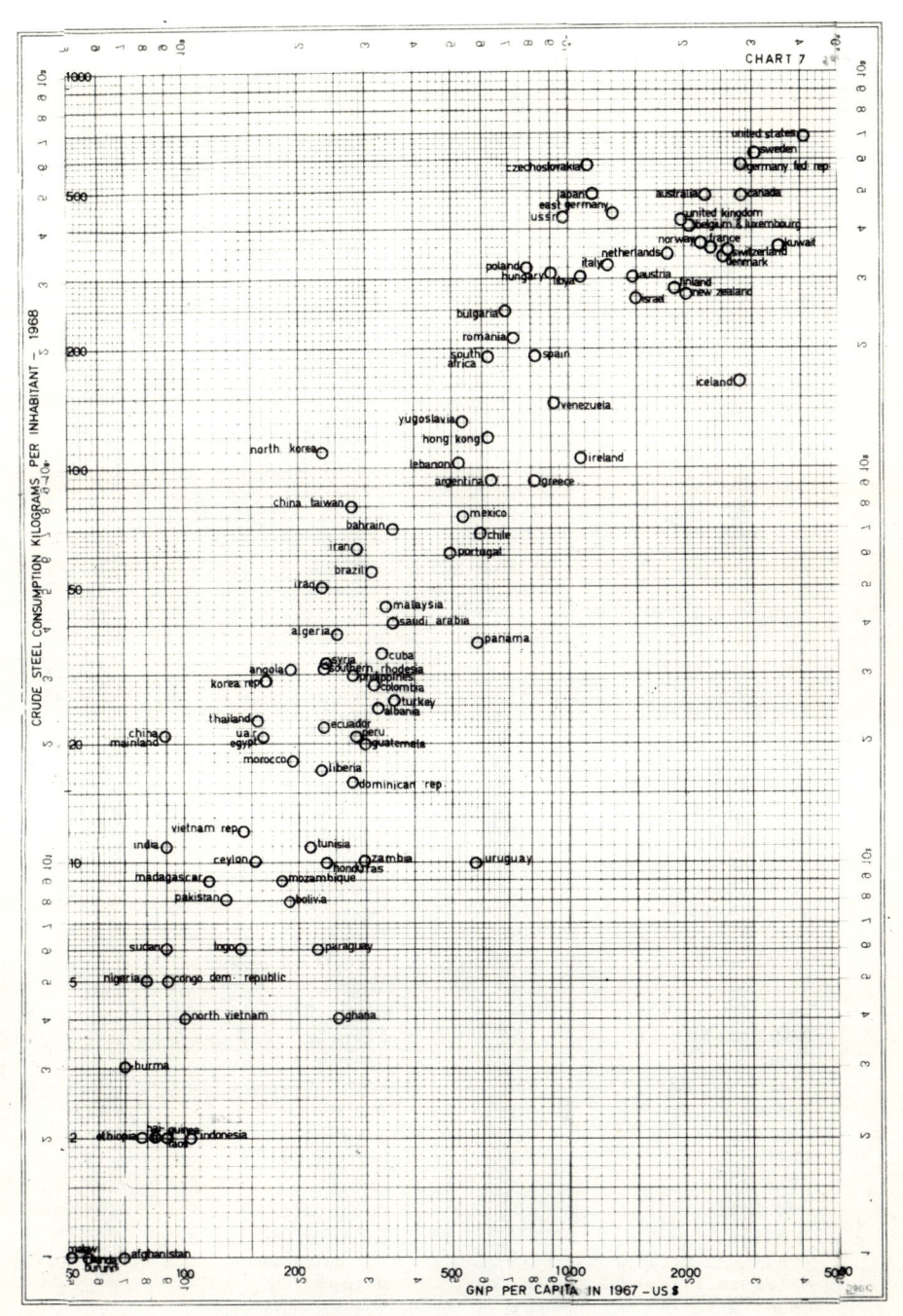

CHART 7—Crude steel consumption

TABLE XVI—Crude steel consumption in kilograms per inhabitant—1968

+ : 67   ++ : 66

Country	kg	Country	kg
World Average	147		
United States	685	Algeria	38
Sweden	623	Panama	36
Czechoslovakia	590	Cuba	34
Germany Fed. Rep.	579	Syria	32
Japan	494	Southern Rhodesia	31
Australia	489	Angola	31
Canada	489	Philippines	30
+ East Germany	437	Korea Republic	29
U.S.S.R.	428	Colombia	28
United Kingdom	422	Turkey	26
Belgium & Luxembourg	409	Albania	25
Norway	371	Thailand	23
Kuwait	363	Ecuador	22
France	359	China Mainland	21
Switzerland	357	Peru	21
Netherlands	347	U.A.R. Egypt	21
Denmark	339	Guatemala	20
Italy	325	Morocco	18
Poland	323	Liberia	17
Hungary	307	Dominican Republic	16
Austria	306	Vietnam Republic	12
Libya	305	India	11
Finland	286	Tunisia	11
New Zealand	276	Ceylon	10
Israel	270	Honduras	10
Bulgaria	251	Uruguay	10
++ Romania	212	Zambia	10
South Africa	189	Madagascar	9
Spain	188	Mozambique	9
Iceland	164	Bolivia	8
Venezuela	147	East Africa	8
Yugoslavia	130	Pakistan	8
Hong Kong	119	Paraguay	6
North Korea	109	Sudan	6
Ireland	107	Togo	6
Lebanon	104	Congo Dem. Republic	5
Argentina	94	Nigeria	5
Greece	94	Ghana	4
China Taiwan	80	North Vietnam	4
Mexico	75	Burma	3
Bahrain	70	Ethiopia	2
Chile	68	Guinea	2
Iran	63	Haiti	2
Portugal	61	Indonesia	2
Brazil	55	Laos	2
Iraq	50	Afghanistan	1
Malaysia	45	Malawi	1
Saudi Arabia	41	Ruanda Burundi	1

CHAPTER FOUR

Economic Growth

Economic growth, the rate at which it can be maintained or accelerated, is a fundamental, common concern of all countries of the world.

To the highly industrialized as well as to the low-income, developing countries (throughout the entire scale of yearly *per capita* GNP which ranges from $50 to nearly $5,000), it gives expression to:

(i) hopes that increasing prosperity will help meet the aspirations of expanding populations,
(ii) hopes for a greater dignity of life,
(iii) hopes for a broader base of employment,
(iv) hopes for higher standards of living and well-being.

Economic growth has been discussed and GNP forecasts have been presented for a number of countries. In most cases, with the exception of Japan's star performance, there has been little indication of the performance trends to be expected from each country during this coming decade let alone into the next 30 years.

This is understandable. Development plans set 5-year targets to achieve legitimate goals determined by current economic conditions and national needs, and each country's performance is subject to many uncertainties.

A comparison of long-term trends in the light of a country's current economic conditions and aspirations would be difficult and the wide margin of contingencies involved would tend to diminish the significance of the comparison.

We have chosen to look as far back into recorded economic history as valid and comparable data allow and correlate our findings into long-range projections of growth potential letting past performance define the patterns for the future.

Of the two factors: Economic Growth *per capita* and Population Growth, the product of which measures the economic growth of a country, the first is of overriding importance, and to its analysis as well as the 'pattern' method of forecasting it we have given a major part in this report.

Its more technical aspects are printed in smaller type enabling the reader to skip these, if he prefers, without losing continuity.

To achieve related projections of the Gross National Product of all countries, we have developed forecasts of demographic growth specifically tailored to each country's past record of population increase.

Thus, we hope to have provided a valid and dynamic insight into the economic prospects of all countries as well as into their market potential.

GROSS NATIONAL PRODUCT

Gross National Product—which we shall refer to as GNP—is the total value, at market prices, of all goods and services produced by a nation's economy.

It is equal to the total of: the consumption expenditure, the private and public gross domestic capital formation (which measures the investment in additional fixed assets, including expenditures or repairs over and above what is needed to keep the capital equipment and goods in continuous good working condition), the *net* balance of exports and imports of goods and services, the *net* balance of investment incomes received from abroad and of income payments made to the rest of the world.

GROSS NATIONAL PRODUCT 'PER CAPITA'

In the following chapters we shall focus attention on the GNP *per capita* which is obtained by dividing the country GNP by the population in mid-year.

For each of the 186 countries reviewed in this volume, its 1967 GNP *per capita* is shown in Table VIII, already presented in Chapter Two.

PER CAPITA ECONOMIC GROWTH

It should be remembered that the growth rate of GNP *per capita* is always smaller than the growth rate of the country GNP, due to the annual percentage increase in population.

For instance, 5% growth rate for the GNP of a country in which the population expands at the rate of 2% per year, is equivalent to a 3% rate of growth for the GNP *per capita*.

Economic Growth 43

This is particularly pertinent for developing countries which have a high rate of population growth; for instance, a country with a 4% GNP growth and a 3½% population growth will have no measurable *per capita* GNP growth.

HOW IS ECONOMIC GROWTH PROJECTED?

For most of the major countries of the world, including the United States, economic growth has generally been projected by estimating the labour force, the hours worked per week and the productivity per man-hour.

We have developed an entirely different approach, which we believe will provide a new insight into the mechanism of growth not only in a number of factors classified as GNP input or output but also in a wide range of aspects of human progress.

Apart from constituting a more comprehensive approach, our pattern concept, derived from the analysis and study of global data recording GNP growth, energy use and electricity use, has provided us with a full set of '153 answers'.

There is one of these answers for each country.

In a global feedback each country has benefitted from having contributed its own record towards a better insight into, and appraisal of, the prospects of all other countries.

This has enabled us to arrive at detailed analyses and forecasts of the *per capita* GNP, each tailored to, and reflecting, the statistical and historical record over the past ten to twenty years of each country of the world.

PATTERNS OF 'PER CAPITA' ECONOMIC GROWTH AND ENERGY CONSUMPTION

For the past 15 years, the author has carried out year-by-year analyses of the growth of the economy and of energy consumption for all countries of the world, now totaling 186. From this study has been established the fact that, on a *per capita* basis, a family of fundamental patterns could be developed, and that—in the absence of major economic or military disruptions or a substantial investment effort to achieve faster growth rates—the trend of each country could be fitted into one of these patterns with a surprising degree of accuracy and consistency.

This single family of patterns, which constitutes the basic theme of our analysis, is shown in fold-out Chart 12, as used for the study of the growth of *per capita* GNP.

In abscissae, we have shown the years elapsed as countries progress along these patterns and, in ordinates, we have shown the stage of growth.

This ordinate scale can be read in $ U.S. *per capita* GNP when multiplied by the appropriate constant, a different one for each country whose constant is shown in Table XXV.

Circles identified with the name of each country pinpoint their respective 1967 *per capita* GNP status and pattern of growth, for each of the 153 countries, except those for which the 'reference year' was beyond 180.

PATTERNS OF GROWTH: HOW WERE THESE PATTERNS OBTAINED?

The basic patterns presented in fold-out Chart 12 were obtained by a simple mathematical calculation, the technique for which is the following:

The yearly percent increase of a 'growth' variable is plotted at various stages in a graph similar to Chart 8, which is the same as Fig. 3 of Item (6), where it is explained in pages 5-10.

Such a chart provides a complete record of annual growth rates expressed in percentages at each stage of development.

To illustrate: Suppose a new species of reptiles has been discovered. They are of all ages, from new-born to full-grown, and we wish to determine, if possible, how old each of them is, at what rate their length has grown, and what length they will eventually attain?

In order to achieve this, we tag each animal and record its length, say on 1st January 1970 and again on 1st January 1971, calculating the yearly increase in percent, thus:

$$\frac{\text{Added length from 1970 to 1971}}{\text{Length as of 1 January 1970}}$$

Plotting these yearly percentage increases for each animal, on the vertical line corresponding to its length on 1 January 1970, we observe a strong concentration of points along a clearly defined 'median' pattern from which we draw the 100% curve.

Here we employ the mathematical technique which converts the graph of Chart 8, showing yearly percentage growth at all stages of development, into a growth pattern in terms of years.

Let us take the first point on the horizontal scale: 2½, which, in our simile serves as the length of the new-born animal. We observe that it grows at the rate of 18% per year during the first weeks of its existence.

How long will it take this new-born, 2½ inches long animal, to reach a length of 5 inches?

We know that when this length is reached the yearly growth rate will have tapered down to 14.8%. Thus we have established that during the elapsed

Economic Growth

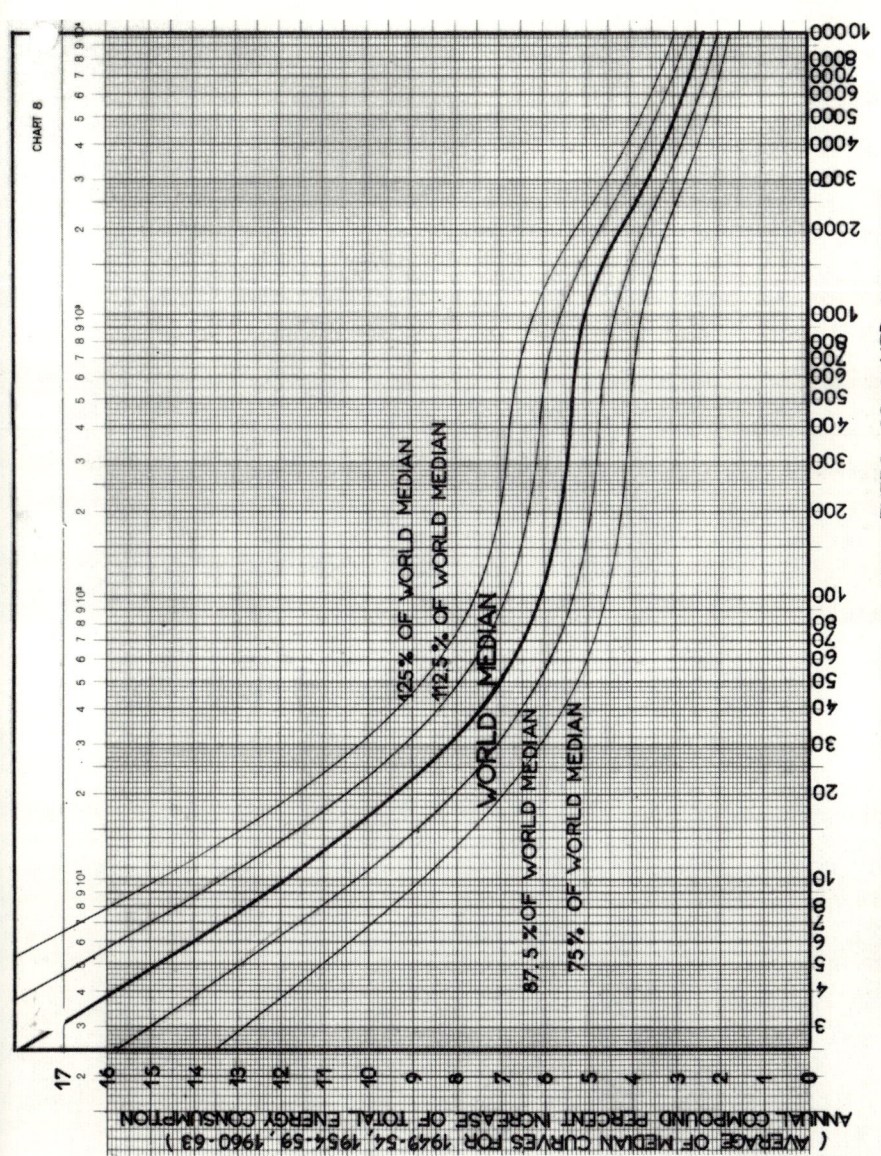

CHART 8—Annual percent increase v. stage of growth
(AVERAGE OF MEDIAN CURVES FOR 1949-54, 1954-59, 1960-63)

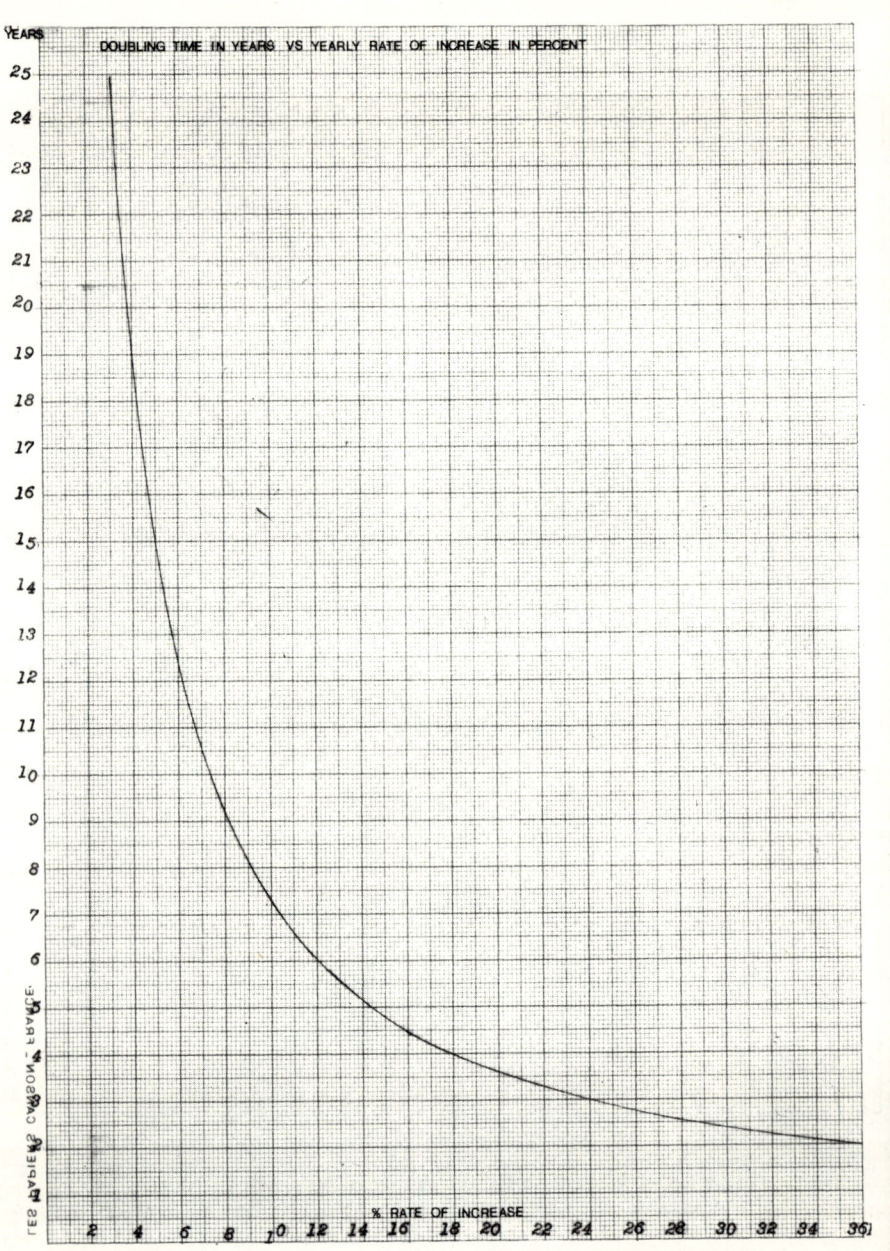

CHART 9—Doubling time in years in term of annual rate of increase

Economic Growth 47

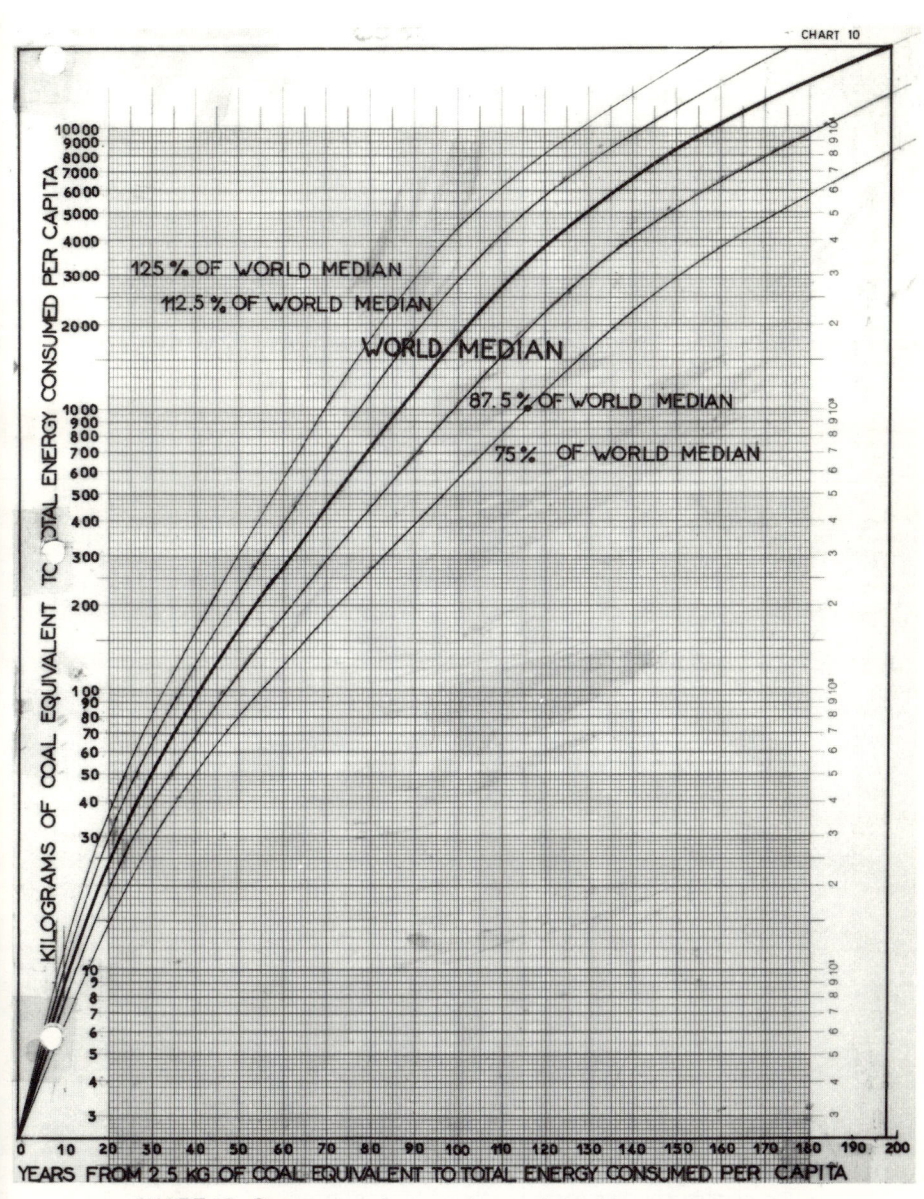

CHART 10—Growth curve in term of years, derived from basic pattern

number of years the average yearly rate of growth will be, as read from the 'World Median' curve of Chart 8:

$$\frac{18 + 14.8}{2} = 16.4\%$$

The problem is simple: What is the doubling time at 16.4% yearly rate of increase?

The answer is 4.6 years, as seen from Chart 9. On the curve of Chart 10, we therefore plot a first point: 5 inches after 4.6 years.

Now we take the next step of growth: from '5 to 10'. When the latter stage is reached, the yearly rate of increase will have tapered down to 11.9%. So, between the '5' and '10' stage, the average yearly rate of increase will have been; as read from Chart 8:

$$\frac{14.8 + 11.9}{2} = 13.35\%;$$

for which the doubling time is 5.6 years.

Thus we have obtained a second point. 10 will be reached after 4.6 + 5.6 = 10.2 years. Repeating this process, step-by-step, enables one to plot the entire curve of Chart 10, which curve shows us that the animals which have reached a length of 1,000 are 86 years old, etc.

It is of interest to note that through this process, even though our record of data accumulation started only on January 1st, 1970, we have a growth history which goes back to 1884, since this is the date on which the 1000 inches long reptile, now 86 years old, was born.

JUSTIFICATION OF THE VALIDITY OF THE APPROACH USED: WORLD MEDIAN PATTERN

The exercise just explained is valid only if we are assured that in 1884 the yearly percentage increases for a new-born animal of this species was the same as was measured for animals born in 1970.

To answer this question, let us return to our analysis of energy use, as follows.

The yearly percentage increase in the energy use *per capita* plot of Chart 8 was calculated for 4 separate periods: 1949 to 1954, 1954 to 1959, 1960 to 1963 and 1963 to 1967.

Each of these analyses was conducted independently of the others, looking only at the span of years under consideration, as if it were the only period of recorded use of energy.

For each of these periods an individual 'shot-gun' array of these average increases was plotted in terms of *per-capita* use of energy in the respective starting year.

In our averaging the percentage increases for all of these countries, at various stages of use of *per capita* energy consumption, we have given the same weight to the most important and to the least important countries, in the same way as, in the United Nations Assembly, the vote of each country has the same weight.

Economic Growth 49

The 'median' curve, which left as many countries above it as below it, was individually plotted for each 5-year period.

There was so little difference between these 4 medians that their average was regarded as fully representative of the relationship between yearly increase in the use of energy and *per capita* use of energy for any year between 1949 and 1968.

In other words, the median of each of the patterns of 150 to 180 countries has remained the same.

The pattern shown as 100% has been proved to be valid over a period spanning the entire industrial development of the United States; this is brought out towards the end of this Chapter under the heading: 'Why introduce a more complex notion for a pattern?'

FAMILY OF GROWTH PATTERNS

Whereas, in an initial approach only two slower patterns: 87.5% and 75% and two faster patterns: 112.5% and 125% were shown, in Chart 8, the complete study of the economic growth of 186 countries brought out that their growth record spanned a much wider range. Yet, the records of countries which had progressed twice as fast as the world median as well as those for countries which had progressed only a quarter as fast as the world median showed that the patterns of growth corresponding to these extreme conditions could be derived from the 100% pattern by the simple proportionality which Chart 11 shows.

At every stage of growth, as plotted in abscissas, the percentage growth rate is obtained from the one on the 100% curve by a direct proportionality: For the 200% pattern, each growth rate is twice that of the world median, for the 25% the ratio is ¼, etc.

We have shown how growth patterns showing stages of growth in terms of years can be derived from charts showing rates of growth increase in terms of stages of growth. The patterns shown in Global Chart 12 are in the same relation to those shown in Chart 11 as the Growth Curve in Chart 10 is to Chart 8. As a matter of fact, the curves identified as 100% are practically identical in both Chart 8 and Chart 11, the same as in Chart 10 and 12.

In Chart 11 there are shown only 10 patterns, 25% apart.

In Chart 12, we have shown approximately 50 of these and, were it not for the limitations imposed by clarity of presentation, we could have shown many more to emphasize that the growth model—an entirely empirical one—that we have defined, can be fitted, as we have done for 150 countries with widely different growth characteristics, to any recorded history of economic progress.

ARE THESE PATTERNS EMPIRICAL OR THEORETICAL?

We wish to emphasize that there has been no theorizing involved in the determination of this basic pattern. Up to a *per capita* use of energy of 10,000 KEC, there was abundant statistical data and we have simply let the 20-year record of all countries, speak for itself.

No attempt has been made to fit an empirical growth curve into a mathematical formula and the patterns used throughout this study cannot serve as input to a computer.

50   *World Markets of Tomorrow*

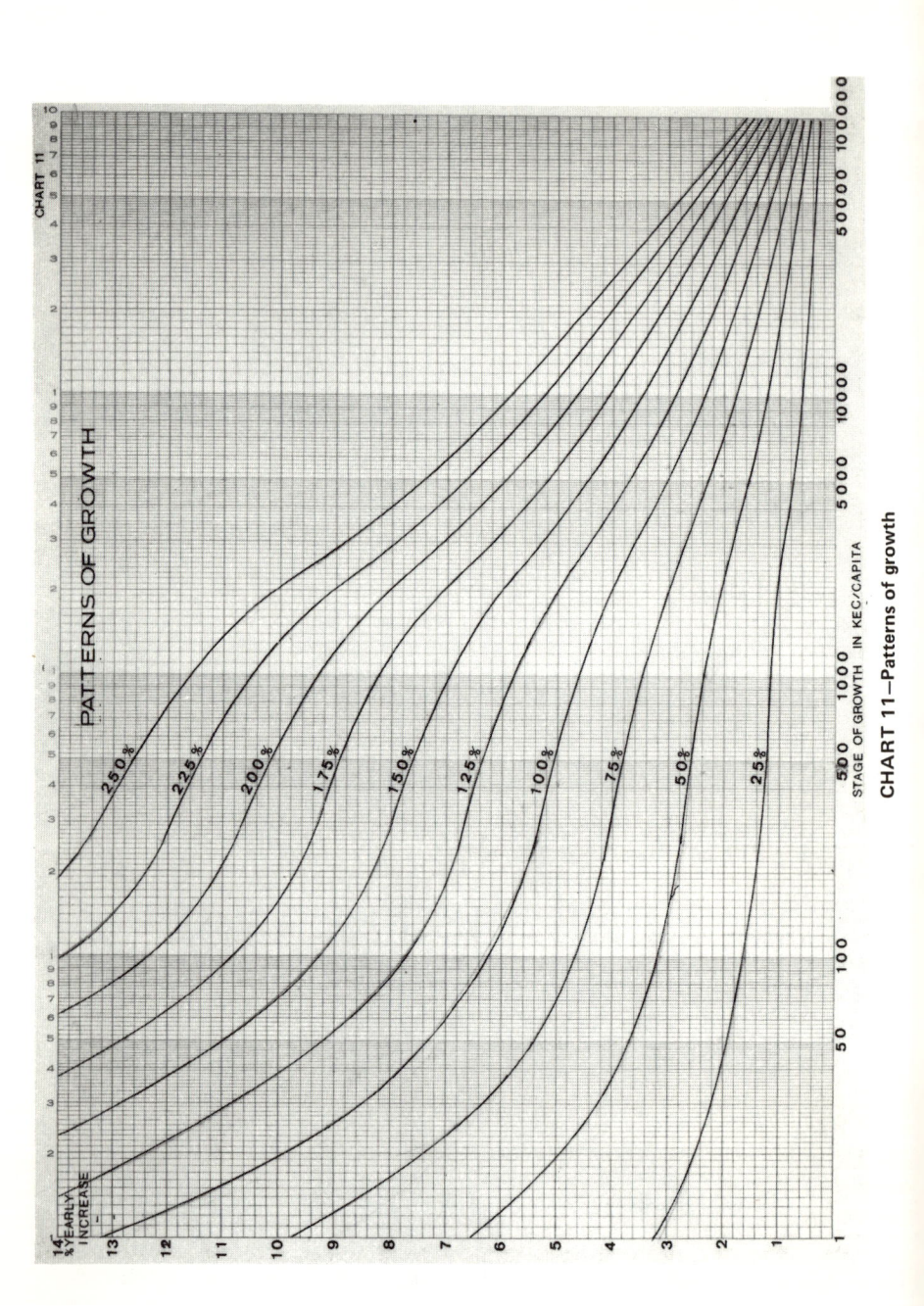

CHART 11—Patterns of growth

Economic Growth 51

'PER CAPITA' GNP VALUES WHICH WOULD CORRESPOND TO MORE THAN 10,000 KEC

For purposes of projection beyond this value, it has been necessary to extrapolate the pattern and, for that purpose a thorough investigation has been made of all the various mathematical formulas to which the empirical pattern could be equated most closely.

It was determined that the Gompertz equation, which provides a favorably regarded form of long-term projection of the trend it recognizes in the data supplied to it, was the most appropriate.

Under 'Complementary Notes' additional comments will be found on the Gompertz equation and its applicability to the population growth projections, as well.

JUSTIFICATION OF THE PATTERNS

1. Why have these verifications of the 'permanence' of the world-median pattern not been carried out over a more extended period?

    They have been carried as far back as the availability of reliable and consistent data permitted. The United Nations statistical series J-1 through J-13 have been our most important source and tribute must be rendered to the completeness of the data made available year after year.

    Our particular analysis demands a 'quality' which the contributing countries have not all provided from the start. It is only since 1948 that U.N. data has made it possible to deduce the results analysed here:

    (i) In part because the aftermath of the war had subsided, bringing to an end all the economic and statistical disturbances attendant thereon.
    (ii) In part because the United Nations continued to improve its own methods of compilation and presentation.
    (iii) And in part because of the emergence of many new nations that contributed additional data for countries in the early stages of development.

2. Recognizing, therefore, that the world-median growth patterns have a high degree of permanence, the question which arises is: Why? How is it that, for over more than 20 years, the world-median rate of growth in energy use has remained the same at a given stage of development?

    How do we explain that these past two decades of surging technological improvement have not resulted in 'world median' countries achieving a much faster growth than countries at the same stage of development 10 or 15 years ago?

    Even in small print, it would be difficult to give here an answer which would not be too lengthy. It may, however, be summarized: For each country, the cost of all the energy used bears a certain relation to the total expenditure for capital investment: 10% is a convenient approximation.

    Since any substantial increase in the cost of the energy used could only occur if there was a ten-fold increase in the total capital formation investments (so that additional industries, etc, could use the extra energy) it is easily realised that the limitations which govern the allocation of all the investments that are demanded for the economic growth of the country have acted, throughout the years, as a regulating factor contributing to the permanence we have noted.

Under 'Complementary Notes' the composition of Capital Formation is explained in detail.

Another question might be asked: Recognizing that for any one country there is an infinity of patterns to choose from, the fact that these are all mathematically related could be interpreted as proof that the 'pattern' approach is forcing each country to fit into a pattern of a specific family.

For the answer one only needs to look at Charts 16 a, b, c and d of *per capita* GNP, from 1970 to 2020, from which it is apparent that no two countries follow similar curves. Thus the approach we have defined can be regarded as responsive and sensitive to the past history and to the status of each country.

GLOBAL CHART OF PATTERNS OF GROWTH

On a *per capita* basis, chart 12 encompasses a comprehensive image of the economic past, present and future of the economy of each of the 153 countries we have analysed.

The base year of 1967 for each country, is identified by locating on its respective pattern, found in Table XVII, each country point at the ordinate corresponding to the relative stage of growth.

There is no difficulty in interpreting the identification of each country with its respective pattern, as read from Table XVII, which, similarly to other yardsticks, measures rate of growth.

PATTERNS OF GROWTH FOR ALL COUNTRIES

Both the horizontal and the vertical scale of global Chart 12 which presents the complete family of patterns encompassing the recorded and forecasted economic growth for all countries of the world, incorporate unusual features which we shall explain in detail.

The horizontal scale is in terms of years and the vertical scale plots the use of energy *per capita* as well as a scale proportional to GNP *per capita*. which, by use of a coefficient, different for each country, can be translated into stage of growth.

For instance, Japan and Romania are on the same point on the same curve, the same point on the scale of stage of growth reading 2,200 for both countries, corresponds to a 1967 GNP *per capita* of $720 for Romania and of $1,155 for Japan.

It was necessary to incorporate this particular feature of a different ratio for each in order to retain and bring out clearly, the

Economic Growth

fundamental basis of the pattern approach. The advantage of this presentation will be immediately realised if the reader turns to Charts 16 a, b, c and d, and notes that the totality of the information contained in these 4 charts is contained in the one Chart 12. Moreover, the course of their economic growth can be read for 150 countries in Chart 12, whereas, for the sake of clarity of presentation, only 50 countries are shown in Charts 16 a, b, c and d.

There is also a special feature about the horizontal scale of years. All the colored circles correspond to the stage of growth recorded in 1967. Thus, for any particular country, note must be made of the years corresponding to the colored circle and the years are counted from then on.

For example, taking the point for Romania and Japan already noted, we read approximately 57 on the scale of years corresponding to that point. Since this is the point for 1967, it means that for any year in which we are interested for the growth of Japan or Romania, we read on the horizontal scale the point corresponding to 10 years less than the calendar year. The point for the Year 2000 will correspond to 90. If 57 corresponds to 1967, 60 corresponds to 1970, 70 to 1980 and so on.

The reader will naturally wonder: Why are not all the 1967 points lined up on the same vertical?

To answer this, let us take the point colored in purple for Switzerland for which we read 148 on the scale of years. If 1967 corresponds to 148, then the point at which all curves converge would correspond to 1967 less 148, or 1819. 1819 is not too remote from the beginning of the Industrial Revolution, and we might interpret the status of Switzerland in 1967 on the 75% pattern as meaning that the economic growth of Switzerland has followed uninterruptedly this pattern ever since shortly after the beginning of the Industrial Revolution, which could well be the case since Switzerland has maintained its territorial continuity since long before that.

But, this raises immediately a question about Kuwait, the high stage of industrial growth of which plotted for a reference year 172, would make its development go back to 1967 less 172, or 1795, which, obviously is meaningless. Conversely, we could take the United Kingdom whose blue circle is plotted at 115, making its industrial development start only in 1967 less 115, or 1852, more than a century *after* James Watt invented the steam engine which started England on the Industrial Revolution.

This wide departure, both ways, from what might be interpereted as an unbroken course of economic growth points to an immediate answer: there has not been an unbroken continuity of development.

Taking 1800 as a convenient starting point for the type of industrial development we are charting, which would correspond to 167 as the base year on Chart 12 we can say that for the majority of the countries, for which the 1967 circle comes before 167, this means that their present rate of development has been preceded by a slower rate than the one with which they are now identified.

Let us take Japan's present place for instance which indicates that it is only 57 years away from the start of its industrial development at its present rate of growth. Our analysis has shown that Japan has approximately followed since

1949 the 187.5% pattern with which we have identified it. We may obtain an approximate image of its previous rate of development by saying that from 1875 until 1949, it followed, on the average the 93.75% pattern, i.e. half as fast as its present one.

Where, on the other hand, we note countries the circles for which are beyond the vertical of 167 years, we can state, without any question that they have known a much faster rate of growth and that they are now cruising on a slower pattern than the one which has launched them initially. For instance, Kuwait was catapulted to its present high stage of economic growth in less than a quarter of a century at a rate which even the 400% pattern, the fastest we have used, could not match. It is now cruising on a consolidating pattern which we have associated with the 81.25% pattern.

To summarize these first comments, we have located each country with its status and pattern of growth which matched its demonstrated and potential record of growth.

The composite image of these 153 countries shows the expected development and gives both the stage of growth and the rate of growth, not a constant one for a given pattern but one which is modulated in keeping with the very nature of most growth mechanisms.

The individual projections of *per capita* GNP growth presented separately for each country in the second part of the book and analysed in global charts were all prepared from these prospective patterns.

We can now turn our attention to the overall conclusions that appear from the composite presentation: for which the following color scheme has been followed:

(A)		(B)	
North America	Dark Blue	Central & Latin America	Green
Oceania	Light Blue	Asia	Yellow
Western Europe	Purple	Africa	Grey
Eastern Europe & Communist Asia	Red	Middle East	Brown

The same color coding has been used in *per capita* GNP Charts 16 a, b, c and d and in GNP Charts 21 a, b, c and d, respectively in Chapter Five and Chapter Eight.

Attention is called at this time to the arbitrary grouping under (A) and (B) of four each of the eight major world areas color-coded above. This was done in order to obtain a clearer presentation of the charts 16 a and c and 21 a and c which pertain to Group A and 16 b and d and 21 b and d which pertain to Group B, as will be explained in Chapter Five.

PATTERN INDEXES OF GROWTH FOR ALL COUNTRIES

Table XVII lists, in descending scale, in the first column of figures, the pattern indexes of growth, resulting from our analyses. These are

Economic Growth 55

TABLE XVII—GNP 'per capita' growth pattern and recorded 6-year annual increase

	Country	Pattern	Ann.Inc.		Country	Pattern	Ann.Inc.		Country	Pattern	Ann.Inc.
1	Japan	187.50%	10.0%		Sweden	112.50%	3.8%		Pakistan	62.50%	3.4%
	Romania	187.50	8.6		Trinidad & Tobago	112.50	4.3		Peru	62.50	1.5
	Libya	✱187.50	21.4		United Kingdom	112.50	2.6		Syria	62.50	3.9
	Trucial Oman	✱187.50	32.5	52	Cyprus	106.25%	5.8%	102	Brunei	56.25	-1.9%
5	Bulgaria	181.25%	7.9%		Netherlands	106.25	4.4		Guam	56.25	2.0
					Panama	106.25	4.3		Guatemala	56.25	2.7
6	U.S.S.R.	168.75%	5.6%		Portug.Guinea	106.25	4.4		Guinea	56.25	2.5
7	Zambia	162.50%	7.2%	56	Austria	100.00%	3.8%		Philippines	56.25	1.5%
	Qatar	✱162.50	2.2		France	100.00	4.1		Sierra Leone	56.25	1.3
					Ireland	100.00	3.7		U.A.R. Egypt	56.25	3.6
9	Ivory Coast	156.25%	5.4%	59	Australia	93.75%	3.8%		Uganda	56.25	3.0
					Bermuda	93.75	4.8	110	Morocco	50.00%	1.5%
10	Muscat & Oman	150.00%	10.2%		Iraq	93.75	3.5		Nigeria	50.00	1.8
					Liberia	93.75	1.5		Tanzania	50.00	2.5
11	Korea Rep.	143.75%	8.1%		New Caledonia	93.75	0.5	113	Afghanistan	43.75%	-0.5%
	Ryukyu Isl.	143.75	10.1		Turkey	93.75	4.2	**	Algeria	43.75	-3.5
	Surinam	143.75	2.0		Communist Asia:				Guadeloupe	43.75	-0.2
	Yugoslavia	143.75	5.0	65	China Mainland ⎤				Niger	43.75	0.1
15	Bahama Isl.	137.50%	8.9%		Korea - North ⎬ 87.50%				Paraguay	43.75	1.3
	Hungary	137.50	5.5		Vietnam-North ⎦			118	Burma	37.50%	0.6%
17	Germany-East	131.25%	3.7%		Mongolia				Cameroun	37.50	0.6
	Germany-West	131.25	3.2		Congo Brazzav.	87.50	1.7		Chad	37.50	0.1
	Poland	131.25	6.9		French Guyana	87.50	11.6		Colombia	37.50	1.7
	Saudi Arabia	131.25	8.4		New Zealand	87.50	1.9		Congo Kinshasa	37.50	-0.5
	Spain	131.25	7.9		Panama Canal Zone	87.50	0.1		Cuba	37.50	-0.3
	US Virgin Isl.	131.25	7.5		Thailand	87.50	5.2		Dominican Rep.	37.50	-1.0
23	Iceland	130.00%	2.1%	74	Bolivia	81.25%	4.5%		Ecuador	37.50	1.7
					Ceylon	81.25	3.4		Ghana	37.50	-1.0
24	Denmark	125.00%	3.4%		Kuwait	81.25	-3.5		Honduras	37.50	2.4
	Finland	125.00	3.4		Mexico	81.25	4.0		Indonesia	37.50	-0.1
	French Oceania	✱125.00	12.0		Mozambique	81.25	3.3		Kenya	37.50	1.1
	Portugal	125.00	5.1		Tunisia	81.25	1.8		Laos	37.50	-0.1
	Reunion	125.00	4.5		Vietnam-South	81.25	1.8		Mali	37.50	0.7
	United States	125.00	3.6						Ruanda	37.50	1.7
				81	Ethiopia	78.75%	3.0%		Senegal	37.50	-0.1
30	China-Taiwan	118.75%	7.8%						Yemen	37.50	1.8
	Gabon	118.75	3.5	82	Cambodia	75.00%	1.1%				
	Greece	118.75	6.8		Malawi	75.00	2.9	135	Nepal	31.25%	0.1%
	Hong Kong	118.75	7.9		Malaysia	75.00	3.1		Sudan	31.25	0.2
	Iran	118.75	4.8		Switzerland	75.00	1.8				
	Italy	118.75	4.2					137	Madagascar	28.13%	-0.5%
	Mauritania	118.75	6.9	86	Angola	68.75%	2.1%				
	Puerto Rico	118.75	5.4		Chile	68.75	2.0	138	Uruguay	25.00%	-1.1%
	Singapore	118.75	2.9		Jamaica	68.75	2.4		Upper Volta	25.00	-0.6
					Lebanon	68.75	2.3				
39	Albania	112.50%	5.7%		Martinique	68.75	2.3	140	Burundi	18.75%	-0.1%
	Bahrain	112.50	2.5		Nicaragua	68.75	4.1		Centr.Afric.R.	18.75	-1.0
	Belgium & Lux.	112.50	3.4		Venezuela	68.75	1.5				
	Canada	112.50	3.7					142	Dahomey	12.50%	0.2%
	Czechoslovakia	112.50	5.6	93	Argentina	62.50%	1.9%		Mauritius	12.50	-2.0
	Israel	112.50	4.8		Barbados	62.50	2.6		South Yemen	12.50	-1.1
	Jordan	112.50	5.8	**	Brazil	62.50	0.8				
	Malta	112.50	6.2		Costa Rica	62.50	1.7	145	Somalia	9.38%	-1.6%
	Norway	112.50	4.3		El Salvador	62.50	1.8				
	South Africa	112.50	4.0		India	62.50	0.4	146	Haiti	6.25%	-0.4%

✱ For the countries thus marked, the indicated growth pattern was maintained only to 1975.
A slower pattern was calculated and followed for the subsequent years.
** For the countries thus marked, the indicated growth pattern was maintained only to 1970.
A faster pattern was calculated and followed for subsequent years.

based on the potential for progress that each country has demonstrated during the period from 1949 to 1968.

ARE PATTERN INDEXES OF GROWTH COMPARABLE TO PERCENTAGE GROWTH RATES?

One reason why these potentialities for growth are not to be related to the 1961-1967 recorded growth rates shown in the second column of figures should be mentioned here:

Among the countries analysed we have identified many whose record of *per capita* economic growth was uniform and unbroken. For these the pattern growth index comes closest to being comparable with the percentage growth rates listed in the second column.

For some countries, however, economic *per capita* growth has been interrupted or slowed down by political upheaval, local wars, or by major disturbances such as acts of God, or major catastrophes as too vividly illustrated by the typhoon which struck East Pakistan. Conversely, economic growth may have been abnormally stimulated by non-recurring events, the impact of which is likely to decrease in years to come.

For these countries, we have disregarded the troubled periods and we have retained the growth achieved during the period regarded as meaningful and indicative of the demonstrated potential for growth.

In thus fitting the recorded growth of *per capita* GNP of each country to the particular pattern which could best be associated with it, we have used the longest period of continuous growth within the 1948-1967 period. We felt that it was more important to bring out the capability for growth of each country rather than be influenced by occasional periods of economic or other upset.

Thus, our analysis has not detected for any country a slower potential for growth than could be associated with approximately 6% of the reference rate. The full span from 190% to 10% corresponds approximately on the % scale to the span from 8% to minus 2%.

HOW SENSITIVE IS THE SELECTION OF THE APPROPRIATE PATTERN?

The accuracy of our method of selection of the appropriate pattern makes it possible to select, say, between a 187.5% and a 193.75% pattern. In terms of the more conventional percent rate of

Economic Growth

growth this would correspond to selecting between a 5% and a 4.75%, which represents a satisfactory degree of accuracy.

We have grouped in alphabetic order the countries associated with the same index. For convenience in calculation, we have used index values selected from the steps 6.25% apart, which were found to approximate most closely the country's growth.

WHICH ARE THE ECONOMICALLY FASTEST GROWING COUNTRIES?

The Growth Patterns Indexes listed in Table XVII are the same as those which can be read from Chart 12. They come nearest to answering the question in most people's minds: which are the economically fastest growing countries?

The 4 countries marked with an asterisk in the first column are those which are now rising at an exceptionally fast rate of growth, but which are not expected to maintain that rate beyond 1975.

The countries marked with two asterisks in the first column are those which are expected to attain beyond 1970 a faster growth pattern than the one which their best performance in the course of the past twenty years had indicated as likely to be maintained.

WHY CANNOT CONSTANT GROWTH RATES BE MAINTAINED INDEFINITELY?

Recognizing the permanence of the pattern associated with the median performance of all the countries of the world and recognizing that each country's economy may be associated with its own pattern 'within the family', why do all these patterns show a 'declining' trend?

Once a country has found its rate of growth, or 'cruising rate' so to speak, why cannot this percentage rate of growth be maintained, for a number of years?

For the answer to this question, we need only turn to Charts 16 a, b, c and d of GNP/Capita growth. With the logarithmic scale used in ordinates, a constant percent yearly rate of growth would be represented by a straight line, tangent to the initial portion of each of the country graphs.

If yearly percent growth rates could be maintained at the rate now projected for the 1970-1980 decade:

(i) the United Kingdom, with a 3.0% *per capita* annual growth rate projected for this period, would see its GNP/Capita

multiplied by 4.4 in 50 years, instead of by 3.6, as forecast,
(ii) the U.S.S.R. with a 5.0% projected *per capita* growth rate for the 1970-1980 decade would see its GNP *per capita* multiplied by 11.5 in 50 years, instead of by 6.2 as forecast.
(iii) Japan with a 9.7% annual growth rate projected for 1970-1980 would see its GNP/Capita multiplied, in 50 years, by 103 instead of by 9.7 as forecast.

TAPERED CHARACTER OF THE PATTERN

It will be noted that the extent to which exponential increase, synonymous of a constant percent rate of growth, departs from the 'tapering pattern', is quickly exaggerated when higher values of the 1970-1980 GNP growth rate are considered, as in the case for Japan.

For the three cases mentioned, we have shown below the ratio between the 'exponential' straight line projection and our tapered pattern for the year 2020, while starting from the same 1970-1980 rate:

	1970-1980 rate	Ratio in 2020 between exponential and tapered growth achieved: 1970 to 2020
United Kingdom	3.0%	1.22
U.S.S.R.	5.0%	1.86
Japan	9.7%	10.60

The above explains why, with a moderate growth rate, projections based on an exponential straight-line continuation of the initial rate do not appear greatly out-of-line, allowing for the usual uncertainties.

On the other hand, the expectation that 'Japan which has been able to maintain a "miraculous" growth rate since her post-war recovery can be expected to keep the same pace and overtake the U.S.A. by the year 2000' is highly problematical.

Throughout this analysis, we have maintained that a country which has shown its ability to grow along any one of our family of patterns can be expected to continue to do so. The pattern inherently recognizes that growth cannot be a straight-line exponential for more than a limited number of decades.

In fact, the above may well be regarded as our thesis' 'test under extreme conditions'. It does indeed appear that the 'tapering pattern' type of projection, because it has been established on the basis of a

Economic Growth

world-wide analysis (which makes it sensitive to any unusual condition such as Japan's precedent-shattering growth), may well be regarded as a most stimulating guide-line to the future:

A constant yearly percentage rate of growth cannot be maintained in any process which is bound to encounter ultimate limitations.

A tapering rate of growth, which is the only growth pattern which can be expected to apply over prolonged periods of time, will provide challenging opportunities for even the most dynamic economies.

In spite of this steadily decreasing rate of growth shown in Chart 29 for the use of electricity in the U.S.A. and in Table XXI, Summary, for *per capita* GNP, the pattern we have established is associated with dynamic progress portrayed in Charts 16 a, b, c and d and in Chart 26.

The pattern's built-in restraint (tapering of growth rate) provides reassurance that even the most spectacular growths will not mushroom into economic monstrosities.

COMPARISON OF PROJECTIONS OF GNP 'PER CAPITA' IN THE YEAR 2000

In the following table, we present a comparison of the projections which will be found in the second part of this volume, also in Tables XXI, with the 'Low', 'Medium' and 'High' *per capita* GNP's presented in *The Year 2000*.[7]

The last column shows that our figures are consistently lower than the 'Medium' estimates of Messrs. Kahn & Wiener, the spread being greatest for Japan 69% and least for Communist China 99%. (To reconcile 1965 and 1967 U.S. $ figures, the latter were reduced by 9% when calculating the ratio in the last column)

	Kahn & Wiener 'The Year 2000' (Based on 1965 U.S. $)			Our Projection (1967 U.S. $)	Ratio: Our Projection Kahn & Wiener 'Medium' (1967 U.S. $ thruout)
	LOW	MEDIUM	HIGH		
United States	4,760	10,160	12,480	9,250	83%
U.S.S.R.	1,880	4,650	7,890	3,975	78%
West Germany	5,150	7,790	10,410	6,245	73%
France	4,480	6,830	9,070	5,905	78.5%
Japan	3,990	8,590	10,000	6,540	69.5%
United Kingdom	3,570	6,530	8,440	4,985	69.5%
Communist China	106	321	969	350	99%
Italy	2,940	4,450	5,930	4,350	89%

ARE GROWTH PATTERNS 'RESTRICTIVE'?

A study of the array of growth patterns may prompt the following questions.

Do they represent 'grooves' into which a country's growth is expected to fit?

If not, how does a country get out of the growth pattern it may have been following and into a faster one?

To the first question, the answer is: Definitely not.

The only 'groovy' aspect of these patterns is that they are likely to continue as long as a country adheres to the same broad economic policy, and maintains approximately the same ratio of total investments to Gross National Product.

The injection of appropriate 'growth-stimulating' factors, such as those reviewed under 'Factors of Growth' in Chapter Five, including an appropriate increase in the investment ratio, may be expected to place the country on a correspondingly faster pattern.

As a simple illustration of this mechanism let us look at Jordan for which the use of energy *per capita* in 1967, in KEC, is the same as the GNP *per capita* in U.S. $. Its past record has identified it with the 75% growth pattern which it has followed prior to 1970.

We assume that in 1970, when the GNP *per capita* reached $ 267, the country took proper steps, through the implementation of a new 5-year plan, towards achieving a 1/6 faster rate of economic growth, bringing it to the 87½% pattern.

This would require increasing the investment ratio from 13% to 15.15%, by allocating the necessary funds from savings and loans. At this higher growth rate, the country's *per capita* GNP reaches $300 in 1975.

The success of the first operation encourages it, in a second 5-year plan, to increase the percentage of Gross Capital Formation from 15.15% to 17.3% so that together with other steps such as those we have reviewed in Chapter Five, a 100% growth pattern can be reached and maintained from 1975 to 1980.

In Chart 13, we have assumed the same process repeated at 5 year intervals, each time increasing by 12.5 percentage points in the growth pattern index. We have carried out these operations to the year 2020, by which time the country has completed 5 years on the 175% growth pattern and has reached $5,100 *per capita* GNP.

This same chart also shows what the *per capita* GNP growth would have been if any one of these intermediate patterns, once started, had been followed to the year 2020.

ANY COURSE OF ECONOMIC GROWTH CAN BE DISSECTED INTO SEGMENTS OF PATTERNS

The purpose of this exercise is to show the wide range of economic growth histories and plans which can be 'categorized' into specific patterns selected from the full span presented in Chart 12.

Economic Growth 61

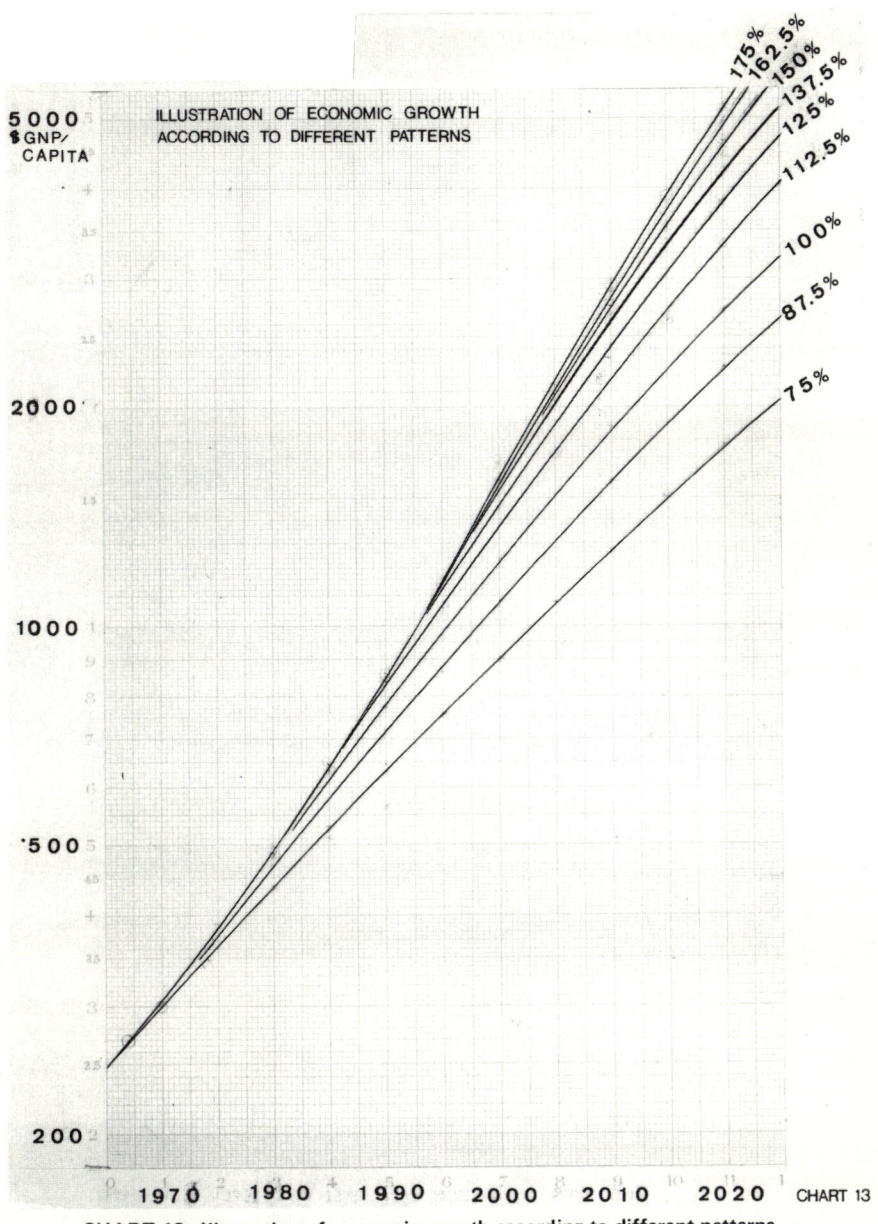

CHART 13—Illustration of economic growth according to different patterns

We shall return later to several of the aspects left untouched in order to emphasize this point:

Any forecast of per capita *economic growth can be dissected into pattern elements which can be found in Chart 12 and matched to the country's performance.*

WHY INTRODUCE SO COMPLEX A PATTERN NOTION?

The question might well be asked: Since the notion of annual rate of growth expressed in percent is so widely accepted and well understood, what is the justification for introducing a more complex notion of pattern which can only be described by reference to a curve plotted on semi-logarithmic paper?

We could justify this by similes drawn from various growth processes, such as that of a human being, in which the yearly rate of growth, expressed in percent, decreases rapidly from birth to maturity.

A more direct justification is immediately afforded by Chart 11 which, plotted against a multiplier of the GNP *per capita*, shows the variation of the yearly increase of the GNP *per capita*, expressed in per cent.

On the 100% pattern, which we may regard as a world median, the percent yearly increase varies from 13% to 6% in 30 years, from 6% to 4.6% in the following 45 years and from 4.6% to 3% in the following 45 years.

The justification of our pattern lies in the fact that, with minor variations, a single pattern may closely approximate the economic growth of a country over many decades or even the span of a century, as shown in the following presentation of stages of economic growth for the United States.

Instead of limiting ourselves to defining growth by a percentage, we are now in possession of a far more sensitive and sophisticated yardstick: the index of a pattern which we can associate with the normal growth pattern of an economy over an extended period of time to emphasize what the continuation of a given trend would lead to.

In order to show why the definition of growth by means of a pattern is far more meaningful than the use of a given percentage, we have shown in the table below the longest span of development history for which we have continuous records of the United States.

We have taken the median world pattern of economic growth shown as 100% on Chart 11, and we have tabulated below the average 'in-between' percent growth rate while progressing from one stage to the next, also the time it would take a country which follows the 'median' pattern to achieve this growth.

According to the table opposite, the United States would have taken 32 + 48 + 80 = 160 years to progress to its present stage of development starting from where Nepal is today. This span of time: 160

Economic Growth

Stage of Economic Growth	10	100	1,000	10,000	100,000
Approximately corresponds to	Nepal in 1968	Indonesia in 1968	Greece in 1968	U.S.A. in 1968	U.S.A. in 2020
Approximate average yearly growth percentage	7.50%	5%	3%	1.25%	
Years to reach from one stage to the next	32	48	80	185	

years is not too different from that elapsed since the beginning of the industrial revolution, about 1800.

There has not been, so far, a satisfactory yardstick to compare the growth performance of countries of widely different characteristics geographically politically, socially and culturally speaking and the above which encompasses countries at stages of growth more than a century apart suggests that the more complex method presented here might prove particularly helpful in the investigation and comparison of growth, from an international point of view.

Obviously, the pattern concept of which we which we have shown the value as a tool for the analysis of economic growth does not provide as 'easy' an answer as that which is given by the straight percentage growth achieved, or planned for and the reader will note that, following Chapter Five, growth is compared only through the usual 'percent increase'.

For a very approximate indication as to how to compare the pattern index of growth with the percent rate of increase, the following may be used as read from Chart 11 for a stage of growth corresponding to 500 KEC/capita which is in the range of countries in early stages of industrialization:

Pattern Index of Growth %	20	40	60	80	100	120	140	160	180	200
Percent rate of Increase	1	2	3	4	5	6	7	8	9	10

For a stage of growth corresponding to 2,000 KEC/capita, which is in the industrialized countries range, the correlation below would apply:

Pattern Index of Growth %	25	50	75	100	125	150	175	200
Percent rate of Increase	1	2	3	4	5	6	7	8

CHAPTER FIVE

Factors of Growth

WHY DO GROWTH RATES DIFFER?

As one studies the array of growth patterns in Chart 12, one is impressed by the diversity of economic identities it portrays and by the realization that some countries are maintaining growth rates much faster than the median of the world, while others are barely holding their own.

Yet that same chart suggests that common factors, albeit in different degrees, are present in each country to shape their respective patterns.

This more accurate basis of comparison recognizes that while a country is progressing on an orderly course of economic expansion, the growth rate can be expected to decrease gradually from year to year, from decade to decade.

Because each of these patterns is 'modulated' to reflect more closely the fundamental character of development, this new approach promises the economist a more sensitive tool, and invites its use for searching analyses and comparisons of economic growth on an international scale.

In *Why Growth Rates Differ*[8] which has attracted considerable attention, 23 different sources of growth were explored on the basis of the performance in the years 1950-1962 of 9 European Countries and of the U.S.A.

Even if a greatly enlarged format had been available, an analytical treatment of 150 countries could not have been attempted here. It is to be hoped though, that, adding to the specific answers some countries have already provided, additional approaches will emerge from the range of 'case histories' reviewed in this volume and will bring us closer to the solution of a number of crucial questions:

(1) Which factors stimulate economic growth?
(2) Why do growth rates differ?
(3) What is 'par for the course?'

Factors of Growth

(4) How wide is the range which at a given stage of development encompasses manageable rates of growth? What is the most desirable rate?
(5) Can accelerated expansion be forced to meet the threat of competition? And could a country's future be endangered if the effort should misfire?
(6) Does planned allocation of resources offer better chances of success than if left largely to voluntary market mechanisms?
(7) How can productive forces be induced to expand their investment in themselves as well as improve the efficiency of their operations?
(8) To what extent is economic growth benefitted by an enviroment favorable to savings and to investment?
(9) How can balanced economic and welfare growth be achieved?
(10) Do some countries have opportunities for growth that are not present in others?
(11) Which actions raising the growth rate entail costs of one sort or another which may appear to be more than the gain in the growth rate is worth?
(12) What effect do shifting consumption patterns have on the rate of economic growth?
(13) To what extent can, or should, individuals, groups, organisations, contribute to an improved rate of national growth?

To these and to a number of other questions the study of economic growth suggests, we hope that this volume will contribute at least partial answers which may not have been available so far.

From the Tables and Charts which are presented and particularly from Chart 12 encompassing 153 'case histories,' we believe that there have already appeared aspects of growth which should make international comparisons more meaningful.

We shall now enumerate many of the 'factors of growth' and we shall give close attention to those for which we may have additional evidence to contribute.

SOURCES OF GROWTH

There are many sources of growth and these vary greatly from time to time and from place to place.

From various sources, including those mentioned in the Bibliography, we are listing, not necessarily in the sequence of importance, a number of factors recognized as promoting growth.

Many of these are overlapping or partly repetitious, but we thought it of value to present an extensive list from which the reader could select the factors potentially most significant to countries of interest.

(1) Increase in physical capital by a higher level of capital investment in non-residential structures and equipment.
(2) Increasing the capital per worker.
(3) A system which encourages adequate saving and investment so as to make available the resources for the formation of fixed capital and the funds for their financing.
(4) Basic availability of national resources.
(5) Investment in the development of new ideas, new products, new scientific advances, new technical research, new methods and new materials, which add to productive capacity.
(6) New discoveries of mineral resources.
(7) Drawing upon the accumulated knowledge and capital of other countries.
(8) Advances and diffusion of knowledge, both technological and material which permit more output to be produced within the same imput.
(9) Increase in the quality of labor, as a result of improved education.
(10) Willingness to invest in 'human capital'.
(11) Progress of knowledge in organization and managerial techniques.
(12) Increase in the quantity of land under cultivation.
(13) Increase in employment.
(14) More use of shift work.
(15) Obtaining the most favorable age-sex combination of man-hours worked.
(16) Encouraging mobility of labor to optimize the availability of needed skills and talents.
(17) Employment of women.
(18) Part-time student employment.
(19) Employment of foreign single male labor.
(20) Improved health of labor force.
(21) Reduction of excessive allocation of resources to activities adding little to the national income.
(22) Transferring resources, mostly labor, to activities to which their addition makes a substantial contribution.

Factors of Growth 67

(23) Transfer of resources from agriculture to non-agricultural employment.
(24) Reducing the number of self-employed and unpaid family workers in non-agricultural industries.
(25) Economies of scale resulting from expansion of demand in the volume of transactions, and increase in the size of producing units and capacity of the means of production.
(26) Enlargement of markets which, by making possible the reduction of unit costs by greater specialization, increases the output realized per unit of input.
(27) Gains in productivity.
(28) Progress evidenced by systematic improvement in the quality of capital equipment embodying technical advance and means of production resulting from planned research and development.
(29) Optimizing the allocation and stimulating the most efficient utilization of available resources. This encompasses specialization, substitution, innovation, efficiency, economy, maximization of production, selection of the best talents, etc.
(30) Profit encouragement to those who innovate successfully.
(31) Improved motivation.
(32) Spirit of enterprise.
(33) Minimization or elimination of institutional obstacles, restrictions, constraints, or untimely interventions, whether imposed by government, agencies, public authorities, labor unions, etc., which detract from the most efficient utilization of resources in the use to which they are put.
(34) Economies of infrastructure of public character.
(35) Improved major public services, transport, communications, etc., can contribute to stimulating gains in productivity.
(36) Reduction of international trade barriers.
(37) Ownership of international assets.
(38) Optimum international allocation of resources.

INDEX OF GROWTH *v* INVESTMENT RATIO

The earlier mention that being able to draw on 150 'case histories' would offer new avenues to the analyst because of the broader base thus provided is illustrated in Chart 14, the vertical scale of which transcribes the *per-capita* growth indexes read from Table XVII and

World Markets of Tomorrow

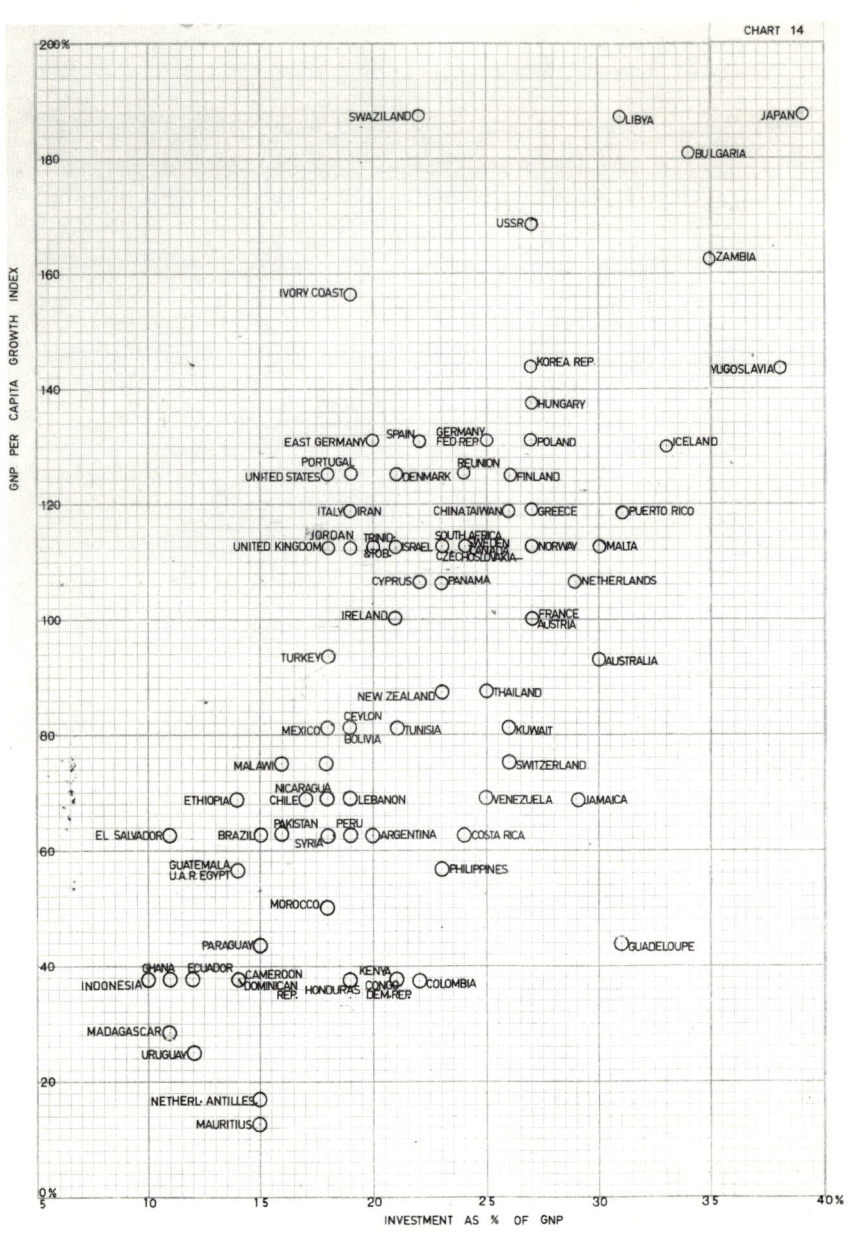

CHART 14—Investment ratio

TABLE XVIII—Investment ratio: gives domestic capital formation as a percentage of GNP

(68)	Japan	39 %	(68)	Congo Dem. Rep.	21 %
(68)	Yugoslavia	38	(68)	Denmark	21
(68)	Zambia	35	(68)	Ireland	21
(68)	Bulgaria	34	(68)	Israel	21
(67)	Iceland	33	(68)	Kenya	21
(67)	Guadeloupe	31	(68)	Southern Rhodesia	21
(68)	Libya	31	(68)	Tunisia	21
(68)	Puerto Rico	31	(68)	Argentina	20
(68)	Australia	30	(68)	Germany East	20
(68)	Malta	30	(68)	Trinidad & Tobago	20
(68)	Jamaica	29	(68)	Bolivia	19
(68)	Netherlands	29	(68)	Ceylon	19
(68)	Austria	27	(68)	Honduras	19
(68)	France	27	(67)	Iran	19
(68)	Greece	27	(68)	Italy	19
(68)	Hungary	27	(67)	Ivory Coast	19
(68)	Korea Rep.	27	(68)	Jordan	19
(68)	Norway	27	(67)	Lebanon	19
(68)	Poland	27	(68)	Peru	19
(68)	U.S.S.R.	27	(68)	Portugal	19
(68)	China Taiwan	26	(67)	Mexico	18
(68)	Finland	26	(68)	Morocco	18
(67)	Kuwait	26	(68)	Nicaragua	18
(68)	Switzerland	26	(68)	Syria	18
(68)	Fiji Islands	25	(68)	Turkey	18
(68)	Germany Fed. Rep.	25	(68)	United Kingdom	18
(67)	Luxembourg	25	(68)	United States	18
(67)	Thailand	25	(68)	Chile	17
(68)	Venezuela	25	(68)	Malawi	16
(68)	Canada	24	(67)	Pakistan	16
(68)	Costa Rica	24	(67)	Brazil	15
(68)	Sweden	24	(68)	Mauritius	15
(67)	Reunion	24	(67)	Netherl. Antilles	15
(68)	Czechoslovakia	23	(68)	Paraguay	15
(67)	Equatorial Guinea	23	(67)	Cameroon	14
(68)	Guyana	23	(68)	Dominican Republic	14
(68)	New Zealand	23	(67)	Ethiopia	14
(68)	Panama	23	(68)	Guatemala	14
(68)	Philippines	23	(67)	U.A.R. Egypt	14
(68)	South Africa	23	(68)	Ecuador	12
(68)	Belgium	22	(68)	Uruguay	12
(68)	Colombia	22	(68)	El Salvador	11
(68)	Cyprus	22	(68)	Ghana	11
(68)	Spain	22	(67)	Madagascar	11
(67)	Swaziland	22	(68)	Indonesia	9

the horizontal scale of which transcribes the investment ratios from Table XVIII.

The wide dispersion on each side of a likely median gives many proofs that some countries have found it possible by the mobilization of human resources, their access to abundant natural resources, or other factors of growth we have enumerated, to make up for a low investment ratio. A contributing reason to the wide dispersion noted may well be in the uncertainties attached to the proper evaluation of the investment ratio.

The median trend which can be drawn may be regarded as portraying the average expectation for the rate of economic growth, measured by the index of the corresponding pattern.

This median trend approaches a straight line which starts from a 5% investment ratio. This may show that it takes more than this minimum to 'break the stagnation wall' and get the country moving along the path of economic growth.

This indication is in keeping with the generally accepted 10% investment ratio as the minimum a country must achieve before it reaches the 'take-off' stage.

The fairly clear evidence of a median trend invites investigation of the sources of economic growth *other than investment*, which have contributed to the higher growth rate of the countries clearly above the median line or to the lower growth rate of those clearly below the median line.

To this end, Chart 14 provides a convenient backdrop in illustration of the wide range spanned by growth rates when plotted in terms of one specific factor—in this case, the rate of investment.

In fact, our attempt to focus on this one factor is likely to raise as many questions as it answers:

Is a high rate of investment the cause or the effect of a high growth rate?

Is not it possible that, in the initial stages of a country's growth, a high rate of investment proves to be the catalyst of economic 'take-off' while, as the country progresses, high investment rates may be an effect of faster growth since the more buoyant prospects for future sales that growth generally engenders will tend to stimulate investment?

DO HIGH RATES OF POPULATION INCREASE SLOW DOWN PER CAPITA ECONOMIC GROWTH?

In order to illustrate the applicability of Chart 14 to a number of different investigations, we shall endeavor, as an example, to answer

Factors of Growth 71

the above question; to this end, we could draw, on each side of the median trend, boundary lines respectively 20% higher and 20% lower in terms of *per capita* growth index. These correspond approximately to 1% higher and to 1% lower *per capita* growth rate than the median.

By so doing, we can 'categorize' the countries noted in the higher brackets as having a growth rate clearly above the median and the countries in the lower brackets as having a growth rate clearly lower than the median, for a given investment ratio.

From their respective profiles in Part Two, we read their yearly rate of population growth—which is also found in Table VII—and we calculate the average yearly rate of population increase for the 'high' countries and for the 'low' countries: these are, for the 'high' countries, 1.33% and, for 'low' countries, 3.17%.

In other words, the countries with a lower rate of *per capita* economic growth have, in this simplified approach, nearly 2% higher rate of population increase than the countries with a higher rate of *per capita* growth.

This is not surprising: the investment ratio can be a yardstick of the impact of *total investment* on *total economy*. When *per capita* rates of economic growth are calculated, they are directly 'diluted' by the rate of population increase.

The same as most of the aspects discussed in this Chapter, the above should be interpreted with a certain flexibility: For instance, if we turn to the six countries selected in Table XIXb, later in this Chapter, as being close to the upper limit of *per capita* economic growth and if we list their respective rates of population increase we note that two of these: Iran and South Korea have nearly 3% yearly population increase. The access to natural resources for one, and the mobilization of human resources for the other, are two factors, among others, which can overcome the potential retarding effect of a relatively high rate of population increase. It will be noted, too, that the average rate of population increase for the six countries is only $\frac{1}{2}$ of 1% higher than the average for the 14 'high' countries previously cited.

	%
Ethiopia	1.90
Mauritania	1.90
Korea Republic	2.91
Iran	2.84
Romania	0.73
Japan	0.96
Average	1.87

NATURAL RESOURCES AS A STIMULUS TO GROWTH

The 'shot-in-the-arm' that the discovery and exploitation of natural resources can impart to economic growth is evident from the high rank in the growth index (Table XVII) enjoyed by the oil-rich countries of the world.

Other countries rich in natural resources, such as Zambia, world's third largest producer of copper and Surinam, whose bauxite deposits are among the richest in the world, also rank high in economic growth.

It is noteworthy, however, that in a number of countries without a substantial natural resource base, economic growth has been stimulated at a rate equal to or greater than in countries with abundant natural wealth. Some of the prime examples are: Japan, Greece, Taiwan, Israel, South Korea and Hong Kong. These countries were able to develop human resources to overcome shortages of natural resources.

The *per capita* resources for 12 developing countries were totaled on the following basis[10]:

(i) Agriculture, Forest and Fisheries, were valued at 10 times the exports of the latest reporting year.
(ii) Reserves of coal presumably minable, were valued at $5 per ton.
(iii) Iron Ore was priced at $5 for 55-60% Ore.
(iv) Petroleum was valued at $1 per barrel of probable reserves.
(v) Non-fuel, non-ferrous reserves were figured at 10 times the export values in the latest reporting year.
(vi) Hydroelectric power was assessed at the coal equivalent of 10 years full plant output.

To the tabulation extracted from the reference study we have added our figures for Zambia's copper and Surinam's bauxite, alumina and aluminium. From Table XVII we have entered, in the right-hand column, our own index of economic growth.

For the first 12 countries, until one comes to oil-rich Iran, there is no evidence of correlation between the economic growth index and the importance of natural resources.

On the other hand, Iran, Surinam and Zambia rank high both in resources and in the rate of economic growth.

From this partial sampling of an approach deserving a far more comprehensive analysis, one can infer that natural resources have a

Factors of Growth 73

	$ 'Per Capita' Natural Wealth	Index of Economic Growth
Pakistan	27	62.5%
U.A.R. Egypt	80	56.25%
Thailand	158	87.5%
Turkey	172	93.75%
Nigeria	184	50%
Burma	192	37.5%
Indonesia	200	37.5%
Philippines	471	56.25%
India	566	62.5%
Republic of Korea	672	143.75%
China—Mainland	800	87.5%
Iran	3,029	118.75%
Surinam (bauxite)	2,050	143.75%
Zambia (copper)	1,800	162.5%

substantial impact on the rate of economic growth mainly when they correspond to a *per capita* natural wealth level well in excess of $1,000. At lower *per capita* levels of natural resources, other factors such as human resources, investment policies, etc, are likely to prove of greater impact.

EXPORTS STIMULATE GROWTH THROUGH INDUSTRIALIZATION STRATEGY

The fullest contribution to growth to be expected from an export-oriented national policy will be dependent on the achieving of internationally competitive cost structures which, in turn, will require the mobilization of a number of the sources of growth previously listed.

'Exports contribute to efficiency in the use of resources as long as the domestic resources that go into them are less than the resources which would have to be used to produce, at home, an equivalent value of imports'[33].

The industrialization strategy and related investments in manufacturing which are part and parcel of a comprehensive export-minded program bring in their wake 'indirect employment in various directions, not only for other industrial products but also for agricultural and mineral raw materials, public utilities and services, building and construction and commercial services and the employment created has repercussions on the demand not only for consumer goods but also for services and housing. The indirect labor creation will be most pronounced if there is sufficient concentration to create a demand for urban facilities and services'[33].

In view of the 'chain reaction' amplifying benefits reviewed above as well as others in the areas of social gains and technical skills stimulated by industrialization, it is not surprising that countries such as Taiwan, Korea and Singapore which have made determined efforts to meet the international challenges raised by export programs have achieved 'higher and more consistent rates of growth than those that have relied on import substitution at all costs and failed to take advantage of export possibilities'[33].

The country which in Chart 14 ranks highest above a median trend is Ivory Coast, the richest and most economically self-sufficient state in former French West Africa[19].

'In the years before World War II with emphasis on cash crops, coffee and cocoa increased in importance while subsistence agricultural sector declined. It even became necessary to import food. Workers migrated to coastal zones to pick cocoa and coffee beans and to work on bridges and roads.

After World War II, migration to coastal areas accelerated. The great urban agglomeration of Abidjan grew from 16,000 in 1936 to its present estimated 550,000. The French Government adopted a new philosophy of economic development, stressing grant aid for development projects for infrastructure and amelioration of social conditions. The traditional subsistence economy diminished in importance as migratory workers moved into the money economy.

When the Ivory Coast became an Overseas Territory under the Fourth Republic, it benefitted from the French Overseas Development Fund—FIDES (Investment Fund for Economic and Social Development). Between 1947 and 1957 FIDES granted $109 million to the Ivory Coast for development. The country has continued to benefit from extensive French economic assistance, which amounts to about $30 million a year in direct grant and loan assistance alone.

Upon attaining independence in 1960, the Government drew up a development plan whose realistic but ambitious goals for the 1960-65 period were, in general, exceeded. The annual growth of Ivory Coast's GDP in recent years has averaged about 8% in real terms.

Ivory Coast's Development Law-Plan for the 1967-70 period provides for $470 million in public investments: $184 million (39%) in infrastructure, $140 million (30%) in agriculture, $34 million (7%) in cultural development (education), $26 million (6%) in sanitation, $36 million (8%) in administration, $30 million (6%) in participation in mixed enterprises, and $20 million (4%) in studies and research.

Under infrastructure, the plan places major emphasis on the development of electric power, railways, and ports. Of particular importance is the construction in the southwest of the seaport of San Pedro at the total cost of $35 million. The Government hopes that this port will provide the necessary impetus for settlement and farming in the still sparsely populated southwest region.

Tentative projections for the 1971-80 period indicate that the Ivory Coast should be able to maintain a Gross Domestic Product growth rate of 6% a year

Factors of Growth 75

(constant prices). The most important development project during this period, as well as the largest in Ivory Coast's history, will be the $100 million Bandama hydroelectric and irrigation complex which the United States is supporting with a $36.5 million loan from the Export-Import Bank. Located in the interior of the Ivory Coast near Kossou, the project will help balance Ivory Coast's economic development, supply water resources to promote agricultural diversification, and provide electrical energy for the rapidly growing needs of industry.'

Several factors of growth we have cited in this chapter are found in the above. In addition there has been greater emphasis on a capably conceived and administered Development Law-Plan.

HOW WIDE IS THE RANGE WHICH, AT A GIVEN STAGE OF DEVELOPMENT ENCOMPASSES MANAGEABLE RATES OF GROWTH?

This will be reviewed in the next chapter, specifically in connection with Chart 15 which, based on the experience of all countries of the world, provides a documented answer to this question.

For any value of *per capita* GNP one may measure, from the lower to the upper boundary, the full range which the combined economic history of countries at all stages of development has helped to outline.

There are distinct limits within which a country can accelerate its economic development and achieve growth with stability.

The implementation of development projects should be in tune with available means of domestic and foreign financing. Available resources should not be overtaxed, treasury deficits should not be incurred, and investment expenditures should be curtailed if financial resources fall short of expectation.

In their approval and surveillance of the investments to which they contribute, the enlightened vigilance of the major international lending institutions provides safeguards along every step of the development process.

WHAT IS 'PAR FOR THE COURSE'?

The median pattern index of growth for the 146 countries charted is about 85%. It should be mentioned here that this study was originally intended to be limited to the 50 countries with the largest GNP (see Table XXI–1 through 4) totalling 96% of the Gross World Product. For these 50 largest countries, the median index of growth is indeed 100%.

CHART 15—GNP 'per capita' in 1990

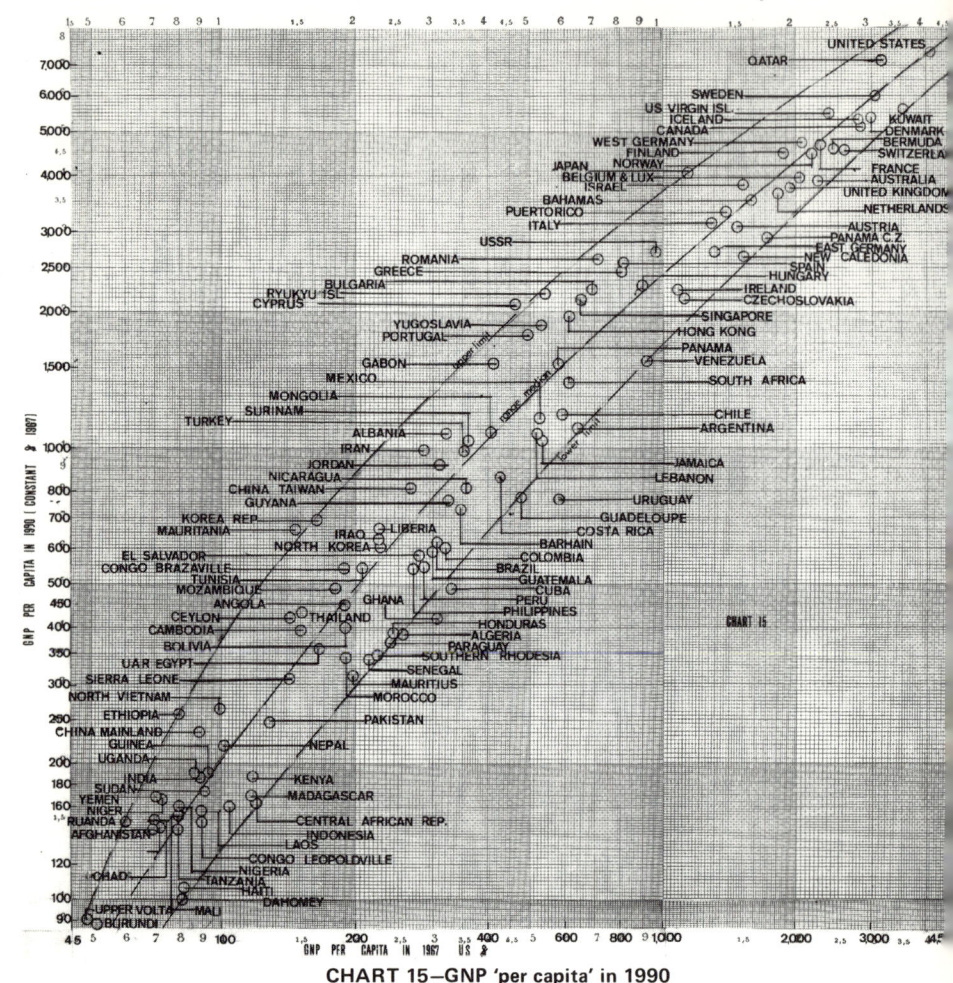

It was later decided to expand this detailed analysis to the next 70 countries (Table XXI—5 through 10). Since, as a group, these 70 countries, which total only 4% of the GWP, have a substantially lower growth rate, they have pulled the world median down from 100 to 85%.

This does not mean that size and rate of growth go together. Had we taken all of the 112 top countries of the world down to Tanzania, we would still have come up with a median of 100%.

Since the last 40 countries represent only 4/10 of 1% of the GWP, it may be said that an index of 100% is indeed 'par for the course'.

Factors of Growth 77

Thus being able to identify a single, median, index of growth—the 100% pattern—as a guideline or yard-stick of comparison applicable to *any* country demonstrates one of the justifications of the concept:

We have given, at the end of Chapter Four, an approximate correlation between the pattern index and the percent rate of increase: For 100% pattern index, we have indicated 5% yearly increase *per capita* for countries in early stages of industrialization and 4% in the industrialized countries range but, had we wanted to span a wider range of stages of growth, we should have said that a 100% pattern corresponds to 7% for an emerging country, to 6% for a developing country or to 3% for a country in a very advanced stage of industrialization.

Therefore, it would be impractical to attempt to define 'par for the course' in terms of percent rate of increase.

GROWTH RATES WHICH ARE QUITE DESIRABLE FOR INDUSTRIALIZED COUNTRIES MAY BE TOTALLY INADEQUATE FOR DEVELOPING COUNTRIES

It is important to emphasize the point made above:

A 3% *per capita* rate of economic growth for a country in a very advanced stage of industrialization, such as the United States, is just as appropriate and desirable as a 6% *per capita* growth rate for a developing country.

Too often, the rates of growth for countries in very early stages of development have been compared with those of industrialized countries and a certain measure of satisfaction was derived from this, whereas it should have been interpreted as a danger signal.

Convenient as they are, to use, rates of economic growth expressed in percent must be interpreted in full awareness that 7% *per capita* growth for an emerging country is not any better than 4% for an industrialized country.

WHAT IS THE MOST DESIRABLE RATE OF GROWTH?

The most desirable rate of growth should be regarded as that which will meet the total of three separate growth requirements:

(i) Growth in population, so that additional employment, additional capital and consumer goods can be provided for the additions to the population.

(ii) Extra growth should be provided to raise the underprivileged classes now living at near poverty level and to provide jobs for the unemployed.

(iii) Finally, additional growth should be achieved in order to ensure that, every year, every one will be slightly better off than the year before and be able to enjoy a slightly higher standard of living.

To translate this into figures, let us look for example at the world summary figures at the foot of Table XXI. For (i) we see 1.5%, for (ii) and (iii) together our forecast for the World as a whole shows 3.5%. Thus we verify that the Development Decade target of 6% for the developing countries is indeed a minimum since the rate of economic growth for developing countries should be at least 2% faster than for industrialized countries.

For Latin America, attaining during the 1970-1980 decade an 8% rate of growth was recommended[24]. By providing a vigorous boost to the needs listed as the 2nd growth requirement, such a rate of growth, if it could be attained by the entire developing world, would indeed be conducive to satisfactory distribution and social equity.

CAN, OR SHOULD, INDIVIDUALS, GROUPS, CONTRIBUTE TO IMPROVED NATIONAL GROWTH?

Each citizen, both as an individual and as a member of a group, can contribute much by constructive steps as well as by taking a stand against misinformed or ill-advised action.

Individuals should recognize that greater productivity is the only real means of achieving growth.

Institutions of learning, at all levels, should teach the importance of sound economics and should aim to turn out creative citizens who recognize that performance is the basis of rewards.

The Press should exercise maximum caution...

'In dealing with the complexities of our technological society. It must make clear to its public the distinction between fact and opinion. This is very difficult at a time when so many experts are speaking out on so many subjects, often beyond, or not related to, their area of competence, to a confused and frightened public.'[23]

Labor unions should not persist in programs which impede growth and they should avoid demands for the perpetuation of unnecessary jobs.

| | 1970 | 1980 | 1990 | 2000 | 2010 | 2020 |

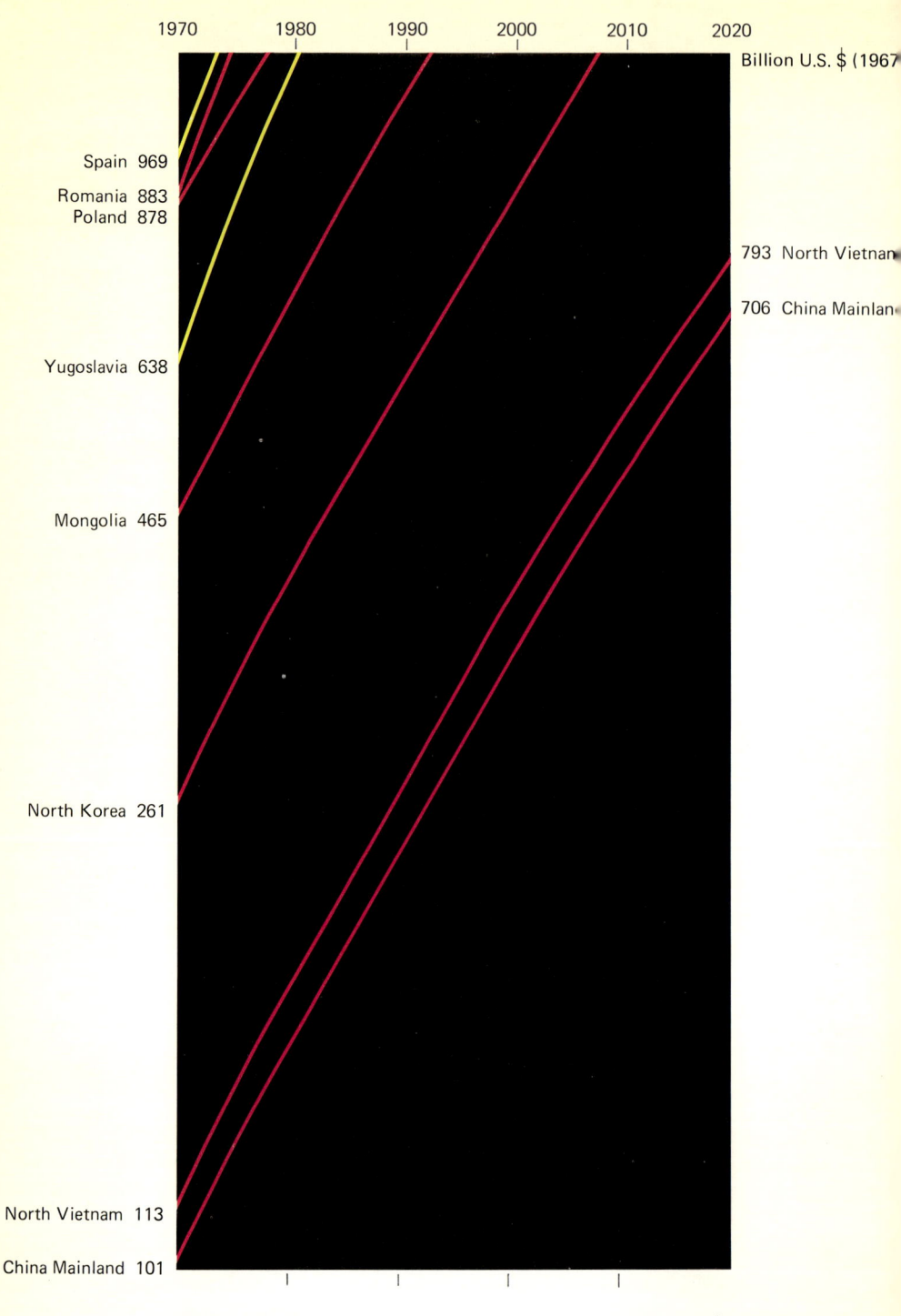

Billion U.S. $ (1967

Spain 969
Romania 883
Poland 878

793 North Vietnam
706 China Mainland

Yugoslavia 638

Mongolia 465

North Korea 261

North Vietnam 113
China Mainland 101

CHART 16a—Forecasted growth of GNP *per capita* in 1967 U.S. $
—group A—lower range

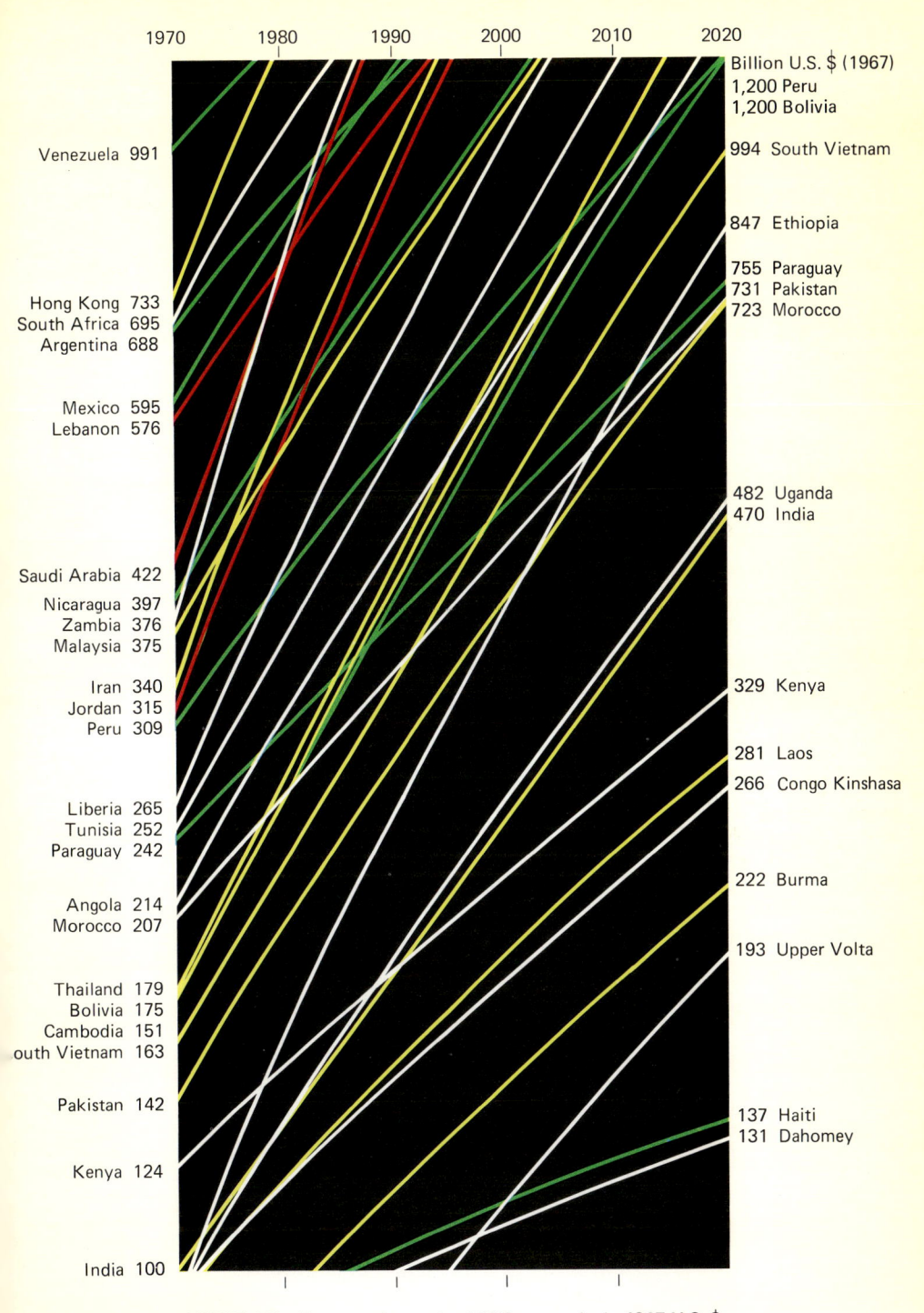

CHART 16b—Forecasted growth of GNP *per capita* in 1967 U.S. $
—group B—lower range

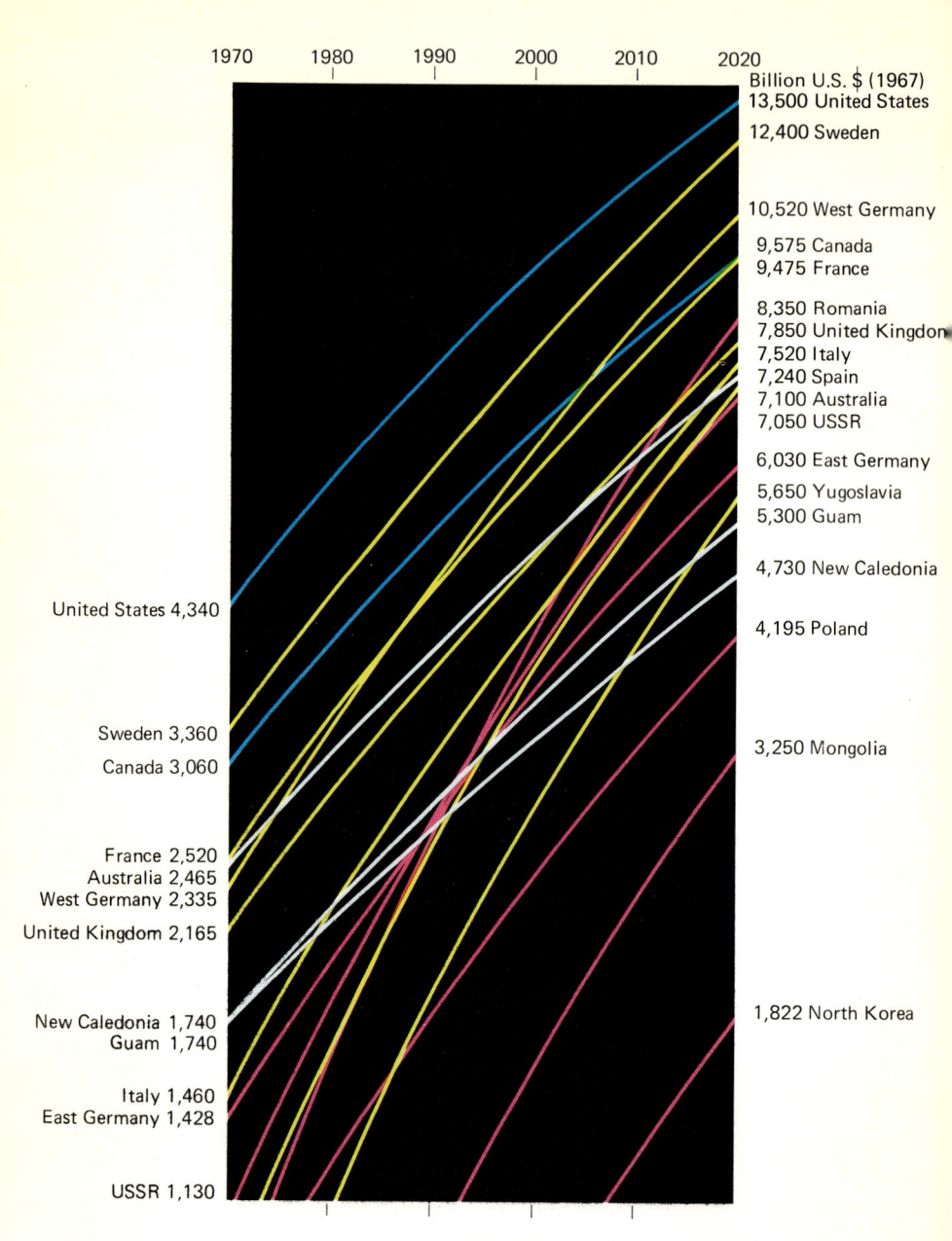

	1970	1980	1990	2000	2010	2020	
							Billion U.S. $ (1967)
							13,500 United States
							12,400 Sweden
							10,520 West Germany
							9,575 Canada
							9,475 France
							8,350 Romania
							7,850 United Kingdom
							7,520 Italy
							7,240 Spain
							7,100 Australia
							7,050 USSR
							6,030 East Germany
							5,650 Yugoslavia
							5,300 Guam
							4,730 New Caledonia

United States 4,340

4,195 Poland

Sweden 3,360
Canada 3,060

3,250 Mongolia

France 2,520
Australia 2,465
West Germany 2,335
United Kingdom 2,165

New Caledonia 1,740
Guam 1,740

1,822 North Korea

Italy 1,460
East Germany 1,428

USSR 1,130

CHART 16c—Forecasted growth of GNP *per capita* in 1967 U.S. $
—group A—upper range

1970	1980	1990	2000	2010	2020	

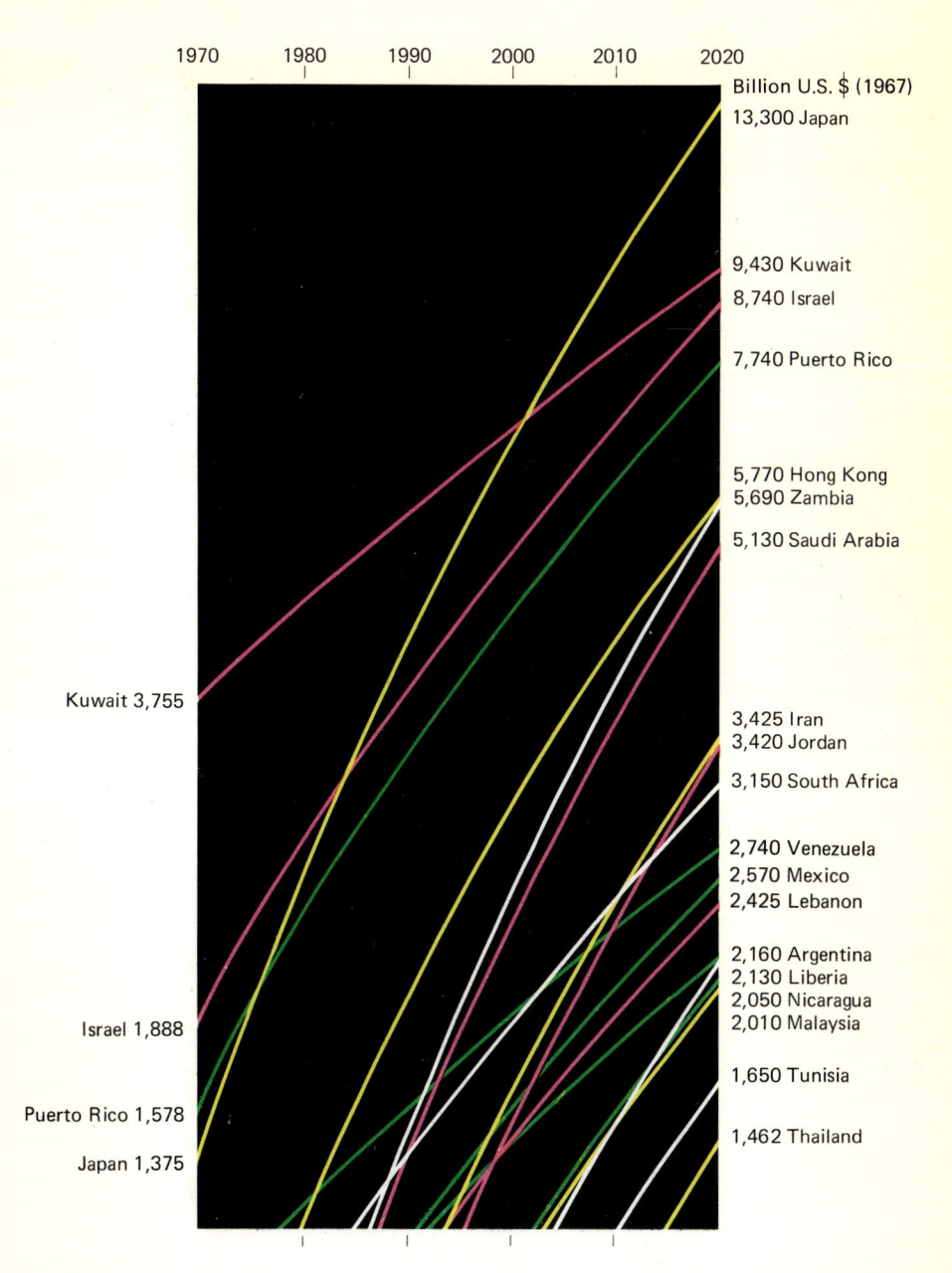

Billion U.S. $ (1967)
13,300 Japan

9,430 Kuwait
8,740 Israel

7,740 Puerto Rico

5,770 Hong Kong
5,690 Zambia

5,130 Saudi Arabia

Kuwait 3,755

3,425 Iran
3,420 Jordan

3,150 South Africa

2,740 Venezuela
2,570 Mexico
2,425 Lebanon

2,160 Argentina
2,130 Liberia
2,050 Nicaragua
2,010 Malaysia

Israel 1,888

1,650 Tunisia

Puerto Rico 1,578

1,462 Thailand

Japan 1,375

CHART 16d—Forecasted growth of GNP *per capita* in 1967 U.S. $
—group B—upper range

	1970	1980	1990	2000	2010	2020

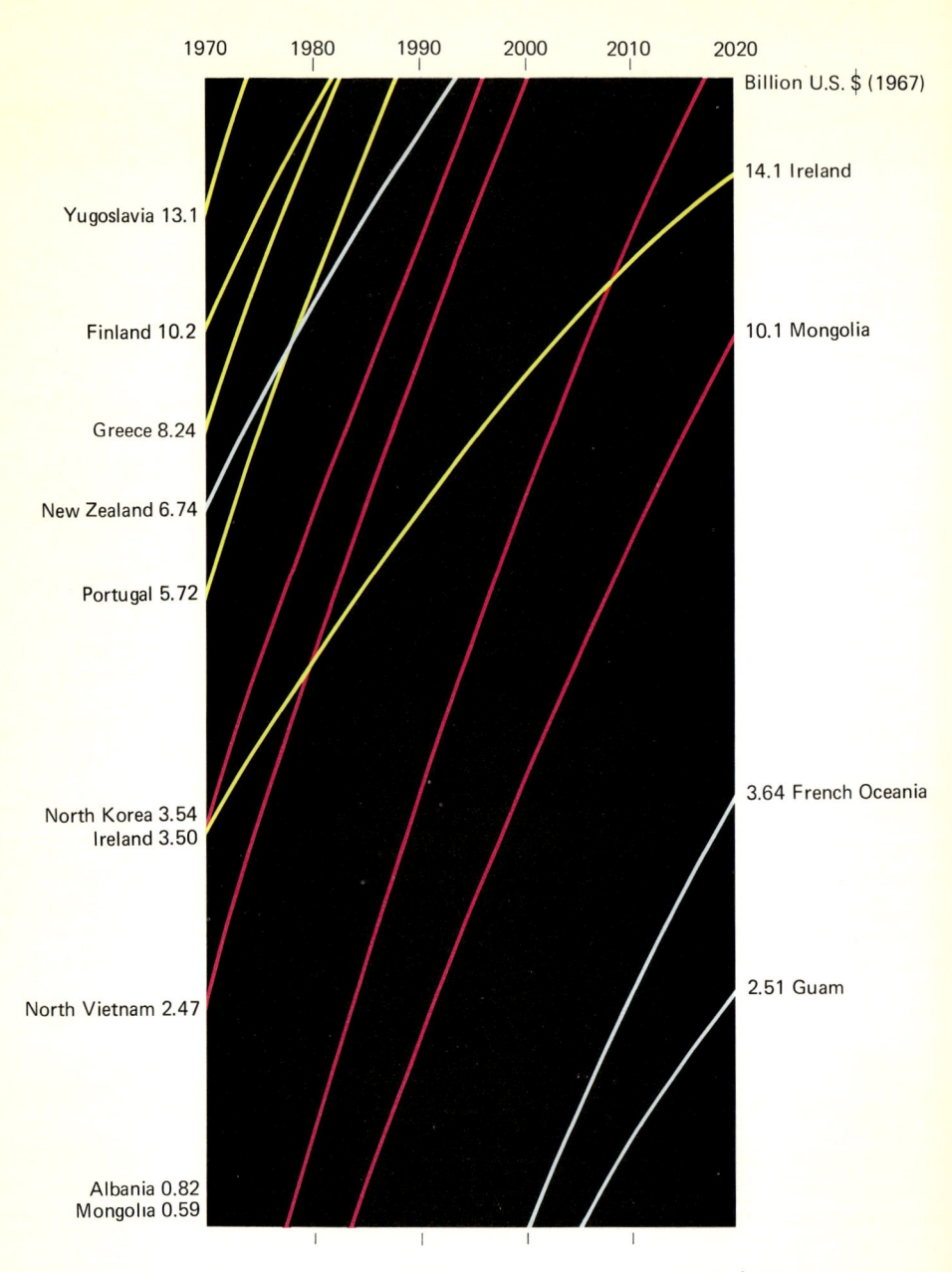

Billion U.S. $ (1967)

14.1 Ireland

Yugoslavia 13.1

Finland 10.2

10.1 Mongolia

Greece 8.24

New Zealand 6.74

Portugal 5.72

3.64 French Oceania

North Korea 3.54
Ireland 3.50

2.51 Guam

North Vietnam 2.47

Albania 0.82
Mongolia 0.59

CHART 21a—Forecasted growth of GNP in Billion 1967 U.S. $
—group A—lower range

1970	1980	1990	2000	2010	2020	

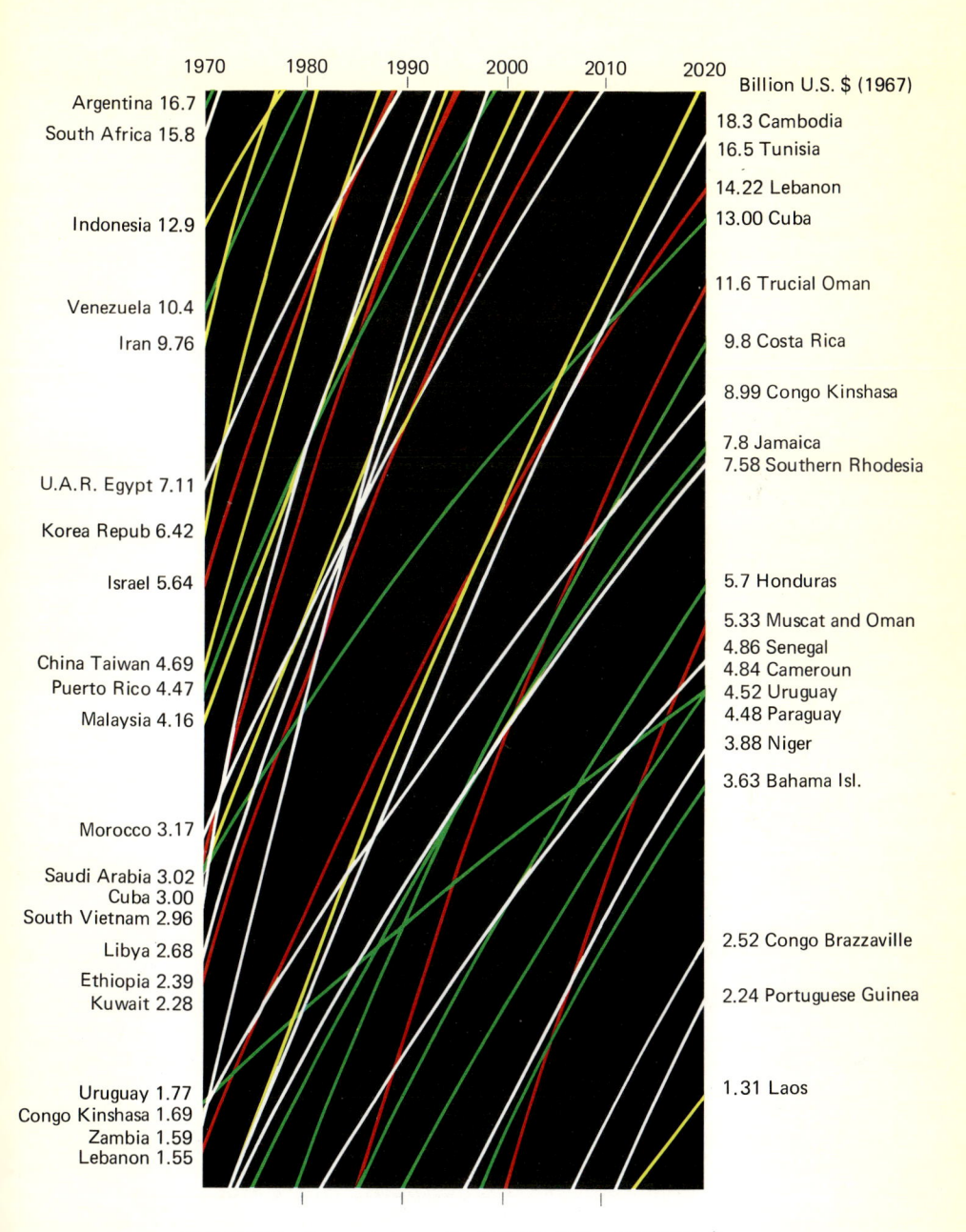

Billion U.S. $ (1967)

Argentina 16.7
South Africa 15.8
  18.3 Cambodia
  16.5 Tunisia
  14.22 Lebanon
Indonesia 12.9
  13.00 Cuba
  11.6 Trucial Oman
Venezuela 10.4
Iran 9.76
  9.8 Costa Rica
  8.99 Congo Kinshasa
  7.8 Jamaica
U.A.R. Egypt 7.11
  7.58 Southern Rhodesia
Korea Repub 6.42
Israel 5.64
  5.7 Honduras
  5.33 Muscat and Oman
  4.86 Senegal
China Taiwan 4.69
  4.84 Cameroun
Puerto Rico 4.47
  4.52 Uruguay
Malaysia 4.16
  4.48 Paraguay
  3.88 Niger
  3.63 Bahama Isl.
Morocco 3.17
Saudi Arabia 3.02
Cuba 3.00
South Vietnam 2.96
Libya 2.68
  2.52 Congo Brazzaville
Ethiopia 2.39
Kuwait 2.28
  2.24 Portuguese Guinea
Uruguay 1.77
  1.31 Laos
Congo Kinshasa 1.69
Zambia 1.59
Lebanon 1.55

CHART 21b—Forecasted growth of GNP in Billion 1967 U.S. $
—group B—lower range

1970	1980	1990	2000	2010	2020

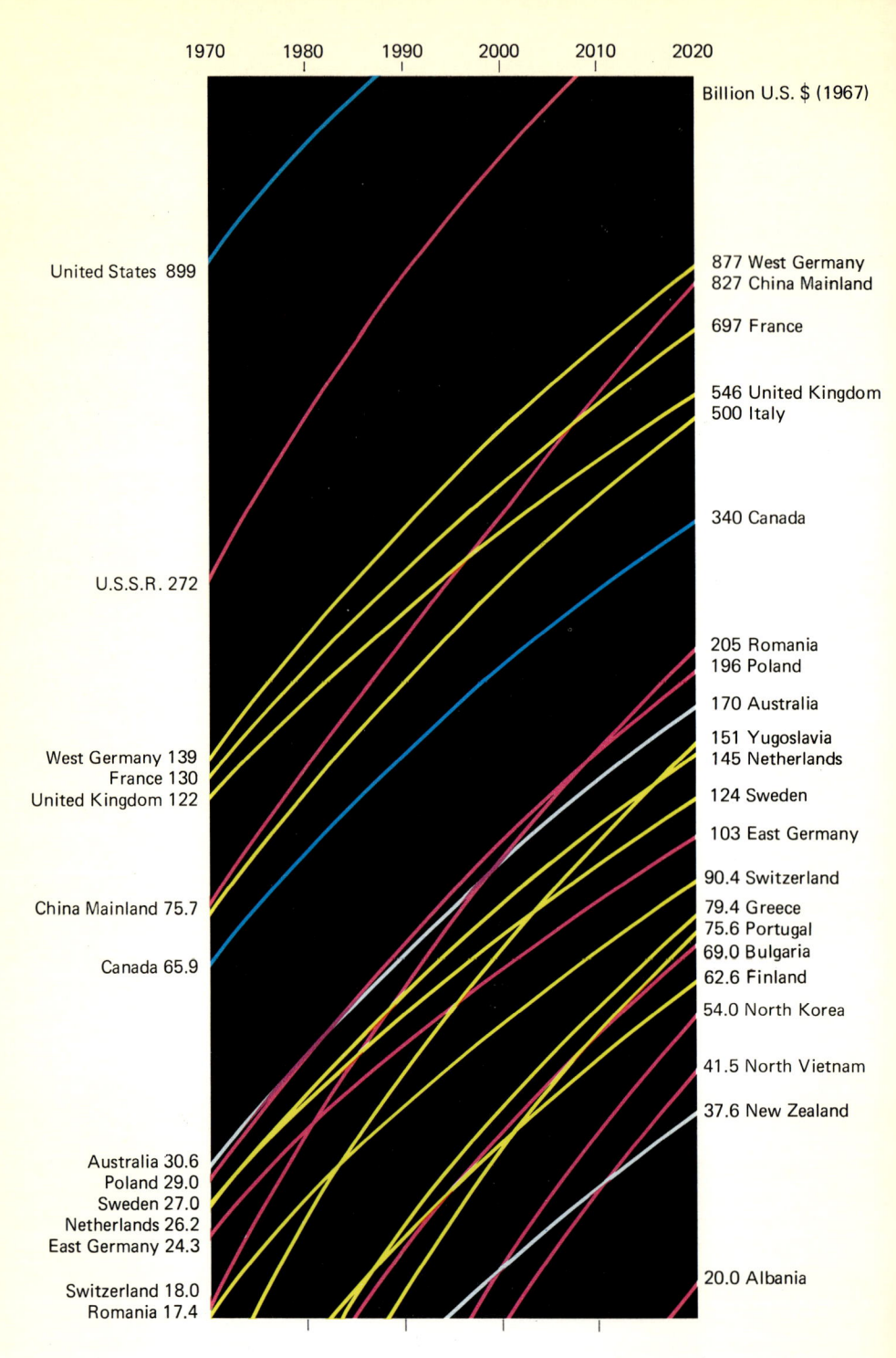

Billion U.S. $ (1967)

United States 899

877 West Germany
827 China Mainland

697 France

546 United Kingdom
500 Italy

340 Canada

U.S.S.R. 272

205 Romania
196 Poland

170 Australia

151 Yugoslavia
145 Netherlands

124 Sweden

103 East Germany

West Germany 139
France 130
United Kingdom 122

90.4 Switzerland

China Mainland 75.7

79.4 Greece
75.6 Portugal
69.0 Bulgaria
62.6 Finland

Canada 65.9

54.0 North Korea

41.5 North Vietnam

37.6 New Zealand

Australia 30.6
Poland 29.0
Sweden 27.0
Netherlands 26.2
East Germany 24.3

Switzerland 18.0
Romania 17.4

20.0 Albania

CHART 21c—Forecasted growth of GNP in Billion 1967 U.S. $
—group A—upper range

1970　1980　1990　2000　2010　2020

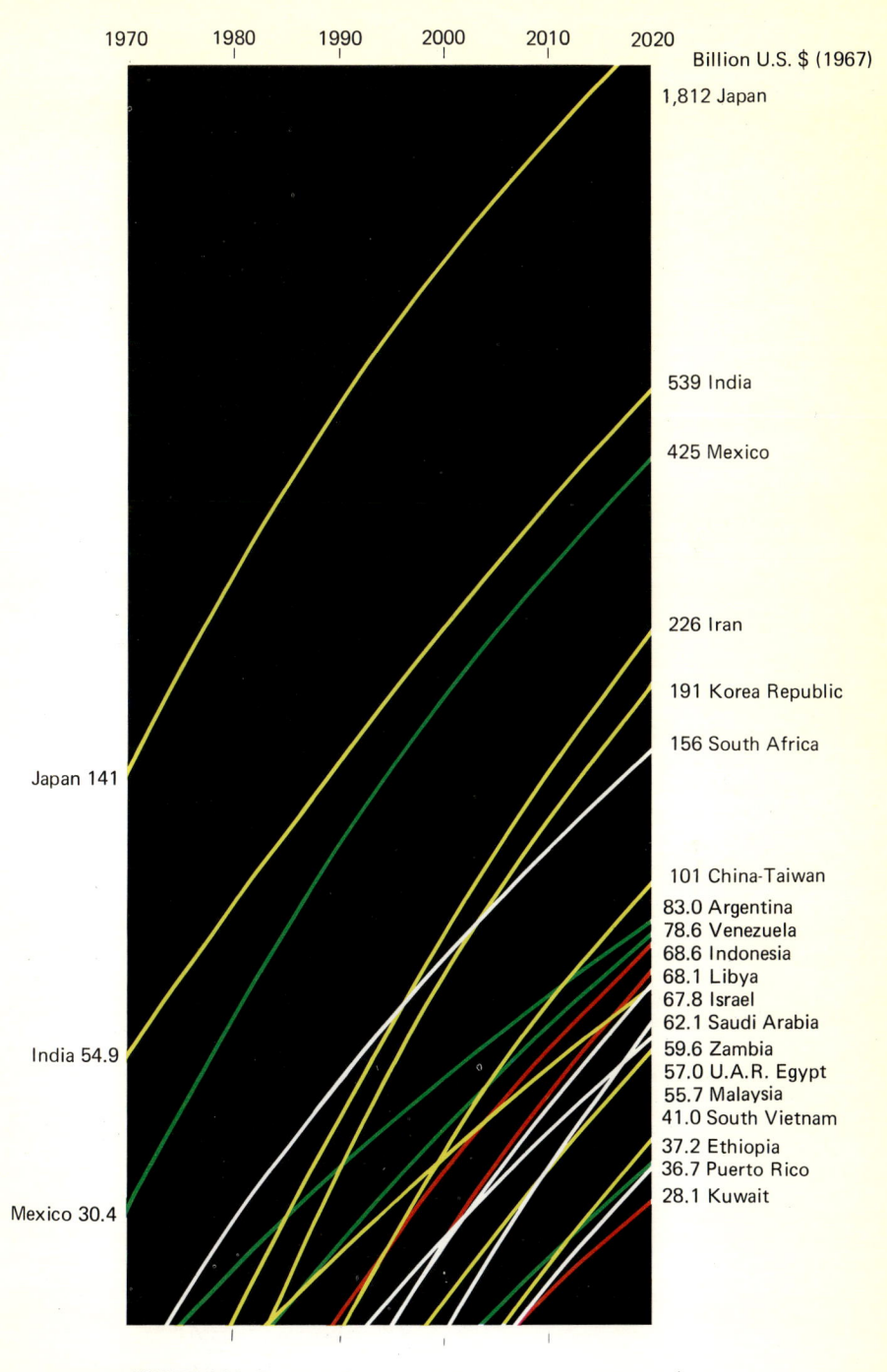

Billion U.S. $ (1967)

1,812 Japan

539 India

425 Mexico

226 Iran

191 Korea Republic

156 South Africa

Japan 141

101 China-Taiwan
83.0 Argentina
78.6 Venezuela
68.6 Indonesia
68.1 Libya
67.8 Israel
62.1 Saudi Arabia
59.6 Zambia
57.0 U.A.R. Egypt
55.7 Malaysia
41.0 South Vietnam
37.2 Ethiopia
36.7 Puerto Rico
28.1 Kuwait

India 54.9

Mexico 30.4

CHART 21d—Forecasted growth of GNP in Billion 1967 U.S. $
—group B—upper range

Factors of Growth

'PER CAPITA' GNP

Continuing the preceding comments on the pattern method and on growth, we shall review the steps which have resulted in the *per capita* GNP tables and charts presented in this volume:

Table VIII is the base of reference from which the calculations for each country were initiated.

Through the use of 'stage of growth factor', a different one for each country—which can be read from Table XXV—the *per capita* GNP since 1948 was matched to the particular pattern which best fitted it. This established the 'reference year' corresponding to 1967 for this country which was pinpointed as circled in Chart 12.

The assumption was then made that the trend—or pattern—thus determined would continue to be followed and the 'stage of growth' for 1970, 1975, etc, to 2020 was read on the ordinate scale.

Using the 'stage of growth factor' in reverse, gave the *per capita* GNP to the year 2020 which the reader will find:

(a) In tabulated form, for each country, individually, in the 'country page' in Part Two, at 5-year intervals from 1970 to 2020

(b) In tabulated form, for all countries, for 1967, 1980, 2000 and 2020 in Table XXI

(c) In Graph curves, from which *per capita* GNP can be read for any desired year, in Charts 16a, b, c and d.

The plotting of the charts on the logarithmic scale (proportional scale) provides two advantages: It makes it possible to portray, with equal accuracy, figures within a 100/1 range, also the slope of the curves, at any point, gives an immediate indication of the rate of growth, since, on this logarithmic scale, a constant annual rate of growth would be portrayed as a straight line.

Parallel slopes indicate equal rates of growth. The curves which cut across in an upward thrust bring out the future potential for extra growth as proved by the results that are being achieved by certain countries.

The spacing in years, read along the horizontal scale between any two countries, at the same *per capita* stage, indicates the number of years 'lead' of one country over the other.

It is hoped that this study will contribute to encouraging more countries of the developing world towards aiming for the results already achieved by some.

For instance, a curve can be drawn, from the point at which any country stands in 1970, parallel to that of another country whose course it feels it can or would like to emulate, which will provide an indication of what lies within the realm of possibilities.

HOW ARE DIFFERENT DEGREES OF INFLATION ACCOUNTED FOR?

Because its impact on economic growth—substantial as it may be—is not easily predictable, inflation is not discussed in depth in this volume of which the aim has been to present, for all countries, GNP data on the basis of a U.S. $ of constant purchasing power.

Questions may arise in the mind of the readers: Is not the method likely to prove at fault if, as is certain to be the case, the currency of a particular country is subject to less or to more inflation than the U.S.$? How can a GNP forecast in terms of constant U.S.$ be converted in terms of current Francs, Pesetas, Marks, etc?

We may answer these questions as follows:

Once we accept the premises that we have a valid approach to the forecasting of *real* economic growth our only problem is to make sure that we have the correct relationship between constant Francs and current Francs, between constant Pesetas and current Pesetas, between constant Marks and current Marks, etc.

This is discussed under the following headings from which the reader may also derive a clearer understanding of the method by which the forecasts presented in this volume were prepared.

GNP DEFLATOR

The United Nations Yearbook of National Accounts[1] provides for many of the countries of which we have analysed the growth, GNP data both on a current market price basis and on a 'constant' basis referred to as the market price as of a certain base year or sometimes two different base years.

These have enabled us to calculate, starting from 1948, an unbroken series of GNP price 'deflators' defined as the factor by which the GNP value in terms of the current prices for any year must be 'deflated' in order to be expressed in terms of the market price on a given base year.

Since our aim was to use as base year, for all countries, the latest year for which consistent, valid data were available for the largest number of countries, we selected 1967, for which the deflator became 100%—unity—for all countries.

Factors of Growth

TABLE XIX—Reciprocal of GNP deflator for 65 countries, referred to 1967 as 1.00

	1958	1959	1960	1961	1962	1963	1964	1965	1966	1967	1968	1969	1970	1971
Argentina	11.2	5.39	4.46	4.00	3.19	2.51	2.00	1.55	1.27	1.00				
Australia	1.30	1.22	1.20	1.20	1.17	1.12	1.10	1.06	1.03	1.00				
Austria	1.39	1.36	1.31	1.25	1.20	1.17	1.14	1.07	1.03	1.00				
Belgium&Lux.	1.25	1.25	1.23	1.22	1.21	1.17	1.12	1.07	1.02	1.00				
Bolivia	1.68	1.52	1.33	1.25	1.21	1.19	1.11	1.04	1.00	0.96				
Brazil	25.2	18.2	15.9	11.0	7.06	4.03	2.34	1.44	1.00					
Burma	1.14	1.12	1.10	1.08	1.05	1.05	1.06	1.06	1.05	1.00				
Canada	1.24	1.21	1.19	1.18	1.17	1.15	1.11	1.07	1.03	1.00				
Ceylon	1.02	1.01	1.01	1.03	1.00	1.02	1.01	1.01	1.01	1.00				
Chile	8.05	6.30	5.64	5.27	4.59	3.26	2.24	1.66	1.28	1.00				
China-Taiwan	1.45	1.35	1.18	1.14	1.12	1.07	1.04	1.03	1.03	1.00				
Colombia		2.46	2.27	2.09	1.96	1.59	1.36	1.25	1.09	1.00				
Cyprus	1.04	1.04	1.03	1.04	1.02	0.99	0.99	0.97	1.00	1.00				
Denmark	1.58	1.53	1.47	1.42	1.36	1.29	1.21	1.14	1.06	1.00				
DominicanRep.	1.19	1.23	1.24	1.24	1.11	1.03	1.00	1.01	1.01	1.00				
Ecuador	1.33	1.33	1.30	1.24	1.21	1.16	1.13	1.09	1.04	1.00				
Finland	1.56	1.55	1.51	1.47	1.43	1.35	1.25	1.11	1.06	1.00				
France		1.33	1.30	1.25	1.19	1.13	1.08	1.06	1.03	1.00	0.95			
West Germany	1.34	1.32	1.28	1.23	1.18	1.15	1.12	1.08	1.01	1.00				
Ghana		1.56	1.57	1.52	1.48	1.39	1.27	1.08	0.97	1.00				
Greece	1.25	1.25	1.21	1.18	1.15	1.13	1.10	1.06	1.02	1.00				
Guatemala	1.03	1.10	1.01	1.01	0.98	1.01	0.98	0.99	0.99	1.00				
Guyana			1.12	1.09	1.04	1.00	1.04	1.02	1.01	1.00				
Honduras	1.09	1.09	1.11	1.09	1.08	1.07	1.05	1.02	1.02	1.00				
Iceland	2.62	2.38	2.17	1.89	1.67	1.52	1.27	1.13	1.01	1.00				
India	1.56	1.55	1.69	1.67	1.61	1.48	1.35	1.25	1.08	1.00				
Iran		1.15	1.08	1.06	0.97	1.05	1.01	1.00	1.00	1.00				
Ireland	1.38	1.35	1.34	1.31	1.25	1.22	1.12	1.09	1.03	1.00				
Israel	1.78	1.68	1.61	1.47	1.35	1.26	1.19	1.09	1.00	1.00				
Italy	1.40	1.40	1.26	1.32	1.24	1.16	1.10	1.05	1.03	1.00				
Jamaica	1.28	1.25	1.22	1.17	1.14	1.11	1.12	1.09	1.05	1.00				
Japan	1.45	1.41	1.37	1.30	1.24	1.18	1.14	1.09	1.04	1.00				
Korea Repub.	3.37	3.30	3.02	2.61	2.30	1.80	1.36	1.27	1.12	1.00				
Libya				1.47	1.41	1.22	1.16	1.07	1.00					
Malaysia	1.10	1.01	0.99	1.04	1.06	1.04	1.02	1.00	1.01	1.00				
Mexico	1.39	1.34	1.28	1.24	1.20	1.15	1.10	1.08	1.04	1.00				
Morocco	1.33	1.28	1.21	1.18	1.12	1.07	1.02	0.99	0.99	1.00				
Netherlands	1.47	1.44	1.40	1.37	1.33	1.27	1.17	1.11	1.04	1.00				
New Zealand	1.23	1.20	1.17	1.16	1.12	1.08	1.05	1.04	1.03	1.00				
Nicaragua	1.11	1.09	1.08	1.07	1.06	1.05	1.03	1.03	1.02	1.00				
Nigeria	1.12	1.14	1.13	1.07	1.01	1.03	1.02	1.01	1.00					
Norway	1.36	1.32	1.29	1.26	1.22	1.19	1.13	1.08	1.04	1.00				
Pakistan	1.38	1.28	1.22	1.23	1.21	1.22	1.17	1.11	1.00	1.00				
Panama			1.10	1.10	1.07	1.08	1.07	1.06	1.05	1.00				
Paraguay	1.70	1.51	1.31	1.20	1.11	1.07	1.04	1.02	0.99	1.00				
Peru	2.26	2.05	1.82	1.75	1.66	1.58	1.40	1.23	1.10	1.00				
Philippines	1.42	1.40	1.33	1.29	1.24	1.16	1.10	1.08	1.03	1.00				
Portugal	1.27	1.24	1.22	1.20	1.18	1.17	1.14	1.11	1.02	1.00				
Puerto Rico	1.28	1.24	1.21	1.16	1.12	1.12	1.10	1.07	1.03	1.00				
South Africa	1.23	1.20	1.18	1.16	1.15	1.12	1.09	1.05	1.03	1.00				
South Vietnam			1.41	1.37	1.33	1.26	1.23	1.05	1.07	1.00				
Spain	1.64	1.50	1.54	1.51	1.43	1.32	1.24	1.12	1.06	1.00				
Sweden	1.43	1.42	1.36	1.31	1.26	1.21	1.17	1.11	1.05	1.00				
Switzerland	1.43	1.42	1.37	1.32	1.25	1.20	1.14	1.10	1.05	1.00				
Tanzania			1.21	1.11	1.10	1.05	1.04	1.04	1.03	1.00				
Thailand	1.13	1.17	1.17	1.14	1.10	1.14	1.13	1.11	1.04	1.00				
Tunisia		1.12	1.21	1.22	1.19	1.17	1.08	1.05	1.00					
Turkey	1.69	1.43	1.38	1.29	1.23	1.16	1.13	1.10	1.04	1.00				
Uganda	1.21	1.25	1.26	1.26	1.21	1.18	1.13	1.03	1.04	1.00				
UnitedKingdom	1.28	1.27	1.26	1.22	1.17	1.15	1.12	1.07	1.03	1.00				
Uruguay	14.5	10.5	7.12	5.75	5.16	4.28	2.99	1.90	1.00					
United States	1.18	1.15	1.13	1.12	1.10	1.09	1.08	1.06	1.03	1.00	0.95			
Venezuela	1.15	1.17	1.21	1.20	1.19	1.17	1.04	1.03	1.02	1.00				
Yugoslavia	3.12	2.94	2.64	2.40	2.24	2.08	1.76	1.38	1.20	1.00				
Zambia	1.25	1.12	1.10	1.14	1.15	1.12	1.13	1.16	1.09	1.00				

Instead of the conventional deflator, the value of which generally rises from one year to the next in response to the gradual erosion of the currency, we have found it preferable to calculate the reciprocal of the deflator, which Table XIX shows for 65 countries, for every year since 1958 through 1967.

Actually, our calculations of this deflector—or its reciprocal—as well as of all the other factors which have contributed to our country forecasts go as far back as 1948 but only the values since 1958 have been shown in Table XIX.

It should also be pointed out, here, that none of the United Nations Statistical Accounts we have used for the years from 1948 through 1967 actually included GNP data on the basis of 1967 market prices but it only required simple proration to make 1967 the base year throughout. A glance at the array of data in Table XIX will show the advantage of this uniform basis of comparison.

CONTINUOUS RECORDS OF GNP DEFLATORS FOR 65 COUNTRIES OF THE WORLD

In addition to its statistical interest, and to its usefulness towards answering several of the questions which our forecasts may raise—to which we shall return under a subsequent heading—Table XIX provides what is probably the most complete record available of the impact of inflation on the GNP of 65 countries over the 9-year period from 1958 to 1967. A number of statistics give consumer price indexes, wholesale price indexes, wages hourly earnings indexes from year to year, for many countries but, to our knowledge, GNP deflators, often called 'implicit' GNP deflators because the GNP price index is implicit in the way the GNP is measured, are not available, in continuous series as we have shown, on a comparable basis; for a large number of countries.

In illustration of the diverse weight given to various price indexes which is 'implicit' in the GNP deflator, we note the 1967 values for the United States of the three other indexes mentioned in the preceding paragraph. These are all equal to 100 for 1958 taken as the base year.

Index for 1967 (1958 = 100)	
Wholesale Prices	106
Consumer Prices	114.5
Wages Hourly Earnings	132
GNP Implicit Deflator	118

Factors of Growth

HOW HAVE COUNTRIES RATED, IN TERMS OF INFLATION, FROM 1958 TO 1967?

As stated earlier, we do not propose to discuss inflation in this volume but the reader may find it of interest to obtain from Table XIX a bird's eye view of the extent of inflation in the various countries reported.

The facing row of figures, which gives the value of the reciprocal of the GNP price deflator for 9 years, for various yearly rates of inflation, may be directly compared with the values which can be read under 1958, for any country (except Brazil, Nigeria and Uruguay which have a 1966 base year) in Table XIX.

We may quickly summarize our observations as follows:

Countries which have had from 1958 to 1967 an inflation per year of:

Yearly rate of inflation	9-year Reciprocal of GNP Deflator
1%	1.093
2%	1.195
3%	1.304
4%	1.423
5%	1.551
6%	1.689
7%	1.838
8%	1.999
9%	2.171
10%	2.357

Less than 1%:   Ceylon, Cyprus, Guatemala, Honduras
Between 1% and 2%:   Burma, Dominican Republic, Iran, Malaysia, Nicaragua, Thailand, United States, Venezuela
Between 2% and 3%:   Australia, Belgium & Luxembourg, Canada, Greece, Jamaica, New Zealand, Portugal, Puerto Rico, South Africa, Uganda, United Kingdom, Zambia
Between 3% and 4%:   Austria, Ecuador, France, West Germany, Ireland, Italy, Mexico, Morocco, Norway, Pakistan, Philippines
Between 4% and 5%:   China Taiwan, Netherlands, Sweden, Switzerland
Between 5% and 6%:   Bolivia, Denmark, Finland, Ghana, India, Spain, Turkey

In the light of the much higher rates of inflation that the United States and other major countries have been experiencing in recent years, the short summary above is, obviously, only of historical interest; however, we hope that, together with Table XIX, these records and the blank columns left for 1968 through 1971, the availability of this data will make it easier for the reader interested in any countries to update the series on inflation as affecting the GNP.

GNP AND GNP 'PER CAPITA' SERIES FROM 1948 TO 1967 FOR EACH COUNTRY

Using the data in Table XIX made it very easy to convert the GNP of any country given in current market prices into constant 1967 prices, for each year from 1948 to 1968 always in the currency of the country. As an example, this is shown for France, since 1958, in lines (a), (b) and (c) opposite.

The next step shown in line (d) was to convert the GNP values in constant 1967 French Francs to constant 1967 U.S.$, using the official exchange rate in 1967 of 4.937 Francs for $1[1]

Line (e) records the population for each year from 1958 through 1968[3]

Line (f) gives the GNP *per capita*, in Constant 1967 U.S.$, simply obtained by dividing line (d) by line (e)

ESTABLISHING THE GROWTH PATTERN FOR EACH COUNTRY

Recapitulating the various steps reviewed above, we have explained how the GNP implicit price deflator was obtained for each country and we have presented the complete record of the reciprocal of this deflator for 65 countries. In lines (a) through (f) of the table of calculations which illustrates the method followed specifically for France, we have shown the series of calculations through which a valid record of GNP *per capita* in constant 1967 U.S.$ was obtained for the 65 countries for which consistent current and constant prices GNP series were available.

We shall now explain, by referring to lines (g), (h) and (i) in the table opposite how the growth pattern for each of these 65 countries was determined.

CONTRIBUTION OF THE ANALYSES OF ENERGY USE TO THE FORECASTING OF ECONOMIC GROWTH

Anticipating somewhat on Chapter Ten, where Energy is discussed at length, also on Chapter Eleven, where the mutual impact of Energy and of Quality of Life is reviewed, it is proper to note that, throughout our investigations of economic growth, as measured by GNP and GNP *per capita*, the availability of a parallel—and in some cases more complete—set of data on energy use has proved of considerable value.

Factors of Growth

		1958	1959	1960	1961	1962	1963	1964	1965	1966	1967	1968
GNP Current Francs (Billions)	(a)		267.4	296.2	319.7	367.2	411.9	456.7	489.8	531.9	572.1	628.5
Reciprocal Of Deflator (From Table XIX)	(b)		1.332	1.295	1.250	1.192	1.125	1.080	1.059	1.028	1.000	0.950
GNP—Constant 1967 Francs (Billions)	(c)		356.0	384.0	400.0	438.5	464.0	494.0	518.5	548.0	572.1	595.0
GNP—Constant 1967 U.S.$ (Billions)	(d)		72.1	77.8	81.0	88.6	94.1	100.1	104.9	111.0	116.0	120.2
Population—Mill.	(e)		45.24	45.68	46.16	47.00	47.82	48.31	48.76	49.16	49.55	49.92
GNP 'per capita' 1967 U.S.$	(f)		1,595	1,700	1,752	1,888	1,975	2,080	2,150	2,260	2,340	2,420
Total Energy Use 'per capita' (KEC)	(g)		2,332	2,425	2,483	2,604	2,828	2,944	2,955	2,952	3,092	3,282
GNP $/Energy KEC	(h)		0.685	0.701	0.706	0.725	0.700	0.706	0.728	0.767	0.758	0.737
GNP $/Capita: 0.758	(i)		2,105	2,242	2,315	2,492	2,615	2,745	2,840	2,965	3,092	3,200

This was particularly helpful wherever series of GNP at constant market prices were not available, which was the case for the 88 countries not included in Table XIX. Complete series of *per capita* use of energy, available for all 153 countries[4], have made it possible to make up, at least partially, for the lack of complete national accounts data for these 88 countries and to achieve practically comparable quality of forecasting throughout.

STEPS IN THE PROCESS OF DETERMINING THE PATTERN INDEX OF GROWTH OF GNP, ALSO OF ENERGY

For each of the 153 countries for which we have prepared forecasts of economic growth, our calculations have progressed through the same steps as we are reviewing, in the following, for France:

In line (g), we have transcribed the yearly *per capita* use of total energy[4].

In line (h), we have shown the ratio between line (f) and line (g) for each year. The trend of this ratio and, should this be the case, any abrupt reversals of this trend from year to year have been used as a sensitive indicator of either the continuity of the growth process or of economic or other disturbances.

There is not a single country in the world for which the *per capita* use of energy increases at the same rate as the *per capita* GNP. This is reviewed in detail in Chapter Ten (Chart 27 and Table XXVI) and the comparison of the two rates of growth has proved of considerable assistance in the evaluation of the respective patterns, particularly where GNP data was not complete.

Line (i) provides a series of values of GNP multiplied by a proportionality factor such that in 1967 the prorated GNP *per capita* reads the same number as the Energy use *per capita* regarded as synonymous of stage of growth.

Line (i) and line (g) have been used, for each country, to determine respectively the pattern of growth of GNP *per capita* and that of Energy *per capita*:

We make sure that out of the 9-years series we have for France, for instance, we select a period for which the ratio on line (h) keeps the same trend. This limits us to either the period from 1959 to 1962 or the period from 1963 to 1966. Matching the growth of the prorated GNP/Capita in line (i) to the family patterns in Chart 12 points to 100% as being the applicable pattern for GNP *per capita*.

Similarly, using the same periods for line (g) points to 93.75% as the applicable pattern for the Energy use *per capita*.

Factors of Growth 87

The ratio of 100% for the GNP *per capita* pattern to 93.75% for the Energy *per capita* pattern is 1.06 which is recorded both in Chart 27 and in Table XXVI.

HOW CAN A GNP FORECAST IN TERMS OF CONSTANT 1967 U.S.$. BE CONVERTED IN CONSTANT 1971 FRANCS?

We can now return to, and answer, the question posed a few pages back, using the forecast for France as an example, the method of conversion being the same for any country. Copying the figures in the profile for France in Part Two we start with

	1967	1970	1975	1980	1985	1990	1995
GNP in Billion 1967 U.S.$	116	129	163	194.9	237.5	283	335.0
Multiplying by 4.937:	572	636	804	961	1,170	1,395	1,700

We need, now, to know the implicit GNP Deflator for the French Franc in 1971 compared to 1967. Let us assume it is 1.30. We simply multiply the last row of figures by 1.30 and we obtain:

	1967	1970	1975	1980	1985	1990	1995
GNP in Billion 1971 French Francs	744	827	1,045	1,249	1,527	1,814	2,210

MANY LIMITATIONS HAVE PREVENTED US FROM DESCRIBING THE METHOD USED IN STILL GREATER DETAIL

Lengthy as the above explanatory comments have been, we realize that the reader interested in a detailed appraisal of the method used will wish that much more space had been given to it.

Format limitations, the imperatives of clear reproduction, the sheer physical size of 153 work-sheets spanning the recorded and forecasted economic and energetic history of each country from 1948 through 2020 have deterred us from presenting any more material—than what is included in this volume—on the method used.

We hope, however, to have covered sufficient ground to satisfy the reader, at least partially, that the concept presented, the methods which developed it and the forecasts derived from it offer a valid approach to international economic comparisons.

COMPARISON OF 'PER CAPITA' GNP IN 1967 and in 1990

The 50-year span over which the forecasts presented in this volume have been carried out gives the reader the opportunity to select the years of greatest interest to any particular investigation.

For 'general comparison' purposes, it was deemed desirable to tabulate and compare, by various yardsticks, the performance of all

TABLE XIXa—GNP 'per capita' in 1990 compared to 1967

	GNP/Capita U.S.$ 1990	GNP/Capita U.S.$ 1967	Rank in 1967	Change in Rank	% Incr. 67-90			GNP/Capita U.S.$ 1990	GNP/Capita U.S.$ 1967	Rank in 1967	Change in Rank	% Incr. 67-90			GNP/Capita U.S.$ 1990	GNP/Capita U.S.$ 1967	Rank in 1967	Change in Rank	% Incr. 67-90
1 United States	7,400	4,040	1	0	2.70	52 Trinidad & Tobago	1,560	783	43	– 9	3.00	103 Angola	451	190	108	+ 5	3.84
2 Qatar	7,200	3,250	3	+ 1	3.50	53 Venezuela	1,560	911	38	–15	2.35	104 Thailand	435	155	114	+10	4.55
3 Sweden	5,965	3,041	4	+ 1	3.01	54 Panama	1,530	581	54	0	4.25	105 Dominican Republic	432	275	87	–18	2.00
4 Kuwait	5,560	3,530	2	– 2	2.00	55 Gabon	1,525	418	67	+12	5.75	106 Ghana	420	252	92	–14	2.25
5 US Virgin Islands	5,450	2,380	10	+ 5	3.68	56 Zambia	1,446	298	81	+25	7.15	107 Ceylon	419	152	115	+ 8	4.45
6 Denmark	5,370	2,497	8	+ 2	3.40	57 South Africa	1,392	619	51	– 6	3.50	108 Cambodia	399	148	117	+ 9	4.35
7 Iceland	5,300	2,780	5	– 2	2.95	58 Saudi Arabia	1,372	350	72	+14	6.10	109 Bolivia	396	189	110	+ 1	3.25
8 Canada	5,140	2,805	6	– 2	2.36	59 Netherlands Antill	1,300	1,180	30	–29	0.50	110 Honduras	394	236	94	–16	2.25
9 Bermuda	4,680	2,410	9	0	2.68	60 Brunei	1,288	800	42	–18	2.10	111 Paraguay	385	224	101	–10	2.40
10 West Germany	4,678	2,085	14	+ 4	3.50	61 Chile	1,184	585	53	– 8	3.10	112 Algeria	383	250	93	–19	1.90
11 France	4,555	2,340	11	0	2.94	62 Mexico	1,175	528	61	+ 1	3.53	113 U.A.R. Egypt	371	160	113	0	3.65
12 Switzerland	4,510	2,595	7	– 5	2.44	63 Muscat & Oman	1,170	150	116	+53	9.30	114 Southern Rhodesia	352	233	96	–18	1.80
13 French Oceania	4,480	1,310	27	+14	5.35	64 Martinique	1,168	540	58	– 6	3.40	115 Ecuador	347	231	97	–18	1.80
14 Finland	4,475	1,874	18	+ 4	3.35	65 Argentina	1,115	635	49	–16	2.50	116 Morocco	345	191	107	– 9	2.60
15 Norway	4,460	2,199	13	– 2	3.10	66 Surinam	1,098	363	69	+ 3	4.90	117 Senegal	344	214	102	–15	2.10
16 Japan	4,205	1,155	31	+15	5.75	67 Albania	1,092	320	77	+10	5.30	118 Vietnam South	336	144	120	+ 2	3.75
17 Libya	4,180	1,073	33	+16	6.04	68 Mongolia	1,080	410	68	– 2	4.25	119 Sierra Leone	310	140	121	+ 2	3.60
18 Trucial Oman	4,090	1,050	35	+17	6.05	69 Lebanon	1,078	520	62	– 7	3.20	120 Mauritius	238	257	91	–29	0.80
19 New Zealand	3,920	2,000	16	– 3	2.97	70 Jamaica	1,055	533	59	–11	3.00	121 Togo	235	140	122	+ 1	3.10
20 Belgium & Luxem	3,980	2,250	15	– 5	2.50	71 Swaziland	1,050	280	85	+14	5.90	122 Pakistan	282	129	124	+ 2	3.45
21 Australia	3,950	2,250	12	– 9	2.50	72 Iran	998	283	82	+10	5.60	123 Vietnam North	263	100	130	+ 7	4.25
22 Israel	3,850	1,490	24	+ 2	4.13	73 Mauritania	995	147	118	+45	8.70	124 Ethiopia	259	77	143	+19	5.37
23 United Kingdom	3,820	1,975	17	– 6	2.94	74 Turkey	988	353	71	– 3	3.80	125 Cameroun	238	145	110	–15	4.20
24 Bahama Islands	3,590	1,570	23	– 1	3.80	75 Barbados	936	478	64	–19	3.00	126 China Mainland	215	89	137	+11	4.30
25 Netherlands	3,580	1,804	19	– 6	3.00	76 Jordan	917	268	89	+13	5.45	127 Nepal	215	102	129	+ 2	3.30
26 Puerto Rico	3,315	1,387	26	0	3.85	77 China Taiwan	873	274	88	+11	5.13	128 Uganda	191	95	131	+ 3	3.10
27 Italy	3,160	1,279	29	+ 2	3.98	78 Costa Rica	845	425	66	–12	3.05	129 Guinea	189	90	135	+ 6	3.30
28 Austria	3,030	1,465	25	– 3	3.20	79 Portuguese Guinea	815	210	105	+26	6.05	130 Kenya	187	117	126	– 4	2.05
29 Panama Canal Zone	2,930	1,720	20	– 8	2.35	80 Nicaragua	805	359	70	–10	3.05	131 India	180	90	132	+ 1	3.25
30 Guam	2,830	1,620	22	– 8	2.45	81 Guadeloupe	770	470	65	–16	2.18	132 Southern Yemen	180	130	123	– 9	1.40
31 U.S.S.R.	2,760	970	37	+ 6	4.42	82 Uruguay	768	577	55	–27	1.25	133 Madagascar	171	90	133	0	3.25
32 East Germany	2,740	1,300	28	– 4	3.30	83 Guyana	765	324	76	– 7	3.85	134 Niger	180	116	127	– 7	1.70
33 New Caledonia	2,654	1,620	21	–12	2.18	84 Malaysia	765	335	74	–10	3.65	135 Sudan	170	90	134	– 1	2.82
34 Romania	2,635	720	46	+12	5.75	85 Bahrain	731	350	73	–12	3.50	136 Yemen	169	70	146	+10	3.90
35 Spain	2,599	822	40	+ 5	5.10	86 Korea Republic	698	162	112	+26	6.53	137 Centr. Afric. Rep	165	120	125	–12	1.40
36 Greece	2,595	908	39	+ 1	4.08	87 Liberia	661	230	98	+13	4.68	138 Indonesia	159	80	128	–10	1.93
37 Hungary	2,478	900	41	+ 3	4.10	88 Iraq	623	230	99	+ 7	4.40	139 Nigeria	158	80	139	0	3.05
38 Bulgaria	2,260	690	47	+ 9	5.25	89 Syria	621	234	95	+ 6	4.25	140 Mali	156	80	141	+ 1	3.00
39 Ryukyu Islands	2,239	540	57	+18	6.35	90 Brazil	613	309	79	+11	4.25	141 Laos	152	60	149	+ 7	4.10
40 Ireland	2,220	1,067	34	– 6	3.25	91 Korea North	605	230	98	+ 7	4.25	142 Rwanda	149	70	148	+ 1	3.35
41 Channel Islands	2,160	980	36	+ 6	3.35	92 Colombia	603	313	78	–14	2.00	143 Chad	149	80	140	–11	2.20
42 Singapore	2,145	646	48	– 6	5.33	93 Windward Islands	598	212	104	+11	4.60	144 Congo Kinshasa	144	90	133	–11	1.45
43 Czechoslovakia	2,130	1,110	32	–11	2.53	94 Guatemala	591	300	80	–14	3.00	145 Tanzania	144	80	136	– 1	3.16
44 Cyprus	2,060	750	45	– 1	4.45	95 Salvador	585	280	84	–11	3.25	146 Afghanistan	143	70	144	– 1	3.16
45 Reunion	2,050	560	56	+11	5.75	96 Peru	549	283	83	–13	2.95	147 Malawi	141	51	150	+ 3	4.50
46 Hong Kong	1,965	620	50	+ 4	5.10	97 Tunisia	549	214	103	+ 6	4.15	148 Burma	119	70	144	– 4	2.32
47 Yugoslavia	1,882	530	60	+13	6.08	98 Congo Brazzaville	549	190	109	+11	4.70	149 Haiti	105	84	138	–11	1.00
48 Poland	1,800	780	44	– 4	3.70	99 Philippines	542	278	86	–13	2.95	150 Dahomey	100	80	142	– 8	1.00
49 Portugal	1,785	493	63	+14	5.73	100 Papua & New Guinea	542	200	106	+ 6	4.00	151 Upper Volta	89	50	151	0	2.55
50 Malta	1,782	587	52	+ 2	4.95	101 Mozambique	490	180	111	+10	4.42	152 Burundi	89	50	152	0	2.55
51	1,722					102	486	330	75	–27	1.70	153 Somalia	60	50	153	0	0.80

Factors of Growth 89

countries in 1990. This 1990 *per capita* GNP is shown in Table XIXa, which includes various elements of comparison and in Chart 15 which we recommend for its comprehensiveness.

LOWER AND UPPER BOUNDARIES OF 'PER CAPITA' GNP IN 1990

Chart 15 presents a graphic condensation of the prospects of all countries. In order to show, effectively, values ranging from $70 to $4,000 in 1967 and from $100 to $8,000 in 1990, we have used a double logarithmic (proportional) scale which gives the same space from 50 to 500 as from 500 to 5,000, thereby spacing more clearly points which, on a conventional arithmetic scale, would be crowded together.

Along the horizontal axis, in the abscissas, we have shown the *per capita* income of all 150 countries in 1967. Along the vertical axis, in ordinates, we have shown the *per capita* income projected for each country in 1990.

The 'shot-gun' array of these 150 points has made it easy to identify the lower and upper boundaries which have been drawn as straight lines.

TABLE XIXb—GNP / capita range of 1990 GNP / capita (in 1967 $) and of percent yearly increases (1967-1990)

1967 GNP/Capita	Range of 1990 GNP/Capita (in 1967 $) & of % Yearly Increases (1967-1990)						% Yearly Increase for Selected Countries close to Upper Limit of Range	
	Low		Median		High			
	$	%	$	%	$	%	%	
100	131	1.2	205	3.2	382	6.0	5.6	Ethiopia
							4.5	Mauritania
							4.3	Korea Republic
200	298	1.8	485	4.0	855	6.5		
							5.7	Iran
500	815	2.2	1,290	4.2	2,045	6.3		
							5.9	Romania
1,100	1,670	2.3	2,400	3.9	3,750	6.0		
							5.8	Japan
Average		1.9%		3.8%		6.2%		

The median (not average) line has been obtained by finding the line which leaves as many points above as it does below it.

In order to derive some specific growth targets from this chart, we have tabulated the lowest, the median and the highest expectations for countries with $100, $200, $500 and $£1,000 *per capita* income in 1967. These are shown in Table XIXb.

These have been shown in terms of both GNP *per capita* attained in 1990 and average annual growth rate in percent between 1967 and 1990. The percentage growth rates have been averaged for each column in order to provide an overall indication of the 'spread' between the low, median and high.

In terms of years required to achieve the same percentage gains in their *per capita* income, the faster progressing countries with a 6.2% *per capita* growth rate will achieve in five years what the median countries with a 3.8% rate will accomplish in ten years, and the slowest countries with a 1.9% rate will reach in fifteen years.

COUNTRIES WHICH WILL ACHIEVE THE GREATEST GAINS IN RANK OF 'PER CAPITA' GNP

Gain in Rank: 1967-1990

Muscat & Oman	+ 53
Mauritania	+ 47
Ivory Coast	+ 39
Korea Rep.	+ 38
Portugu. Guinea	+ 28
Zambia	+ 25
Saudi Arabia	+ 24
Ethiopia	+ 21
Ryukyu Isl.	+ 18
Trucial Oman	+ 17
Libya	+ 16
Japan	+ 15
Liberia	+ 15
Niger	+ 15
Portugal	+ 14
China Mainland	+ 13
China Taiwan	+ 13
Yugoslavia	+ 13
Windward Isl.	+ 13
Romania	+ 12
Thailand	+ 12
Gabon	+ 12
Iraq	+ 12
French Oceania	+ 12
Guinea	+ 12
Mozambique	+ 12
Korea North	+ 11
Peru	+ 11
Reunion	+ 11

In the facing tabulation, we have shown, in decreasing order, the countries for which the gain in rank, as read from the 'Change in Rank' column in Table XIXa is greater than 10.

This is only one of several yardsticks by which the estimated progress in *per capita* GNP can be compared. Because it greatly magnifies the gains achieved by countries which previous to the discovery of important natural resources were far down the ladder, only partial significance should be attached to it.

COUNTRIES WHICH WILL ACHIEVE THE GREATEST GAINS IN PERCENTAGE POINTS IN 'PER CAPITA' GNP

Another, partial, yardstick may be derived from the line-up of the countries which will have achieved the greatest gain in percentage points in *per capita* GNP. This is shown in the following tabulation.

Since percentage gains are slower for the industrialized than for the developing countries, this yardstick, too, tends to emphasize the progress achieved by the latter category of countries.

	GNP 'per capita' percent Annual Gain
Muscat & Oman	9.30
Mauritania	8.70
Yugoslavia	8.65
Ivory Coast	8.35
Zambia	7.15
Korea Rupublic	6.53
Ryukyu Islands	6.35
Trucial Oman	6.06
Portuguese Guinea	6.05
Libya	6.04
Gabon	5.75
French Oceania	5.35

CHAPTER SIX

'Have' and 'Have Not' Countries

CAN THE GAP BETWEEN THE HIGHLY-INDUSTRIALIZED COUNTRIES AND THE DEVELOPING COUNTRIES BE MINIMIZED?

We hope that the implications of our analysis will prove of specific help in problems which are of major concern to today's world, especially the widening gap between the industrialized and the developing nations.

Concern for the environment has inspired a swelling uproar of protests against growth, but the fact remains that, at both ends of the scale, the need for substantial growth is more pressing than ever before.

The industrialized nations need the extra resources that only increasing prosperity can provide in order to meet successfully the challenge to the environment.

These extra resources are also required to contribute more than they have in the past to needs in the 'underdeveloped' areas within their own borders, as well as to reduce the growing gap between the industrialized nations as a whole and the developing world.

Attempts have been made to distinguish various categories throughout the progress of economic growth, ranging all the way from the pastoral stage to the post-industrial stage as they traverse the takeoff stage, the transitional stage, and the industrial stage.

We prefer to regard this road to economic growth, as encompassing the recorded and projected growth of each country, within a wide-band spectrum, for which our charts show that the doubling time of GNP *per capita* ranges from 12 to 25 years.

It is clear that a doubling time of 25 years which may be acceptable for a highly industrialized country, is too slow a rate of progress for a developing country now at the $100 GNP *per capita* level.

In this respect, the example of Japan, Iran, Taiwan, etc. provide most effective evidence that a doubling time of 10 years can be

'Have' and 'Have Not' Countries

achieved and that the gap between the developed and developing nations, though bound to increase, may be contained.

Table XIXb provides a direct measure of the often-mentioned gap between the 'have-not' and the 'have' countries.

Comparing for instance, a country in the $100 *per capita* range with one having $1,000 *per capita*, thus starting with a gap of $900 in 1967, by the year 1990:

	$
If both countries are in the 'low' category, the gap will become	1,539
If both countries are in the 'high' classification, the gap will become	3,368
If the $100 country is in the 'high' group and the $1,000 country in the low group, the gap will still increase but only by	1,288

However, in this last assumption, the developing country will have seen its *per capita* income nearly triple in the space of a generation—which would bring the fulfilment of many aspirations, whereas the country which started with a *per capita* income of $1,000 will have achieved a 2/3rd increase only.

Thus, in spite of the growth prospects that lie ahead for the developing countries, it is to be expected that the 'absolute' gap in $ *per capita* will continue to increase but this should not be interpreted to mean solely that the rich nations are getting richer while the poor grow poorer.

The scale of $ *per capita* should not be read as a 'Happiness Scale'. The most important goal to achieve is substantial dynamic growth.

It is the challenge of the industrialized nations to help a larger number of developing countries to approach or achieve high rates of economic growth.

Of course any effort a country makes toward helping less developed countries is limited by the demands which it faces within its own boundaries and among its own people, but we are convinced that to an increasing extent the achieving of higher GNP *per capita* levels for the developing countries will contribute a 'feed back' to the donor countries. In the long run, this will prove beneficial to overcoming disparities of wealth within the industrialized countries themselves.

There is also an interrelationship between the growth requirements of the developed and of the developing countries. Leaving aside humanitarian reasons, there are potent self-interest reasons why the 'have' countries should regard their own economic growth prospects as likely to be enhanced if the developing nations are helped to achieve faster progress.

Political developments increasingly remind us that economic

frustration and despair are at the source of much of the discontent which drives to reckless violence those who should contribute productively to the growth of their country. When such discontent erupts on a national scale into political instability, the overseas assets and interests of the industrialized nations are further endangered.

Economic growth is the major way out of the poverty that afflicts such a large proportion of mankind. As President Nixon said, 'Economic development will not, by itself, guarantee the political stability which all countries seek, certainly not in the short run, but political stability is unlikely to occur without economic development'.

Conversely, greater economic prosperity in the developing countries makes them much better customers of the industrialized nations. In a recent speech, Mr. Bert Tollefson, Assistant Administrator of the Agency for International Development, has cited that:

'In 1963, when Greece, Israel, Iran and Taiwan were receiving U.S. aid, they imported a total of $231,000,000 worth of goods from the United States.

Five years later, in 1968, after the aid program was terminated, they imported $1,000,000,000 worth of goods from the U.S.

Other countries which have effectively put to use relatively modest amounts of U.S. aid are Republic of Korea, Cyprus, Mexico, Zambia, Brazil, Costa Rica, Thailand'.

With the help of the better instruments and techniques now available, it is apparent that, barring major catastrophes and upheavals, the mechanisms of growth are becoming more stabilized when one thinks in terms of decades.

The increased effectiveness of regulating functions supervised by the major international institutions, the improvement in communications, the mounting realisation that, in our 'spaceship economy' all efforts must be directed towards minimizing the gap between the industrialized and developing world, have already contributed much towards correcting imbalanccs.

An excellent illustration is provided by the fact that those countries which helped write the 'success stories' of the United States Agency for Industrial Development also stand out in our portrayal of projections of economic growth: Taiwan, Korea, Iran, Greece, etc.

FIRST AND SECOND UNITED NATIONS DEVELOPMENT DECADES

In the expectation that an annual rate of economic growth of 5% might be attained by the developing world, the past ten years have

'Have' and 'Have Not' Countries   95

been proclaimed by the United Nations as the 'Development Decade'.

The 'First Development Decade' did, indeed, achieve an all-time high average growth rate of 5% for the developing countries. There was, however, considerable variation in the growth rates achieved by individual countries and in many cases it was all but absorbed by the population increase.

In his 1969 address to the annual meeting in Washington, the World Bank President Robert McNamara commented as follows:

'As the peoples of the world looked at the Sixties—the United Nations' Development Decade—they felt a deep sense of frustration and failure. The rich countries felt that they had given billions of dollars without achieving much in the way of development; the poor countries felt that too little of the enormous increase in the wealth of the developed world had been diverted to help them rise out of the pit of poverty in which they have been engulfed for centuries past.

'How far is this mood and frustration and failure justified by the events of the past decade? I have sought to find out the truth about this, but, though there have been many voices only too anxious to answer my question, each with a panoply of statistics to prove its point, there is no agreed situation report, nor any clear joint strategy for the future'.

On September 25th, 1970 the General Assembly of the United Nations has been asked to proclaim the 1970 to 1980 decade as the 'Second Development Decade', following the 'First Development Decade'.

At the same meeting from which we quoted Mr. McNamara's remarks, Lester B. Pearson, Chairman of the Commission on International Development, said:

'The choice is between slow, halting growth in an environment of desperation with declining levels of assistance and embittered international relations, or growth as part of a positive, concerted campaign to accelerate and smooth the absorption of the technological revolution in the poorer countries, with a reasonable chance that the spirit of shared concern and effort will reduce the frictions and the dangers, and facilitate and expedite positive results. If the developing countries have no choice, developed countries have. But do they realize how a choice for disengagement would affect their own societies?'

We shall develop this theme in subsequent chapters. Here we have stressed the value of being able to reach specific forecasts of *per capita* growth, on a basis which will be likely to lead to accurate and specific 'cost : benefit ratios' when plans and programs are being formulated.

HOW CAN THE INDUSTRIALIZED NATIONS SPEED UP THE GROWTH OF THE DEVELOPING COUNTRIES?

Among the various suggestions which have been put forward towards achieving a greater contribution from the industrialized countries towards speeding-up the economic development of the 'have-not' countries, one has been that, referring say to 1970, the industrialized countries allocate each year 1% of their added GNP since that year to the financing of projects most likely to speed-up the growth of the developing countries.

We have not attempted an exact breakdown of all countries of the world between the two categories but, referring to Table XXIIb in Chapter Nine, we can arrive at a line-up somewhat as follows:

Average Annual Increase 1967-1990 Industrialized Countries	Billion $	Average GNP 'Have-not' Countries	1967-1990 Billion $
North America	1,215	Caribbean & Other America	228
Western Europe	803	Africa less South Africa	98
Eastern Europe	919	Non-Communist Asia less Japan	264
Japan	389	Communist Asia	158
Oceania	55		
South Africa	35		
Total:	3,416	Total:	748

We can see that 1% of the total on the left column would represent 5% of the total in the right column. If we refer to Chart 14 showing the rate of growth as related to the investment ratio, and if we assume that the 5% addition to the investment ratio to be derived from the allocation reviewed here would raise the investment ratio for the developing countries from 10% to 20%, for instance, this would increase the pattern index of growth from say 50% to 90%, or, in terms of percentage growth rate, from 1½% to 3½%. In effect, this would make it possible, if judiciously administered for optimum results, to raise the rate of economic growth of these countries from the 'low' to the 'median', or from the 'median' to the 'high' rate of progress.

Increasing the rate at which private investment and public aid are injected in the economy is being stressed in all meetings of international agencies or financial institutions. In the words of Dirk

U. Stiiker, Former Secretary-General of the North Atlantic Treaty Organisation:

'Notwithstanding the experience, technology and skills it brings with it, private investment can only be a complement but never a substitute for public aid. An adequate basic infrastructure needs to be created in each developing country both for 'pump priming' purposes and to provide the base on which private industry can build. Private funds cannot be attracted to pay for roads, railways, power stations, medical and educational facilities and the like, because they do not earn any financial return. Yet they are essential in every country if private industry is to come in and make its full contribution to economic growth.

As we have said, a substantial share of the increased *per capita* income of the industrialized countries will, in the decades to come, be allocated to enhancing the quality of life within their borders.

Another much smaller share of their increased income will, by stimulating economic growth in the developing countries, contribute to greatly accelerated improvement in their standards of living and growth, prove to be a major factor towards enchancing the quality of life in the developing countries.

'HAVE' AND 'HAVE-NOT' COUNTRIES

In an earlier chapter, we expressed the hope that, because it provides a valid panorama of prospects for growth for all countries of the world, this study would contribute towards helping to minimize the disparity between the future prospects of the developing countries and of the highly industrialized ones.

In presenting Chart 15 and Table XIXa we have had this particular aim in mind. The clearly defined range of expectations that these are providing will make it possible to bring into focus what needs to be—and can be—achieved.

From the range of legitimate aspirations that countries at various stages of development could deduce from this summary, we can think of the following.

Developing countries, such as Haiti, Dahomey or the Central African Republic, now in the $100 *per capita* range could expect to raise their present prospect of a 1.2% annual increase in *per capita* income to 3.2% which is the median. This would increase by more than 50% the *per capita* wealth they would reach in 1990.

Similarly, a country, like Senegal, now in the $200 *per capita* range, by raising its low present expectation of a 1.8% annual increase to a median 4.0%, could aim for a *per capita* income in 1990 nearly 2/3 higher than what its present pattern of growth would bring it to.

We could, similarly, look at countries now in the median category, such as Mali, Guinea, Nepal, Pakistan, Sierra Leone, Egypt, Angola, Tunisia, El Salvador, who could expect, by adding 2.1 to 2.5% to their annual growth rate to increase their 1990 income by 60% to 75%.

The targets suggested above would not be just 'wishful thinking'. They are the exact expression of the progress expected to be achieved by countries at fully comparable levels of *per capita* GNP.

CHAPTER SEVEN

Population Stabilization

WHY MAKE ASSUMPTIONS AS TO THE COURSE OF THE POPULATION GROWTH RATE FOR EACH COUNTRY?

One of the aims of this volume is to provide a consistent set of market forecasts for all countries, permitting both respective and relative growths to be evaluated for any country or any geographic, political or economic area.

A consistent set of population assumptions was required so that country GNP's could be developed on a valid basis.

The many intangibles surrounding population growth prevented any but arbitrary assumptions to be made:

To assume that the population would stay frozen at the 1970 level, or that the current population growth rate for each country would be maintained, would have been equally unrealistic.

We have chosen an assumption, in-between these two, which would recognize:

(i) that except for very few exceptions each country would like to see some curtailment in its population increase,
(ii) that the effectiveness of any population stabilization program could not but be responsive to the country's past record.

It was not a coincidence that the same built-in restraint features which the analysis of *per capita* growth of GNP had developed became part of the population stabilization which were finally selected.

This is brought out in the following page where attention is called to the fact that at the end of every 32 years the calculated increase in population will have become 56% of what it was at the outset of that period.

Additional comments on this appertainance to the Gompertz equation will be found in the 'Complementary Notes'.

NET PER CENT INCREASE IN POPULATION FOR EACH COUNTRY

Table VII shows the 1958-67 average annual population growth rates for each country.

For each of the 186 countries, the percent annual growth rate shown in Table VII is the 'base' 1967 growth rate, which, as explained in the following, has been assumed to be reduced, in each successive year, to 98% of what it was in the previous year.

For each country, the population growth obtained by this assumption is detailed in the first line, under the years ranging from 1967 to 2020, identified as: Population: Population in 1967.

It will be noted that the 1961-1967 average annual population growth rate for the world as a whole was 1.9%. There are 120 countries which have higher population growth rates, 60 countries which have lower rates than this average, but, obviously it is the growth rates of the countries with the largest populations which determine the population increase of the world as a whole.

The total population we have forecasted for the world was obtained by summating the population of each of the 186 countries, as listed in the individual country tables in the last chapter.

The universal rapidly amplifying demand for a reduction in the rate of population increase will undoubtedly find in most countries an effective echo.

The targets suggested in this chapter may not be quite as drastic as the advocates of 'instant' holding the line on population growth would like to have it, but they are realistic and they will be found to agree with a number of the individual countries targets.

SELECTION OF A REDUCER OF THE RATE OF POPULATION INCREASE

A comparable set of population projections was obtained as follows: Starting from the percent annual rate of population increase in Table I, regarded as the percent increase in 1967, it was assumed that each year should see the previous years rate of increase reduced by a constant factor which we shall call 'reducer'.

The first step was to select which reducer to use. To this end an extensive series of computerized calculations specifically programmed for this study were carried out and the 'asymptote' (value at which the population assumed to be 100 in 1967 would eventually level-off) was tabulated as shown opposite.

To use this table one has only to select from the upper horizontal row the initial rate of increase and from the vertical column at the left the 'reducer' which is being considered.

The figure, at the intersection of these two lines, is the asymptote for the selected values of 'percent population increase' and 'reducer'.

Population Stabilization 101

	Average Annual Rate of Population Increase—%							
Reducer	0.5%	1.0%	1.5%	2.0%	2.5%	3.0%	3.5%	4.0%
0.965	115	132	152	175	202	232	267	307
0.970	118	139	164	193	227	268	316	372
0.975	122	148	181	220	268	327	398	485
0.980	128	164	210	269	345	441	565	724
0.985	139	194	270	376	523	728	1,013	1,411
0.990	164	270	445	732	1,203	1,979	3,254	5,352
0.995	271	735	1,994	5,405	14,657	39,742	107,759	292,188

Keeping in mind that rates as high as 4% are now encountered, in Mexico for instance, the table above quickly showed that 0.98 was the highest reducer which could be used.

Lower values of the reducer such as 0.975 or 0.97 were considered but they appeared unrealistic, although highly desirable, and population growth was calculated and plotted for all countries on the basis of a reducer of 0.98.

WHERE WOULD POPULATION STABILIZE IN THIS ASSUMPTION?

For example: given the average yearly percentage increase in population for the world, which was 1.9%, we may assume that for every year following 1967, the population yearly percentage increase will be:

    in 1968   1.9% x 0.98
    in 1969   1.9% x 0.98 x 0.98
    in 1970   1.9% x 0.98 x 0.98 x 0.98, etc.

In about 200 years, the world population would stabilize at 255/100 = 2.55 times what it was in 1967.

The data summarized in the above table were thus used to select the yearly percentage reduction in the rate of population increase which appeared most applicable.

Year	Population	
1930	2,070 Million	
1940	2,295	
1950	2,517	
1960	3,005	
1963	3,176	Average yearly increase
1967	3,420	from 1960 to 1968: 1.9%
1968	3,483	

Looking at the historic record above, the prospect of eventually reaching and stabilizing a population of 2.55 times the present number—equalling nearly 9 billion people—seems a suitable compromise between unbounded population growth and restriction to an extent which would be unrealistic.

As the tabulation shows, if the percentage rate of yearly reduction were to be 0.975 instead of 0.98, the world population would stabilize at 2.08 times the present which would be most desirable if it could be achieved. Conversely, if this were 0.985 instead of 0.98, the world population would eventually grow to 3.45 times the present number.

From Chart 17 we see that 90% of this ceiling would be reached in 2074.

Actually, because of the different 'mix' taken into account in our calculations, the world population growth curve as shown in Chart 18 differs somewhat from the nearest 'pattern' in Chart 17, but it is plotted as calculated and provides a reasonable indication of the total world population assuming each country accepts the arbitrary target of a 0.98 yearly reducer to the annual rate of growth.

Of course, both the assumption of a constant reduction of the percentage increase in population and the choice of 0.98 for the purpose of this study are entirely arbitrary, but they have the advantage of providing through specific numbers, a basis of comparison for all countries and, incidentally, bringing out how a relatively minor reduction each year would result in holding the population growth within reasonable boundaries.

Because the full stabilization in this assumption would not be achieved, as calculated, before two centuries, we have shown on Chart 17 the date at which the population would reach 90% of its ultimate total.

For instance, for the United States, which the table shows as having a 1.47% 'starting' rate, we have calculated the following:

	1967	1970	1975	1980	1985	1990	1995	2000	2005	2010	2015	2020
Population in millions	199	207	222	236	250	261	274	285	295	304	313	322

In fact, population in the United States has increased by an average of 1.07% for the past two years, but we have preferred, for such a long term projection, to use a yearly population percentage increase based on a longer period: 1958-1967.

Population Stabilization 103

The population would eventually stabilize at 400,000,000 but 90% of the total would be reached in the year 2062 with a population of 360,000,000.

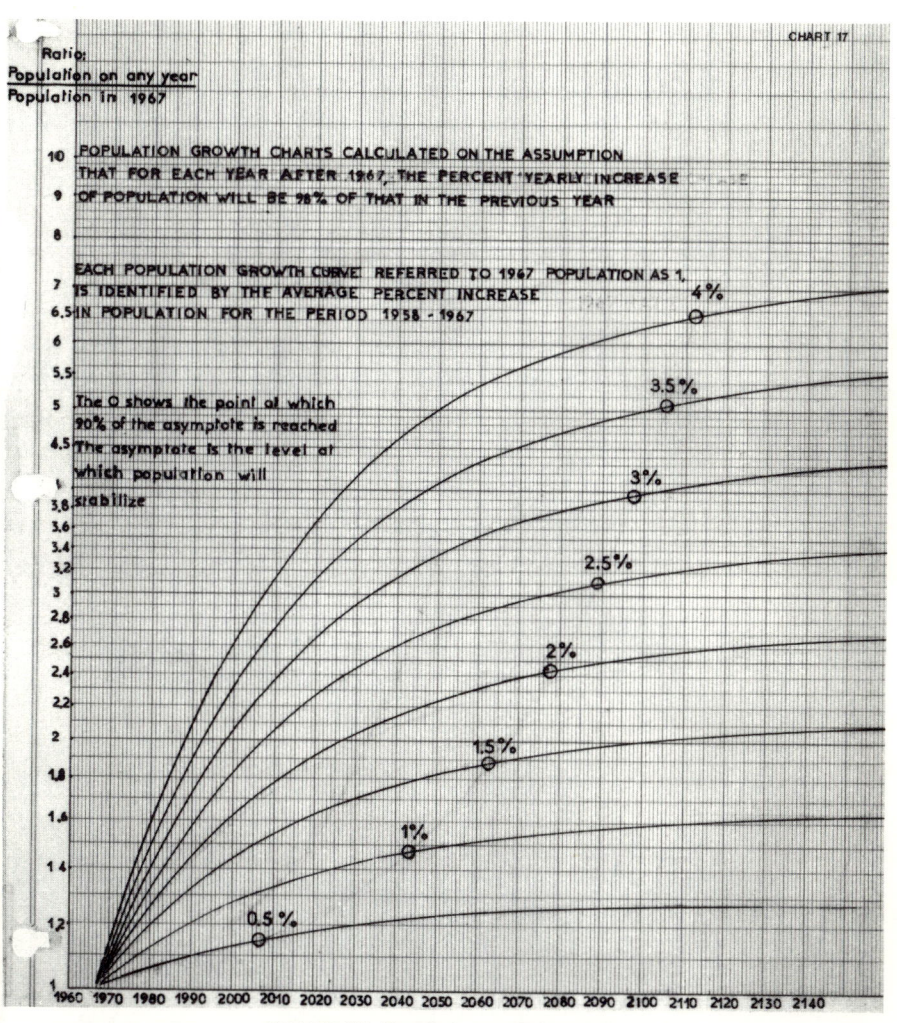

CHART 17—Population growth curves

Most of the population projections made for the United States have estimated 300,000,000 for the year 2000. Our figure of 285,000,000 above is more where we hope it will be.

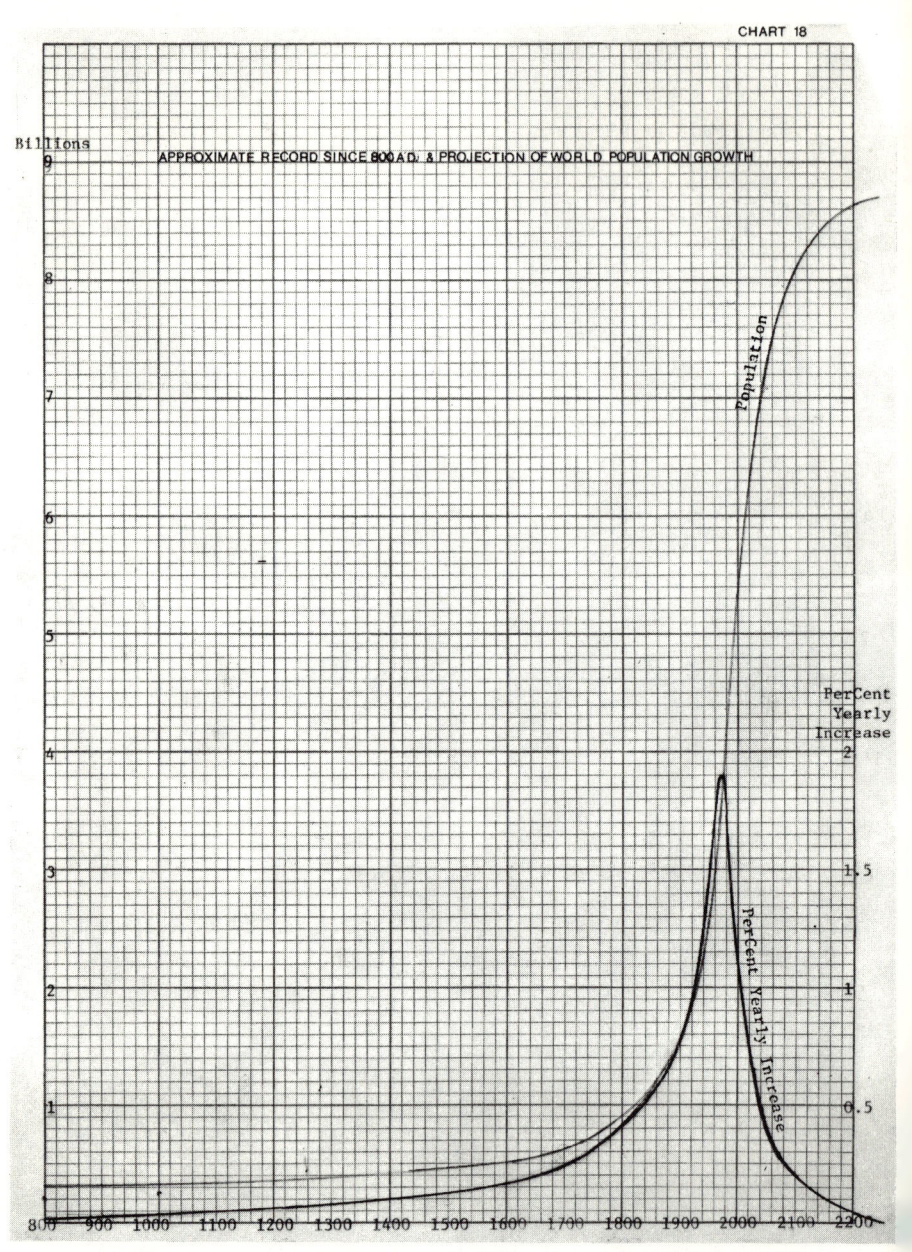

CHART 18—World population from A.D. 800 and projection to the year 2020

Population Stabilization

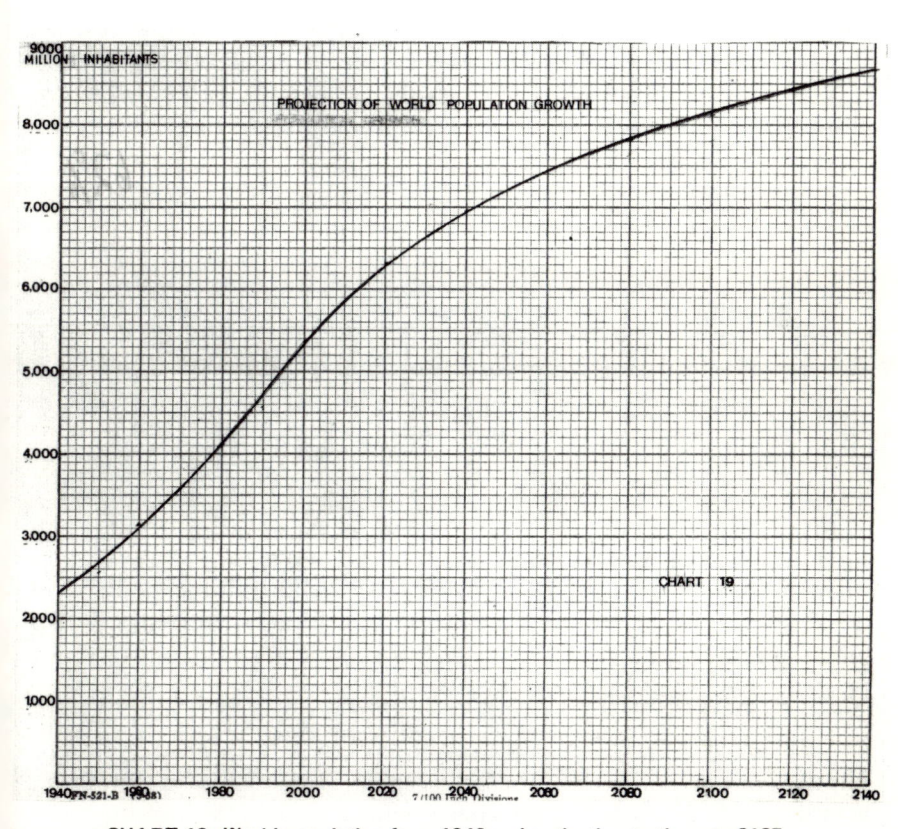

CHART 19—World population from 1940 and projection to the year 2125

From the population growth figures we have calculated for each of the countries the world population growth shown on Chart 19.

In Chart 18, we have included the world population growth record and projection of Chart 19, which extends from 1940 to 2125, into a recorded population chart starting in 800. We have also extended the projected world population total to the year 2300, on the assumption that the 0.98 year-to-year reducer of the net percentage increase in population would continue to apply.

Chart 18 also shows as a curve which 'peaks up' sharply in 1970, the percent yearly increase in the population of the world which was:

    0.03% in the year 1000
    0.25%   1500
    0.75%   1900

and which has averaged 1.90% from 1958 to 1968.

As will be seen from the chart, if the 0.98 reducer of the yearly percent increase applies from now on, this yearly percent rate of increase of population will have come down to:

    1.07% in the year 2000 (56% of the 1968 rate)
    0.59%   2032 (56% of the 2000 rate)
    0.32%   2064 (56% of the 2032 rate)

Zero population growth will be reached in the year 2300, but it will be noted that, already in the year 2000, the yearly rate of population increase will have been reduced by one half, and the population 'explosion' will have become very manageable indeed, if this apparently minimal reduction: 2%, each year, of the previous year's percent increase in population, is accomplished, year after year.

Should an ultimate population level of double our present population for the United States, or 2.55 times the present population for the world, not be regarded as enough of a limitation, a multiplier of 0.965, for instance, instead of 0.98, would limit the U.S. population to one and a half time the present and the world population to double the present total.

A GRADUATED REDUCTION OF THE RATE OF POPULATION INCREASE MUST BE ACHIEVED

It is not our purpose to propose the means by which such a reducer might be controlled or otherwise achieved. We simply want to suggest that, as 'zero population growth' is ultimately essential, an important share of the benefits it will confer can be obtained, by gradual means with only minimal disruption of the growth

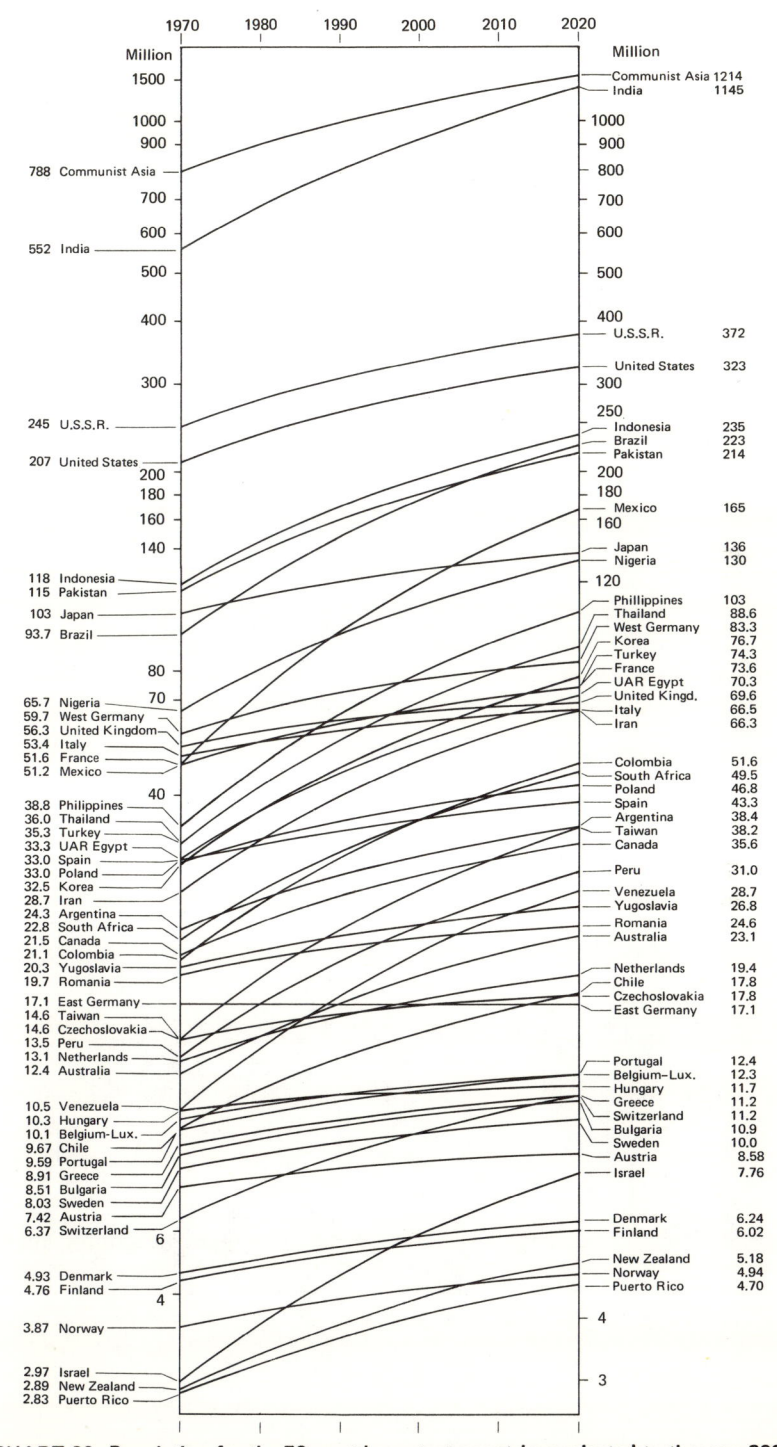

CHART 20—Population for the 50 most important countries projected to the year 2020

1970	2020
788 Communist Asia	Communist Asia 1214
552 India	India 1145
245 U.S.S.R.	U.S.S.R. 372
207 United States	United States 323
118 Indonesia	Indonesia 235
115 Pakistan	Brazil 223
103 Japan	Pakistan 214
93.7 Brazil	Mexico 165
65.7 Nigeria	Japan 136
59.7 West Germany	Nigeria 130
56.3 United Kingdom	Phillippines 103
53.4 Italy	Thailand 88.6
51.6 France	West Germany 83.3
51.2 Mexico	Korea 76.7
38.8 Philippines	Turkey 74.3
36.0 Thailand	France 73.6
35.3 Turkey	UAR Egypt 70.3
33.3 UAR Egypt	United Kingd. 69.6
33.0 Spain	Italy 66.5
33.0 Poland	Iran 66.3
32.5 Korea	Colombia 51.6
28.7 Iran	South Africa 49.5
24.3 Argentina	Poland 46.8
22.8 South Africa	Spain 43.3
21.5 Canada	Argentina 38.4
21.1 Colombia	Taiwan 38.2
20.3 Yugoslavia	Canada 35.6
19.7 Romania	Peru 31.0
17.1 East Germany	Venezuela 28.7
14.6 Taiwan	Yugoslavia 26.8
14.6 Czechoslovakia	Romania 24.6
13.5 Peru	Australia 23.1
13.1 Netherlands	Netherlands 19.4
12.4 Australia	Chile 17.8
10.5 Venezuela	Czechoslovakia 17.8
10.3 Hungary	East Germany 17.1
10.1 Belgium-Lux.	Portugal 12.4
9.67 Chile	Belgium-Lux. 12.3
9.59 Portugal	Hungary 11.7
8.91 Greece	Greece 11.2
8.51 Bulgaria	Switzerland 11.2
8.03 Sweden	Bulgaria 10.9
7.42 Austria	Sweden 10.0
6.37 Switzerland	Austria 8.58
4.93 Denmark	Israel 7.76
4.76 Finland	Denmark 6.24
3.87 Norway	Finland 6.02
2.97 Israel	New Zealand 5.18
2.89 New Zealand	Norway 4.94
2.83 Puerto Rico	Puerto Rico 4.70

mechanism to which our social and economic life is attuned. Unless a 'crash program' is imperative, greatly improved conditions can be achieved through orderly slowdowns, the fast effectiveness of which is demonstrated by the 'mathematics' supporting a number of our charts and presentations.

Our projection for the United States is very close to what would be achieved if the number of births per woman were to be held at 2.45. The present rate is 2.11 which, taking account of child deaths, corresponds to practically zero population growth.

CHAPTER EIGHT

Gross National Product

The building-block method followed:
   1st: Projection of the *per capita* GNP
   2nd: Projection of the population

has now brought us to the 3rd step, obtained by simple multiplication, the GNP.

Table XX has been provided for convenience in finding any country in Table XXI; it lists the countries in alphabetic order and gives for each its 1967 GNP rank in Tables XXI.

WHERE CAN GNP PROJECTIONS FOR ANY COUNTRY BE FOUND IN THIS VOLUME?

The reader will find the GNP projections:
(a) In tabulated form, individually, for each country, in the 'country page' at 5-year intervals from 1970 to 2020.
(b) In tabulated form for all countries, for 1967, 1980, 2000 and 2020 in Table XXI.
(c) In graph curves, from which GNP can be read for any desired year, in Charts 21 a, b, c, d.

ALL GNP DATA IS ON THE BASIS OF 1967 U.S. $

The GNP deflator measures the ratio of the GNP expressed in current $ to the GNP expressed in constant $ as of a certain year.

It is of interest to note that the National Industrial Conference Board, whose analyses of the economy of the United States are the most highly regarded and most often quoted, are changing from 1958 to 1967 the reference year for all their figures when expressed in constant U.S. $. Thus, the 1967 constant U.S. $ which we have used throughout is going to be the new 'standard constant U.S. $'.

If, as may be possible the U.S. $ will be worth in June 1971

TABLE XX—Alphabetical listing showing GNP ranking in 1967

Country	Rank	Country	Rank	Country	Rank
Afghanistan	79	Gibraltar	177	Pakistan	24
Albania	98	Gilbert & Ellice Isl.	175	Panama	93
Algeria	52	Greece	37	Panama Canal Zone	149
American Samoa	179	Greenland	167	Papua & New Guinea	107
Angola	84	Guadeloupe	139	Paraguay	104
Argentina	22	Guam	137	Peru	50
Australia	12	Guatemala	70	Philippines	31
Austria	29	Guinea	112	Poland	14
Bahama Islands	122	Guyana	123	Portugal	46
Bahrein	153	Haiti	108	Portuguese Guinea	146
Barbados	144	Honduras	100	Portuguese Timor	162
Belgium & Lux.	19	Hong Kong	58	Puerto Rico	48
Bermuda	143	Hungary	32	Qatar	118
Bhutan	161	Iceland	102	Reunion	121
Bolivia	99	Ifni	183	Romania	23
Botswana	158	India	10	Ruanda	128
Brazil	11	Indonesia	28	Ryukyu Islands	103
British Honduras	165	Iran	36	Sao Tome & Principe	176
Brit. Solomon Isl.	185	Iraq	62	Saudi Arabia	59
Brunei	150	Ireland	53	Senegal	92
Bulgaria	39	Isle of Man	157	Seychelles Isl.	184
Burma	66	Israel	47	Sierra Leone	111
Burundi	133	Italy	7	Sikkim	180
Cambodia	88	Ivory Coast	83	Singapore	76
Cameroun	91	Jamaica	85	Somalia	141
Canada	9	Japan	5	South Africa	25
Cape Verde Isl.	172	Jordan	101	Southern Rhodesia	82
Centr. Afric. Rep.	132	Kenya	78	Southern Yemen	138
Ceuta & Melilla	163	Korea-North	54	Spain	13
Ceylon	67	Korea-Republic	45	Spanish Sahara	181
Chad	120	Kuwait	64	Sudan	73
Channel Islands	145	Laos	116	Surinam	140
Chile	41	Lebanon	71	Swaziland	147
China – Mainland	8	Leeward Islands	166	Sweden	16
China – Taiwan	49	Lesotho	159	Switzerland	21
Colombia	38	Liberia	113	Syria	72
Comoro Islands	171	Libya	63	Tanzania	87
Congo Brazzaville	134	Macao	156	Thailand	42
Congo Leopoldville	69	Madagascar	95	Togo	119
Costa Rica	96	Malawi	124	Tonga	174
Cuba	56	Malaysia	51	Trinidad & Tobago	90
Cyprus	106	Mali	109	Trucial Oman	129
Czechoslovakia	20	Maldive Islands	182	Trust Ter. Pacif. Isl.	173
Dahomey	125	Malta	130	Tunisia	86
Denmark	26	Martinique	131	Turkey	27
Dominican Rep.	81	Mauritania	135	U.A.R. Egypt	43
Ecuador	75	Mauritius	126	Uganda	94
El Salvador	89	Mexico	15	United Kingdom	6
Equatorial Guinea	154	Mongolia	105	United States	1
Ethiopia	65	Morocco	55	Upper Volta	114
Faeroe Islands	155	Mozambique	74	Uruguay	68
Fiji Islands	178	Muscat & Oman	151	U.S.S.R.	2
Finland	33	Nepal	80	US Virgin Islands	148
France	4	Netherlands	17	Venezuela	34
French Guyana	169	Netherl. Antilles	115	Vietnam – North	61
French Oceania	142	New Caledonia	136	Vietnam – South	57
Fr. T. Afars & Issas	160	New Hebrides	170	Western Samoa	186
Gabon	127	New Zealand	40	West Irian	164
Gambia	168	Nicaragua	97	Windward Islands	152
Germany – East	18	Niger	117	Yemen	110
Germany – West	3	Nigeria	44	Yugoslavia	30
Ghana	60	Norway	35	Zambia	77

Gross National Product 111

approximately $0.83 in terms of the 1967 U.S. $, *all the GNP and GNP/Capita U.S. $ given in 1967 $, should be multiplied by 1.20* in order to change these to June 1971 prices, for instance.

COMPARISON OF THE FORECASTED GROWTH OF THE GNP FOR ALL COUNTRIES

For each country the information in Table XXI is the same as that listed in each country page. Grouped as it is for all countries in descending order of GNP in 1967, it does contribute to a fuller understanding of the present and future place of any country in relation to any of the others.

A visual comparison of the same relative standing of all countries for any year between 1970 and 2020 is provided by Charts 21.

RECAPITULATION OF GNP AND POPULATION TABLES AND CHARTS

Tables XXI provide in a series of 7 tables, 6 of these in facing pages, a comprehensive record for 1967 and set of projections, for 1980, 2000 and 2020, of population, GNP *per capita* and country GNP, for the 186 countries we have investigated and which, to all intents and purposes, total the entire world.

For the convenience of the reader and to help in quickly locating the growth data of any country, in comparison with others, the Tables XXI are preceded by Table XX in which all countries are listed in alphabetic order and identified with their 1967 GNP rank in Tables XXI.

Of these 186 countries, the growth prospects of 153 have been individually analysed and presented, not only in the Tables XXI but also, in greater detail and with additional data in the 153 separate market profiles, alphabetically arranged in Part Two.

Population, GNP/Capita and GNP are shown for 1967, 1980, 2000 and 2020 for the countries numbered 1 through 150 in the following Charts:

Charts 16 a & b and 21 a & b	apply to countries in area group (A)
Charts 16 c & d and 21 c & d	apply to countries in area group (B)

TABLE XXI—GNP 'per capita', population, GNP, in 1967-1980-2000-2020

		1967			1980		
		Population Millions	GNP/Cap. $	GNP Billion $	Population Millions	GNP/Cap. $	GNP Billion $
1	United States	199.120	4,040	803.90	236.00	5,740	1,352.00
2	U.S.S.R.	235.520	970	228.00	274.70	1,838	505.50
3	West Germany	57.700	2,085	120.70	65.40	3,358	219.50
4	France	49.548	2,340	116.00	56.55	3,455	194.90
5	Japan	99.918	1,155	115.20	111.00	2,540	281.50
6	United Kingdom	55.058	1,975	108.70	59.50	2,908	173.10
7	Italy	52.354	1,279	66.96	56.70	2,220	125.80
8	Communist China	720.000	89	64.28	850.00	158	134.00
9	Canada	20.440	2,805	57.12	24.88	3,982	99.50
10	India	511.120	90	45.90	676.00	136	92.20
11	Brazil	85.655	309	26.80	119.80	457	54.80
12	Australia	11.750	2,250	26.60	14.85	3,135	46.50
13	Spain	32.140	822	26.40	35.70	1,637	58.40
14	Poland	31.944	780	24.90	36.41	1,282	46.70
15	Mexico	45.671	528	24.11	71.90	849	60.90
16	Sweden	7.870	3,041	23.93	8.59	4,510	38.78
17	Netherlands	12.598	1,804	22.73	14.62	2,730	39.95
18	East Germany	17.081	1,300	22.20	17.08	2,044	35.05
19	Belgium & Luxem.	9.910	2,045	20.26	10.62	3,010	32.10
20	Czechoslovakia	14.300	1,110	15.90	15.42	1,610	24.85
21	Switzerland	6.071	2,595	15.75	7.43	3,650	27.10
22	Argentina	23.255	635	14.73	27.80	894	24.80
23	Romania	19.285	720	13.87	20.91	1,610	33.62
24	Pakistan	107.260	129	13.85	136.10	202	27.50
25	South Africa	21.180	619	13.09	28.50	1,014	28.90
		2,446.748	Avge 832	2,031.88	2,976.46	Avge 1,320	3,757.95

Gross National Product 113

Table XXI—*continued*

Population Millions	GNP/Cap. $	GNP Billion $	Population Millions	GNP/Cap. $	GNP Billion $	
285.00	9,250	2,635.00	322.50	13,500	4,360.00	1
330.80	3,975	1,315.00	372.00	7,050	2,620.00	2
76.20	6,245	475.50	83.30	10,520	877.50	3
66.60	5,905	392.50	73.60	9,475	697.00	4
126.10	6,540	825.00	163.30	13,300	1,812.00	5
65.50	4,985	326.10	69.60	7,850	546.30	6
62.60	4,350	272.20	66.50	7,520	500.00	7
1,037.00	350	363.00	1,172.00	706	827.00	8
30.95	6,460	200.00	35.60	9,575	340.00	9
922.00	255	235.00	1,145.00	470	538.00	10
173.10	814	141.10	222.50	1,430	318.50	11
19.50	4,915	95.80	23.05	7,400	170.10	12
39.90	3,810	151.90	43.29	7,240	314.50	13
42.40	2,450	103.90	46.80	4,195	196.20	14
116.20	1,570	183.00	165.20	2,570	425.00	15
9.30	7,740	72.50	10.00	12,400	124.00	16
17.38	4,625	80.50	19.42	7,460	144.80	17
17.08	3,650	62.40	17.08	6,030	103.00	18
11.62	5,230	60.90	12.28	8,360	102.65	19
16.90	2,740	46.40	17.78	4,310	76.60	20
9.52	5,550	52.90	11.15	8,105	90.40	21
33.82	1,450	49.10	38.40	2,160	83.00	22
23.10	4,110	95.00	24.57	8,350	205.00	23
178.20	406	72.50	213.80	731	156.00	24
39.60	1,843	73.10	49.50	3,150	155.90	25
3,650.44	Avge 2,300	8,380.30	4,379.72	Avge 3,600	15,784.05	

Table XXI—*continued*

		1967			1980	
		Population Millions	GNP/Cap. $	GNP Billion $	Population Millions	GNP/Cap. $	GNP Billion $
26	Denmark	4.839	2,497	12.08	5.270	3,940	20.75
27	Turkey	32.724	353	11.54	43.650	640	27.95
28	Indonesia	110.079	104	11.48	143.400	131	18.80
29	Austria	7.320	1,465	10.72	7.720	2,260	17.42
30	Yugoslavia	19.750	530	10.46	21.910	1,138	24.90
31	Philippines	34.656	278	9.64	50.900	409	20.75
32	Hungary	10.217	900	9.20	10.680	1,600	17.08
33	Finland	4.666	1,874	8.74	5.099	3,140	15.99
34	Venezuela	9.352	911	8.54	13.900	1,250	17.40
35	Norway	3.784	2,199	8.32	4.141	3,370	13.93
36	Iran	26.284	283	7.45	36.400	600	21.84
37	Greece	8.720	808	7.04	9.500	1,552	14.72
38	Colombia	19.191	313	6.01	27.100	457	12.38
39	Bulgaria	8.310	690	5.74	9.110	1,410	12.82
40	New Zealand	2.726	2,000	5.45	3.400	3,085	10.49
41	Chile	9.140	585	5.34	11.550	894	10.32
42	Thailand	32.680	155	5.07	46.400	280	12.99
43	U.A.R. Egypt	30.907	160	4.95	41.250	283	11.64
44	Nigeria	61.450	80	4.92	79.800	119	9.50
45	Korea Republic	29.784	162	4.78	41.490	381	15.77
46	Portugal	9.382	493	4.62	10.290	1,050	10.79
47	Israel	2.669	1,490	3.98	3.090	2,790	10.86
48	Puerto Rico	2.695	1,387	3.74	3.268	2,340	7.65
49	Taiwan	13.145	274	3.61	19.110	542	10.37
50	Peru	12.385	283	3.51	17.090	411	7.03
		506.855	Avge 349	176.93	665.558	Avge 575	382.47

Gross National Product

Table XXI—*continued*

Population Millions	GNP/Cap. $	GNP Billion $	Population Millions	GNP/Cap. $	GNP Billion $	
5.850	7,110	41.60	6.240	11,780	73.40	26
60.000	1,488	89.40	74.250	2,980	221.50	27
192.500	196	37.75	234.500	292	68.60	28
8.260	3,960	32.70	8.580	6,380	54.60	29
24.800	2,830	70.30	26.780	5,650	151.10	30
77.600	711	55.15	103.000	1,225	126.30	31
11.280	3,160	35.60	11.690	5,760	67.40	32
5.650	6,040	34.10	6.020	10,400	62.60	33
21.480	1,906	41.00	28.710	2,740	78.60	34
4.610	5,890	27.18	4.940	9,660	47.60	35
52.100	1,590	82.95	66.250	3,425	226.50	36
10.490	3,700	38.80	11.160	7,110	79.40	37
39.920	804	32.05	51.600	1,360	70.20	38
10.150	3,390	34.41	10.880	6,340	68.98	39
4.390	4,890	21.40	5.180	7,280	37.62	40
14.920	1,530	22.91	17.800	2,390	42.55	41
68.400	662	45.30	88.600	1,462	129.90	42
56.700	485	27.50	70.250	812	57.00	43
106.600	212	22.65	130.100	362	47.20	44
59.990	1,145	68.70	76.700	2,490	190.80	45
11.530	2,884	33.30	12.380	6,110	75.60	46
5.850	5,150	30.10	7.760	8,740	67.80	47
4.065	4,515	18.38	4.700	7,800	36.65	48
28.900	1,330	38.43	38.150	2,640	100.70	49
24.390	725	17.68	31.010	1,200	37.20	50
910.435	Avge 1,100	999.34	1,127.230	Avge 1,960	2,209.80	

Table XXI—continued

	1967 Population Millions	1967 GNP/Cap. $	1967 GNP Billion $	1980 Population Millions	1980 GNP/Cap. $	1980 GNP Billion $
51 Malaysia	10.071	335	3.37	14.400	589	8.48
52 Algeria	12.540	250	3.18	16.080	320	5.14
53 Ireland	2.899	1,067	3.09	2.989	1,602	4.97
54 North Korea	12.700	230	2.83	17.020	401	6.83
55 Morocco	14.140	191	2.70	19.520	270	5.28
56 Cuba	8.033	330	2.65	10.400	412	4.29
57 South Vietnam	16.973	144	2.44	23.100	226	5.225
58 Hong Kong	3.834	620	2.37	5.520	1,210	6.68
59 Saudi Arabia	6.990	350	2.34	8.460	795	6.73
60 Ghana	8.139	252	2.05	11.080	368	4.07
61 North Vietnam	20.100	100	2.01	29.100	174	5.07
62 Iraq	8.440	230	1.94	11.650	405	4.72
63 Libya	1.803	1,073	1.86	2.700	2,750	7.42
64 Kuwait	0.520	3,530	1.83	0.988	4,590	4.54
65 Ethiopia	23.667	77	1.82	29.400	165	4.85
66 Burma	25.811	70	1.80	32.700	95	3.10
67 Ceylon	11.701	152	1.77	15.440	274	4.23
68 Uruguay	2.783	577	1.61	3.215	670	2.16
69 Congo Kinshasa	16.354	90	1.47	20.700	121	2.55
70 Guatemala	4.717	300	1.41	6.750	444	3.00
71 Lebanon	2.520	520	1.32	3.390	796	2.70
72 Syria	5.570	234	1.30	7.780	468	3.64
73 Sudan	14.355	90	1.29	20.000	144	2.87
74 Mozambique	7.124	180	1.28	8.120	322	2.65
75 Ecuador	5.508	231	1.27	8.150	291	2.37
	257.292	Avge 198	51.000	329.202	Avge 348	114.435

Gross National Product 117

Table XXI—*continued*

Population Millions	2000 GNP/Cap. $	GNP Billion $	Population Millions	2020 GNP/Cap. $	GNP Billion $	
21.150	1,188	25.25	27.700	2,217	61.40	51
21.225	456	9.68	25.600	642	16.42	52
3.120	2,900	9.06	3.200	4,410	14.10	53
23.750	903	21.60	29.650	1,802	54.00	54
27.750	443	12.29	35.200	723	25.60	55
13.900	568	7.90	16.920	766	12.95	56
32.400	498	16.18	41.000	994	40.75	57
8.280	2,965	24.55	10.900	5,770	62.80	58
10.490	2,190	22.95	12.100	5,130	62.10	59
15.540	482	7.49	19.600	629	12.31	60
43.600	393	17.12	57.400	723	41.50	61
16.530	905	14.97	21.025	1,675	35.25	62
4.290	6,230	26.75	5.790	11,740	68.10	63
2.000	6,730	13.46	2.980	9,430	28.12	64
37.450	391	14.64	43.900	847	37.20	65
42.600	148	62.80	50.900	222	11.33	66
20.700	630	13.02	25.500	1,370	34.90	67
3.815	835	3.18	4.230	1,104	4.66	68
27.000	182	4.90	32.250	286	9.23	69
9.930	776	7.70	12.980	1,329	17.21	70
4.680	1,440	6.75	5.870	2,425	14.22	71
11.200	708	7.33	14.340	1,396	20.00	72
28.800	198	5.73	36.950	275	11.18	73
9.550	740	7.07	10.480	1,635	17.12	74
12.500	413	5.70	16.700	596	99.50	75
452.950	Avge 688	311.01	563.165	Avge 1,285	722.40	

Table XXI—continued

		1967			1980		
		Population Millions	GNP/Cap. $	GNP Billion $	Population Millions	GNP/Cap. $	GNP Billion $
76	Singapore	1.956	646	1.26	2.620	1,318	3.45
77	Zambia	3.945	298	1.17	5.550	786	4.36
78	Kenya	9.928	117	1.15	13.850	152	2.11
79	Afghanistan	15.751	70	1.10	19.525	106	2.08
80	Nepal	10.463	102	1.07	12.960	159	2.58
81	Dominican Rep.	3.889	275	1.06	5.980	355	2.12
82	South'n Rhodesia	4.530	233	1.05	6.550	295	1.93
83	Ivory Coast	4.010	263	1.05	7.460	783	5.83
84	Angola	5.293	190	1.00	6.190	311	1.92
85	Jamaica	1.876	531	0.99	2.344	787	1.85
86	Tunisia	4.560	214	0.97	5.900	366	2.16
87	Tanzania	12.181	80	0.97	16.200	108	1.15
88	Cambodia	6.415	148	0.95	8.410	272	2.29
89	El Salvador	3.889	280	0.88	4.730	428	2.03
90	Trinidad&Tobago	1.010	783	0.79	1.372	1,167	1.60
91	Cameroun	5.470	145	0.79	7.040	192	1.35
92	Senegal	3.670	214	0.78	4.805	283	1.36
93	Panama	1.329	581	0.77	1.962	1,034	2.03
94	Uganda	7.994	95	0.75	10.550	137	1.45
95	Madagascar	6.350	116	0.73	8.320	145	1.21
96	Costa Rica	1.594	425	0.67	2.495	630	1.57
97	Nicaragua	1.783	359	0.64	2.640	567	1.50
98	Albania	1.965	320	0.63	2.742	654	1.79
99	Bolivia	3.801	154	0.59	5.340	265	1.41
100	Honduras	2.445	236	0.57	3.520	316	1.11
		126.097	Avge 177	22.375	167.085	Avge 316	52.814

Gross National Product

Table XXI—*continued*

Population Millions	2000 GNP/Cap. $	GNP Billion $	Population Millions	2020 GNP/Cap. $	GNP Billion $	
3.655	3,340	12.20	4.565	6,880	31.35	76
8.140	2,480	20.19	10.475	5,690	59.60	77
19.960	228	4.53	25.540	329	8.40	78
24.880	189	4.72	29.150	321	9.35	79
16.520	283	4.68	19.350	456	8.82	80
9.490	522	4.95	12.890	758	9.78	81
9.790	423	4.14	12.890	588	7.58	82
14.620	3,250	47.50	22.050	8,950	192.72	83
7.410	642	4.76	8.310	1,298	10.79	84
3.030	1,369	4.14	3.584	2,185	7.84	85
7.880	814	6.42	9.625	1,650	16.15	86
22.170	190	4.20	27.550	317	8.71	87
11.430	608	6.95	14.030	1,305	18.30	88
7.500	803	6.02	10.250	1,450	14.85	89
1.929	2,044	3.95	2.435	3,345	8.15	90
9.250	292	2.70	11.170	433	4.85	91
6.530	418	2.74	8.025	605	4.86	92
2.945	2,140	6.31	3.925	3,770	13.32	93
14.420	265	3.82	17.920	482	8.63	94
11.315	99	2.02	13.900	277	3.85	95
3.700	1,130	4.18	4.975	1,975	9.82	96
4.040	1,112	4.50	5.400	2,050	11.08	97
3.942	1,768	6.96	5.055	3,950	19.98	98
6.380	607	3.87	7.160	1,200	8.60	99
5.545	495	2.75	7.410	768	5.69	100
236.471	Avge 759	179.181	297.634	Avge 1,690	502.48	

Table XXI—*continued*

	1967 Population Millions	1967 GNP/Cap. $	1967 GNP Billion $	1980 Population Millions	1980 GNP/Cap. $	1980 GNP Billion $
101 Jordan	2.039	268	0.547	2.770	545	1.510
102 Iceland	0.199	2,720	0.541	2.440	4,070	0.994
103 Ryukyu Islands	0.956	540	0.516	1.103	1,285	1.418
104 Paraguay	2.161	224	0.484	3.090	305	0.943
105 Mongolia	1.170	410	0.480	1.643	715	1.178
106 Cyprus	0.614	750	0.460	0.688	1,360	0.936
107 Papua & NewGuinea	2.257	200	0.452	3.000	340	1.020
108 Haiti	4.580	84	0.385	5.720	84	0.480
109 Mali	4.697	80	0.376	5.950	120	0.713
110 Yemen	5.330	70	0.373	6.850	118	0.810
111 Sierra Leone	2.439	140	0.342	2.820	226	0.638
112 Guinea	3.702	90	0.333	5.030	138	0.695
113 Liberia	1.110	230	0.256	1.342	424	0.562
114 Upper Volta	5.054	50	0.253	6.500	71	0.458
115 Netherl. Antilles	0.212	1,180	0.250	0.248	1,252	0.311
116 Laos	2.763	90	0.249	3.680	123	0.453
117 Niger	3.546	70	0.248	4.985	120	0.600
118 Qatar	0.075	3,250	0.244	0.143	6,260	0.881
119 Togo	1.724	140	0.242	2.310	210	0.485
120 Chad	3.410	70	0.238	4.795	100	0.480
121 Reunion	0.414	560	0.232	0.577	1,271	0.733
122 Bahama Islands	0.144	1,570	0.226	0.216	2,600	0.562
123 Guyana	0.680	387	0.263	0.924	538	0.497
124 Malawi	4.130	51	0.210	5.415	93	0.503
125 Dahomey	2.505	80	0.200	3.496	91	0.318
	55.911	Avge 150	8.387	73.535	Avge 247	18.178

Gross National Product 121

Table XXI—*continued*

Population Millions	GNP/Cap. $	GNP Billion $	Population Millions	GNP/Cap. $	GNP Billion $	
\-\-\- 2000 \-\-\-			\-\-\- 2020 \-\-\-			
3.890	1,508	5.850	4.900	3,420	16.730	101
0.306	6,760	2.066	0.356	10,690	3.805	102
1.310	3,885	5.080	1.452	8,620	12.500	103
4.560	480	2.188	5.945	755	4.480	104
2.408	1,610	3.880	3.100	3,250	10.080	105
0.780	2,930	2.280	0.853	5,200	4.430	106
0.410	735	3.010	0.509	1,470	7.490	107
7.390	84	0.621	8.740	84	0.734	108
7.750	204	1.578	9.250	320	2.960	109
9.000	233	2.090	10.865	396	4.300	110
3.340	441	1.472	3.705	811	3.005	111
7.070	254	1.790	8.910	446	3.497	112
1.665	1,010	1.680	1.920	2,130	4.090	113
8.550	114	0.971	10.310	193	1.990	114
0.297	1,345	0.400	0.332	1,428	0.474	115
5.040	195	0.982	6.250	291	1.814	116
7.320	233	1.700	9.410	412	3.877	117
0.289	8,240	2.380	0.430	10,450	4.500	118
3.225	375	1.272	4.025	637	2.580	119
7.025	195	1.365	9.040	315	2.840	120
0.830	3,560	2.955	1.063	8,950	9.520	121
0.334	4,850	1.620	0.450	8,080	3.630	122
1.300	1,043	1.263	1.640	2,090	3.425	123
7.360	210	1.547	9.040	457	4.130	124
5.030	106	0.535	6.450	131	0.845	125
96.068	Avge 522	50.575	118.344	Avge 993	117.726	

Table XXI—continued

		1967			1980		
		Population Millions	GNP/Cap. $	GNP Billion $	Population Millions	GNP/Cap. $	GNP Billion $
126	Mauritius	0.774	257	0.199	1.038	283	0.293
127	Gabon	0.473	418	0.198	0.518	890	0.462
128	Ruanda	3.306	60	0.198	4.730	103	0.487
129	Trucial Oman	0.180	1,050	0.189	0.342	2,760	0.945
130	Malta	0.570	587	0.187	0.319	1,138	0.363
131	Martinique	0.330	540	0.178	0.419	850	0.356
132	Centr.Afric.Rep.	1.459	120	0.175	1.940	144	0.279
133	Burundi	3.340	50	0.167	4.175	75	0.313
134	Congo Brazzaville	0.860	190	0.163	1.015	352	0.357
135	Mauritania	1.110	147	0.162	1.376	447	0.615
136	New Caledonia	0.094	1,620	0.152	0.128	2,156	0.276
137	Guam	0.092	1,620	0.152	0.165	2,230	0.367
138	Southern Yemen	1.170	130	0.151	1.515	159	0.241
139	Guadeloupe	0.920	470	0.150	1.192	624	0.744
140	Surinam	0.410	363	0.149	0.512	716	0.366
141	Somalia	2.660	50	0.133	4.230	55	0.232
142	French Oceania	0.097	1,340	0.130	0.133	2,792	0.374
143	Bermuda	0.050	2,410	0.121	0.061	3,705	0.267
144	Barbados	0.249	478	0.119	0.276	698	0.192
145	Channel Islands	0.116	980	0.114	0.127	1,560	0.198
146	Portuguses Guin.	0.528	210	0.111	0.541	462	0.250
147	Swaziland	0.385	280	0.108	0.536	606	0.325
148	US VirginIslands	0.056	2,380	0.105	0.106	3,900	0.415
149	PanamaCanalZone.	0.058	1,720	0.100	0.098	2,345	0.229
150	Brunei	0.108	800	0.086	0.168	1,075	0.181
151	Muscat & Oman	0.565	150	0.085	0.565	518	0.293
152	Windward Islands	0.372	212	0.079	0.474	390	0.185
153	Bahrain	0.193	350	0.068	0.300	545	0.163
		20.525	Avge 191	3.928	27.000	Avge 363	9.767

Gross National Product

Table XXI—*continued*

Population Millions	GNP/Cap. $	GNP Billion $	Population Millions	GNP/Cap. $	GNP Billion $	
2000	2000	2000	2020	2020	2020	
1.448	332	0.481	1.808	379	0.688	126
0.577	2,485	1.433	0.614	5,550	3.412	127
6.965	207	1.437	9.100	360	3.280	128
0.693	5,890	4.065	1.033	11,220	11.600	129
0.319	2,695	0.860	0.319	5,140	1.635	130
0.545	1,578	0.860	0.650	2,810	1.825	131
2.655	187	0.496	3.296	235	0.775	132
5.400	110	0.600	6.380	147	0.935	133
1.240	831	1.030	1.402	1,798	2.525	134
1.753	2,070	3.630	2.054	7,260	14.900	135
0.180	3,255	0.585	0.217	4,730	1.025	136
0.316	3,540	1.140	0.476	5,300	2.410	137
2.024	210	0.426	2.470	270	0.667	138
1.592	942	1.500	1.940	1,397	2.710	139
0.662	1,573	1.040	0.783	3,038	2.375	140
7.130	65	0.464	9.915	75	0.747	141
0.190	7,400	1.405	0.242	15,040	3.635	142
0.077	5,900	0.454	0.090	8,980	0.804	143
0.318	1,235	0.393	0.345	2,100	0.725	144
0.142	2,835	0.401	0.151	4,640	0.698	145
0.557	1,415	0.788	0.568	3,940	2.235	146
0.772	1,735	1.338	0.990	3,920	3.920	147
0.216	7,540	1.625	0.322	12,250	3.940	148
0.177	3,590	0.635	0.258	5,350	1.455	149
0.267	1,528	0.406	0.360	2,090	0.753	150
0.565	2,540	1.433	0.565	9,450	5.330	151
0.616	920	0.566	0.735	2,090	1.540	152
0.476	954	0.454	0.643	1,586	1.018	153
37.871	Avge 791	29.944	47.725	Avge 1,210	57.562	

Table XXI—continued

		1967				1967	
		Population Millions	GNP/Cap. $	GNP Billion $		Population Millions	GNP/Cap. $	GNP Billion $
154	Equatorial Guinea	0.277	240	0.067	171 Comoro Islands	0.250	110	0.028
155	Faeroe Islands	0.038	1,710	0.065	172 Cape Verde Isls.	0.236	110	0.026
156	Macao	0.268	240	0.064	173 Trust Ter. Pacif. Isl	0.093	260	0.024
157	Isle of Man	0.050	1,250	0.061	174 Tonga	0.079	310	0.024
158	Botswana	0.593	90	0.053	175 Gilbert & Ellice Isl	0.055	380	0.021
159	Lesotho	0.885	60	0.053	176 Sao Tome & Principe	0.063	280	0.018
160	Fr.T.Afars&Issas	0.083	580	0.048	177 Gibraltar	0.025	610	0.015
161	Bhutan	0.795	60	0.048	178 Fiji Islands	0.490	290	0.014
162	Portuguese Timor	0.572	80	0.046	179 American Samoa	0.029	490	0.014
163	Ceuta & Melilla	0.161	280	0.045	180 Sikkim	0.183	60	0.011
164	West Irian	0.874	50	0.044	181 Spanish Sahara	0.048	210	0.010
165	British Honduras	0.113	360	0.041	182 Maldive Islands	0.104	80	0.008
166	Leeward Islands	0.140	243	0.034	183 Ifni	0.054	150	0.008
167	Greenland	0.043	760	0.033	184 Seychelles Isls.	0.049	60	0.003
168	Gambia	0.343	90	0.031	185 Brit. Solomon Isl.	0.144	180	0.003
169	French Guyana	0.038	790	0.030	186 Western Samoa	0.134	130	0.002
170	New Hebrides	0.077	280	0.029	154 to 186 Total	7.386	Avge 139	1.021

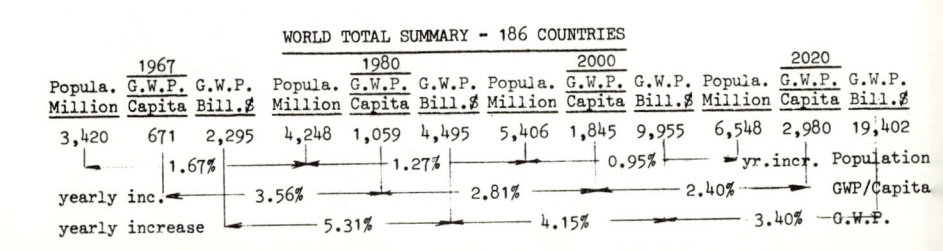

WORLD TOTAL SUMMARY - 186 COUNTRIES

1967			1980			2000			2020		
Popula. Million	G.W.P. Capita	G.W.P. Bill.$	Popula. Million	G.W.P. Capita	G.W.P. Bill.$	Popula. Million	G.W.P. Capita	G.W.P. Bill.$	Popula. Million	G.W.P. Capita	G.W.P. Bill.$
3,420	671	2,295	4,248	1,059	4,495	5,406	1,845	9,955	6,548	2,980	19,402

yearly inc. ← 1.67% → ← 1.27% → ← 0.95% → yr. incr. Population
← 3.56% → ← 2.81% → ← 2.40% → GWP/Capita
yearly increase ← 5.31% → ← 4.15% → ← 3.40% → G.W.P.

Gross National Product 125

In the 13th page of Table XXI, Population, GNP/Capita and GNP are shown, for 1967 only, for the countries numbered 154-186.

GNP IN 1990

Similarly to Table XIX, for the *per capita* GNP, Table XXIIa provides for a specific span of time, 23 years, a convenient comparison of how the various countries will fare over the period of a generation.

The columns marked Rank in 1967 and Change in Rank since 1967 provide interesting elements of comparison which have been noted in the following page. Note that the top 50 countries in 1967, with two exceptions will have remained the top 50 countries in 1990.

The two exceptions are Puerto Rico, which had rank 48 in 1967 and becomes No. 55 in 1990, and Peru which was 50 in 1967 and becomes 56 in 1990. Their places in the Club of the Top Fifties are taken by the Ivory Coast, which makes a huge leap from No. 83 in 1967 to No. 46 in 1990, and by Libya, which advances from No. 63 to No. 50.

Gains in their GNP Rank		GNP percent Annual Increase
Ivory Coast	37	12.9
Trucial Oman	29	11.1
U.S. Virgin Islands	25	9.8
Guadeloupe	24	9.0
Zambia	20	9.7
Albania	20	8.0
Korea Republic	18	9.1
Mauritania	18	10.3
French Oceania	15	7.8
Panama	15	7.2
Libya	13	9.4
Jordan	13	5.0
Iran	12	8.0
Cambodia	12	6.4
Qatar	12	8.5
Reunion	11	8.3

GAINS IN RANKING OF THEIR GNP

The facing column of figures show in descending order the countries which from 1967 to 1990 will have achieved gains in rank of their GNP greater than 10.

Whereas 29 countries had achieved gains in their GNP *per capita* rank greater than 10, there are only 16 countries in the same category when their GNP gains are compared.

The difference lies of course in the demographic factor which gives additional weight to the countries with the larger population thereby minimizing the magnitude of the changes in rank proper.

TABLE XXIIa—GNP in 1990 compared to 1967

		GNP.Bill.1967 $		Rank				GNP.Bill'67$		Rank	
		1990	1967	67	Chg			1990	1967	67	Chg
1	United States	1,930.00	803.90	1	0	65	Algeria	7.22	3.18	52	-13
2	USSR	845.00	228.00	2	0	66	Ireland	6.83	3.09	53	-13
3	Japan	503.80	115.20	5	+2	67	Singapore	6.75	1.26	76	+ 9
4	Germany-West	334.50	120.70	3	-1	68	Syria	6.05	1.30	72	+ 4
5	France	283.00	116.00	4	-1	69	Cuba	6.00	2.65	56	-13
6	United Kingdom	240.90	108.70	6	0	70	Ghana	5.61	2.05	60	-10
7	China-Mainland	222.50	64.28	8	+1	71	Guatemala	4.910	1.41	70	- 1
8	Italy	190.50	66.96	7	-1	72	Burma	4.525	1.80	66	- 6
9	India	149.50	45.90	10	+1	73	Lebanon	4.375	1.32	71	- 2
10	Canada	144.00	57.12	9	-1	74	Mozambique	4.370	1.28	74	0
11	Mexico	111.00	24.11	15	+4	75	Sudan	4.170	1.29	73	-2
12	Spain	98.20	26.40	13	+1	76	Cambodia	3.98	0.95	88	+12
13	Brazil	89.90	26.80	11	-2	77	Tunisia	3.80	0.97	86	+ 9
14	Poland	71.50	24.90	14	0	78	Panama	3.760	0.77	93	+15
15	Australia	68.20	26.60	12	-3	79	Albania	3.715	0.63	99	+20
16	Romania	58.60	13.87	23	+7	80	Congo Kinsh	3.675	1.47	69	-11
17	Netherlands	57.90	22.73	17	0	81	Ecuador	3.585	1.27	75	- 6
18	Sweden	53.50	23.93	16	-2	82	El Salvad.	3.38	0.88	89	+ 7
19	Turkey	51.45	11.54	27	+8	83	Domin. Rep	3.340	1.06	81	- 2
20	South Africa	47.80	13.09	25	+5	84	Afghanist.	3.205	1.10	79	- 5
21	Germany-East	46.85	22.20	18	-3	85	Nepal	3.200	1.07	80	- 5
22	Pakistan	44.60	13.85	24	+2	86	Kenya	3.165	1.15	78	- 8
23	Belgium-Luxemb	44.60	20.26	19	-4	87	Angola	3.105	1.00	84	- 3
24	Iran	44.30	7.45	36	+12	88	Jordan	3.055	0.54	101	+13
25	Yugoslavia	44.30	10.46	30	+5	89	South.Rhod	2.860	1.05	82	- 7
26	Switzerland	38.60	15.75	21	-5	90	Jamaica	2.855	0.99	85	- 5
27	Korea Republic	35.40	4.78	45	+18	91	Tanzania	2.770	0.97	87	- 4
28	Argentina	35.30	14.73	22	-6	92	Uruguay	2.715	1.61	68	-24
29	Philippines	34.85	9.64	31	+2	93	Ryukyu Isl	2.695	0.51	103	+10
30	Czechoslovakia	34.00	15.90	20	-10	94	Nicaragua	2.690	0.64	97	+ 3
31	Denmark	30.10	12.08	26	-5	95	Trin. Tobo	2.584	0.79	90	- 5
32	Indonesia	27.20	11.48	28	-4	96	Costa Rica	2.575	0.67	97	+ 1
33	Venezuela	27.02	8.54	34	+1	97	Uganda	2.387	0.75	94	- 3
34	Hungary	25.19		32	-2	98	Bolivia	2.340	0.72	96	- 2
35	Greece	25.08	7.04	37	+2	99	Mongolia	2.190	0.48	105	+ 6
36	Thailand	24.95	5.07	42	+6	100	Trucial Om.	2.095	0.18	129	+29
37	Austria	24.38	10.72	29	-8	101	Senegal	1.958	0.78	92	- 9
38	Finland	24.13	8.74	33	-5	102	Cameroun	1.942	0.79	91	-11
39	Bulgaria	21.91	5.74	39	0	103	Honduras	1.810	0.57	100	- 3
40	China-Taiwan	20.88	3.61	49	+9	104	Papua	1.780	0.45	107	+ 3
41	Columbia	20.20	6.01	38	-3	105	Madagascar	1.682	0.73	95	-10
42	Norway	19.64	8.32	35	-7	106	Qatar	1.570	0.24	118	+12
43	Portugal	19.61	4.62	46	+3	107	Mauritania	1.568	0.16	135	+18
44	Israel	18.70	3.98	47	+3	108	Cyprus	1.515	0.46	106	+ 2
45	U.A.R. Egypt	18.19	4.95	43	-2	109	Paraguay	1.472	0.48	104	- 1
46	Ivory Coast	18.12	1.05	83	+37	110	Reunion	1.445	0.23	121	+11
47	Chile	15.78	5.34	41	-6	111	Iceland	1.411	0.54	102	- 9
48	New Zealand	15.34	5.45	40	-8	112	Yemen	1.350	0.37	110	- 2
49	Nigeria	14.92	4.92	44	-5	113	Guinea	1.147	0.33	112	- 1
50	Libya	14.65	1.86	63	+13	114	Mali	1.090	0.37	109	- 5
51	Malaysia	13.60	3.37	51	0	115	Guadeloupe	1.076	0.15	139	+24
52	Hong-Kong	13.55	2.37	58	+6	116	Niger	1.044	0.24	117	+ 1
53	Saudi Arabia	13.12	2.34	59	+6	117	Liberia	1.005	0.25	113	- 4
54	Korea North	12.38	2.83	54	0	118	Bahama Isl	0.988	0.22	123	+ 5
55	Puerto Rico	12.22	3.74	48	-7	119	Sierra Leo	0.982	0.34	111	- 8
56	Peru	11.39	3.51	50	-6	120	Malawi	0.908	0.21	124	+ 4
57	Zambia	9.90	1.17	77	+20	121	Ruanda	0.885	0.19	128	+ 7
58	Vietnam North	9.58	2.01	61	+3	122	Chad	0.880	0.23	121	- 1
59	Vietnam South	9.26	2.44	57	-2	123	US VirginI	0.870	0.10	148	+25
60	Iraq	8.78	1.94	62	+2	124	Guyana	0.854	0.26	113	-11
61	Ethiopia	8.71	1.82	65	+4	125	Gabon	0.840	0.19	127	+ 2
62	Kuwait	8.24	1.83	64	+2	126	Togo	0.782	0.24	119	- 7
63	Morocco	8.14	2.70	55	-8	127	Fr. Ocean.	0.726	0.13	142	+15
64	Ceylon	7.60	1.77	67	+3	128	Haiti	0.702	0.38	108	-20

Gross National Product

	GNP gains in Billion 1967 $	GNP percent Annual Increase
United States	1,107	3.9
U.S.S.R.	617	5.8
Japan	388	6.6
Germany-West	214	4.5
France	167	5.5
China-Mainland	158	5.5
United Kingdom	132	3.5
Italy	124	4.6
India	114	5.3
Canada	87	4.1
Mexico	87	6.9
Spain	72	5.9
Brazil	63	5.4
Poland	57	4.7
Romania	45	6.4
Australia	42	4.3
Turkey	40	6.7
Iran	37	8.0
Netherlands	35	4.1
South Africa	35	5.8
Yugoslavia	34	6.4
Pakistan	31	5.2

GNP GAINS IN BILLION 1967 U.S. $

In line with each country, we have also shown its annual percent gain in GNP.

In actual magnitude gains in GNP, the countries line-up in descending order as in the facing column. It is interesting to note that, except for Iran, none of the countries in the top 'gains in rank' line-up is found in the top gains in GNP proper. Also, here, we have shown the annual percentage gains for the same countries.

CHAPTER NINE

Gross Area Product and Gross World Product

DETERMINATION OF GROSS WORLD PRODUCT

We have referred to our use of a building block method to arrive at the GNP of each country.

Table XXI which extends over 13 pages shows the further use of building block approach to arrive at an exact definition of the Gross World Product in 1967 and a valid estimate of its progress up to the year 2020.

Before reaching the grand total for the world, at the end of Table XXI, each page provides a total for the population and the GNP, thus available 25 countries by 25 countries, also an average of the GNP *per capita*.

The following table summarizes the information at the foot of each page:

Countries:	Population 1967 Millions	% of World	Population 2000 Millions	% of World	GNP per Capita 1967	GNP per Capita 2000 in 1967 $	GNP (1967 $) 1967 Billions	% of World	GNP (1967 $) 2000 Billions	% of World
1 to 25	2,477	71.6	3,650	67.5	832	2,300	2,032	88.5	8,380	84.0
26 to 50	507	14.8	910	16.9	349	1,100	177	7.7	999	10.0
51 to 75	257	7.3	453	8.4	198	688	51	2.2	311	3.2
76 to 100	126	3.7	236	4.4	177	759	22	1.0	179	1.8
101 to 125	56	1.6	96	1.8	150	522	8	0.4	51	0.5
126 to 153	21	0.7	38	0.7	191	791	4	0.2	30	0.3
154 to 170	7	0.3	13	0.3	139		1		5	0.05
World:	3,420	100	5,396	100	671	1,850	2,295	100	9,955	100

Among the various observations suggested by the above, we note the following: Between 1967 and 2000, the 25 top countries recede slightly in percent of the world population and in percent of the Gross World Product.

For the 25 top markets of the world which represent 88.5% of the

Gross Area Product and Gross World Product 129

Gross World Product, their average GNP *per capita* is higher than the world average.

For the balance of the world, the average GNP *per capita* is substantially lower than the world average.

WHAT WILL BE THE CHANGES IN THE MAJOR AREAS' SHARE OF THE GROSS WORLD PRODUCT IN THE NEXT 20 YEARS?

In order to provide 'area answers' we have prepared Table XXIIb which regroups into their geographic or economic areas 'our' 186 countries, and we have compared their importance in relation to the Gross World Product in 1967 and in 1990.

TABLE XXIIb—GNP in 1967 and 1990 compared for 11 major areas of the world

	G.A.P. 1967 Billion $	% of World	G.A.P. 1990 Billion $	% of World	G.N.P. % Annual Increase 1967–1990
NORTH AMERICA	861.174	37.4	2.076.325	31.1	3.95
CARIBBEAN & OTHER AMERICA	108.943	4.7	347.356	5.2	5.15
EUROPEAN COMMON MARKET	346.650	15.1	910.500	13.6	4.25
WESTERN EUROPE LESS COMMON MARKET	240.876	10.5	628.009	9.4	4.25
EASTERN EUROPE & U.S.S.R.	320.440	14.1	1.106.765	16.6	5.50
MIDDLE EAST	33.817	1.5	165.873	2.5	7.20
AFRICA	53.954	2.3	204.332	3.0	5.95
NON COMMUNIST ASIA	226.686	9.9	911.190	13.6	6.20
COMMUNIST ASIA	69.600	3.0	246.650	3.7	5.65
OCEANIA	33.113	1.5	87.900	1.3	4.30
WORLD	2.295.253	100.0	6.684.900	100.0	4.75
JAPAN	115.200	5.0	503.800	7.5	6.70
NON COMMUNIST ASIA LESS JAPAN	111.486	4.8	417.390	6.3	5.90

World Markets of Tomorrow

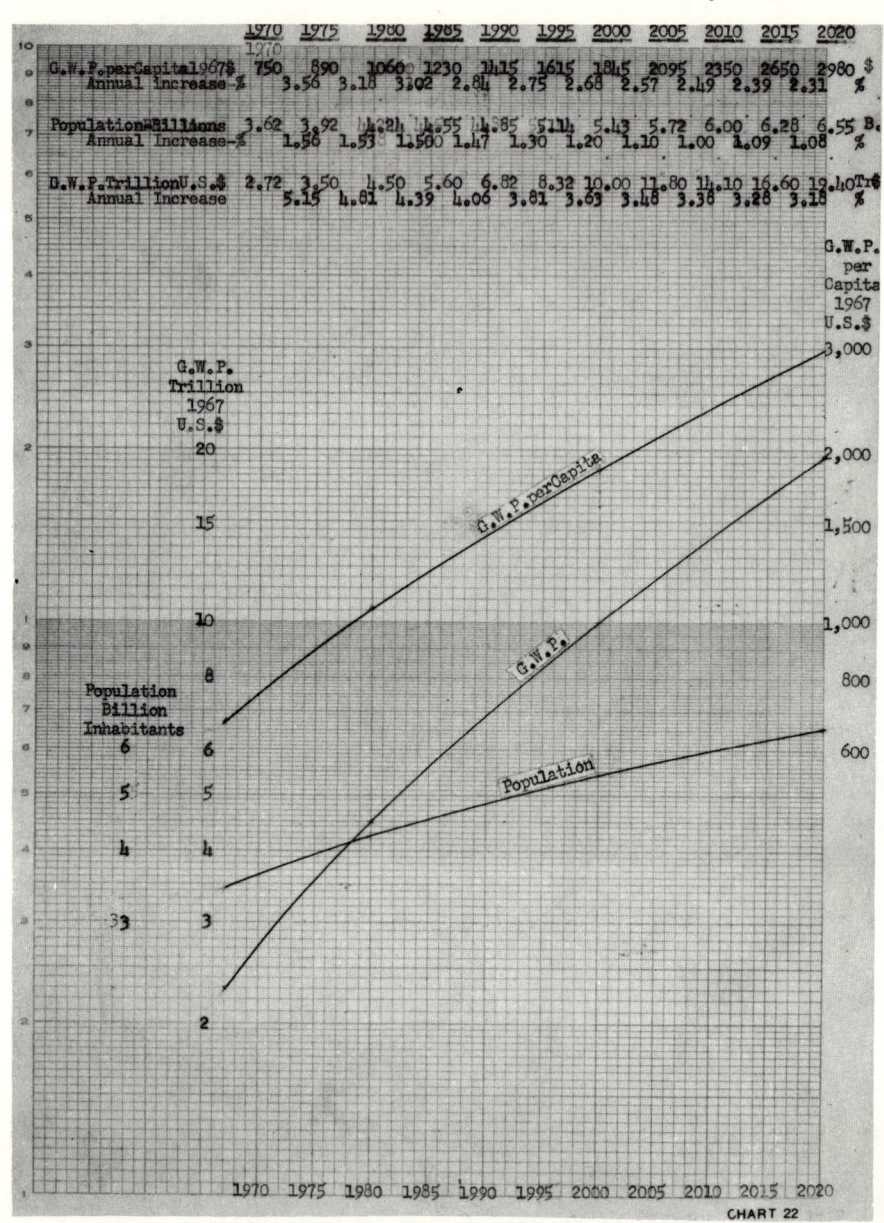

	1970	1975	1980	1985	1990	1995	2000	2005	2010	2015	2020
G.W.P. per Capital 1967 $	750	890	1060	1230	1415	1615	1845	2095	2350	2650	2980 $
Annual increase %		3.56	3.18	3.02	2.84	2.75	2.68	2.57	2.49	2.39	2.31 %
Population Billions	3.62	3.92	4.24	4.55	4.85	5.14	5.43	5.72	6.00	6.28	6.55 B.
Annual Increase %		1.56	1.53	1.50	1.47	1.30	1.20	1.10	1.00	1.09	1.08 %
G.W.P. Trillion U.S. $	2.72	3.50	4.50	5.60	6.82	8.32	10.00	11.80	14.10	16.60	19.40 Tr$
Annual Increase		5.15	4.81	4.39	4.06	3.81	3.63	3.48	3.38	3.28	3.18 %

CHART 22—Gross world product and world population projected to 2020: Summation of Forecasts for 186 Countries

Gross Area Product and Gross World Product

Bar charts are generally used to portray percentage shifts, but here, these are fairly minimal (except for North America's share of the Gross World Product), and a direct comparison of the two columns captioned '% of World' is quite revealing:

The biggest 'loser' is North America which gives up 6.3% (down to 31.1% from 37.4%) of its share of the GWP.

Next comes Western Europe, down to 23.0% from 25.6%

The biggest 'gainer' is Non-Communist Asia, up 3.7%, from 9.9% to 13.6%; Japan, up to 7.5% from 5.0% of GWP. contributes two-thirds of this gain.

The next largest gain is registered by the countries of Eastern Europe, which includes the U.S.S.R. up 2.5%, from 14.1% to 16.6%.

The Middle East, Africa, Communist Asia and Latin America complete the list of gainers, in that order, as far as percentage points are concerned.

WHICH OF THE MAJOR WORLD MARKETS, IN TERMS OF ECONOMIC AREAS, WILL HAVE THE MOST DYNAMIC GROWTH IN THE NEXT 20 YEARS?

When looking at each area's share of a Gross World Product, which will have nearly tripled in the 23 years we are attempting to span, percentage points, gains or losses are a very inadequate yardstick.

A more meaningful index of growth is afforded by the last column which gives the average percent annual increase in GNP for each of the areas.

From the figures in this column, it is evident that *there are no losers*! The largest gainer is the Middle East, with a 7.20% annual increase, on the average, over the entire 23-year period, thanks to its oil wealth.

Next comes Non-Communist Asia, again largely because of Japan's contribution, followed by Africa, etc., with North America at the foot of the list with a 3.95% average annual gain.

In addition to our brief comments on the Middle East and Japan, the review above suggests a number of observations: It may be a source of surprise to some that the growth rate of Africa and of 'Non-Communist Asia less Japan' be so near to that for Japan, but if we look at Chart 12 as well as at Chart 11, this will be easily explained:

Whereas Japan's stage of growth, as read on the vertical scale of Chart 12 is 2,250, the average for Africa and the average for

GAP Average % Yearly increase 1967 to 1990	
7.20	Middle East
6.70	Japan
5.95	Africa
5.90	Non-Communist Asia less Japan
5.65	Communist Asia
5.50	Eastern Europe incl. U.S.S.R.
5.15	Caribbean & Other America
4.30	Oceania
4.25	European Common Market
4.25	Western Europe Less Common Market
3.95	North America
4.75	World

'Non-Communist Asia less Japan' are at a much earlier stage of growth, say around 100.

If we now turn to Chart 11, we see that, on the 187.5% pattern for Japan, the percentage growth rate at its stage of growth is 7.5% whereas on the 100% pattern that we may identify with Africa and with Asia less Japan, their stages of growth point to growth rates very near that for Japan.

In other words, a less rapidly advancing economy at an earlier stage of growth may be expected to have the same percentage growth rate as a more dynamic economy at a higher stage of development.

This same consideration explains, to a certain extent, the 'foot of the ladder' status of North America: Taking the respective pattern indexes for Japan and for the United States will show a ratio of 187.5 : 125, i.e. 1.5 to 1, whereas the percentage growth rates which are influenced by more mature stage of development in the U.S. show a ratio of 1.7 to 1. An adult grows less rapidly than a boy!

The same consideration of 'stage of growth' in relation to 'index of dynamism' explains why Communist Asia and Eastern Europe are so close together in the percentage ladder.

Communist Asia's lower stage of development and slower pattern combine to match Eastern Europe's much more advanced stage of development on a more dynamic pattern.

We can turn our attention to the two Europes: Western and Eastern. The latter's growth rate, more than one percentage point higher than that of the former, reflects the emphasis on industrial output which is characteristic of the Eastern bloc economies, and, in a subsequent Chapter, the reader will note the related disparity in the use of energy per unit of GNP.

Gross Area Product and Gross World Product

The extent to which these gains have not permeated into the consumer goods sector and the well-being of the individual can be noted in the comparison of *per capita* GNP for the two Europes in 1967.

	G.N.P.	Population	GNP 'per Capita'
Eastern Europe	320 Billion $	338.5 Million	945 $
Western Europe	587 Billion $	348 Million	1,690 $

As we close this review, we note that the forecasted growth rates for the Common Market and for Western Europe less the Common Market are identical.

WHICH WORLD MARKETS WILL BE THE LARGEST GAINERS, IN ABSOLUTE TERMS?

Again proving how difficult it is to settle on an 'all-purpose' yardstick a different perspective is provided from the following:

1990 G.A.P. (Billion 1967)	Increase in G.A.P. from 1967 to 1990 (in Billion 1967 $)	
2,076	1,215	North America
1,107	786	Eastern Europe, incl. U.S.S.R.
911	564	European Common Market
628	388	Western Europe less European Common Market
504	388	Japan
407	296	Non-Communist Asia less Japan
347	238	Caribbean & Other America
247	177	Communist Asia
204	150	Africa
166	132	Middle East
88	55	Oceania

Next to North America, which will account for 27.7% of the total world gain, Eastern Europe, including the U.S.S.R. will be the largest gainer in absolute terms and will account for 17.9% of the total.

Third in line, will be the European Common Market (12.8%) and, tied for 4th place, Western Europe less the Common Market and Japan: 8.8% each.

For the reader interested in other groupings or areas than those presented above, the desired figures for each country can be obtained either from Table XXI for 1980, 2000 and 2020 or, more completely, from the alphabetically listed country profiles in the second part.

PROFILES OF GROWTH FOR 150 COUNTRIES

The reader will have noted that a 'building block' approach has been followed throughout:
1. The starting search was the definition of the 'index' of growth for each country and its identification with one of the patterns of Chart 12.

    From this pattern and beginning with the stage of growth corresponding to 1970, as circled in Chart 12, the GNP *per capita* was read at five-year intervals through to the year 2020.

    These values of the GNP *per capita* were entered in the 4th row of figures in the growth profile which extends from the bottom to the top of each country page, on the left side.

    They provide a direct measure of the average *per capita* income and are entirely unaffected, as far as our analysis is concerned, by the rate of population growth.
2. The method by which population growth was estimated for each country was explained in Chapter Seven. The second row of figures shows the multiplier used to arrive at the population for any of the years in the first row.

    Multiplying the 1967 population by this multiplier gave the population at 5-year intervals in the third row of figures.

    If, as is quite likely to happen, the reader interested in a particular country does not agree with the population estimates we have calculated all he needs to do is to write, in their place, the figures he would rather use.
3. Multiplying the population figures in the third row by the GNP *per capita* in the fourth row gave, also at 5-year intervals, the country GNP in the fifth row, always expressed in 1967 $.
4. The last row of figures, shown in-between the 5-year steps, are the average yearly increase for that period in percent. The rapid diminution of this rate of yearly increase may be a source of surprise but it is explained on two counts:
    (a) The taper of the pattern accounts, as an average, for two thirds of this decrease. This is the fundamental characteristic of growth phenomena on which we shall comment again in subsequent chapters.

Gross Area Product and Gross World Product 135

(b) The continuous decrease in the rate of population increase, on an average, account for one third of the decrease in the growth of the GNP. Incidentally, this calls attention to the fact that were 'zero population growth' to be attained overnight the increasing impact of man on the environment would be reduced by only one third.

5. The substantial reduction in the rate of growth of the GNP which is associated with each of the country forecasts presented might appear disquieting. We have, as a nation, become used to regarding unemployment as directly increased by any slowdown in the economy and the prospect of at least 1% reduction in our growth rate every twenty years could be so interpreted.

Actually, even with this gradual reduction in our rate of economic growth, the economy of every country will keep on expanding, in absolute terms, as shown by the summary below, prepared for the world as a whole, up to the year 2000:

	1970	1975	1980	1985	1990	1995	2000
GWP in Billion 1967 U.S. $	2.72	3.52	4.46	5.56	6.94	8.39	10.00
5-year Increase:		0.80	0.90	1.10	1.28	1.45	1.61
GWP per Capita 1967 U.S. $	750	890	1,040	1,205	1,390	1,605	1,845
5-year increase		140	150	165	185	215	230

The same figures as above for the GWP and for the GWP *per capita* are in Chart 22, where the 5-year annual increases are shown in percent. In the summary above we are showing the increases in absolute terms.

As we note from the above figures both the GWP and the GWP *per capita* increase each year in absolute terms and they increase each year by a greater absolute amount than the increase in the year before.

6. We may well focus our attention on the significance of the pace of growth that this 'world average' and the related world total portend:

In order to bring this 'closer to home' we may say that we are looking at a country where the *per-capita* wealth is near that of Argentina, Singapore or Bulgaria today. The reader who likes to know as much as possible of 'the facts' can see from

Table VII that these three countries straddle the 1967 world average: $671 *per capita*.

For the wage-earner of this country assuming 40% as the population as the size of the labor force his income of 2½ times the *per-capita* GNP will increase from $1,880 in 1970 to $2,230 in 1975 to $2,600 in 1980 to $3,000 in 1985 to $3,480 in 1990.

On successive 5-year intervals, he will find himself richer by:

$350 $370 $400 $463

In other words, he will have not only a little more to spend each year, but that 'little more' will be, each year, more than it had been in the previous year. From market expansion standpoint, this may be regarded as a healthy growth: The disposable income of Mr. World Average wage-earner will increase even more rapidly than the above indicates and the goal that we have set in a previous chapter will be met. Yet, the yearly percent increase will have been gradually coming down:

5.2%   4.8%   4.4%   4.1%

7. Let us note that all figures we have cited are in terms of constant 1967 $, meaning that each $ indicated will retain the same purchasing power. Inflation will increase all these figures to an extent that cannot be predicted but on a constant purchasing power basis, the estimates given here have a fair probability of being verified provided that disruptive forces are kept in check.

8. The above provides us also with an approximate yardstick for the productivity goals which should be achieved if inflation is to be held in check in relation to the approximate increase in the wage-earner's income.

ALL THE WORLD MARKETS OF THE FUTURE

In the preparation of this volume, the aim has been to develop through a valid evaluation of the growth of the GNP, a direct measure of the overall market potential of each country or area.

In addition, we intend to show how the approach presented in this volume can lead to a sounder evaluation of the growth of demand and how future markets in specific areas can be analysed with greater precision.

For some illustrative cases, tabulated in Chapter 3, we have shown how their trend can be determined in response to increasing *per*

Gross Area Product and Gross World Product 137

capita GNP. From this partial sampling, the reader, the manufacturer or the exporter interested in the market for certain product lines, be they television sets, automobiles, etc. can, starting from the point plotted for the country in which he is interested, derive an estimate of future trend.

In order better to illustrate this we shall assume that we would like to determine the number of television sets in 1980, in the United Kingdom.

We start from the point shown in Table XIII and in Chart V which shows that in 1968 there were 280 sets per 1000 inhabitants and we draw a trend line, letting our eye be guided by the cluster of points. We prepare the first column, marked 1968, of the tabulation below in which we have shown by letters a, b, c, etc, the sequence in which we enter figures.

	1968	1980	1980 High	1980 Low
(1967 U.S. $) Per Capita GNP	a 2,040	e 2,908	e 2,908	e 2,908
Television Sets per 1000	b 280	f 350	365	338
Millions Population	c 55.46	g 59.50	g 59.50	g 59.50
Total Number of Television Sets	d 15,500,000	h 20,800,000	21,700,000	20,100,000

The GNP *per capita* (a) and the population in 1968 (c) were taken as 1/3 of the way between the 1967 and the 1970 figures shown in the United Kingdom profile on page 000. The total number of sets in 1968 (d) is obtained as the product of b x c.

From the same profile, we note the *per capita* GNP (e) and the population (g) in 1980.

From the trend line we have sketched, we read that to a *per capita* GNP of $ U.S. 2,908 in 1980, there will correspond (f) 350 television sets per 1,000.

The product of g x f gives (h) the total number of sets in 1980. 20,800,000.

Looking at this figure, we wonder whether we have either overestimated or underestimated the market: so we draw two trend lines, one faster one slower, shown lightly dotted which should bracket the range and we repeat our estimates in the next two columns marked 1980 high and 1980 low. In there we enter the new figure for (f) but we repeat the *per capita* GNP (e) and the population (g).

In final analysis we have determined that there will be by 1980 between 20,100,000 and 21,700,000 television sets with 20,800,000 as a possible medium estimate.

CHAPTER TEN

Energy, Electricity and the Environment

WORLD GROWTH PROJECTIONS OF CONSUMPTION OF ENERGY, ETC

Table XXIIc has been prepared to indicate, in a very general way, our expectations of the world demand for various sources of energy, and for the total, from all sources, shown in the first row of figures.

It is very interesting to compare the forecasted growth of the world use of energy with that of the Gross World Product, as tabulated in Chapter Nine. We note that whereas the GWP will, in 2000, reach 370% of its total in 1970 the total consumption of energy will reach 311%.

In a subsequent chapter, where we discuss the 'elasticity coefficient' of GNP as related to Energy, we shall mention that this coefficent is 104.5% which means that, for the world as a whole, every year the GNP is expected to increase 4.5% faster than the use of energy for the next decade, for instance.

The two forecasts estimates are not conflicting if we consider, which will probably be the case, that in the following decades, the growth of GNP in relation to the use of Energy may slow down somewhat.

This may also be interpreted by saying that over the next 30 years, the elasticity coefficient will average only 1 for the world as a whole.

In anticipation of the added attention which, in the following chapters, will be given to the use of energy and electricity, Table XXIIc as well as Charts 23 and 24 present some forecasts of the world future demand for the various sources of energy.

Note that the demand for all sources will gain in absolute terms, but in gradually varying extent.

The use of coal which is currently evidencing its 'short-supply' status will increase least of all, and its percentage of contribution to the total demand, will dwindle from 33% to 9%.

Natural gas, greatly in demand in the chemical field, will also see

TABLE XXIIc—World growth projections: use of energy including electricity, hydro and nuclear

	1970	1980	1990	2000
Energy : Million MetricTons Coal Equivalent	6,450	9,740	14,200	20,050
" PerCent	100	151	220	311
Solid Fuels : Million MetricTons of Coal/Year	2,165	2,300	2,555	2,815
" " PerCent	100	106	118	130
Liquid Fuels : Million Barrels of Oil/Day	35	57	83.50	107
" " PerCent	100	163	238	306
Natural Gas : Trillion CubicFeet/Year	35	57	73.50	78
" PerCent	100	163	210	222
HydroElectricity : Trillion KilowattHours	1.22	1.85	2.80	4
" PerCent	100	152	229	328
NuclearElectricity : Trillion KilowattHours	0.50	1.57	5.25	13
ElectricityGeneration : ✱ Trillion KilowattHours	4.86	8.66	15.85	26.45
" PerCent	100	178	326	524

(✱ includes Hydro&Nuclear above)

Note : The fuel use for the balance of the electricity generation is included as part of Coal, Oil & Natural Gas Consumptions shown under Energy.

its percentage contribution as a source of energy come down drastically, from 20% to 6%.

Liquid Fuels will average the greatest contribution, both in absolute terms and as a percentage of the total which will stay practically unchanged at 40%.

However, shortly after the turn of the next half-century it is expected to be supplanted by nuclear power as the most important

Energy, Electricity and the Environment 141

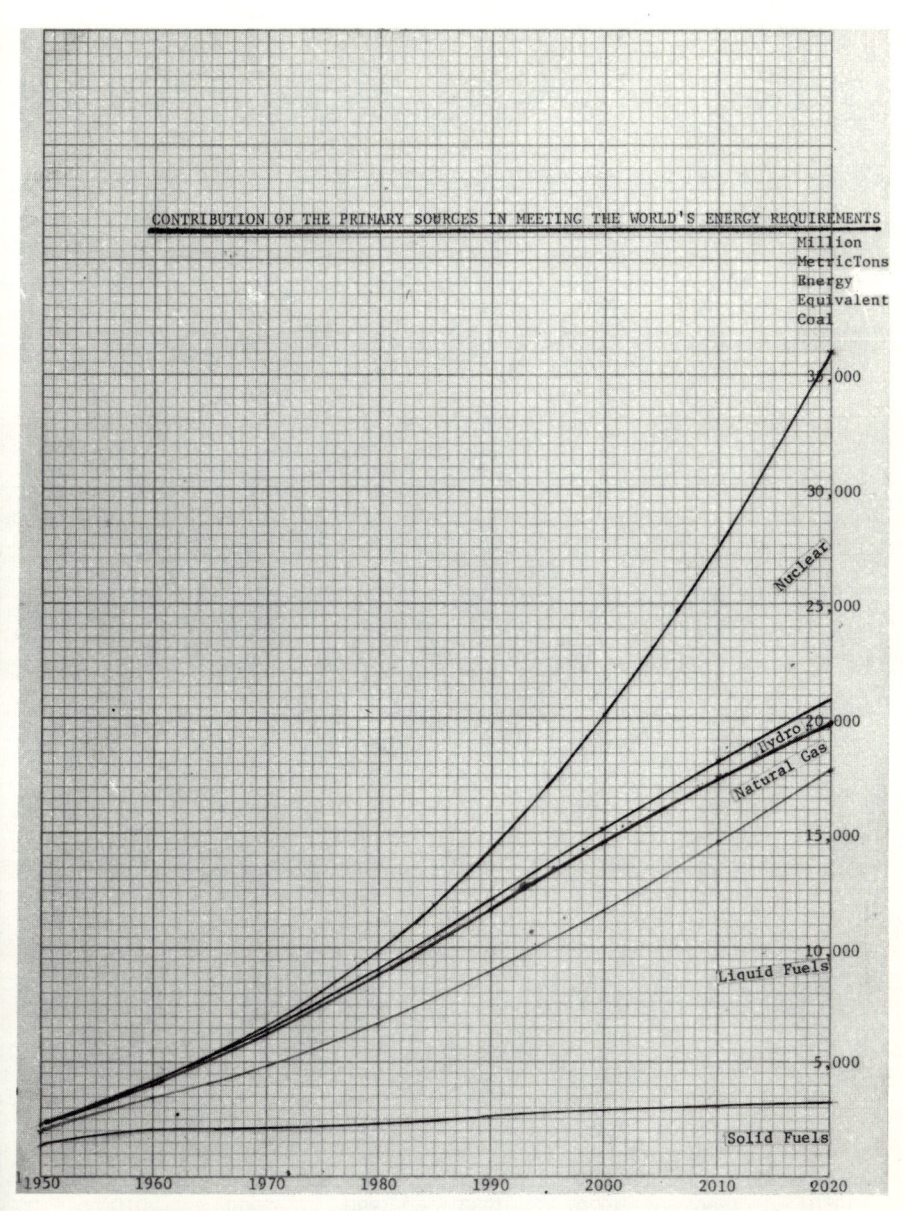

CHART 23—Contribution of the primary sources in meeting world's energy needs

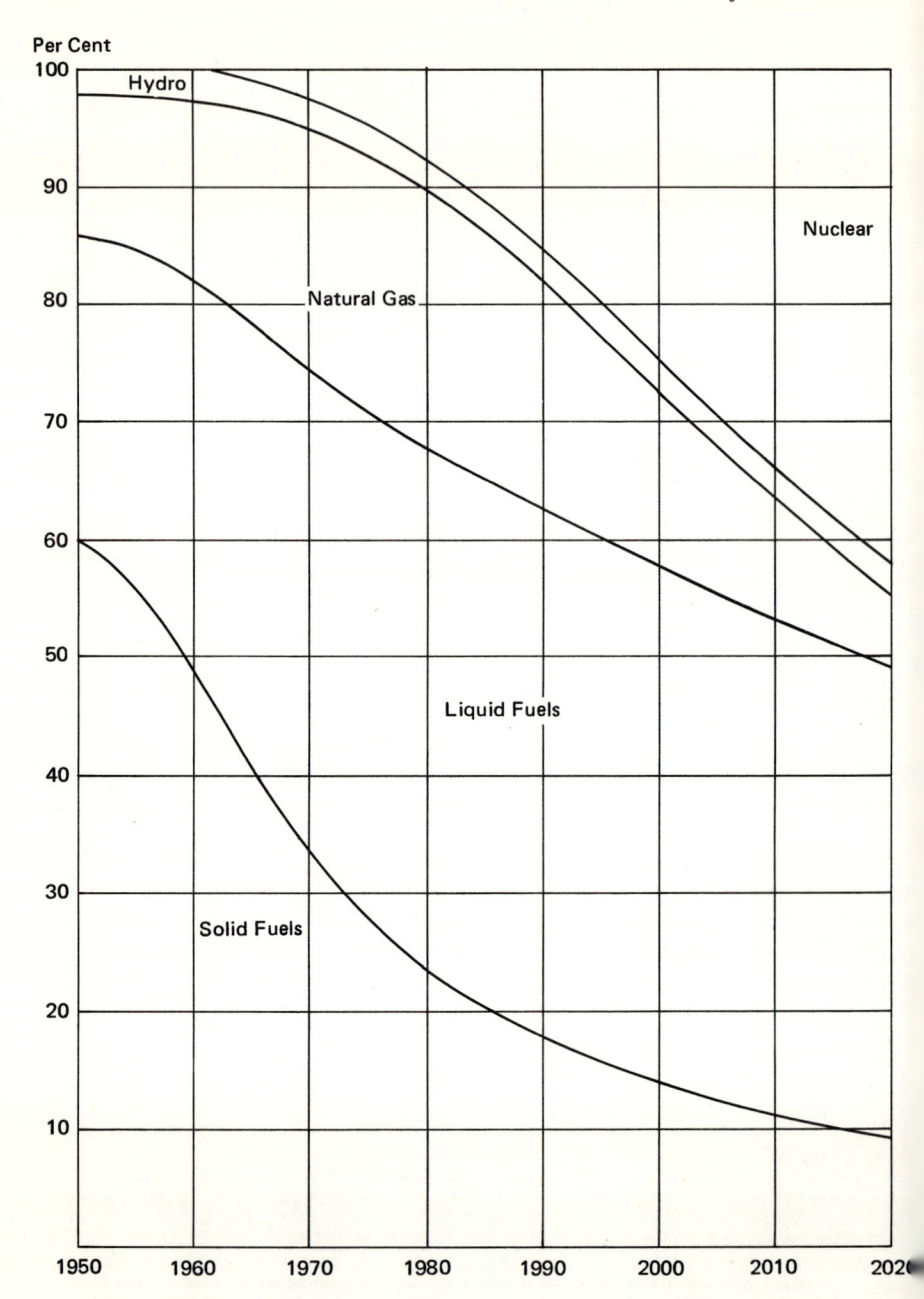

CHART 24—Percentage share of primary sources in meeting world's energy needs

Energy, Electricity and the Environment 143

single source of energy. In the year 2000, 25% of the world's total needs of energy will be met by nuclear power and this share will double by the year 2030.

We shall see in the chapters on environment that this emergence of nuclear power as the largest single source of energy in the world will not only provide the required amounts of energy, critically needed to meet the growing demands of our economy and of our social progress, but will accomplish this in the most desirable form, from the point of view of the environment.

CONTROL OF THE ENVIRONMENT

The growing public concern for the preservation of the environment has led to searching analyses of 'deteriorating' factors, both actual and potential, emanating from a number of sectors of the economy.

The use of energy in all its forms and, among these, the generation of electricity have been prominently identified as major causes of environmental damage.

There is a considerable volume of data on Energy which is not available on anywhere near the same basis of reliability in connection with GNP. Also, the use of energy is independent of currency exchange fluctuations, devaluation in one form or another, and many of the uncertainties which enter into the evaluation of economic growth, such as the differentiation between 'good' GNP and 'bad' GNP.

Since our GNP forecasts have derived considerable support from the study of energy use which, concurrently with GNP, we have carried out over the 20 year period which has served as the base for our analysis, we are reviewing in the following chapters a number of aspects of the use and growth of use of energy and electricity throughout the world. Both through the statistical answers and the evaluation of their contribution to the economy which shall be developed, we hope to provide a clearer understanding of the mutual impact of energy, the economy and the environment.

These shall be reviewed in a succession of steps.

TOTAL USE OF ENERGY FOR ALL COUNTRIES OF THE WORLD

In the next page, Table XXIII shows in descending order of magnitude the total use of energy in 1968 for the 172 countries for which this is available.

TABLE XXIII—Total use of energy-billion kilograms energy equivalent coal—1968

Country	Value	Country	Value	Country	Value
WORLD TOTAL	6,015.815	West Malaysia	3.731	Malta	0.313
United States	2,078.156	Saudi Arabia	3.622	Brunei	0.282
U.S.S.R.	965.215	Hong Kong	2.991	Greenland	0.250
Communist Asia	350.448	Southern Rhodesia	2.766	Sabah	0.249
United Kingdom	277.270	Morocco	2.638	Gabon	0.212
Germany Fed. Rep.	269.793	Syria	2.475	Congo Brazzaville	0.178
Japan	254.247	Zambia	2.259	Leeward Islands	0.177
Canada	176.164	Uruguay	2.230	Fiji Islands	0.174
France	163.986	Jamaica	1.913	Malawi	0.174
Poland	123.666	Panama	1.790	KuwaitNeutralZone	0.151
Italy	116.883	Nigeria	1.745	Sierra Leone	0.151
India	96.378	Lebanon	1.739	Haiti	0.146
Germany East	92.041	Burma	1.519	Mauritius	0.142
Czechoslovakia	82.954	Ecuador	1.492	Barbados	0.138
Australia	61.619	Kenya	1.479	Bermuda	0.128
South Africa	59.033	Congo Kinshasa	1.426	Martinique	0.127
Netherlands	52.459	Ceylon	1.368	Trucial Oman	0.123
Belgium & Luxem.	52.131	Singapore	1.364	Qatar	0.115
Mexico	50.300	Sudan	1.321	Guadeloupe	0.113
Romania	47.062	Albania	1.168	Nepal	0.112
Spain	43.035	Guatemala	1.167	Mali	0.104
Sweden	42.439	Mozambique	1.109	Guam	0.100
Brazil	39.735	Tunisia	1.099	Faeroe Islands	0.096
Argentina	33.325	Ghana	1.058	Togo	0.095
Hungary	28.889	Bolivia	0.970	Reunion	0.086
Bulgaria	27.765	Libya	0.890	Laos	0.084
Yugoslavia	25.152	Iceland	0.842	Papua	0.082
Venezuela	24.636	Dominican Rep.	0.841	Macau	0.080
Denmark	22.843	New Caledonia	0.815	Dahomey	0.078
Austria	20.978	Cyprus	0.805	Somalia	0.075
Switzerland	18.583	Surinam	0.780	Windward Islands	0.075
Korea Republic	17.643	Angola	0.777	American Samoa	0.073
Norway	16.214	Ivory Coast	0.687	Afars & Issas	0.068
Finland	15.655	Bahama Islands	0.669	Mauritania	0.067
Turkey	15.120	Tanzania	0.654	Yemen	0.067
Iran	12.920	El Salvador	0.653	Chad	0.061
Colombia	11.423	Guyana	0.647	British Honduras	0.058
Indonesia	11.234	Nicaragua	0.642	Niger	0.057
China Taiwan	10.984	Jordan	0.588	Centr. Afric. Rep.	0.054
Chile	10.764	Ethiopia	0.543	Upper Volta	0.052
Pakistan	10.611	Senegal	0.541	West Irian	0.052
U.A.R. Egypt	9.540	Costa Rica	0.529	Equatorial Guinea	0.045
Greece	8.959	Honduras	0.524	Gibraltar	0.039
Philippines	8.912	Afghanistan	0.516	French Guyana	0.037
Ireland	8.344	Ryukyu Islands	0.513	Wake Islands	0.036
Cuba	8.281	South Yemen	0.512	Ruanda	0.035
Peru	8.086	Uganda	0.504	Portuguese Guinea	0.031
Puerto Rico	7.385	Cameroun	0.462	Burundi	0.031
New Zealand	7.368	Bahrain	0.423	Cape Verde Isl.	0.024
Thailand	6.873	Sarawak	0.414	Nauru	0.024
Kuwait	6.429	Madagascar	0.392	Muscat & Oman	0.024
South Vietnam	5.653	US Virgin Islands	0.390	Christmas Islands	0.022
Iraq	5.560	Guinea	0.372	St.Pierre&Miquelon	0.021
Israel	5.530	Cambodia	0.333	Brit.Solomon Isl.	0.019
Algeria	5.441	Liberia	0.324	Gambia	0.019
Portugal	5.122	Panama Canal Zone	0.322	Western Samoa	0.018
Trinidad & Tobago	4.310	Paraguay	0.316	Falkland Islands	0.012
Netherlands Antilles	3.805				

Energy, Electricity and the Environment

The energy use in 1968, was calculated by totalizing, on the basis of their calorific values, the contribution from all commercial sources of energy: solid fuels, liquid fuels, natural gas, and hydro-electricity, as 'Equivalent' Kilograms of Coal (KEC), on the basis of the coefficients of equivalence currently used in the United Nations Statistical Papers shown in the table below:

	Coal Equivalent (Metric Tons)	Energy Content 10 Kilocalories
1 metric ton anthracite & bituminous coal	1	7,000
1 metric ton of coke of anthracite or bituminous coal	0.9	6,300
1 metric ton of lignite	0.3 to 0.6	2,100 to 4,200
1 metric ton of crude petroleum	1.3	9,100
1 metric ton of gasoline, kerosene, fuel oil	1.5	10,500
1000 cubic meters natural gas	1.33	9,310
1000 cubic meters manufactured and coke oven gases	0.6	4,200
1000 kilowatt-hour electrical energy	0.125	875
The above energy contents are consistent with		BTU
1 pound of coal		12,600
1 pound of liquid fuel		18,000
1000 cubic feet of natural gas		1,050,000
1 barrel of fuel oil		6,300,000

The totals thus arrived at are not 'ideally' representative and comparable.

They include only the 'commercial' forms of energy listed in the table; they completely omit the non-commercial sources forms such as animal wastes, wood, etc., the total of which may, for some developing countries, amount to 50% of the total energy actually consumed.

Even where the coefficients of equivalence are correct from the calorific point of view, varying utilization factors may affect the economic value of the respective Btu's, (for instance, one Btu of natural gas or of petroleum might prove more valuable than one Btu of coal).

The value shown in the table above for the coefficient of equivalence used for electrical energy, until recently mostly hydro, but which includes a rapidly increasing contribution from nuclear power, results in a considerable distortion of the contribution from these two sources. This goes beyond the scope of this volume but we may simply mention here that unless the coefficient of 0.125 now used is replaced by one which, every year, reflects the coal equivalent of the average amount of energy consumed in the production of electricity by steam power plants, the totals for the years to come will become increasingly distorted and not suitable for analysis without being recalculated.

In spite of the above limitations it should be stated that the energy consumptions listed in this volume represent a unique group of data and that the discrepancies we have noted do not, as of today, noticeably affect the comparisons which may be made.

'PER CAPITA' USE OF ENERGY FOR ALL COUNTRIES OF THE WORLD

The data in Table XXIV, along with its electricity corresponding number, Table XXIX, have been for selected countries the most often cited—and sometimes misquoted as has been the case when it is stated that one United States citizen, identified with 10,331 KEC, is 55 times more polluting than the average Indian who can only claim 183 KEC.

It is precisely because the average Indian consumes only 1/55 of the energy consumed by an average U.S. citizen that the environmentally disastrous conditions which prevail in Calcutta including cholera in the endemic stage for instance, exist. The progress of India's population limitation program and of its economy will, at the same time as it raises the *per capita* energy consumption, remove such environmental blights.

This table calls for a number of comments supplementing those in Table XXIII. The United Nations data does not take into account the energy furnished by draft animals, neither does it include the energy consumed in the form of food intake by each individual.

It is of interest to evaluate how the latter compares with the energy consumed *outside* each individual: If we take 2,500 kilocalories as a representative daily food intake, this is equivalent to the burning of 0.35 kilogram of energy equivalent coal, which is the same as 130 KEC per year.

Thus, the average citizen of Ghana consumes as food intake, the same amount—additional—as the energy consumed from commercial fuels. At higher levels of *per capita* use, the personal consumption of energy becomes less and less significant.

Note that throughout these tables and related comments, we are talking only of energy consumed by the country, not the energy produced.

TABLE XXIV—Kilograms of energy equivalent coal 'per capita'—1968

Country	Value	Country	Value	Country	Value
Netherl. Antilles	17,460	Mexico	1,064	Bolivia	207
Kuwait	11,905	French Oceania	1,051	Congo Brazzaville	205
United States	10,331	Cuba	1,025	Thailand	203
New Caledonia	8,491	Greece	1,017	Reunion	201
Canada	8,480	Guam	1,004	Windward Islands	200
US Virgin Islands	6,718	Jamaica	999	El Salvador	199
Czechoslovakia	5,775	Malta	979	India	183
Panama Canal Zone	5,741	French Guyana	937	Morocco	180
Christmas Islands	5,625	Trucial Oman	924	Mauritius	180
Greenland	5,566	Guyana	899	Ivory Coast	167
East Germany	5,387	Afars & Issas	825	Equatorial Guinea	161
Sweden	5,359	Taiwan	815	Mozambique	152
Belgium & Luxem.	5,236	Uruguay	791	Senegal	146
Australia	5,121	Hong Kong	761	Angola	144
United Kingdom	5,004	Singapore	685	Kenya	144
Denmark	4,690	Lebanon	673	Paraguay	141
West Germany	4,484	Iraq	644	Brit.Solomon Isl.	131
St.Pierre&Miquelon	4,299	Peru	633	Papua	131
Norway	4,245	Korea Republic	579	Ghana	128
Trinidad & Tobago	4,221	Albania	578	Ceylon	114
Iceland	4,188	Colombia	576	Western Samoa	104
Netherlands	4,116	Southern Rhodesia	559	Indonesia	99
U.S.S.R.	4,058	Zambia	553	Guinea	97
Nauru	4,000	Barbados	546	Cape Verde Isl.	97
Poland	3,828	Portugal	541	Sudan	89
Bahama Islands	3,780	Ryukyu Islands	531	Pakistan	87
Finland	3,339	Saudi Arabia	510	Congo Kinshasa	85
Bulgaria	3,317	British Honduras	504	Cameroun	83
France	3,282	Libya	493	Sierra Leone	61
Switzerland	3,012	Iran	478	Uganda	61
Ireland	2,867	Communist Asia	458	Mauritania	60
Austria	2,854	Brazil	450	Madagascar	60
Hungary	2,816	Turkey	450	Portuguese Guinea	59
South Africa	2,721	Sarawak	448	West Irian	58
Puerto Rico	2,712	Gabon	442	Burma	57
New Zealand	2,678	Syria	434	Tanzania	53
Bermuda	2,560	South Yemen	428	Togo	53
Venezuela	2,543	Malaysia	425	Cambodia	50
Faeroe Islands	2,539	Algeria	420	Gambia	42
Brunei	2,519	Sabah	407	Muscat & Oman	42
Japan	2,515	New Hebrides	399	Malawi	40
Romania	2,386	Martinique	390	Centr. Afric. Rep.	36
American Samoa	2,370	Guadeloupe	355	Afghanistan	32
Italy	2,215	Nicaragua	348	Haiti	31
Bahrain	2,114	Fiji Islands	345	Dahomey	30
Surinam	2,081	South Vietnam	324	Laos	29
Israel	2,014	Costa Rica	323	Nigeria	27
WORLD AVERAGE	1,727	Macau	309	Somalia	27
Gibraltar	1,559	U.A.R. Egypt	301	Ethiopia	22
Qatar	1,443	Liberia	286	Mali	21
Argentina	1,411	Jordan	279	Chad	17
Spain	1,312	Ecuador	261	Niger	14
Panama	1,304	Philippines	248	Yemen	13
Cyprus	1,294	Guatemala	239	Upper Volta	10
Yugoslavia	1,247	Tunisia	235	Nepal	10
Leeward Islands	1,246	Honduras	216	Ruanda	10
Chile	1,151	Dominican Rep.	208	Burundi	8

For an oil producing country, for instance, none of the oil loaded in the tankers or fed to the pipelines is included, but the energy consumed on the soil of this country in the refineries, port loading facilities, etc, is, which accounts for the top figures in Table XXIV: Netherlands Antilles, Kuwait, etc. Also in top position, we note New Caledonia, an energy-intensive nickel producing country with low population.

WHAT IS THE COST OF ENERGY?

Owing to a number of conditions which have been labeled as part of the energy crisis there have been recently substantial increases in the cost of energy. For that reason the costs shown below are to-day minimum costs and are generally exceeded in most areas of the world. They provide a convenient means of comparison of up-to-date costs of various fuels.

An average cost of energy equivalent to $12.60 per metric ton of coal would be the same as $18.00 per metric ton of oil, or $2.75 per barrel of oil, or 35.0 cent/million Btu.

HOW DOES THE AMOUNT OF ENERGY USED FOR THE PRODUCTION OF $1 OF GNP VARY THROUGHOUT ALL COUNTRIES OF THE WORLD?

The universally accepted relationship between the use of energy and the productive output of a country measured in $ of GNP might well

GAP 1967 Billion U.S. $	Energy Use Billion KEC	$ GAP. KEC	
861.174	2,127.468	0.405	North America
108.838	170.883	0.634	Caribbean & Other America
587.342	536.996	1.098	Western Europe
320.440	1,315.961	0.244	Eastern Europe
33.817	52.417	0.646	Middle East
53.281	92.609	0.575	Africa
226.511	394.021	0.575	Non-Communist Asia
69.600	268.970	0.260	Communist Asia
32.936	65.746	0.502	Oceania
100% 2,295.253	100% 5,612.315	0.409	Total World
17% 390.040	28% 1,584.931	0.246	Eastern Europe and Communist Asia
83% 1,905.213	12% 4,027.384	0.474	Rest of World

Energy, Electricity and the Environment

lead one to believe that the energy contents of one $ of GNP are fairly predictable in any area of the world.

Rather surprisingly, the facing Table XXV and the summary-by-areas below show, respectively, for 164 countries and for 9 areas of the world that wide variations are found in the ratio $ GNP or GAP/KEC.

TABLE XXV—GNP $ per kilogram of energy equivalent coal and reciprocal—1967

#	Country	GNP/Kec	Kec/GNP	#	Country	GNP/Kec	Kec/GNP	#	Country	GNP/Kec	Kec/GNP
1	Netherl.Antil.	0.0599	18.550	55	Norway	0.5550	1.800	110	Guadeloupe	1.1370	0.880
2	South Yemen	0.0640	15.600	56	Columbia	0.5550	1.800	111	Tanzania	1.1420	0.875
3	Bahrain	0.0972	10.290	57	Jamaica	0.5590	1.790	112	Congo Kinshasa	1.1500	0.870
4	American Samoa	0.1260	7.920	58	Puerto Rico	0.5850	1.710	113	Gabon	1.1530	0.866
5	Dominican Rep.	0.1550	6.440	59	Denmark	0.5850	1.710	114	Philippines	1.1620	0.860
6	Greenland	0.1710	5.830	60	Algeria	0.5920	1.690	115	Martinique	1.2340	0.810
7	Trinidad&Tobago	0.1855	5.390	61	Syria	0.5950	1.680	116	Costa Rica	1.3000	0.770
8	Angola	0.1862	5.370	62	Italy	0.5990	1.670	117	Nicaragua	1.3240	0.755
9	Surinam	0.1880	5.330	63	U.A.R. Egypt	0.6020	1.660	118	Burma	1.3700	0.730
10	Czechoslovakia	0.2020	4.950	64	Finland	0.6200	1.610	119	Ceylan	1.3700	0.730
11	New Caledonia	0.2075	4.820	65	Iran	0.6290	1.590	120	Western Samoa	1.3700	0.730
12	Poland	0.2140	4.680	66	Sweden	0.6330	1.580	121	Guatemala	1.3890	0.720
13	Bulgaria	0.2160	4.430	67	Uruguay	0.6400	1.560	122	Pakistan	1.4080	0.710
14	South Africa	0.2300	4.350	68	Bermuda	0.6400	1.560	123	Honduras	1.4280	0.700
15	Germany East	0.2440	4.100	69	Afars & Issas	0.6450	1.550	124	Guam	1.4500	0.690
16	U.S.S.R.	0.2470	4.030	70	Spain	0.6500	1.540	125	Equat. Guinea	1.5150	0.660
	Communist Asia:			71	Israel	0.6580	1.520	126	Senegal	1.5500	0.645
	Commun. China			72	Cyprus	0.7140	1.400	127	Brit.Solomon Isl.	1.5880	0.630
	North Korea	0.2600	3.840	73	Iceland	0.7190	1.390	128	Mozambique	1.5900	0.628
	North Vietnam			74	Liberia	0.7250	1.380	129	El Salvador	1.6480	0.607
	Mongolia			75	Faeroe Islands	0.7300	1.370	130	Ivory Coast	1.7530	0.570
17	Korea Republic	0.2860	3.500	76	Brit. Honduras	0.7460	1.340	131	Paraguay	1.7530	0.570
18	Romania	0.3165	3.160	77	Malta	0.7460	1.340	132	Mauritius	1.8200	0.550
19	Cuba	0.3180	3.140	78	France	0.7580	1.320	133	Uganda	1.8200	0.550
20	Bahama Islands	0.3320	3.010	79	New Zealand	0.7700	1.300	134	Cameroun	1.8900	0.530
21	Hungary	0.3380	2.960	80	Hong Kong	0.7810	1.280	135	French Oceania	1.9600	0.510
22	Canada	0.3472	2.880	81	New Hebrides	0.7880	1.270	136	Madagascar	2.0400	0.490
23	Brunei	0.3472	2.880	82	Malaysia	0.7880	1.270	137	Papua&NewGuinea	2.0400	0.490
24	PanamaCanalZone	0.3680	2.720	83	Brazil	0.7880	1.270	138	Gambia	2.0400	0.490
25	Iraq	0.3760	2.660	84	Saudi Arabia	0.8000	1.250	139	Laos	2.0820	0.480
26	Guyana	0.3760	2.660	85	West Irian	0.8060	1.240	140	Somalia	2.1750	0.460
27	China - Taiwan	0.3785	2.640	86	Kenya	0.8130	1.230	141	Reunion	2.2200	0.450
28	United Kingdom	0.3950	2.530	87	Bolivia	0.8130	1.230	142	Libya	2.2500	0.444
29	Ireland	0.4050	2.470	88	Lebanon	0.8160	1.225	143	Ghana	2.3550	0.425
30	United States	0.4100	2.440	89	Turkey	0.8400	1.190	144	Qatar	2.3800	0.420
31	Venezuela	0.4100	2.440	90	Macao	0.8480	1.180	145	Togo	2.5000	0.400
32	Gibraltar	0.4230	2.360	91	Fiji Islands	0.8700	1.150	146	Nigeria	2.5600	0.390
33	Belgium & Lux.	0.4365	2.290	92	Portugal	0.8770	1.140	147	Afghanistan	2.5900	0.386
34	US Virgin Isls.	0.4390	2.280	93	Albania	0.8930	1.120	148	Haiti	2.6360	0.380
35	Yugoslavia	0.4550	2.220	94	Thailand	0.8930	1.120	149	Mauritania	2.7800	0.360
36	Peru	0.4570	2.190	95	French Guyana	0.9100	1.100	150	Cambodia	2.8600	0.350
37	Argentina	0.4600	2.170	96	Tunisia	0.9170	1.090	151	Trucial Oman	3.0300	0.330
38	Panama	0.4650	2.150	97	Guinea	0.9250	1.080	152	Sierra Leone	3.3330	0.300
39	Australia	0.4690	2.130	98	Barbados	0.9350	1.070	153	Centr.Afric.Rep	3.4450	0.290
40	South'nRhodesia	0.4760	2.100	99	Greece	0.9350	1.070	154	Mali	3.5700	0.280
41	Netherlands	0.4810	2.080	100	Switzerland	0.9350	1.070	155	PortugueseGuin.	3.7000	0.270
42	South Vietnam	0.4880	2.050	101	Singapore	1.0100	0.990	156	Ethiopia	4.2700	0.234
43	Mexico	0.4900	2.040	102	Jordan	1.0100	0.990	157	Chad	4.3500	0.230
44	Germany Fed.Rep.	0.4975	2.010	103	Sudan	1.0410	0.960	158	Upper Volta	4.5400	0.220
45	Chile	0.5025	1.990	104	Ecuador	1.0520	0.950	159	Niger	5.2600	0.190
46	Japan	0.5050	1.980	105	Ryukyu Islands	1.0520	0.950	160	Dahomey	6.2500	0.160
47	India	0.5130	1.950	106	Malawi	1.0640	0.940	161	Burundi	7.1500	0.140
48	Zambia	0.5150	1.940	107	Cape Verde Isl.	1.0640	0.940	162	Ruanda	7.6900	0.130
49	Kuwait	0.5300	1.890	108	Morocco	1.0750	0.930	163	Yemen	7.690	0.130
50	Austria	0.5500	1.820	109	Indonesia	1.0750	0.930	164	Nepal	11.360	0.088

We shall attempt to elucidate this and review some of the factors likely to cause discrepancies in a listing such as in Table XXV.

We may choose to overlook, as extreme cases, at one end of the scale, the countries ranked 1 through 9, where either an intensive use of energy or a very low value of GNP is responsible for abnormally high values of the ratio: KEC/GNP.

We may also choose to overlook, at the other end of the scale, the countries ranked 150 through 164 which may be regarded as still in a pastoral stage where the very low use of energy accounts for the lowest values of the ratio of energy to GNP.

Even with these eliminations we still note a spread of 14 to 1 in the contents of energy per $ of GNP. As mentioned in the preceding pages the energy totals used throughout this report do not include any of the non-commercial forms of energy (wood, animal wastes, etc.,) These could account for as much as 50% or more of the total energy consumed. This however, could not account for the wide range that we note from one end of Table XXV to the other.

Sometimes, too, the differences in efficiency of large industrial installations or power plants as compared to inefficient or antiquated installations are cited and often labeled inefficiency in the use of energy.

There are other less substantial differences which are often cited when comparing energy use statistics as we are doing: difference in climate might account for greater use of energy for space heating although air-conditioning requirements may be an offsetting factor. However, these could not account for the 14 to 1 spread we have noted.

A major reason for this extremely wide range is that, whereas industrial processes are 'energy-intensive', services and agriculture are not.

This could be further analysed; for instance, mining generates fairly low GNP, in relation to the energy consumed, etc. Surinam, New Caledonia, Poland, South Africa are among the 14 countries which show the lowest ratio of GNP to KEC.

At the same low end of this ratio, we note Southern Yemen, the former British naval base of Aden, with its heavy energy requirements in connection with oil bunkering, etc., and relatively little generation of GNP.

Refinery requirements such as are present in the Netherland Antilles, Southern Yemen, Bahrain, Trinidad and Tobago, also appear to account for a high use of energy in relation to GNP.

Energy, Electricity and the Environment

At the other end of the scale, we note, from the Central African Republic to Nepal, 12 countries close to the pastoral stage where substantial amounts of GNP are generated with little expenditure of commercial energy, which accounts for the very high ratios of GNP to KEC.

The same general concept can be explained as follows:
Whether an economy consumes in energy the equivalent of 5 kilograms, or 360 grams, of coal for every $ of GNP it generates, the energy contents are still very low representing, if we accept 1 cent as the price of a kilogram of coal, between 5 cents and less than ½ cent out of every dollar.

It is not surprising therefore that, according to the type of the economy: industrial or agricultural, and according to the importance of services and of residential and private use, wide variations are noted even between countries which may, at first glance, appear to be at comparable stages of development.

Because of this wide range, which makes generalizations difficult, we shall now direct our comments to the summary-by-areas above:
On an area basis, we have narrowed the range to a little more than 4 to 1.

Western Europe generates $1 of GNP with approximately 1 Kg. of Energy Equivalent Coal.

At the other end, we find both Communist Asia and the Eastern Europe Communist countries with approximately $0.250 of GNP per KEC, but this concordance between two widely separated areas of the world is coincidental.

Communist Asia, although removed from the Great Leap Forward era with its proliferation of 'backyard blast furnaces', may still be making relatively inefficient use of its coal resources. It is however quite striking to note the disparity in the value of this ratio between the two Europes: 1 in Western Europe, 0.25 in Eastern Europe.

Since the similarity of technical standards excludes any possibility that there could be wide differences in the technological efficiency between one side and the other of the Iron Curtain, one may deduce that economic efficiency, in so far as the generation of GNP as the end product is concerned, is responsible for the disparity.

The emphasis placed by the Eastern bloc countries on industrial activity at the expense of consumer well-being is responsible for the high rate of growth noted in the industrial output, which is associated with the lower *per capita* income that we note.

From a global standpoint, it is noteworthy that, whereas the Communist World consumes 28% of the World energy while generating 17% of its GNP, the Free World uses 72% of the World energy while generating 83% of its GNP.

To a certain extent, the 2 to 1 disparity between the two Germanys is just as striking and is not very far from the disparity between their respective GNP *per capita* in 1967: $2,085 in West Germany, $1,300 in East Germany.

COMPARISON OF GROWTH TRENDS OF GNP AND ENERGY

We have investigated separately the growth trends of both GNP and of Energy and Table XXVI shows, for each country, the ratio between the two pattern indexes:

$$\frac{\% \text{ Pattern Index for GNP}}{\% \text{ Pattern Index for Energy}}$$

We define this ratio as the coefficient of elasticity of GNP in relation to Energy.

As we have stressed throughout this report, the Pattern Index is comparable to the percentage which measures Yearly Growth, the main difference being that *for a given pattern index* the percentage growth rate varies according to stages of growth, as shown in Chart 11.

Table XXVI, in which the countries are ranked in decreasing magnitude sequence of the coefficient of elasticity, shows that this coefficient is highest for the industrialized countries and lowest for the developing countries.

In other words, we can expect the GNP of industrialized countries to show decreasing contents of energy per unit of output, while developing countries will find that they have to use increasing amounts of energy per unit of GNP output.

Table XXVI indicates that, in spite of the impressive performance of countries such as Japan and Italy, their economy may be regarded as still in evolution from an agricultural to an industrial structure.

We can gauge the gradual transition from an agricultural economy to an industrial economy by looking at Table XXVI from which it appears that at the lower values of the elasticity ratio, in countries such as Sudan, Nepal, Algeria, etc, the GNP grows only 31% as fast as the use of energy, whereas in West Germany, Belgium and Luxembourg, the GNP increases more than twice as fast as the use of energy.

Although the correlation is far from impressive, it will be noted that, on the whole, low values for the elasticity coefficient are associated with high values of the ratio of GNP:KEC shown on Table XXV.

Since the elasticity coefficient gives a dynamic comparison of the same two quantities which the ratio GNP:KEC compares statically, this would indicate that, where the value of the GNP generated by one unit of energy is high, the trend is for the energy to increase faster than the GNP, towards reducing the spread between the two.

Conversely, where, in a highly industrialized country, the ratio of GNP to KEC is low, the tendency is for the GNP to increase faster than the energy, to bring the two closer together.

Energy, Electricity and the Environment

TABLE XXVI—Coefficient of elasticity—GNP pattern: energy pattern—1967

#	Country	Value	#	Country	Value	#	Country	Value
1	Belgium & Lux.	2.190	46	Singapore	0.715	93	Barbados	0.535
			47	Morocco	0.707	94	New Caledonia	0.530
2	Germany West	2.000				95	Italy	0.528
3	South Africa	1.878	48	Guatemala	0.693	96	Puerto Rico	0.525
4	Poland	1.700	49	Mauritania	0.691	97	Turkey	0.523
5	United Kingdom	1.575	50	Israel	0.690	98	Portuguese Guinea	0.506
6	Austria	1.370	51	French Guyana	0.688			
7	U.S.S.R.	1.318	52	Hungary	0.687	99	Malawi	0.500
8	Iceland	1.300	53	Switzerland	0.685	100	El Salvador	0.493
9	Germany East	1.250	54	Bolivia	0.685	101	Philippines	0.493
10	Australia	1.165	55	India	0.685	102	Uganda	0.483
11	Romania	1.100	56	Afghanistan	0.675	103	Burma	0.478
12	Taiwan	1.090	57	Brazil	0.675	104	Sierra Leone	0.476
13	Canada	1.070	58	Gabon	0.672	105	Trinidad & Tobago	0.476
14	France	1.060	59	Mauritius	0.667	106	Centr.Afric.Rep.	0.468
15	United States	1.044	60	Malaysia	0.660	107	Liberia	0.468
16	Czechoslovakia	1.010	61	Mexico	0.660	108	Ecuador	0.457
			62	Bahrain	0.658	109	Comecon Asia	0.453
17	Portugal	1.000	63	Bulgaria	0.658	110	Cuba	0.450
18	Yugoslavia	0.971	64	Mali	0.655	111	Uruguay	0.450
19	Iran	0.971	65	Cyprus	0.655	112	Upper Volta	0.438
20	Sweden	0.966	66	Reunion	0.654	113	Cameroun	0.412
21	Spain	0.931	67	Yemen	0.653	114	Ruanda	0.410
22	Denmark	0.912	68	Muscat & Oman	0.652	115	Senegal	0.407
			69	Finland	0.652	116	Indonesia	0.405
23	Albania	0.900	70	Tunisia	0.650	117	Panama	0.405
24	Netherlands	0.897	71	Iraq	0.641	118	Peru	0.401
25	Japan	0.875	72	Korea Republic	0.640			
26	Argentina	0.858	73	Cambodia	0.634	119	Tanzania	0.400
27	New Zealand	0.825	74	Honduras	0.625	120	Thailand	0.389
28	Ryukyu Islands	0.812	75	Guam	0.609	121	Ireland	0.389
29	Ivory Coast	0.808				122	Madagascar	0.388
			76	Brunei	0.600	123	French Oceania	0.381
30	Libya	0.790	77	Congo Brazzaville	0.600	124	Panama CanalZone	0.380
31	Kenya	0.789	78	U.A.R. Egypt	0.598	125	US Virgin Islands	0.375
32	Zambia	0.783	79	Angola	0.597	126	Dominican Rep.	0.375
33	Kuwait	0.782	80	Syria	0.595	127	Bermuda	0.371
34	Qatar	0.774	81	Mozambique	0.595	128	Bahama Islands	0.370
35	Hong Kong	0.766	82	Chile	0.587	129	Niger	0.370
36	Venezuela	0.765	83	Chad	0.586	130	Laos	0.366
37	Jordan	0.765	84	Martinique	0.583	131	Vietnam South	0.366
38	Nigeria	0.760	85	Nicaragua	0.578	132	Algeria	0.364
39	Norway	0.760	86	Ghana	0.577	133	Paraguay	0.360
40	Saudi Arabia	0.745	87	Ceylon	0.570	134	Jamaica	0.359
41	Ethiopia	0.738	88	Pakistan	0.568	135	Guadeloupe	0.340
42	Colombia	0.727	89	Guinea	0.568	136	Sudan	0.329
43	Congo Kinshasa	0.725	90	Malta	0.563	137	Nepal	0.322
44	Surinam	0.725	91	Costa Rica	0.556			
45	Greece	0.723	92	Lebanon	0.555	138	Somalia	0.234

In simplified terms, in a basically agricultural economy, since the main source of GNP is a low consumer of energy, economic growth is accompanied by the relatively higher uses of energy identified with the non-agricultural sectors of the economy. Therefore the GNP grows more slowly than the use of energy.

In a country which derives its main income from energy-intensive industries, economic growth in the non-industrial sectors of the economy is accompanied by a relatively lower incremental use of energy, and, therefore, the GNP grows faster than the use of energy.

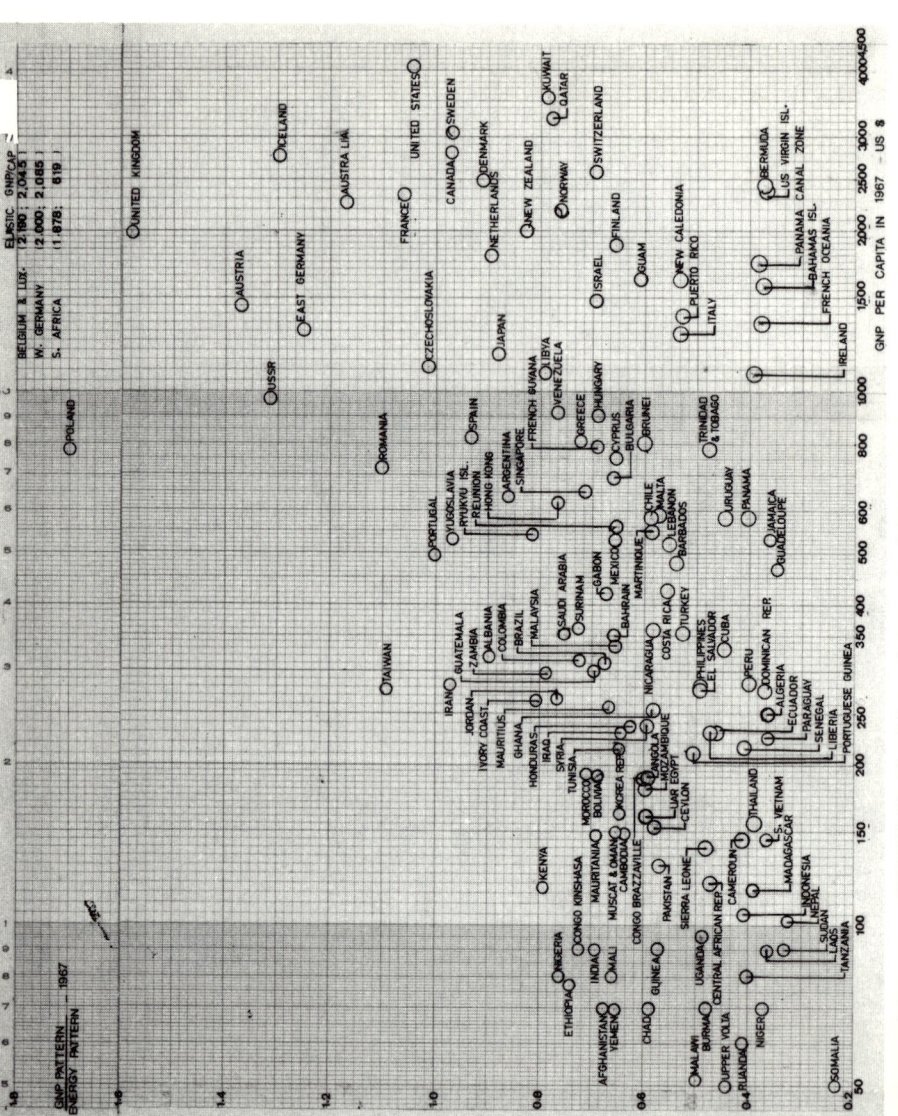

CHART 25 - Elasticity ratio: growth of GNP related to growth of energy

Energy, Electricity and the Environment

Chart 25 which plots the coefficient of elasticity in terms of the GNP per capita gives a comprehensive panorama and assessment of the type of economy with which each country can be identified.

For instance, for a coefficient of elasticity of 0.4—corresponding to the use of energy growing 2½ times as fast as the GNP—we see in succession: Tanzania, Madagascar, Thailand, Peru, Panama, Ireland and the U.S. Virgin Islands.

At about the 0.53 level of coefficient of elasticity, where GNP grows only half as fast as the use of Energy, we find: Pakistan, Ceylon, Turkey, Lebanon, New Caledonia.

At about the 0.67 level, where GNP grows only 2/3 as fast as the use of Energy, we find: Cambodia, Tunisia, Mexico and Finland.

At the 0.8 level, we find, within a 50 to 1 range in GNP *per capita*, Kenya, Zambia, Saudi Arabia, Hong Kong, Venezuela, Libya, Norway, Kuwait and Qatar, including a string of oil-producing countries in different geographical areas.

At the 1.1 level, where the GNP grows 10% faster than Energy, we find countries which may well be at comparable evolutionary stages in their balance of agriculture and of industry: Taiwan, Rumania, France, Canada and the United States.

With Chart 25, we can also travel through countries at the same GNP *per capita* level, but where the coefficient of elasticity varies over a range of 5 to 1, from Bermuda and the Bahamas to New Caledonia, to Finland, to Israel, to the Netherlands, to New Zealand, to Australia, to the United Kingdom, West Germany and Belgium and Luxembourg.

In other words, there are greater areas of similarities, as regards the economic structure, if one compares countries at widely different income *per capita* levels and the same value of the elasticity ratio than if one compares countries at the same *per capita* level and different values of the elasticity ratio.

In spite of the multiplicity of factors which govern the correlation between the rates of growth of GNP as compared with the rate of growth of energy, it is apparent that the GNP/Energy elasticity coefficient contributes a significant insight into the mechanism of growth.

We have seen in Chapter Five that the transfer of resources from agriculture to industry is regarded as one of the major factors of growth. This is confirmed by the analysis just presented.

In the United States, there has been a slight trend reversal as seen here:

	1954	1955	1956	1957	1958	1959	1960	1961	1962	1963	1964	1965	1966	1967	1968
Kilogram of Equivalent Coal per GNP in 1967 $	2.42	2.49	2.56	2.55	2.51	2.45	2.50	2.50	2.48	2.47	2.47	2.44	2.41	2.43	2.45

Since Energy is used less efficiently when output is reduced, it is likely that the past economic slowdown will result in this trend having being maintained through 1970. It is also likely that the steps being taken for the protection and beautification of the environment will initially contribute to a continuation of this trend: for instance, cooling towers, etc., cause a loss in efficiency.

On the other hand, it may also be expected that, as the steps now being taken for the protection of the environment take effect, economic growth will be stimulated due to the additional demands for equipment and services required for ecological reasons. Also the GNP proper will be increased due to the higher value of the higher quality products which will meet the environmental criteria.

It will be noted that, at its place in the elasticity scale, close to unity, the United States is likely to hover on each side of unity.

Because, as we have emphasized, the United States is a low user of energy as related to GNP, deviations such as we are experiencing now are not critical but, in view of the much greater demands expected in the future, these should not and will not be left uncorrected; this is commented upon in a later chapter.

TABLE XXVII—Installed electric capacity kilowatts—1968

Country	kW	Country	kW	Country	kW
United States	310,125,000	Hong Kong	1,054,000	Bermuda	69,600
U.S.S.R.	142,504,000	Israel	1,012,000	Bahrain	66,400
United Kingdom	59,628,000	Algeria	639,000	Malta	55,000
Japan	52,650,000	Ghana	631,000	Malawi	49,100
Germany Fed.Rep.	47,054,000	Morocco	494,000	Bahamas	46,100
Canada	35,933,000	Nigeria	485,000	Fiji Islands	42,800
France	34,133,000	Singapore	464,000	Haiti	40,800
Italy	30,264,000	Vietnam Republic	438,000	Sarawak	39,400
Spain	14,910,000	Lebanon	374,000	Nepal	37,700
India	14,314,000	Ecuador	290,000	Brunei	34,800
Sweden	13,731,000	Angola	288,900	Barbados	31,600
Australia	12,095,000	Ryukyu Islands	287,200	Greenland	31,500
Norway	12,030,000	Afghanistan	275,000	Sabah	30,800
East Germany	11,673,000	Tunisia	262,000	Faeroe Islands	27,000
Poland	11,591,000	Burma	260,000	Papua	25,500
Czechoslovakia	10,071,000	Trinidad & Tobago	253,000	Gabon	25,000
Switzerland	9,500,000	Costa Rica	236,600	Mauritania	25,000
Netherlands	9,296,000	Bolivia	222,000	Togo	22,400
Brazil	8,555,000	Ceylon	217,000	Congo Brazzaville	22,000
Belgium	7,540,000	Syria	216,000	New Guinea	19,500
Austria	7,056,000	Iceland	193,000	Ceuta & Melilla	17,500
Mexico	5,969,000	Dominican Rep.	192,600	Macau	17,500
Argentina	5,836,000	Cyprus	175,000	Gibraltar	16,400
Romania	5,611,000	Saudi Arabia	173,100	French Polynesia	14,000
Yugoslavia	4,700,000	El Salvador	171,000	Centr. Afric. Rep.	12,800
Finland	4,635,000	Cameroon	170,000	American Samoa	11,000
Denmark	3,920,000	Libya	168,500	Upper Volta	10,600
Bulgaria	3,462,000	Nicaragua	156,600	Nauru	7,600
New Zealand	3,138,000	Kenya	153,000	Cayman Islands	7,400
Venezuela	2,740,000	Liberia	152,100	Christmas Islands	7,400
U.A.R. Egypt	2,725,000	Guatemala	149,600	Gambia	7,000
Hungary	2,601,000	Canary Islands	144,000	Somalia	6,200
Colombia	2,368,000	West Malaysia	139,000	British Honduras	6,000
China Taiwan	2,062,000	Panama	128,900	Western Samoa	5,800
Portugal	2,030,000	Panama Canal Zone	110,600	Portuguese Guinea	5,600
Turkey	1,973,000	Paraguay	108,400	Burundi	5,200
Pakistan	1,731,000	Mauritius	101,400	SaoTome & Principe	4,300
Chile	1,720,000	US Virgin Islands	99,300	New Hebrides	3,600
Greece	1,715,000	Sudan	97,400	Spanish Sahara	3,430
Peru	1,629,000	Senegal	95,000	St. Vincent	3,400
Korea Republic	1,453,000	Guyana	92,100	Cape Verde Isl.	3,000
Cuba	1,410,000	Honduras	91,000	Tonga	1,900
Ireland	1,292,000	Guam	90,000	Seychelles Isl.	1,700
Luxembourg	1,153,000	Southern Yemen	82,700	Ifni	1,100
Iran	1,089,000	Cambodia	75,000	St. Helena	230

Energy, Electricity and the Environment

USE OF ELECTRICITY

Facing Table XXVII introduces this section with a list of the total installed electric capacity expressed in kilowatts, for each country.

INSTALLED ELECTRIC CAPACITY FOR ALL COUNTRIES OF THE WORLD

The use of one kilowatt during one hour represents a consumption of one kilowatt-hour which may cost about 3 cents on a residential basis and less than 2 cents to a large industrial user.

Modern electric power plants surpass 1,000,000 Kilowatts in size. On the average, 4,500 hours a year (out of 8,760) may be regarded as corresponding to the normal utilization of electric power capacity but because of the high capital cost of the new large 1,000,000 kw. nuclear power plants, efforts are made to run these at full capacity for a high portion of the time.

Table XXVIII shows the total generation of electricity. This is measured at the power plant and represents the net production at departure of the high voltage transmission lines which transport the electricity. The losses in these transmission lines and subsequent distribution systems are included in the total shown.

As we have already mentioned, the data in Table XXIX is often mentioned for selected countries; Norway, Canada and Sweden are ahead of the United States in *per capita* use of electricity. This and a number of related aspects are discussed in subsequent chapters.

ELECTRICITY AND THE ENVIRONMENT

The surging concern about the degradation of our environment has focused public attention on estimates of future energy requirements. In certain quarters, questions have been raised on whether the expansion of our consumption of electricity is not getting out of hand, also on whether we were making an efficient use of this energy. Simultaneously, fears have been expressed by others that power shortages are imminent in some areas because of low reserve margins in generating capacity.

Because of these concerns, the author was asked to prepare, for the *Electrical World*, two separate articles[20, 21] parts of which were extracted from material prepared for this volume into which,

TABLE XXVIII—Use of electricity—billion kilowatt-hours—1968

Country	Value	Country	Value	Country	Value
WORLD TOTAL	4,203.803	Iraq	2.325	Paraguay	0.179
United States	1,434.908	Indonesia	2.080	Southern Yemen	0.178
U.S.S.R.	636.191	Kuwait	1.970	Jordan	0.156
Japan	265.074	Uruguay	1.825	Sierra Leone	0.144
United Kingdom	223.972	Singapore	1.639	Fiji Islands	0.132
Germany Fed. Rep.	210.325	Algeria	1.591	Cambodia	0.128
Canada	176.841	Morocco	1.543	Malawi	0.117
France	119.404	Netherl. Antilles	1.215	Haiti	0.115
Italy	106.127	Ryukyu Islands	1.211	Barbados	0.110
Communist Asia	82.567	Trinidad & Tobago	1.139	Brunei	0.104
Germany East	63.309	Nigeria	1.105	Reunion	0.092
Sweden	58.039	Surinam	1.076	Sarawak	0.088
Norway	56.707	Jamaica	1.068	Gabon	0.074
Poland	55.844	Lebanon	1.036	Qatar	0.074
India	48.000	Cameroon	1.006	Guadeloupe	0.072
Australia	46.504	Ecuador	0.850	Martinique	0.072
Spain	44.099	Saudi Arabia	0.850	Ruanda	0.069
Czechoslovakia	43.607	Costa Rica	0.833	Sabah	0.068
South Africa	43.485	South Vietnam	0.830	Papua & New Guinea	0.068
Brazil	38.181	Syria	0.773	Faeroe Islands	0.063
Netherlands	33.345	Albania	0.730	Greenland	0.063
Belgium & Luxem.	29.590	Iceland	0.729	Togo	0.056
Romania	25.605	Dominican Rep.	0.699	Kuwait Neutr. Zone	0.055
Switzerland	25.210	Tunisia	0.678	Congo Brazzaville	0.055
Mexico	22.872	Bolivia	0.672	Nepal	0.055
Austria	21.216	Panama	0.663	Macau	0.046
Yugoslavia	20.235	Ceylon	0.650	Leeward Islands	0.046
Finland	18.103	New Caledonia	0.643	French Oceania	0.045
Argentina	17.851	Kenya	0.626	Mauritania	0.044
Bulgaria	15.764	Guatemala	0.610	Gibraltar	0.039
Hungary	15.764	Panama Canal Zone	0.599	Windward Islands	0.035
New Zealand	12.295	Guam	0.597	Mali	0.035
Denmark	11.834	El Salvador	0.582	American Samoa	0.034
Venezuela	10.814	Liberia	0.573	Centr. Afric. Rep.	0.034
China Taiwan	10.036	Burma	0.553	Afars & Issas	0.034
Greece	7.360	Uganda	0.541	Laos	0.033
Colombia	7.000	Cyprus	0.510	Chad	0.031
Philippines	7.000	Nicaragua	0.484	Niger	0.028
Chile	6.918	Angola	0.457	Dahomey	0.025
Turkey	6.886	Mozambique	0.390	Upper Volta	0.023
U.A.R. Egypt	6.735	Ivory Coast	0.372	Nauru	0.019
Pakistan	6.500	Ethiopia	0.361	Yemen	0.017
Korea Republic	6.400	Bahrain	0.350	Christmas Islands	0.017
Portugal	6.281	Sudan	0.334	Burundi	0.017
Puerto Rico	6.182	Afghanistan	0.325	French Guyana	0.016
Israel	5.506	Tanzania	0.299	British Honduras	0.016
Iran	5.008	Senegal	0.287	Somalia	0.016
Ireland	4.980	Guyana	0.287	Equatorial Guinea	0.015
Peru	4.880	Honduras	0.280	West Irian	0.012
Cuba	4.780	Libya	0.274	Gambia	0.012
Hong Kong	3.948	US Virgin Islands	0.258	Portuguese Guinea	0.009
Thailand	3.137	Guinea	0.225	Western Samoa	0.009
Zambia	3.413	Malta	0.219	Cape Verde Isl.	0.009
Malaysia	2.920	Bahama Islands	0.215	Brit. Solomon Isl.	0.008
Southern Rhodesia	2.898	Mauritius	0.203	New Hebrides	0.008
Congo Kinshasa	2.599	Madagascar	0.195	Falkland Islands	0.002
Ghana	2.589	Bermuda	0.190	ST. Pierre & Miquelon	0.002

Energy, Electricity and the Environment

TABLE XXIX—Use of electricity—kilowatt-hours 'per capita'—1968

Norway	14,847	Greece	836	Saudi Arabia	119
Panama Canal Zone	10,696	Singapore	824	Honduras	116
Canada	8,513	Cyprus	819	Sabah	111
Sweden	7,730	Argentina	755	Papua	109
United States	7,133	Taiwan	745	Communist Asia	107
New Caledonia	6,697	Chile	739	Morocco	105
Guam	5,962	Malta	686	New Hebrides	102
Netherl. Antilles	5,651	Portugal	663	Sarawak	95
Kuwait Neutral Z.	5,500	Uruguay	647	Windward Islands	93
New Zealand	4,469	Cuba	592	Thailand	93
Christmas Islands	4,250	Southern Rhodesia	586	India	91
US Virgin Islands	4,448	Jamaica	558	Ivory Coast	90
Switzerland	4,087	Costa Rica	509	Angola	85
United Kingdom	4,042	Liberia	507	Paraguay	80
Australia	3,865	Mexico	483	Senegal	77
Finland	3,861	Panama	483	Jordan	74
Bermuda	3,799	French Oceania	449	Uganda	66
East Germany	3,705	Barbados	436	Western Samoa	65
Kuwait	3,648	Brazil	432	Congo Brazzaville	63
Iceland	3,626	Afars & Issas	414	Kenya	61
West Germany	3,495	Lebanon	401	Guinea	59
Nauru	3,166	St.Pierre&Miquelon	399	Sierra Leone	58
Czechoslovakia	3,036	French Guyana	399	Ceylon	54
Belgium & Luxem.	2,972	Guyana	399	Brit. Solomon Isl.	54
Austria	2,886	Peru	382	Mozambique	53
Surinam	2,869	Albania	361	Equatorial Guinea	53
U.S.S.R.	2,675	Colombia	353	Pakistan	53
Japan	2,622	Malaysia	332	South Vietnam	47
Netherlands	2,616	Leeward Islands	323	Mauritania	39
Denmark	2,429	Ghana	309	Cape Verde Isl.	36
France	2,389	Iraq	269	Gambia	34
Puerto Rico	2,270	Nicaragua	262	Togo	31
Italy	2,011	Fiji Islands	261	Madagascar	29
South Africa	2,005	Mauritius	257	Malawi	27
Israel	2,005	Guadeloupe	226	Haiti	24
Bulgaria	1,883	Martinique	222	Tanzania	24
Bahrain	1,750	Reunion	215	Sudan	22
Poland	1,728	U.A.R. Egypt	212	Centr. Afric. Rep.	22
Ireland	1,711	Korea Republic	210	Afghanistan	20
Faeroe Islands	1,657	Turkey	205	Burma	20
Gibraltar	1,559	Philippines	195	Ruanda	20
Hungary	1,501	Iran	185	Cambodia	19
Greenland	1,399	Cameroon	180	Indonesia	18
Spain	1,345	El Salvador	178	Nigeria	17
Romania	1,298	Macao	176	Portuguese Guinea	17
Ryukyu Islands	1,254	Dominican Republic	173	Ethiopia	14
Bahama Islands	1,214	Congo Kinshasa	155	West Irian	13
WORLD AVERAGE	1,207	Gabon	154	Laos	11
Venezuela	1,116	Libya	151	Dahomey	9
Trinidad & Tobago	1,115	Ecuador	149	Chad	8
American Samoa	1,096	Southern Yemen	148	Mali	7
Yugoslavia	1,038	Tunisia	145	Niger	7
Hong Kong	1,005	Bolivia	143	Nepal	5
Falkland Islands	1,000	British Honduras	137	Somalia	5
Brunei	928	Syria	135	Upper Volta	4
Qatar	924	Guatemala	125	Burundi	4
Zambia	836	Algeria	122	Yemen	3

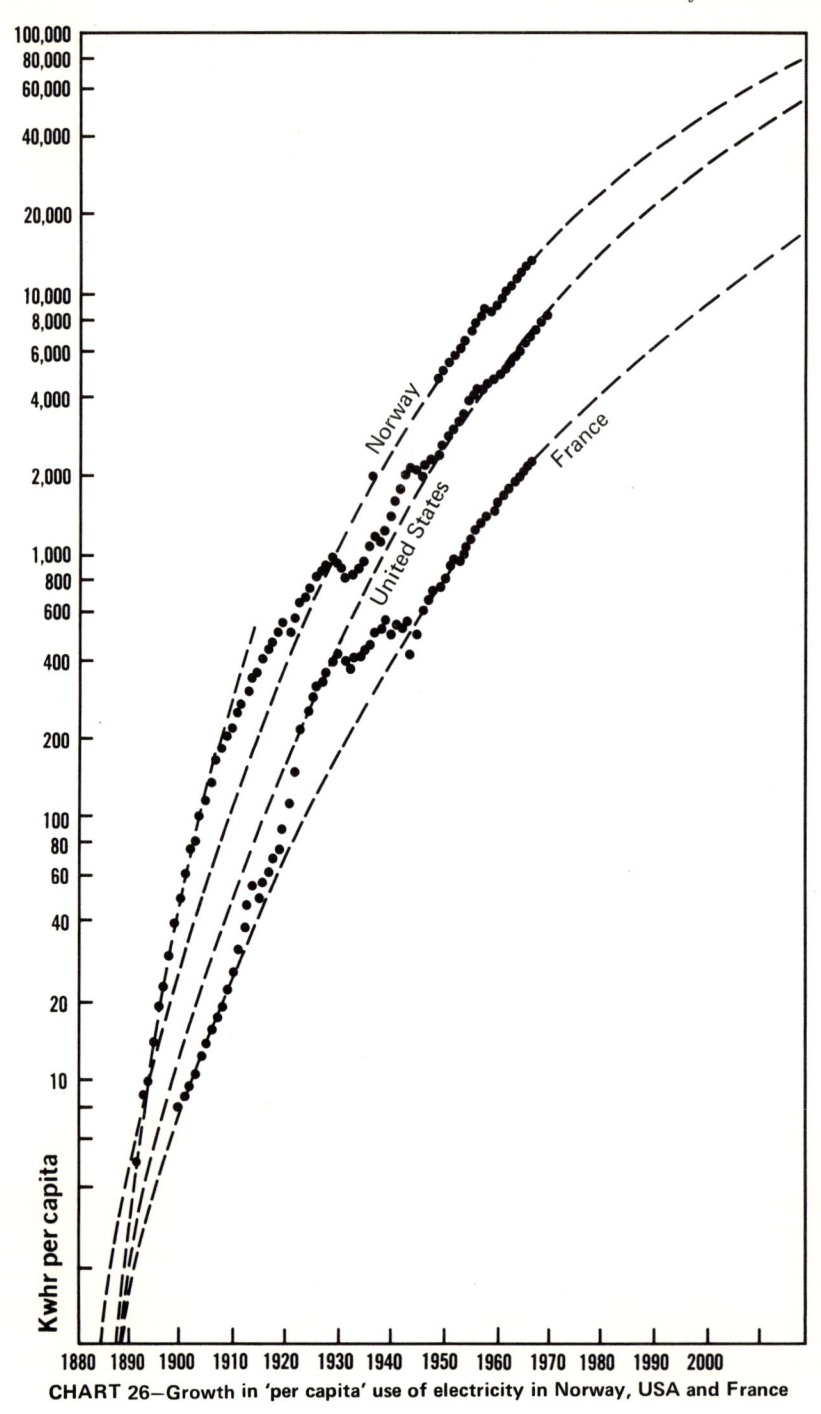

CHART 26—Growth in 'per capita' use of electricity in Norway, USA and France

Energy, Electricity and the Environment

through the courtesy of McGraw-Hill Inc., they are now incorporated in a re-edited form.

After studying, for all countries of the world, data on the growth of use of electricity, it was found that, similarly to the growth of energy use, the *per capita* kwhr of any national economy adhered— with the same reservations as were voiced for the growth of GNP—to a single family of curves.

Chart 26, shows the Kwh *per capita* recorded, point by point, since 1891 for the U.S. since 1900 for France, and since 1949 for Norway.

Out of the family of mathematically related patterns into which the recorded growth history of all countries of the world fit, the patterns for these three countries have been shown in dashed trend lines.

It is of interest to note that, except for easily recognized major disruptions such as the 1929-1933 depression and World War II, Chart 26 shows a fairly smooth growth, either along the pattern identified with the 1946-1968 history or along other patterns of the same family.

The U.S. and France are two countries for which the most complete series of unbroken data are available. Empirical curves fitted to the period 1946 to 1967, when carried back to 1.0 Kwh *per capita*, show a 'starting date' in the early 1880s. This checks closely with the startup of the Pearl Street Station by Thomas Edison in 1882. It also concurs with the 1881 date for the Exposition Universelle in France, at which the use of 'Gramme' generators identified Paris as the 'Ville Lumière' or City of Light.

As a matter of interest, the present program for France's new Five-Year Plan incorporates a 20% faster rate of growth of electricity use than the continuation of the pattern of the past 20 years would indicate.

This same historic record of U.S. generation growth has been used to arrive at the long-term trends shown in the accompanying charts and tables. These are presented to bring out different aspects as explained in the following.

Table A tabulates statistical data from 1891 through 1970. These are extrapolated, through the Gompertz equation, to the year 2020.

The historic record for the U.S. (Table A) shows the yearly rate of increase in electricity generation fluctuating above and below 7.0% over the period from 1925 to 1970. Because of the unusual prolongation of this plateau (due to the 1929-33 depression, World War II, etc.) the impression has been gained that the 7% rate is here

TABLE A—US History and Projections

	Millions population	KWH 'per capita'	Total kwhr millions	Average annual growth rate during 10-year period	
1891	64	2	129		
1895	70	14	974	1891-1900	45 %
1900	76	49	3,729	1895-1905	25.9 %
1905	84	116	9,723	1900-1910	18.4 %
1910	92	220	20,330	1905-1915	13.8 %
1915	100	355	35,695	1910-1920	11 %
1920	106	540	57,499	1915-1925	9.2 %
1925	116	742	85,939	1920-1930	7.3 %
1930	123	944	116,229	1925-1935	3.5 %
1935	127	945	120,272	1930-1940	4.3 %
1940	132	1,379	182,021	1935-1945	8.6 %
1945	132	2,067	273,817	1940-1950	7.95 %
1950	151	2,582	390,460	1945-1955	8.8 %
1955	164	3,853	633,078	1950-1960	8.1 %
1960	180	4,718	849,097	1955-1965	3.15 %
1965	194	5,969	1,156,781	1960-1970	6.95 %
1970	205	8,100	1,660,000	1965-1975	7.15 %
1975	221	10,450	2,310,000	1970-1980	7.05 %
1980	236	14,000	3,300,000	1975-1985	6.85 %
1985	249	17,350	4,300,000	1980-1990	5.65 %
1990	261	21,800	5,690,000	1985-1995	5.15 %
1995	273	25,900	7,090,000	1990-2000	4.55 %
2000	285	31,000	8,850,000	1995-2005	4.25 %
2005	295	36,350	10,710,000	2000-2010	3.95 %
2010	304	42,500	13,000,000	2005-2015	3.65 %
2015	313	49,000	15,320,000	2010-2020	3.35 %
2020	322	55,800	17,950,000		

to stay. In fact, this figure is the median yearly rate of growth associated only with the industrialization stage of most economies.

The assumption of a continued high growth rate has led to genuine apprehension as to the problems it would create. In Table A, we do project that an average rate of 7.05% will be maintained during the next decade. However, from then on the annual rate of growth will be about one-sixth less every 10 years. Thus, the growth rate drops to 6% after 1980, 5% after 1990, etc.

To maintain the 7% annual increase through 1990 would require a very high level of general economic growth and a severe strain on the economy.

It is believed that this long-range pattern permits continuation of the rhythm of economic growth to which the U.S. economy is

Energy, Electricity and the Environment 163

accustomed without slamming the brakes on orderly and balanced growth. Yet it, in itself, constitutes a built-in, constructive, restraint on unchecked growth.

Lately the question is being asked: 'Why not start right now to curtail our growth in the use of electric power, and thereby preserve our environment from further degradation?' This can be best answered in two steps:

First, what would such a 'pulling of the plug' do to our economy?

Table A and Charts 27 and 28 show that the yearly rate of increase, in percent, of the United States use of electricity *per capita* will be decreasing substantially, at the same time as the use of electricity grows.

Any further curtailment of our rate of growth in the use of electricity and of energy and, consequently of the rate of GNP growth, would plunge the economy of the country into a recession followed by a full fledged depression leading to catastrophic chaos.

The patterns of growth for *per capita* consumption of electricity, for the total use of energy and for the Gross National Product are indissolubly and inseparably related (Chart 29). Any attempt to achieve a faster rate in any of these would have to be 'matched' with a corresponding acceleration in the other two. Conversely, any slowdown in the rate of expansion for electricity generation below what is implied in the natural growth pattern would cause a corresponding slowdown in the rate of economic growth.

Electricity has a high 'amplification factor' on the Gross National Product. On the average, every dollar of GNP requires the simultaneous availability of 3 cents worth of electricity. Any reduction in the amount of electric power available is likely to result in a relatively greater reduction of GNP, until equilibrium is restored at a lower level. And, since as much as 70% of electric power consumption is for commercial and industrial purposes, a forced reduction in the availability of this vital form of energy will have an adverse effect on employment.

Secondly, an answer should be given to the question, 'Why not accept a decline in the rate of economic growth, and aim toward a zero-growth economy?'

A normal pace of economic growth is the answer. One which provides the resources needed to preserve our progress, to enhance social justice and beautify the environment.

To imply that growth should be curtailed or arrested so that we shall not be afflicted by some of its by-products makes as much

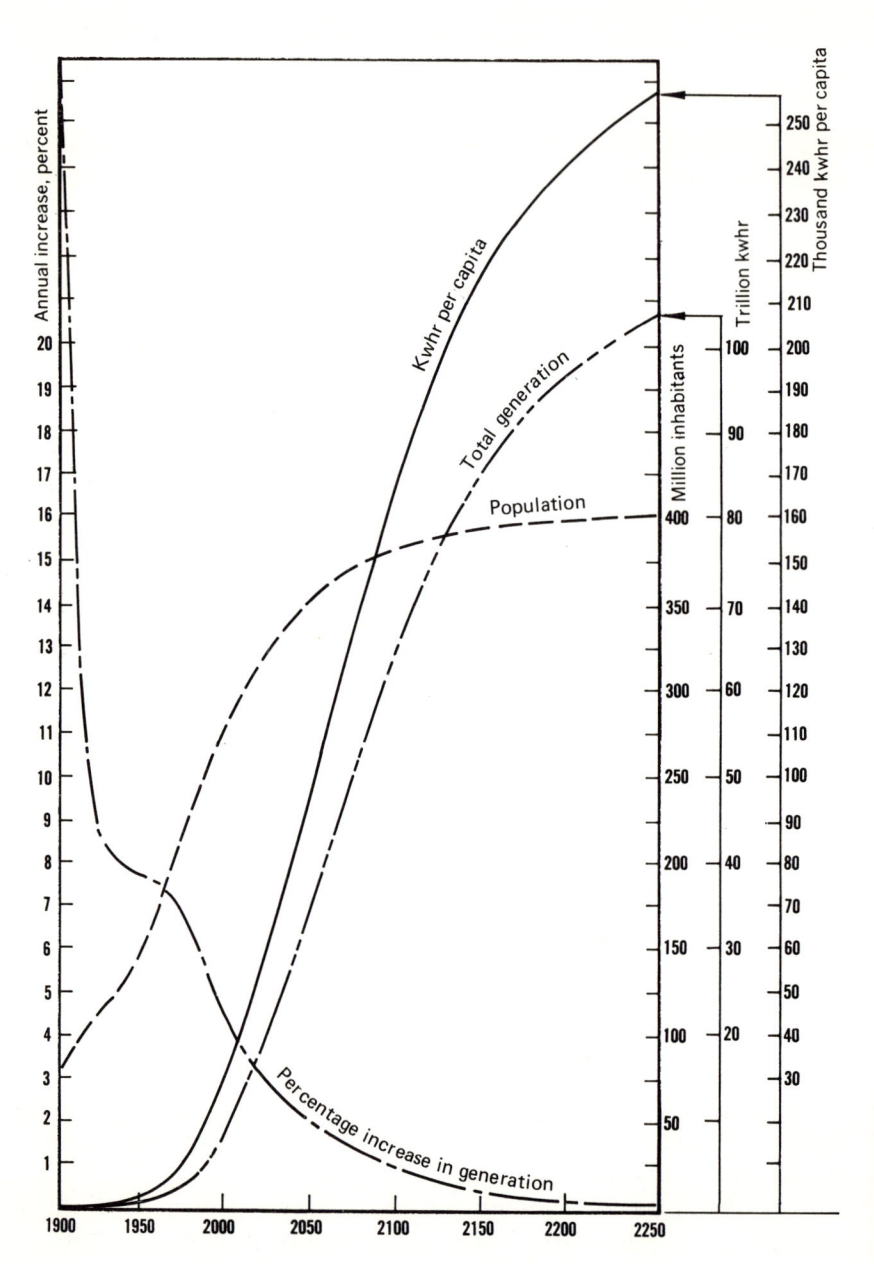

CHART 27—Growth of use of electricity in the U.S.A.

Energy, Electricity and the Environment 165

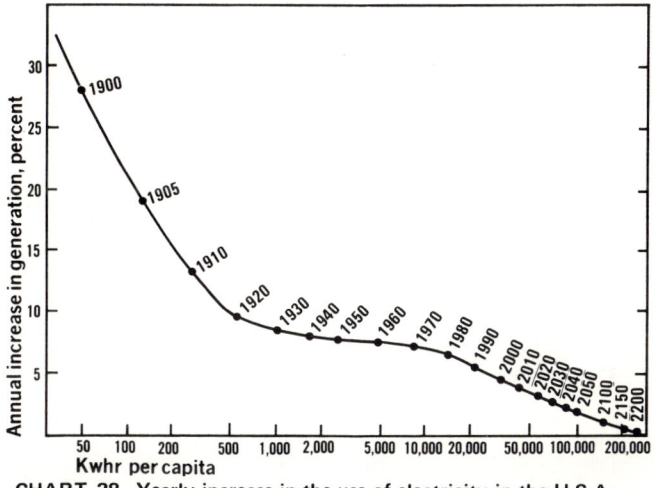

CHART 28—Yearly increase in the use of electricity in the U.S.A.

social and economic sense as a father wishing that his boy's growth should be stunted so that he can keep on wearing the same clothes year after year!

For those who would take exception to this simile on the grounds that we have reached maturity and should readjust our programs accordingly, we would call attention to Chart 29. We will continue growing, in terms of annual *per capita* use, for many years. Today, with only 8,100 kWh *per capita*, the U.S. stands at only 6% of the 130,000 kWh expected one century from now.

The consumption of 31,000 kWh *per capita* which we forecast for the U.S. in the year 2000 is only twice the recorded *per capita* use in Norway for 1968. And Norway must be considered one of the most environmentally conscious nations of the world. Thus, our forecast should contain no element of surprise, and should certainly not constitute any cause for alarm.

The promises of the benefits to be expected from future growth to 130,000 kWh *per capita* in the next hundred years are already within our present horizon. The use of electricity is destined to augment:

(i) In transportation within cities, by the greater use of battery-operated cars and buses;
(ii) In high-speed trains for mass transportation in suburban and interurban services, where much higher speed will permit green spaces to be conveniently reached; and

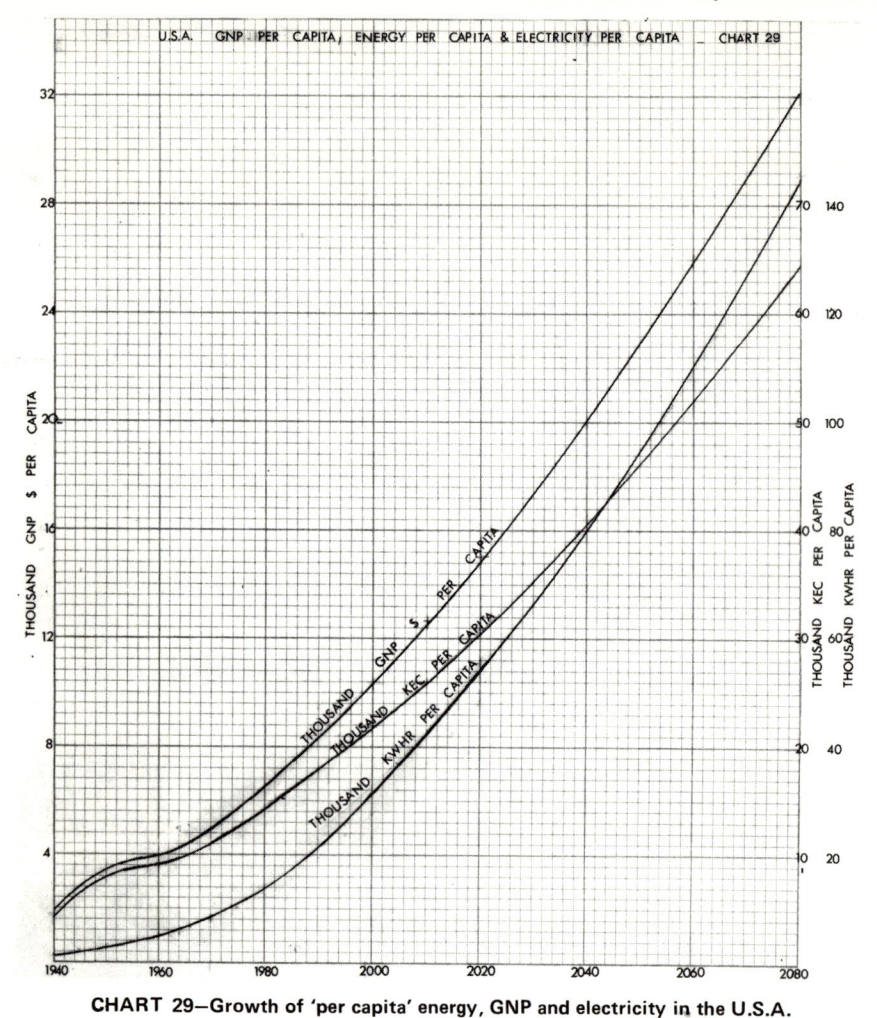

CHART 29—Growth of 'per capita' energy, GNP and electricity in the U.S.A.

(iii) In chemical, petroleum, mining and metal industries, where electric energy will make possible new and improved extraction, refining and conversion processes.

A substantial share of the additional power will be used in recycling the wastes produced in other sectors of the economy and in eliminating other sources of pollution. Electricity—generated largely from pollution-free nuclear power plants—will be increasingly substituted for other forms of energy, particularly those forms which tend to cause air and water pollution.

Energy, Electricity and the Environment 167

Electric power will also make it economically possible to tap vast sources of wealth—for instance, in the large-scale use of water-desalting, in the reclamation of desert or infertile areas, in the use of waste heat from power plants to increase agricultural yields, in the exploration of offshore oceanic and mineral resources.

Because of its unique adaptability to a wide range of needs, increased use of electricity is an exceptionally effective tool for improving the overall quality of life. It will continue to be a powerful future resource in our drive for social improvement, with which the use of electricity has always been identified.

AT ITS 'PER CAPITA' GNP LEVEL, THE UNITED STATES IS A MINIMUM USER OF ELECTRICITY AND OF ENERGY IN RELATION TO THE GNP THESE CONTRIBUTE TO GENERATE

Table XXX lists the electricity contents, expressed in kilowatthours, of a dollar of GNP for all countries. This is also shown, plotted in terms of kWh *per capita* in Chart 30.

In addition Chart 30 also incorporates curves of constant GNP *per capita*, by means of which the eye can follow countries at the same GNP *per capita* level. This global presentation, which provides a clear definition of the upper and lower boundaries of the kWh per $ GNP range covered by all 163 countries, brings out that the United States use of 1.64 kWh per $ of GNP is, actually, at the very bottom of the range, right on the lower boundary.

Let us analyse what this means: At the 1967, 6,662 kWh *per capita* use or at the $ 4,040 GNP *per capita* level, the kWh contents of one $ of GNP are lower for the United States than for any other country, at anywhere near the same GNP *per capita* level.

Since it might appear that plotting the chart in terms of kWh *per capita* might not be as meaningful as it would be in terms of GNP *per capita*, we have shown in chart 31 the 30 countries which have the highest *per capita* kWh use and for which the GNP *per capita* is 970 or higher. (In 1967 the GNP *per capita* of the U.S.S.R. was 970).

Even more strikingly than Chart 30, this plot brings out that the United States achieves the highest GNP *per capita* in the world with minimum use of electricity in relation to GNP.

The same as in Chart 30, the countries which, at their own level of *per capita* wealth also have minimum use of electricity are Denmark, closely approached by France.

TABLE XXX—Kilowatt-hours per $ of gross national product—1967

#	Country	Value	#	Country	Value	#	Country	Value
1	Southern Yemen	7.01	52	Chile	1.29	106	Algeria	0.45
2	Panama Canal Zone	6.95	53	Uruguay	1.28	107	Western Samoa	0.45
3	Surinam	6.41	54	U.A.R. Egypt	1.27	108	Paraguay	0.42
4	Norway	6.18	55	Cameroun	1.25	109	Guadeloupe	0.42
5	Netherl. Antilles	4.80	56	Pakistan	1.19	110	Honduras	0.39
6	Bahrain	4.74	57	US Virgin Islands	1.16	111	Angola	0.38
7	New Caledonia	4.43	58	Brunei	1.16	112	Guatemala	0.37
8	Guam	3.48	59	Argentina	1.13	113	Sierra Leone	0.36
9	South Africa	3.06	60	Singapore	1.13	114	Reunion	0.36
10	Canada	2.89	61	Venezuela	1.11	115	Gambia	0.36
11	Zambia	2.75	62	Costa Rica	1.11	116	Korea Republic	0.35
12	Hong Kong	2.74	63	Puerto Rico	1.10	117	Martinique	0.35
13	East Germany	2.68	64	Mauritius	1.08	118	Senegal	0.34
14	U.S.S.R.	2.57	65	Communist Asia	1.07	119	Saudi Arabia	0.33
15	Czechoslovakia	2.54	66	Malta	1.06	120	Burma	0.33
16	Gibraltar	2.49	67	Colombia	1.05	121	Ceylon	0.32
17	Taiwan	2.48	68	Cyprus	1.04	122	Afghanistan	0.31
18	Bulgaria	2.40	69	France	0.98	123	Ivory Coast	0.30
19	Southern Rhodesia	2.32	70	Greece	0.97	124	Tanzania	0.30
20	Sweden	2.22	71	Jamaica	0.97	125	Qatar	0.30
21	American Samoa	2.18	72	Malaysia	0.92	126	South Vietnam	0.30
22	New Zealand	2.15	73	Faeroe Islands	0.92	127	Ruanda	0.28
23	Ryukyu Islands	2.14	74	India	0.91	128	Gabon	0.28
24	Poland	2.07	75	Guyana	0.91	129	French Oceania	0.28
25	Japan	2.05	76	Denmark	0.89	130	West Irian	0.28
26	United Kingdom	1.92	77	Mexico	0.88	131	Mozambique	0.27
27	Finland	1.92	78	Albania	0.88	132	Jordan	0.27
28	Austria	1.84	79	Fiji Islands	0.84	133	Brit.Solomon Isl.	0.26
29	Yugoslavia	1.81	80	Bolivia	0.83	134	Papua & NewGuinea	0.25
30	Greenland	1.70	81	Kuwait	0.80	135	Sudan	0.24
			82	Bahama Islands	0.80	136	Madagascar	0.24
	World Average	1.68	83	Barbados	0.80	137	New Hebrides	0.24
			84	Ghana	0.76	138	Nigeria	0.23
31	Congo Kinshasa	1.68	85	Iraq	0.73	139	Mauritania	0.23
32	United States	1.64	86	Panama	0.70	140	Haiti	0.20
33	Romania	1.64	87	Lebanon	0.69	141	Togo	0.19
34	Australia	1.62	88	Dominican Rep.	0.66	142	Equatorial Guinea	0.19
35	Hungary	1.56	89	Uganda	0.65	143	Indonesia	0.17
36	Switzerland	1.55	90	Nicaragua	0.65	144	Ethiopia	0.17
37	West Germany	1.53	91	Tunisia	0.63	145	Centr.Afric.Rep.	0.16
38	Ireland	1.52	92	Guinea	0.62	146	Cape Verde Isl.	0.14
39	Liberia	1.52	93	Peru	0.61	147	Laos	0.12
40	Spain	1.50	94	Macao	0.61	148	Libya	0.11
41	Italy	1.48	95	Portugal	0.60	149	Dahomey	0.11
42	Cuba	1.46	96	Ecuador	0.59	150	Cambodia	0.10
43	Philippines	1.45	97	El Salvador	0.59	151	Chad	0.10
44	Bermuda	1.44	98	Afars & Issas	0.55	152	Somalia	0.10
45	Iran	1.43	99	Turkey	0.54	153	Mali	0.09
46	Belgium & Lux.	1.34	100	Morocco	0.53	154	Niger	0.09
47	Netherlands	1.31	101	Syria	0.52	155	Portuguese Guinea	0.07
48	Israel	1.31	102	Kenya	0.50	156	Upper Volta	0.08
49	Trinidad & Tobago	1.31	103	French Guyana	0.50	157	Burundi	0.08
50	Iceland	1.30	104	Malawi	0.47	158	Yemen	0.04
51	Brazil	1.29	105	Thailand	0.45	159	Nepal	0.03

Energy, Electricity and the Environment

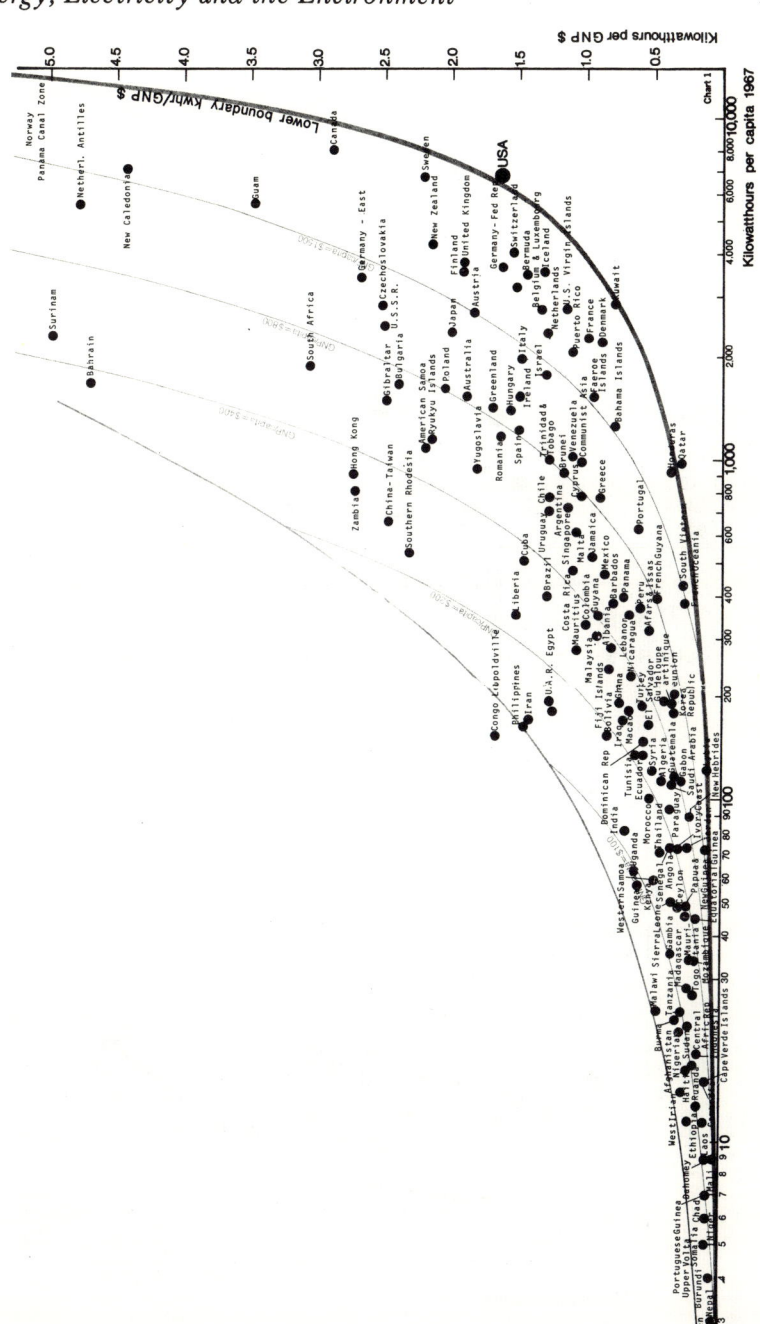

169

CHART 30—Contents of electricity per $ of GNP v. kilowatt-hours 'per capita'

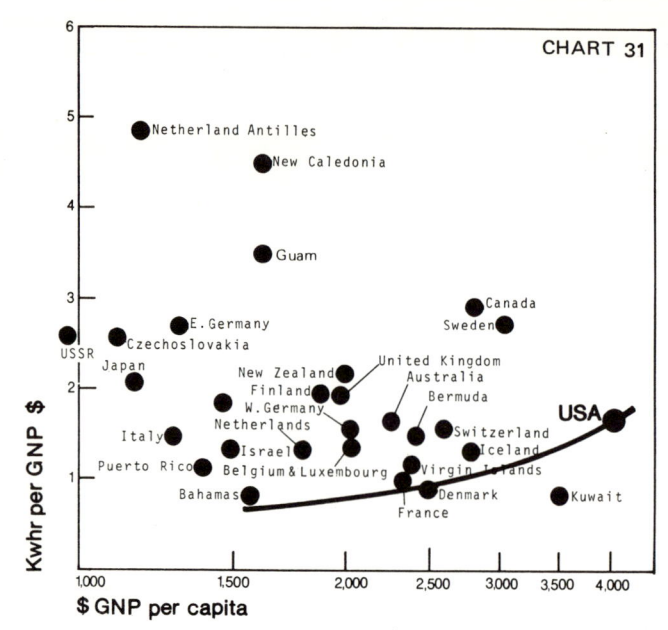

CHART 31—Contents of electricity per $ of GNP, v. GNP 'per capita'

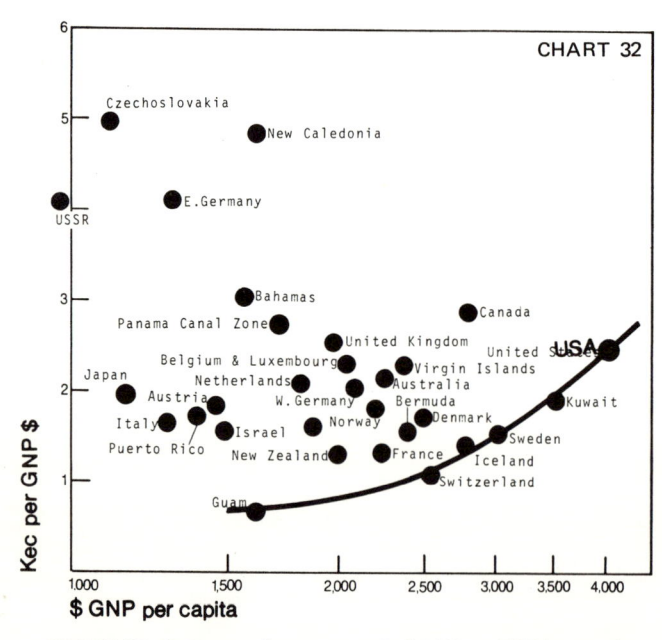

CHART 32—Contents of energy per $ of GNP, v. GNP 'per capita'

Energy, Electricity and the Environment

One reason is the high economic and technological efficiency which is achieved in our agricultural and industrial output as well as in the production of related services.

Another contributing reason to our low use of electricity in relation to GNP is that, as compared to some of the countries, such as Sweden, Canada, Norway, which, owing to the abundance of their hydroelectric resources, are large users of electricity, our own use of electricity represents a relatively lower share of the total consumption of energy, but, also from that point of view: total use of energy, as related to GNP, the United States still proves to be a 'minimum' user.

This aspect has been separately brought out in Chart 32, also plotted in terms of GNP *per capita*, which, for the same countries as in Chart 31, shows an ordinates: kilograms of coal equivalent per $ of GNP.

Summarizing, we have, through these three charts, confirmed and explained the 'rock-bottom' use of electricity and of energy in the United States in relation to the GNP.

It will be noted that, for the United States, the contents of energy per unit of GNP are equivalent to 2.45 kg. of coal or 3.77 lbs. of fuel oil.

Of these, 75.6% are used for purposes other than electricity generation (industry, transportation, heating, etc.) and the balance: 0.6 KEC (equivalent to 0.92 lb. of fuel oil) is used in generating the 1.64 Kwhr electricity component of every $ of GNP.

At the current cost of 1.54 cent per kWh, this means that, on the average, the cost of electricity represents 2.5 cents out of every $ of GNP. The other components of the GNP—most of which in some way depend on the availability of electric power—represent nearly 40 times the cost of power. This, in turn, means that, when shortages threaten in electricity supply, the economy stands to lose up to 40 times the cost of the electricity that is not available when needed.

This is important in considering the current trend in delaying and blocking electric generating and transmission facilities by ecologists and other opposition.

Emphasis has too often been placed on the displeasure and inconvenience for the residential public.

It might be more appropriate that the withholding of power facilities be compared to the damaging effects of a strike in a major industry. The loss of power can prove even more damaging through the curtailment of production in manufacturing industries deprived of electrical service and through the resultant unemployment, not

172   World Markets of Tomorrow

only in the industries directly affected but also in all those to which the blacked-out industries would have contributed.

The following is offered as a simplified yardstick for the economic leverage of electrical power: The US trillion-dollar economy depends on a generation capacity of about 335,000 Mw. Thus, if the economy were deprived of the output of a 1,000-Mw plant for a year (and the energy were not otherwise made available), the damage suffered by the national economy would have an upper limit of $3-billion.

Chart 33 shows that although the contents of electricity per $ of GNP will gradually increase—in answer to greater demands for the industrial and social improvements that only electricity can provide—even by the year 2000, when we will reach 3.02 kWh per dollar of GNP, we will still have a content of electricity, per unit of GNP, exceeded to-day by more than half the nations in Chart 30.

As regards the contents of energy per $ of GNP, Chart 33 points to

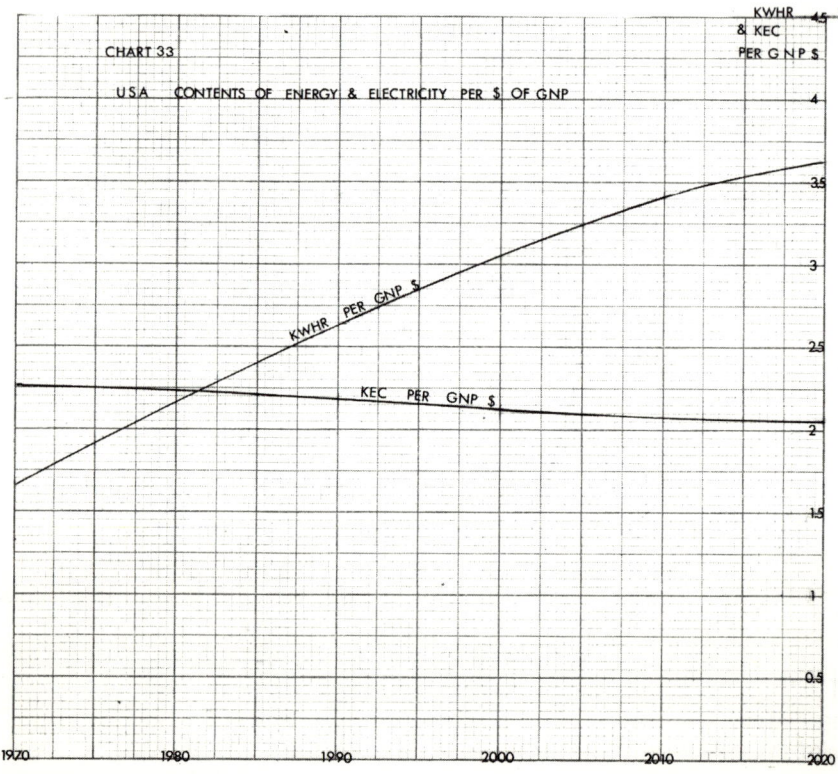

CHART 33—Future trend for the U.S.A. of contents of energy and electricity per $ of GMP

a continuation of the past trend. Even if, as discussed in connection with Table XXVI and Chart 25, this trend should reverse, the U.S.A. will remain the most efficient user of energy at its *per capita* GNP level.

OPTIMUM USE OF ENERGY RESOURCES

The favourable status brought out in Chart 32, as regards the efficient use which the United States economy makes of its energy resources should not be interpreted as representing the best that will be achieved in the coming decades:

On an extrapolated basis, improvements in the thermal efficiencies of the present equipments and systems together with the gains resulting from the economies of scale are expected to result, by the year 2000, in approximately one fifth higher overall efficiency.

Since, by that time, the United States will be requiring 4½ times the amount of energy it uses today, further gains in efficiency should be achieved and these will be obtained by the reduction into practice of new technologies, new energy systems, such as breeder reactors, magneto-hydrodynamic steam plants, fuel cells, etc., will make possible.

Thus, the total use of energy will be minimized without any interference with the economic process, the orderly growth of which is essential to the availability of the extra resources needed for the protection and beautification of the environment, which, by 1980, may require 20 to 25% of our GNP.

Only sustained economic growth will make such resources available.

CHAPTER ELEVEN

Quality of Life

ZERO ECONOMIC GROWTH

One of the purposes of this volume is to make available and relate into the overall scheme of life a number of aspects which are too often overlooked and which, as presented by overzealous groups, can be extremely misleading and dangerous if believed. We have in mind the uninformed clamor for zero economy growth, which has been presented as the panacea for all our environmental ills.

Additional confusion has been created by placing zero population growth, for which a strong case can be made, in the same category as zero economic growth which makes no sense at all and which would lead the world into darkness and chaos.

The argumentation of the proponents of zero economic growth would run somewhat as follows:

We have so many people employed now at so many jobs, so that everyone is more or less taken care of.

By maintaining the population and the economy at a constant level we shall keep the same total number of people employed making the same amount of money and we shall have fuller opportunities to protect our environment.

The first effects of zero economic growth would be immediately to defeat the aimed-for social progress for which the advocates of zero growth are campaigning so zealously:

In attempting to freeze the economy at its present level, zero economic growth would deny to minority groups the chance to accede the higher positions, and to all the underprivileged groups who live at, or near, poverty levels, the opportunity to better their lots and for better social justice.

Also, it would deny to the country the resources needed for more schools, more universities and more hospitals, and to continue the fight against pollution and other environmental ills.

For a clearer perspective of what 'zero economic growth' would mean, we can turn to Table XVIII and to Chart 14, both of which present the investment ratio:

Quality of Life

There is a wide variation in the figures for the different countries but, for the sake of simplification, let us take the United States with an 18% ratio, which is in the lowest quarter.

This ratio gives a direct measure of the share of the GNP which goes into growth. Since all such parts of the GNP can be associated with a corresponding share of the labour force, we can see that, for the United States, 18% of the labor force of approximately 90 millions derive their employment from the continuing process of economic growth.

Zero economic growth would mean that 15,000,000 out of these 90,000,000 would be added to the unemployment rolls.

NO INDUSTRIALIZED NATION HAS THE OPTION TO RETIRE INTO PASTORAL UTOPIA

The United States—or for that matter any of the industrialized nations of the world—do not have the option to retire into a bucolic past. The growth which has increased our culture, our social justice, our wealth must continue—in a balanced and controlled fashion—not just for the sake of growth but simply because there is no other alternative.

Continued, balanced, growth is essential to the generation of the resources needed for reducing and eliminating poverty and want, for providing better opportunities for the minority groups and for financing the considerable costs both for technological research and for the needed equipment that control of the environment and enhancement of the quality of life will imperatively clamor for.

To prove that there is no alternative it is only necessary to think through the consequences of just a forced slow-down of our normal growth pattern. One would soon find that unemployment (this was explained just above), epidemics, famine, social and political unrest would rapidly degrade humanity and the environment as well.

But this is not likely to happen because a clamor infinitely louder than the one which emanates to-day from the advocates of zero economic growth would soon demand a return to 'the good old days'!

RESTRAINT IN FUTURE GROWTH IS IMPLICIT IN OUR PATTERN

We hope that the presentation of patterns of economic growth and industrial development recorded by 150 countries gives ample proof that there need not be an exponential crisis, with its apocalyptic implications that machine-age pollution would cause the earth either to melt or to freeze.

We have already referred to the 'built-in' restraint feature present in our basic growth pattern and in all those derived from it. This is not something invented so that the growth projections would become more acceptable. It is a fundamental characteristic of any process which is bound to encounter internal limitations.

In the context of the comments just presented, this confirms that, to a not unconsiderable extent, the need for restraint in future growth is already implicit in the pattern.

TECHNOLOGY AND ENVIRONMENTAL DISRUPTION

We have been enlarging our horizons and conquering new frontiers on a scale which has never been equalled in the whole of human history. This swift progress has brought in its wake a number of problems which have caused many to question whether we had not progressed too far too fast.

Actually, the danger signals we are noting spell out that the need for further progress, further growth is greater than ever *and* that this progress, this growth will provide the means, and should be used, to correct our neglect of the past.

The accelerating rate of scientific and technological advance, which has given rise to fears that we are precipating the extinction not only of the environment but ultimately of ourselves, should instead be regarded as an all-powerful tool which, if used with wisdom, will maintain the real gains we have achieved and carry civilization to greater heights of human happiness and progress.

The recent debates on the fate of the supersonic transport plane, on the radiation hazards discussions in connection with the operation of nuclear power plants, etc., are bringing increased evidence of the searching scrutiny to which technological advances will increasingly be subjected.

Technology which until recently has been given the green light in its spell-binding prowesses is being pronounced guilty sometimes without a trial, too often on the basis of emotional disregard of what the castrophic consequences that such rash condemnation will have on the economy.

Quality of Life

We are convinced that, eventually, the situation will right itself on any specific object of discussion, wherever there is a legitimate cause for concern and when the technological stage of advancement has not progressed to the point of providing complete reassurance to those who are genuinely concerned.

However, we are concerned with the 'rocking-the-boat' opposition which manifests itself on issues where technology has already proved itself and is placed on the defensive while the economy of the country is being seriously endangered.

The pace of technological change continues to increase in parallel with a growing demand for the new creations that flow from the industrial applications of technology. This demand grows as much in the developed as in the under-developed countries of the world.

'Nothing, nothing can stop the continued growth of scientific knowledge or the emergence of new technologies. The new technologies of the aero-space industry, of computers, of telecommunications, of the chemical and transportation industries, surge forwards, and in their wake impose a world-wide and standard pattern of consumption whose components are very largely the industrial creations of the past few decades. And the new industrial and technological achievements of the advanced countries generate in the less privileged areas of the world a demand to share in the benefits for which modern technology has been responsible'.[35]

It is salutary that ours should be an increasingly questioning era: that we should subject to preexamination our entire social system as well as the future of our economy and our wisdom in the use of energy. But we should not let our justified concern for the abuses blind us to the 'quality of life' benefits which this same economic growth has made possible.

Science and technology can and must be directed toward the betterment of all. Whatever problems they leave in their wake, they can conquer at a cost which will be a fraction of the benefits they can bring to an ever widening segment of the population.

The only unconquerable material and social hardships are those for which correcting resources are lacking. In illustration, we may cite the increasing contribution to be expected from energy—which some would brand as the arch villain of our age—not only towards correcting its own by-products but also towards enhancing the quality of our life.

ECONOMIC DENSITY

For those concerned with the growing specter of inadequate pollution control rendering even the most remote countryside uninhabitable, we have shown in Table XXXI the economic density in sequence of decreasing magnitude for all countries.

This factor, expressed in $ per square kilometer, is obtained by dividing the GNP of the country by its area.

The same as for the population densities shown in Table VII, such comparisons are valid only between different countries; they do not take into account the concentration of population in metropolitan centers where the population density or the economic density may be 1,500 times greater than the average for the country, as is the case for Manhattan.

The sparsely-populated areas which are responsible for the low country average do constitute an important potential for additional forests and parks or for moderate-sized communities and cities which will be linked by 300 miles per hour aerotrains with the megalopolae of finance and government.

ENERGY'S CONTRIBUTION TO THE QUALITY OF LIFE

In a recent talk Dr. Glen Seaborg said that the population of the world 'even though its size may be stabilized in the future through the great and concerted effort we must make, is still going to require the consumption of a huge amount of energy in many forms. To try to ignore, write off, or avoid the responsibility of this vital fact of life does not make one an environmentalist, because the consequences of trying to get along without, or with less than, the amount required to meet the needs of a modern civilization can be just as environmentally disastrous as using such energy thoughtlessly.'

RECYCLING

Recycling of waste materials is the most promising and immediate means of correcting the degradation of our environment while preserving our natural resources to meet the always growing needs of increasing populations.

So long as social costs are not included, the recovery and processing of steel scrap, beverage cans, etc. may not appear

Quality of Life

TABLE XXXI—Economic density: 1967 GNP $ per square kilometers

#	Country	Value	#	Country	Value	#	Country	Value
1	Macao	4,000,000	64	Gilbert & Ellice Isl.	23,600	124	Australia	3,460
2	Gibraltar	2,500,000	65	North Korea	23,500	125	Ivory Coast	3,260
3	Bermuda	2,190,000	66	Cuba	23,150	126	Uganda	3,180
4	Singapore	2,165,000	67	Albania	21,900	127	Brazil	3,150
5	Ceuta & Melilla	1,454,500	68	Dominican Rep.	21,700	128	Portuguese Guinea	3,080
6	Bahrain	1,135,000	69	New Zealand	20,300	129	Portuguese Timor	3,060
7	Netherlands	676,000	70	Yemen	19,150	130	Gambia	2,740
8	Belgium & Lux.	613,000	71	Sao Tome & Principe	18,000	131	Peru	2,730
9	Malta	592,000				132	Southern Rhodesia	2,700
10	Channel Islands	585,000		WORLD AVERAGE	17,000	133	Burma	2,675
11	United Kingdom	445,000				134	Equatorial Guinea	2,390
12	Puerto Rico	421,000	72	Malaysia	16,750	135	Liberia	2,300
13	West Germany	420,000	73	Trinidad & Tobago	15,400	136	Trucial Oman	2,260
14	Switzerland	381,000	74	Brunei	14,920	137	Fr.Ter. Afars & Issas	2,180
15	Japan	312,000	75	Turkey	14,800	138	Kenya	1,978
16	US Virgin Islands	306,000	76	Pakistan	14,650	139	New Hebrides	1,950
17	Denmark	280,000	77	India	14,050	140	Malawi	1,780
18	Guam	276,500	78	South Vietnam	14,050	141	British Honduras	1,780
19	Barbados	276,500	79	Haiti	13,880	142	Dahomey	1,778
20	Netherl. Antilles	260,000	80	Trust Ter. Pacif. Isl.	13,500	143	Lesotho	1,740
21	Ryukyu Islands	235,000	81	Costa Rica	13,200	144	Afghanistan	1,700
22	Hong Kong	229,000	82	Guatemala	12,980	145	Cameroun	1,665
23	Italy	222,500	83	Comoro Islands	12,700	146	Mozambique	1,635
24	France	212,000	84	North Vietnam	12,650	147	Sikkim	1,568
25	East Germany	206,000	85	Mexico	12,220	148	Zambia	1,555
26	Bahama Islands	198,000	86	Qatar	11,080	149	Ethiopia	1,490
27	Israel	192,500	87	South Africa	10,800	150	Guinea	1,360
28	Martinique	162,500	88	U.S.S.R.	10,180	151	Algeria	1,337
29	Austria	129,200	89	Panama	10,150	152	Madagascar	1,242
30	Lebanon	127,000	90	Thailand	9,850	153	Guyana	1,225
31	Czechoslovakia	124,500	91	Venezuela	9,380	154	Paraguay	1,192
32	Kuwait	114,200	92	Ghana	8,600	155	Saudi Arabia	1,090
33	Isle of Man	103,000	93	Uruguay	8,200	156	Libya	1,058
34	Taiwan	100,500	94	New Caledonia	8,000	157	Laos	1,050
35	Hungary	99,000	95	Seychelles Isl.	8,000	158	Tanzania	1,034
36	Mauritius	97,500	96	Indonesia	7,700	159	Bhutan	1,000
37	Reunion	92,500	97	Nepal	7,600	160	Papua & NewGuinea	980
38	Jamaica	90,500	98	Ruanda	7,530	161	Upper Volta	924
39	United States	85,800	99	Syria	7,020	162	Surinam	913
40	Guadeloupe	84,400	100	Chile	6,970	163	Angola	804
41	Poland	79,800	101	China - Mainland	6,730	164	Fiji Islands	767
42	American Samoa	71,000	102	Cape Verde Isl.	6,500	165	Gabon	745
43	Panama Canal Zone	69,900	103	Swaziland	6,220	166	Western Samoa	704
44	Romania	58,400	104	Morocco	6,080	167	Bolivia	655
45	Sweden	53,300	105	Burundi	6,000	168	Congo Kinshasa	627
46	Greece	53,300	106	Tunisia	5,800	169	Southern Yemen	526
47	Spain	52,300	107	Canada	5,700	170	Sudan	514
48	Bulgaria	51,800	108	Jordan	5,600	171	Nicaragua	492
49	Portugal	50,400	109	Ifni	5,340	172	Congo Brazzavile	477
50	Cyprus	49,800	110	Nigeria	5,330	173	Muscat & Oman	382
51	Korea Republic	48,700	111	Colombia	5,280	174	Mongolia	306
52	Faeroe Islands	46,400	112	Cambodia	5,250	175	Mali	303
53	Ireland	42,800	113	Iceland	5,250	176	French Guyana	303
54	Yugoslavia	41,000	114	Argentina	5,240	177	Centr. Afric. Rep.	281
55	Windward Islands	38,100	115	Honduras	5,070	178	Somalia	209
56	Leeward Islands	37,700	116	U.A.R. Egypt	4,940	179	Niger	196
57	Tonga	34,280	117	Sierra Leone	4,770	180	Chad	185
58	French Oceania	32,500	118	Iran	4,520	181	Mauritania	157
59	Philippines	31,200	119	Ecuador	4,480	182	West Irian	107
60	Ceylon	27,000	120	Iraq	4,470	183	Botswana	88
61	Maldive Islands	26,850	121	Togo	4,230	184	Spanish Sahara	37
62	Finland	25,900	122	El Salvador	4,120	185	Greenland	16
63	Norway	25,700	123	Senegal	3,970	186	Brit. Solomon Isl.	10

profitable, at present, which results in the mounting accumulation of junked automobiles!

Similarly, the recovery and reprocessing of waste paper may, from a very short-sighted perspective which does not take into account the added cost of disposal, appear more costly than the cutting down of more forests!

WILL ANTI-POLLUTION EXPENDITURES LOWER THE PRODUCTIVITY OR PROVE INFLATIONARY?

Some have said that the additional inputs of capital and labor needed to reduce pollution will not be reflected in any increase in output and that by definition, therefore, antipollution measures will tend to lower productivity.

We believe that there will be found, in final analysis, very few areas of environmental improvement where soundly conceived and applied expenditures will not result, directly or indirectly, in substantial gains in productivity.

As a first example, let us look at the production of electric power which has been among the most-mentioned causes of air and thermal pollution, the former through emissions from the stacks, the latter because of the discharge of heated water to the rivers.

The addition of electrical precipitators and filters and the provision of cooling towers will be the chief cost items. Their manufacture will add to the country's production of goods and will create additional employment contributing to increase in the GNP; this was borne out in the flurry of interest in the anti-pollution stocks.

Always in connection with electricity generation, remote siting of nuclear power plants in existing or man-made off-shore islands, twenty or thirty miles distant from the coastal cities they serve, is being considered. Additional employment will be needed to build these facilities which will also be a source of added wealth to the nation the same as the manufacture of the electric cables required to bring the power, but the extra distance of transmission involved will represent a net loss to the economy.

To the chapter of net losses, we should also add the extra power required in connection with the use of precipitators, cooling towers, etc.

Altogether, the items mentioned—which give a fair sampling of what non-polluting and aesthetically pleasing electric power will

Quality of Life

involve—will represent an increase of the order of one billion dollars a year to the GNP providing new employment for approximately 50,000.

Their cost, which will be borne by all industrial and residential users as well, will mean an addition of 10 to 15% to the cost of electricity, which will increase the average residential customer monthly bill, say from $10.00 to $11.50.

It will, probably, be surprising to many that for a cost of one extra taxi ride each month they could pay their full share of removing this one source of pollution and damage to the environment. Far more startling, yet, is the favorable impact on the economy of the country as a whole to be expected from over-all acceptance of a very modest increase in the cost of electric power.

As a second example of the impact of anti-pollution expenditures on productivity, we can conjecture on the probable effect of the cost of passenger automobiles of the measures which require that their emission be reduced by 90% in the next 4 years.

The extra cost of these new devices will also contribute to an increase in economy and employment in the same way as previous additions to passenger automobile equipment: air conditioning, automatic transmission, etc. Here we can point to an indirect improvement in productivity, simply from the health standpoint, reduction of respiratory diseases, thus to be achieved.

WHAT IS THE FULL COST TO SOCIETY OF ENERGY?

It has been said that 'It may be that energy consumption is growing so fast in part because the price does not include the full cost to society of producing it and delivering it'.

Actually, the 'ex-environmental' cost of energy is so low in relation to its value to the economy that even the addition of the 'social cost'—which has, so far, not been reckoned as it should—will still make energy the biggest bargain in our economy.

The financial implications of control of the environment will not all be one way: a number of benefits—which will also have to be evaluated in the concerted approach we are suggesting—will also materialize:

(i) Increase in fish and agricultural yields resulting from irrigation with warmer water available from the discharge of nuclear power plants,
(ii) Decreases in the cost of water treatment equipment,
(iii) Reduction in respiratory diseases.

The difficulty will lie in placing the responsibility and in accurately assessing social costs and benefits which are not easy to calculate. Ecologists, who have been very specific about warnings of disastrous consequences, should, in a concerted world-wide approach, help to arrive at an internationally acceptable allocation of the social costs of all forms of human activity which are liable to have an impact on the environment.

Let us indulge in Monday morning quarterbacking and ask ourselves:

(i) Why did we regard it as normal to cut down new forests instead of reclaiming discarded newspapers even if this were to cost a little more?
(ii) Why did we regard it as normal to allow junked cars to pile up in the countryside instead of promptly recycling them, even if this were to cost a little more?
(iii) Why have we allowed garbage collection to be carried out by methods which were already antiquated centuries ago?
(iv) Why have we allowed beautiful landscapes to be disfigured by billboards and other eyesores?

Obviously, these neglects cannot be imputed to the penalties of an insatiable technology or to impact on the environment which was beyond our control.

The plain answer is that we gave a very poor priority to the correction of such nuisances. Emphasis was on getting each job done at minimum cost and with minimum concern as to what the accumulation of such malpractices and neglects would lead to.

The outcry which we are now witnessing appears akin to the dismay of the husband who, during a prolonged absence of his wife, gets along very well by letting dishes pile up until the day when the sink is so full that he has to do something about reducing the environmental imbalance that his indifference has allowed to build up to a 'crisis' level.

We are finally finding out that our industries, our cities, our automobiles, ourselves, cannot keep on using our environment as a sink.

OUR CHALLENGE

In the first of the two following excerpts[22], as well as in the second[23] in which we have included some of our own words, are reminders that man was never meant to 'leave nature alone'.

'People like to talk about preserving nature in its "pristine" state, which, Mr. Webster says, refers to earlier times and carries with it the implication of purity and cleanliness and even an implication of an unchanging state of cleanliness. We know, of course, that nature itself doesn't act that way. Every mountain formed is being washed into the ocean. Streams carry millions of tons a day of good earth into the sea. Earthquakes change the face of the land. Plagues and pestilence wipe out whole populations of animals, birds, people and vegetation. The flourishing of one form of life is often at the expense of another. So the environment changes and, of course, it changes more rapidly if people are present, since man has a greater impact on his environment—for good or bad—than any other organism.'

'When the Good Lord created the earth, he never finished it. Nothing is all done, nothing is ended. He wisely provided for continuing vibrant and throbbing growth, for creation, throughout all time. He left mountains that are impassable, forests that were impenetrable; wild rivers that were uncrossable and uncontrollable rainfall that was erratic producing deserts and rainforests; storms that brought forth hurricanes and rampaging floods and lack of storms that produced searing droughts. He left the heat of summer and the cold of winter.

He provided ample natural resources for the life of man, but they were resources which require work and knowledge and cooperation and will to develop and use; resources that must be developed on wise and sound principles or the development boomerangs. He provided Nature that would be governed by laws which have no sympathy for ignorance, no matter how well intended. And He gave Adam and Eve the job of subduing the earth and having dominion over it.

We have tremendous problems to be solved. In some ways it appears we have oversubdued the earth—and produced pollution and congestion and ugliness. While we now have a higher standard of living for all our people in this Miracle of America of ours, than ever before in all history, we also have problems without precedent. Our affluence has raised our expectations of life—and our unrest. Our capacity to alter our environment, along with preferences for convenience and speed and sometimes for quick returns, has headed us in some instances in the wrong direction.

But we must not let the idea become rooted in our minds that 'we have become the victims of our technological and economic' growth.

To the contrary, it is only from advances in technology and from continued economic growth that we find the means and draw the resources 'to correct air and water pollution, to correct the traffic congestion our individual freedom of movement has created, and' to put an end to 'the desecration of many of our areas. We have a tremendous job ahead of rebuilding and making our cities' our suburbs, our countryside 'the great places to live that they can be, and must be for our survival.

We have the knowhow and the methods' and the resources 'to resolve' these problems, 'but we need, as a people, much more than this. We need collective recognition of the' true measure of 'the problem and the' clear thinking and 'careful weighing of the various solutions' available to us so that we can continue on with the creation, as we fulfill our responsibilities and hopes for a better world'.

There is no insurmountable technological obstacle in the way of achieving all that our concern for a pure environment and a better quality of life demands. Technologically and economically the solutions are well within what we know how to do and what we can afford to do.

CREATION OF NEW COMMUNITIES

In spite of continued efforts to disperse industries and urban and business centers over wide areas, it is likely that the working day will still be spent largely in high density areas, raising environmental challenges which technology will continue to overcome.

Improved transportation by electric trains powered from pollution-free nuclear plants will permit the industrial worker, office employee and businessman to live in pleasing natural surroundings, commuting daily in comfort and relaxation over distances which today one only associates with week-end travel.

One half-hour commuting time—which is the present day average—will link middle-sized communities well outside of the established population corridors.

In the creation of these new communities, the growth of which will be encouraged, new concepts and new goals will be incorporated benefitting from the investigations now in progress in many industrialized countries.

It is to be expected and hoped that, in the planning of these communities, the lessons of the past will be heeded as fully as the concerns of to-day.

The systems approach which should govern such plans should be truly world-wide in scope, encompassing the greatly varying requirements of all areas of the world and aiming to develop a global set of guidelines for infrastructure, tailored to the specific needs of diverse communities.

Since any 'standardization' would be limited to the infrastructure, to the utilities, to zoning provisions, etc, the individuality of the character of diverse communities would never be interfered with. This would insure, however, that the important and often costly facilities necessary for the protection of the environment are provided for, as efficiently and as economically as possible, all over the world.

Quality of Life

A GLOBAL DEVELOPMENT STRATEGY IS NEEDED

Further emphasized by ecological considerations, the case for international cooperation and understanding is becoming stronger, every day.

The dependence of the industrialized countries upon the resources of the developing countries, the dependence of the developing countries upon the markets of the industrialized countries, and the growing concern about the ecology of the world as a whole which has focused attention on the extent to which the preservation of a continuing balance between growth and quality of life will demand concerted efforts from all countries, are all emphasizing the need for a global development strategy which will encompass economic development and ecology.

THE GREENING OF THE WORLD

Much has been written and is being written about the new awareness of man's responsibility to ecology and about the new sense of urgency with which these problems are being examined.

Great as the resources of the technology and of healthy economy may be, they will be severely taxed and strained to undo the harm already done, and to reverse, wherever it can still be reversed, the impact of man on the environment. However, we hope that this study will have brought to light evidence that new technical means are available to us, and that we shall be able to afford them.

Greatly increased use of pollution-free nuclear power, while requiring only ecologically insignificant inputs from the biosphere, will make available the vast amounts of energy needed.

The potentialities of nuclear desalting which offers a method of meeting water shortages by increasing the water supply without any harm to he environment are an eloquent rebuttal to the prophets of doomsday who see only further aggravation ahead. Its large scale use will make deserts bloom and increase the forest areas of countries which have been practically denuded of trees, nature's means of reducing CO_2.

The conjunction of the two new technologies—nuclear power and desalting—adds a vast new dimension to man's search for energy and water. Large dual-purpose nuclear plants will enable us to take advantage of both the atom as a resource for energy and the ocean as a resource from which to obtain fresh water.

The concept of tying together nuclear power and desalting can be expanded even further to encompass nuclear energy centers surrounded by industrial or agro-industrial complexes. Such a grouping might include interrelated industrial processes for the production of fertilizers, aluminum, phosphorous, caustic-chlorine and ammonia. The complex could also include large-scale desalting of seawater for a highly intensified program of irrigating food crops[3,4].

While the cost of desalted water is, today, still too high for irrigation uses, the forces of the market will tend to minimize the difference. The realization that all projects, all programs will have to be evaluated on a 'systems' basis which will assign their due weight to the otherwise hidden social costs will develop a new awareness that nuclear-desalted water is not uneconomical; this will result in greatly extending the arable areas of the world and in stimulating the creation of new communities, new 'natural' parks, new green pastures. Literally, a new Greening of the World!

HOW WILL THESE INCREASED INCOMES THAT WE HAVE BEEN PROJECTING BE USED?

We hope that the reader who is interested in any particular country will derive from the growth profiles in the second part, evidence that the cost of a higher quality of life can well be afforded. As an average for the world, a *per capita* growth rate of 3½ per year will after ten years make every individual wealthier by 40% in constant prices.

As an example, in terms of constant 1967 $, the U.S. *per capita* will be:

$4,340 in 1970
$5,740 in 1980, i.e. 1.32 times the 1970 income
$7,400 in 1990, i.e. 1.70 times the 1970 income

As we have said, a substantial share of the increased *per capita* income of the industrialized countries will, in the decades to come, be allocated to enhancing the quality of life within their borders.

Another, much smaller, share of their increased income will, by stimulating economic growth in the developing countries, contribute to greatly accelerated improvements in their standards of living and related dignity of life.

The cost of anti-pollution and environmental protection will climb steadily year after year; at the start it may be only of the order of

5%, but it could well reach 25% by 1980; but, even this last figure, will still leave a substantial margin, say 15%, of extra resources.

This 25% added cost for environmental quality is not just an extra burden which will take away a quarter of our income before we have a chance to enjoy it: it will be reflected in increased enjoyment of every aspect of life. In return for that cost, we will breathe pure air, the water discharged by our industrial plants will be clearer than when taken in, the city noise which impinges on our ears will be quieted down, the countryside will not be disfigured and our health as well as every possession we enjoy will be protected and will become more durable.

Those who would doubt that even a 25% cost for environmental quality could bring all these benefits, can derive reassurance from the fact that we estimate for the United States in 1980 a GNP of $1,351 billion 1967 $: 25% of this should be abmut $340 billion 1967 $, which is equal to our entire GNP in 1946. Obviously, expenditures of this magnitude will call for new government agencies, new administrations, new professional fields, new scientific establishments for environmental research, the aims of which will be to obtain maximum value for our environmental protection dollar.

Can our young people who are searching for new avenues of self-expression, a new sense of participation in the progress of their country, a new area of dedication for social betterment think of a better outlet than the one above, comparable in magnitude to the entire total of services and goods produced by the United States just 25 years ago? The very imperative of a radically improved environment has already begun to create new markets for new skills: new architectural concepts, technological skills, engineering disciplines, legal approaches, management challenges, and above all a new and enlarged sense of responsibility to the preservation of the quality of life. Surely this suggests a vital area in which the searching energy of youth can be channeled into constructive outlets.

TABLE XXXII—Country index for energy 'per capita' growth pattern

In order to chart the growth in energy use per capita for any country:
(1) Find on Chart 12 the pattern for which the index is closest to that of the country. For instance, for the United States (120%) use Pattern 118.75%.
(2) From Table XXXIII, Page 189, read the Kec/Cap. for 1969: 10,773.
(3) Locate on Pattern 188.75% on Chart 12, the point for which the ordinate is 10,773. The corresponding reference year, in abscissa, is approximately 134.
(4) If 1969 corresponds to 134, 1970 corresponds to 135, 1975 to 1940, etc., up to the year 2015 which corresponds to 180, by which time the kec/capita will be 30,400.
(5) The United States Profile Page 328 shows a population of 313 Millions in 2015. Multiplying this by 30,400 gives a total energy use of 9,500 Bill.Kec.

	%		%		%
Trucial Oman	660.0	Jordan	147.5	Kuwait	104.0
Muscat & Oman	507.0	Norway	148.0	Laos	102.5
Bahama Islands	366.0	Congo-Brazzaville	146.0	Czechoslovakia	101.5
U S Virgin Islands	350.0	Iraq	146.0	Dominican Republic	100.0
French Oceania	328.0	Ceylon	142.0	Iceland	100.0
Bulgaria	275.0	Spain	141.0	Guinea	99.0
Ireland	257.0	Denmark	137.5	Nepal	97.0
Panama Republic	255.0	Mozambique	136.0	Sudan	95.0
Bermuda	252.5	Guadeloupe	128.5	France	95.0
Libya	238.0	U S S R	128.0	U A R Egypt	94.0
Trinidad & Tobago	236.0	French Guyana	127.5	Brunei	94.0
Panama Canal Zone	230.0	El Salvador	126.0	Brazil	92.5
Italy	225.0	Albania	125.0	Guam	92.5
Korea Republic	225.0	Portugal	125.0	Indonesia	92.5
Puerto Rico	225.0	Tanzania	125.0	Senegal	92.0
Thailand	225.0	Togo	125.0	India	91.5
South Vietnam	222.0	Tunisia	125.0	Ruanda	91.5
Japan	215.0	Lebanon	124.0	Cameroun	91.0
Qatar	210.0	Iran	122.5	Venezuela	90.0
Zambia	208.0	Mexico	122.5	Cuba	83.5
Portuguese Guinea	204.0	Paraguay	121.5	Guatemala	81.0
Hungary	200.0	United States	120.0	Australia	80.5
Liberia	200.0	Algeria	119.5	Burma	78.5
Malta	200.0	Bolivia	119.0	Poland	77.5
Surinam	199.0	Cambodia	119.0	Argentina	73.0
Ivory Coast	194.0	Netherlands	119.0	Austria	73.0
Communist Asia	193.0	Nicaragua	119.0	Madagascar	72.5
Finland	192.0	Niger	118.5	United Kingdom	71.5
Jamaica	191.0	Martinique	118.0	Morocco	71.0
Reunion	191.0	Sierra Leone	118.0	West Germany	65.5
Turkey	179.5	Barbados	117.0	Nigeria	65.5
New Caledonia	177.0	Chile	117.0	Afghanistan	65.0
Gabon	176.5	Uganda	116.5	Ghana	65.0
Rykuyu Islands	176.5	Sweden	116.0	Chad	64.0
Saudi Arabia	176.0	Angola	115.0	Honduras	60.0
Bahrain	171.5	Malaysia	114.0	South Africa	60.0
Mauretania	171.5	Philippines	114.0	Mali	57.5
Romania	171.0	Costa Rica	112.5	Yemen	57.5
Cyprus	170.0	Pakistan	110.0	Upper Volta	57.0
Singapore	166.0	Switzerland	109.5	Uruguay	55.5
Greece	164.0	Taiwan	108.5	Colombia	52.0
Israel	163.5	Ethiopia	107.0	Congo Kinshasa	52.0
Peru	156.0	New Zealand	107.0	Belgium & Luxembourg	51.5
Hong Kong	155.0	Canada	105.0	Kenya	47.5
Malawi	150.0	East Germany	105.0	Central African Repub	40.0
Yugoslavia	148.0	Syria	105.0	Somalia	40.0
				Mauritius	19.0

Quality of Life

TABLE XXXIII—Use of energy: kilograms of equivalent coal 'per capita'

	Kg of Energy Equivalent Coal per Capita 1969	1968		Kg of Energy Equivalent Coal per Capita 1969	1968		Kg of Energy Equivalent Coal per Capita 1969	1969
US Virgin Islands	65000	35300	Chile	1210	1158	Bolivia	213	203
Netherlands Antilles	18680	20720	Greece	1149	1017	Dominican Republic	212	208
Kuwait	10992	12399	Mexico	1114	1134	Thailand	208	203
United States	10773	10340	Jamaica	1088	1008	Congo Brazzaville	203	199
Canada	8819	8487	Malta	994	974	Morocco	194	186
Christmas Island	8250	7875	Hong Kong	948	752	India	187	181
New Caledonia	7207	8486	Barbados	936	570	Ivory Coast	183	158
Czechoslovakia	6120	5774	Uruguay	914	789	Windward Islands	173	160
Falkland Islands	6000	6000	French Guyana	909	916	Mozambique	168	152
Sweden	5768	5380	Guyana	896	899	Papua	164	131
East Germany	5673	5386	Taiwan	884	814	Mauritius	161	180
Belgium & Luxembourg	5429	5236	French Oceania	860	1047	Equatorial Guinea	158	161
Nauru	5250	4000	Lebanon	764	683	Ghana	155	126
Australia	5214	5055	Singapore	761	685	Angola	151	144
Denmark	5141	4692	Guam	750	1004	Senegal	147	149
United Kingdom	5139	4960	Afars & Issas	742	705	Paraguay	134	141
West Germany	4850	4488	Saudi Arabia	738	504	Ceylon	133	114
Trinidad & Tobago	4727	4205	Trucial Oman	729	674	British Solomon Is	122	125
Netherlands	4659	4119	Gabon	659	626	El Salvador	118	194
Norway	4430	4249	Korea Republic	634	579	Sao Tome	117	121
USSR	4200	4050	Peru	622	644	Indonesia	110	104
St Pierre & Miquelon	4199	3699	Iraq	614	615	Sudan	108	88
Greenland	4053	5566	Albania	607	575	Western Samoa	102	104
Poland	4029	3828	Portugal	603	541	Cape Verde Islands	95	97
Bahrain	3846	2530	Colombia	578	585	Guinea	95	97
Finland	3575	3483	Iran	565	485	Mauritania	93	92
Bahama Islands	3547	3780	Libya	559	483	Sierra Leone	93	58
France	3517	3282	Southern Rhodesia	541	559	Pakistan	90	85
Panama Canal Zone	3503	5806	Ryukyu Islands	530	531	Congo Kinshasa	88	84
Bulgaria	3491	3317	Martinique	518	453	Cameroun	84	81
Iceland	3461	4187	Zambia	509	553	Tanzania	74	52
Switzerland	3175	3012	Communist Asia	505	457	Cambodia	65	50
Puerto Rico	3075	2650	South Yemen	484	467	Portuguese Guinea	65	50
Austria	2994	2854	Guadeloupe	481	427	Togo	65	54
Ireland	2938	2904	Syria	481	434	Madagascar	64	61
Hungary	2895	2816	Brazil	475	446	Uganda	62	61
Faeroe Islands	2894	2539	Algeria	470	424	West Irian	57	58
Japan	2828	2517	Turkey	461	450	Burma	54	48
South Africa	2746	2726	British Honduras	449	400	Gambia	54	51
American Samoa	2718	2370	Malaysia	441	415	Laos	54	29
Romania	2627	2388	Fiji Islands	407	345	Muscat & Oman	50	42
New Zealand	2623	2678	Liberia	390	301	Malawi	40	40
Brunei	2552	2331	South Vietnam	369	318	Haiti	39	31
Italy	2432	2266	Costa Rica	332	323	Comoro Islands	38	34
Israel	2314	2014	Nicaragua	327	337	Central African Rep	38	38
Bermuda	2186	2560	Macau	311	316	Dahomey	30	29
Surinam	2157	2089	Jordan	308	278	Ethiopia	29	22
Venezuela	2096	2532	Pacific Islands	306	281	Nigeria	29	27
WORLD AVERAGE	1805	1727	Gilbert Islands	299	277	Somalia	28	27
Panama Republic	1656	1301	New Hebrides	299	399	Afghanistan	26	39
Argentina	1545	1409	Reunion	272	263	Chad	23	18
Qatar	1469	1443	Ecuador	269	260	Nepal	17	11
Gibraltar	1444	1559	Philippines	266	263	Mali	15	21
Leeward Islands	1374	1246	Tunisia	248	223	Niger	14	17
Spain	1354	1279	Guatemala	236	239	Yemen	14	13
Yugoslavia	1292	1249	Seychelles	235	239	Upper Volta	11	9
Cyprus	1252	1294	U A R Egypt	221	301	Ruanda	10	10
Cuba	1222	1044	Honduras	219	216	Burundi	8	8

TABLE XXXIV—Use of electricity: kilowatt hours 'per capita' (1969-1968)

The reader may note that, generally speaking, the countries which show the greatest increase in per capita use of electricity from 1968 to 1969 are among those with the highest index of economic growth.

Country	1969	1968	Country	1969	1968	Country	1969	1968
Norway	14452	14848	Zambia	865	836	Sabah	125	111
Panama Canal Zone	11298	11232	Argentina	828	760	Honduras	120	111
Canada	8959	8514	Taiwan	823	745	Papua	118	109
Sweden	7743	7331	Malta	801	692	Communist Asia	117	109
United States	7644	7135	Qatar	750	924	Thailand	106	90
New Caledonia	7295	6906	Chile	745	739	Sao Tome	106	93
Guam	6843	5969	Uruguay	732	688	Ivory Coast	104	90
U S Virgin Islands	6466	4607	Portugal	717	663	Sarawak	101	95
Netherlands Antilles	5761	5390	Jamaica	653	554	India	100	91
Kuwait Neutral Zone	5599	5500	Southern Rhodesia	640	586	Angola	99	85
Christmas Island	4750	4250	Cuba	606	582	New Hebrides	99	102
New Zealand	4697	4469	Liberia	549	507	Windward Islands	98	93
Iceland	4497	3626	Costa Rica	534	509	Jordan	90	75
United Kingdom	4291	4042	Mexico	525	484	Paraguay	87	90
Finland	4274	3860	Panama Republic	517	477	Senegal	84	77
Switzerland	4237	4087	Barbados	517	436	Western Samoa	71	66
Kuwait	4192	3722	French Oceania	514	441	Congo Brazzaville	69	61
Austria	4162	3865	Brazil	451	427	Sierra Leone	69	58
Bermuda	4078	3799	Lebanon	430	401	Kenya	64	61
East Germany	3874	3705	Guyana	420	399	Ceylon	61	57
West Germany	3815	3495	Afars & Issas	407	419	South Vietnam	61	49
Nauru	3333	3166	Peru	402	392	Pakistan	58	52
Belgium & Luxembourg	3236	2972	St Pierre & Miquelon	399	399	Uganda	57	66
Czechoslovakia	3212	3041	Albania	379	336	Equatorial Guinea	52	53
Surinam	3192	2869	Colombia	378	350	Guinea	52	53
Australia	3103	2886	French Guyana	354	347	British Solomon Is	50	38
Japan	2972	2622	Leeward Islands	342	324	Mozambique	50	53
Netherlands	2858	2620	West Malaysia	340	332	Mauritania	49	39
U S S R	2847	2669	Ghana	322	309	Zanzibar	46	44
Denmark	2709	2432	Nicaragua	287	262	Australian New Guinea	43	36
France	2598	2390	Iraq	280	257	Cape Verde Islands	39	36
Puerto Rico	2559	2270	Guadeloupe	272	235	Gambia	36	34
Bahama Islands	2251	2067	Fiji Islands	267	261	Sudan	34	22
Israel	2154	2005	Martinique	262	226	Madagascar	31	30
Italy	2123	2011	Korea Republic	256	212	Malawi	29	27
South Africa	2119	2008	Pacific Islands	255	260	Togo	29	27
Bulgaria	2072	1883	Mauritius	250	257	Tanganyka	27	24
Poland	1849	1728	Reunion	240	215	Central African Repub	27	22
Bahrein	1835	1750	Turkey	227	205	Haiti	24	23
Ireland	1807	1685	U A R Egypt	225	212	Burma	21	20
Faeroe Islands	1763	1657	Macau	211	181	Ruanda	21	20
Hungary	1599	1501	Iran	210	184	Afghanistan	19	20
Spain	1502	1345	Philippines	207	195	Nigeria	19	17
Gibraltar	1481	1559	Dominican Republic	204	186	Cambodia	18	19
Greenland	1468	1399	Libya	187	151	Indonesia	18	18
Romania	1440	1298	Cameroun	182	180	Portuguese Guinea	18	17
Ryukyu Islands	1347	1254	El Salvador	182	178	Ethiopia	16	14
WORLD AVERAGE	1285	1206	Syria	174	135	Laos	15	11
Trinidad & Tobago	1166	1095	Gabon	173	154	West Irian	13	13
Venezuela	1164	1116	Congo Kinshasa	164	155	Chad	10	8
American Samoa	1156	1096	Bolivia	152	149	Dahomey	10	10
Hong Kong	1149	1005	South Yemen	147	148	Mali	7	7
Yugoslavia	1140	1038	Ecuador	145	133	Niger	7	7
Brunei	1086	928	Tunisia	145	137	Nepal	6	5
Falkland Islands	1000	1000	Guatemala	145	125	Somalia	6	5
Greece	947	836	British Honduras	141	137	Burundi	5	4
Singapore	930	824	Algeria	135	125	Upper Volta	4	4
Cyprus	876	800	Saudi Arabia	131	121	Yemen	3	3
			Morocco	126	119			

PART TWO

CHAPTER TWELVE

Individual Country Profiles

The table below corresponds to the material found in each of the country profiles. It shows pages to which one may refer, also the Table and the Chart where the same information is given for all the countries of the world.

Each Table and Chart shows the statistical year for the data given. The rates of exchange are as of July 1970.

Refer to PAGES:	TABLE:	CHART:
Map and Page (in Part Two)	I	
Area-Total:	II	
Area-Arable:	III	
Population:	IV	
Population Density:	V	
Birth-Death Rate %:	VI	
Population Rate of Increase:	VII	
1967 GNP *per capita*:	VIII	
Students in Institutions of Higher Learning	IX	1
Hospital Beds:	X	2
Daily Neswpapers:	XI	3
Telephones:		
Television Sets:	XIII	5
Tourist Receipts	XIV	
Passenger Cars:	XV	6
Steel Consumption:	XVI	7
Growth Pattern Index:	XVII	12
Investment Ratio:	XVIII	14
GNP/Capita Annual Increase 67-90:	XIX	15
Energy Total Billion KEC:	XXIII	
Energy *per capita* KEC:	XXIV	
KEC per $ of GNP:	XXV	
Growth Ratio GNP/KEC:	XXVI	27
Electric Capacity Megawatts	XXVII	
Generation Billion Kilowatt-hours	XXVIII	
Kilowatt Hours *per capita*:	XXIX	
Kilowatt Hours per $ of GNP:	XXX	30
Economic Density: GNP $/Sq. Km.	XXXI	

AFGHANISTAN

	1970	1975	1980	1985	1990	1995	2000	2005	2010	2015	2020
Population / 1967 Population	1.060	1.150	1.240	1.330	1.420	1.500	1.580	1.650	1.720	1.790	1.850
Population Millions	16.70	18.11	19.53	21.95	22.35	23.61	24.88	26.00	27.10	28.20	29.15
GNP/Capita 1967 $	77.8	90.7	106.2	123.0	143.3	164.5	189.2	217.5	249.0	280.0	321.0
GNP Billion $ 1967	1.300	1.643	2.075	2.700	3.205	3.885	4.720	5.660	6.750	7.800	9.350
Yearly Increase GNP	4.8%	4.7%	4.5%	4.3%	4.1%	3.9%	3.7%	3.5%	3.3%	3.0%	

Map	Asia & Middle East	H L Students	27 per 100000
Capital	Kabul	Hospital Beds	0.2 per 1000
One U S $ =	81.56 Afghani	Daily Newspapers	7 per 1000
		Telephones	10,000
Area-Total	647,497 Sq Km		
Area-Arable	78,440 Sq Km	Kec per $ of GNP	
		Growth Ratio GNP/Kec	
Population	16,516,000	Passenger Cars	29,200
Population Density	24 per Sq Km	Steel Consumption	1 Kg/Cap
Population Rate of Increase	1.90%	Growth Pattern Index GNP/Capita	43.75%
		Annual Increase 67-90	3.16%
1967 GNP per Capita	70 US $		

Energy Total Billion Kec	0.516
Energy per Capita Kec	32
Kec per $ of GNP	0.386
Growth Ratio GNP/Kec	0.675
Electric Capacity Mw	275
Generation Billion Kwhr	0.325
Kilowatt Hours per Capita	20
Kwhr per $ of GNP	0.31
Economic Density GNP $/Sq Km	1,700

ALBANIA

	1970	1975	1980	1985	1990	1995	2000	2005	2010	2015	2020
Population 1967 Population	1.085	1.240	1.395	1.550	1.705	1.855	2.005	2.155	2.300	2.440	2.575
Population Millions	2.135	2.436	2.742	3.044	3.400	3.645	3.942	4.235	4.520	4.795	5.055
GNP 1967 $ Capita	383	501	654	860	1,092	1,385	1,768	2,202	2,705	3,302	3,950
GNP Billion $ 1967	0.819	1.220	1.792	2.620	3.715	5.055	6.960	9.310	12.220	15.820	19.980
Yearly Increase GNP	8.3%	8.0%	7.9%	7.2%	6.4%	6.6%	6.0%	5.6%	5.3%	4.7%	

Map	Europe	
Capital	Tirana	
One U S $ =	5.00 Lek	
Area-Total	28,748 Sq Km	
Area-Arable	5,010 Sq Km	
Population Density	2,075,000 68 per Sq Km	
Birth-Death Rate %	3.56-0.80	
Population Rate of Increase	2.90%	
1967 GNP per Capita	320 US $	

H L Students	633 per 100000
Hospital Beds	5.9 per 1000
Daily Newspapers	53 per 1000
Television Sets	1,000
Steel Consumption	25 Kg/Cap
Growth Pattern Index GNP/Capita	112.50%
Annual Increase	5.45%

Energy Total Billion Kec	1.168
Energy per Capita Kec	578
Kec per $ of GNP	1.120
Growth Ratio GNP/Kec	0.900
Generation Billion Kwhr	0.730
Kilowatt Hours per Capita	361
Kwhr per $ of GNP	0.88
Economic Density GNP $/Sq Km	21,900

ALGERIA

	1970	1975	1980	1985	1990	1995	2000	2005	2010	2015	2020
Population 1967 Population	1.060	1.230	1.320	1.580	1.740	1.900	2.025	2.205	2.370	2.510	2.660
Population Millions	13.88	16.41	18.55	21.06	23.21	25.35	27.01	29.35	31.55	33.45	35.45
GNP Capita 1967 $	265	326	401	506	625	780	955	1158	1395	1630	1950
GNP Billion $ 1967	3.68	5.38	7.41	10.60	14.50	19.60	25.95	33.40	44.00	55.00	69.00
Yearly Increase GNP	8.0%	7.5%	6.8%	6.5%	6.1%	5.8%	5.6%	5.2%	4.9%	4.6%	

Map	Africa	H L Students	78 per 100000
Capital	Algiers	Hospital Beds	3.5 per 1000
One U S $ =	4.937 Dinar	Daily Newspapers	14 per 1000
		Telephones	156,038
Area-Total	2,381,741 Sq Km		
Area-Arable	67,870 Sq Km	Television Sets	150,000
Population	13,349,000	Passenger Cars	117,000
Population Density	5.27 per Sq Km	Steel Consumption	38 Kg/Cap
Birth-Death Rate %	4.40-1.40		
Population Rate of Increase	2.20%	Growth Pattern Index GNP/Capita	93.75%
		Annual Increase 67-90	4.05%
1967 GNP per Capita	250 US $		

Energy Total Billion Kec	5.441
Energy per Capita Kec	420
Kec per $ of GNP	1.690
Growth Ratio GNP/Kec	0.364
Electric Capacity Mw	639
Generation Billion Kwhr	1.591
Kilowatt Hours per Capita	122
Kwhr per $ of GNP	0.45
Economic Density GNP $/Sq Km	1,337

ANGOLA

	1970	1975	1980	1985	1990	1995	2000	2005	2010	2015	2020
Population 1967 Population	1.043	1.110	1.170	1.235	1.300	1.350	1.400	1.445	1.490	1.530	1.570
Population Millions	5.525	5.875	6.190	6.540	6.880	7.145	7.410	7.650	7.885	8.100	8.310
GNP 1967 $ Capita	214	257	311	382	451	540	642	764	920	998	1,298
GNP Billion $ 1967	1.180	1.508	1.920	2.500	3.105	3.855	4.760	5.850	7.220	8.080	10.790

Yearly Increase GNP	5.1%	4.9%	4.7%	4.5%	4.4%	4.3%	4.1%	3.9%	3.7%	3.5%

Map	Africa		H L Students	14 per 100000		Energy Total Billion Kec	0.777
Capital	Luanda		Hospital Beds	2.4 per 1000		Energy Per Capita Kec	144
One U S $ =	28.50 Escudo		Daily Newspapers	10 per 1000			
			Telephones	22,978		Kec per $ of GNP	5.370
Area-Total	1,246,700 Sq Km					Growth Ratio GNP/Kec	0.597
Area-Arable	9,000 Sq Km						
Population	5,430,000		Passenger Cars	64,400		Electric Capacity Mw	288
Population Density	4.24 per Sq Km		Steel Consumption	31 Kg/Cap		Generation Billion Kwhr	0.457
						Kilowatt Hours per Capita	85
						Kwhr per $ of GNP	0.38
Population Rate of Increase	1.40%		Growth Pattern Index GNP/Capita	68.75%		Economic Density GNP $/Sq Km	804
			Annual Increase 67-90	3.84%			
1967 GNP per Capita	190 US $						

ARGENTINA

	1967	1970	1975	1980	1985	1990	1995	2000	2005	2010	2015	2020
Population 1967 Population	1.000	1.045	1.120	1.190	1.255	1.335	1.390	1.455	1.505	1.560	1.610	1.650
Population Millions	23.26	24.28	25.80	27.80	29.20	30.60	32.30	33.82	35.00	36.30	37.49	38.40
GNP Capita 1967 $	635	688	790	894	1,025	1,115	1,298	1,450	1,615	1,775	1,950	2,160
GNP Billion $ 1967	14.73	16.70	20.40	24.80	29.60	35.30	41.90	49.10	56.20	64.50	73.40	83.00
Yearly Increase GNP		4.1%	3.9%	3.7%	3.6%	3.5%	3.2%	2.9%	2.7%	2.6%	2.4%	

Map	South America
Capital	Buenos Aires
One U S $ =	4 Peso
Area-Total	2,808,602 Sq Km
Area-Arable	330,070 Sq Km
Population	23,983,000
Population Density	8.39 per Sq Km
Birth-Death Rate %	2.20-0.80
Population Rate of Increase	1.60%
1967 GNP per Capita	635 US $

H L Students	1,135 per 100000
Hospital Beds	6.7 per 1000
Daily Newspapers	128 per 1000
Telephones	1,599,861
Television Sets	2,500,000
Tourist Receipt US $	175,000,000
Passenger Cars	1,152,300
Steel Consumption	94 Kg/Cap
Investment Ratio	20%
Growth Pattern Index	62.50%
GNP/Capita Annual Increase 67-90	2.50%

Energy Total Billion Kec	33.325
Energy per Capita Kec	1,411
Kec per $ of GNP	2.170
Growth Ratio GNP/Kec	0.858
Electric Capacity Mw	5,836
Generation Billion Kwhr	17.851
Kilowatt Hours per Capita	755
Kwhr per $ of GNP	1.13
Economic Density GNP $/Sq Km	5,240

AUSTRALIA

	1967	1970	1975	1980	1985	1990	1995	2000	2005	2010	2015	2020
Population 1967 Population	1.000	1.055	1.160	1.260	1.360	1.460	1.550	1.650	1.730	1.815	1.880	1.950
Population Millions	11.81	12.41	13.62	14.85	16.08	17.28	18.40	19.50	20.50	21.45	22.30	23.05
GNP Capita 1967 $	2,250	2,465	2,770	3,135	3,525	3,950	4,415	4,915	5,480	6,060	6,740	7,400
GNP Billion $ 1967	26.6	30.6	37.8	46.5	56.7	68.2	81.2	95.8	112.2	130.5	151.0	170.7
Yearly Increase GNP		4.3%	4.2%	4.0%	3.8%	3.6%	3.5%	3.2%	3.0%	2.9%		2.5%

Map	Oceania	H L Students	1,296 per 100000
Capital	Canberra	Hospital Beds	12.5 per 1000
One U S $ =	.8964 Dollar	Daily Newspapers	363 per 1000
		Telephones	3,392,436
Area-Total	7,686,810 Sq Km	Television Sets	2,700,000
Area-Arable	414,610 Sq Km	Tourist Receipt US $	3,444,800
Population	12,296,000		
Population Density	1.54 per Sq Km	Steel Consumption	489 Kg/Cap
Birth-Death Rate %	2.00-0.91	Investment Ratio	30%
Population Rate of Increase	1.90%	Growth Pattern Index	93.75%
		GNP/Capita Annual Increase 67-90	2.50%
1967 GNP per Capita	2,250 US $		

Energy Total Billion Kec	61.619
Energy per Capita Kec	5,121
Kec per $ of GNP	2.130
Growth Ratio GNP/Kec	1.165
Electric Capacity Mw	12,095
Generation Billion Kwhr	46.504
Kilowatt Hours per Capita	3,865
Kwhr per $ of GNP	1.62
Economic Density GNP $/Sq Km	3,460

AUSTRIA

	1967	1970	1975	1980	1985	1990	1995	2000	2005	2010	2015	2020
Population 1967 Population	1.000	1.012	1.035	1.053	1.072	1.096	1.110	1.128	1.140	1.150	1.160	1.171
Population Millions	7.32	7.42	7.59	7.72	7.86	8.03	8.14	8.26	8.35	8.42	8.50	8.58
GNP Capita 1967 $	1,465	1,628	1,930	2,260	2,635	3,030	3,445	3,960	4,490	5,090	5,695	6,380
GNP Billion $ 1967	10.72	12.08	14.62	17.42	20.75	24.38	28.05	32.70	37.50	42.80	48.40	54.60
Yearly Increase GNP		3.9%	3.7%	3.5%	3.3%	2.9%	3.1%	2.7%	2.6%	2.5%	2.4%	

Map	Europe	H L Students	734 per 100000
Capital	Vienna	Hospital Beds	10.0 per 1000
One U S $ =	25.86 Schilling	Daily Newspapers	249 per 1000
		Telephones	1,242,785
Area-Total	83,849 Sq Km		
Area-Arable	16,720 Sq Km	Television Sets	1,129,000
		Tourist Receipt US $	687,000,000
Population	7,371,000	Passenger Cars	1,056,300
Population Density	87 per Sq Km	Steel Consumption	306 Kg/Cap
Birth-Death Rate %	1.72-1.31	Investment Ratio	27%
Population Rate of		Growth Pattern Index	100%
Increase	0.48%	GNP/Capita	
		Annual Increase 67-90	3.20%
1967 GNP per Capita	1,465 US $		

Energy Total Billion Kec	20.978
Energy per Capita Kec	2,854
Kec per $ of GNP	1.820
Growth Ratio GNP/Kec	1.370
Electric Capacity Mw	7,056
Generation Billion Kwhr	21.216
Kilowatt Hours per Capita	2,886
Kwhr per $ of GNP	1.84
Economic Density GNP $/Sq Km	129,200

BAHAMA ISLANDS

	1970	1975	1980	1985	1990	1995	2000	2005	2010	2015	2020
Population 1967 Population	1.090	1.295	1.500	1.705	1.910	2.115	2.320	2.525	2.725	2.925	3.120
Population Millions	0.157	0.187	0.216	0.246	0.275	0.304	0.334	0.364	0.393	0.421	0.450
GNP/Capita 1967 $	1,815	2,145	2,600	3,035	3,590	4,180	4,850	5,600	6,430	7,250	8,080
GNP Billion $ 1967	0.285	0.400	0.562	0.742	0.988	1.275	1.620	2.100	2.530	3.050	3.630
Yearly Increase GNP	7.0%	6.6%	6.0%	5.6%	5.2%	4.8%	4.4%	4.0%	3.7%	3.5%	

Map	North & Caribbean America
Capital	Nassau
One U S $ =	1 Dollar
Area-Total	11,405 Sq Km
Area-Arable	130 Sq Km
Population	195,000
Population Density	12.62 per Sq Km
Population Rate of Increase	3.50%
1967 GNP per Capita	1,570 US $

H L Students	155 per 100000
Hospital Beds	5.3 per 1000
Daily Newspapers	122 per 1000
Telephones	36,513
Passenger Cars	32,400
Growth Pattern Index	
GNP/Capita	137.50%
Annual Increase 67-90	3.80%

Energy Total Billion Kec	0.669
Energy per Capita Kec	3,780
Kec per $ of GNP	3.010
Growth Ratio GNP/Kec	0.370
Electric Capacity Kw	46,100
Generation Billion Kwhr	0.215
Kilowatt Hours per Capita	1,214
Kwhr per $ of GNP	0.80
Economic Density GNP $/Sq Km	198,000

BAHREIN

	1970	1975	1980	1985	1990	1995	2000	2005	2010	2015	2020
Population 1967 Population	1.090	1.325	1.555	1.785	2.015	2.240	2.465	2.685	2.905	3.120	3.330
Population Billions	0.210	0.256	0.300	0.344	0.388	0.433	0.476	0.519	0.561	0.603	0.643
GNP Capita $ 1967	389	467	545	632	737	836	954	1,090	1,240	1,412	1,586
GNP Billion $ 1967	0.082	0.119	0.163	0.218	0.286	0.362	0.454	0.566	0.696	0.851	1.018
Yearly Increase GNP	6.8%	6.3%	5.8%	5.3%	4.8%	4.6%	4.4%	4.2%	4.0%	3.7%

Map	Asia & Middle East	H L Students	55 per 100000
Capital	Manama	Hospital Beds	7.4 per 1000
One U S $ =	0.468 Dinar		
Area-Total	598 Sq Km	Telephones	10,236
		Television Sets	21,000
Population	207,000		
Population Density	323 per Sq Km	Steel Consumption	70 Kg/Cap
Population Rate of Increase	3.70%	Growth Pattern Index GNP/Capita	112.50%
		Annual Increase 67-90	3.30%
1967 GNP per Capita	350 US $		

Energy Total Billion Kec	0.423
Energy per Capita Kec	2,114
Kec per $ of GNP	10.290
Growth Ratio GNP/Kec	0.658
Electric Capacity Kw	66,400
Generation Billion Kwhr	0.350
Kilowatt Hours per Capita	1,750
Kwhr per $ of GNP	4.74
Economic Density GNP $/Sq Km	1,135,000

BARBADOS

	1970	1975	1980	1985	1990	1995	2000	2005	2010	2015	2020
Population 1967 Population	1.030	1.075	1.117	1.163	1.207	1.245	1.277	1.308	1.335	1.360	1.383
Population Millions	0.256	0.268	0.276	0.289	0.301	0.310	0.318	0.326	0.332	0.339	0.345
GNP Capita 1967 $	520	605	698	805	936	1,067	1,235	1,423	1,620	1,842	2,100
GNP Billion $ 1967	0.133	0.162	0.192	0.232	0.281	0.330	0.393	0.463	0.537	0.625	0.725
Yearly Increase GNP	4.0%	3.9%	3.8%	3.7%	3.6%	3.5%	3.4%	3.2%	3.1%	3.0%	

Map North & Caribbean America		H L Students	151 per 100000	
Capital Bridgetown		Hospital Beds	11.1 per 1000	
One U S $ = 2.00 Dollar		Daily Newspapers	115 per 1000	
		Telephones	24,834	
Area-Total	430 Sq Km			
Area-Arable	260 Sq Km	Television Sets	15,000	
Population	254,000			
Population Density	580 per Sq Km			
Birth-Death Rate %	2.9–0.9	Growth Pattern Index	62.50%	
Population Rate of Increase	1.00%	GNP/Capita		
		Annual Increase 67-90	3.00%	
1967 GNP per Capita	478 US $			

Energy Total Billion Kec		0.138
Energy per Capita Kec		546
Kec per $ of GNP		1.07
Growth Ratio GNP/Kec		0.535
Electric Capacity Kw		31,600
Generation Billion Kwhr		0.110
Kilowatt Hours per Capita		436
Kwhr per $ of GNP		0.80
Economic Density GNP $/Sq Km		276,500

201

BELGIUM & LUXEMBOURG

	1967	1970	1975	1980	1985	1990	1995	2000	2005	2010	2015	2020
Population / 1967 Population	1.000	1.020	1.048	1.072	1.100	1.130	1.150	1.172	1.192	1.205	1.220	1.238
Population Millions	9.92	10.11	10.38	10.62	10.91	11.20	11.40	11.62	11.81	11.95	12.09	12.28
GNP/Capita 1967 $	2,045	2,262	2,625	3,010	3,480	3,980	4,575	5,230	5,910	6,675	7,500	8,360
GNP Billion $ 1967	20.26	22.85	27.25	32.10	38.00	44.60	52.20	60.90	69.90	79.80	90.60	102.65
Yearly Increase GNP		3.6%	3.5%	3.4%	3.3%	3.2%	3.1%	2.8%	2.6%	2.5%	2.4%	

Map   Europe
Capitals   Brussels – Luxembourg
One U S $ =   49.65 Franc

Area-Total   33,099 Sq Km
Area-Arable   8,860 Sq Km

Population
Population Density   298 per Sq Km   9,983,000

Birth-Death Rate %   1.48–1.28
Population Rate of
  Increase   0.65%

1967 GNP per Capita   2,045 US $

H L Students   603 per 100000
Hospital Beds   7.9 per 1000
Daily Newspapers   295 per 1000
Telephones   1,937,435

Television Sets   1,946,000
Tourist Receipt US $ 288,000,000
Passenger Cars   1,891,100
Steel Consumption   409 Kg/Cap

Investment Ratio   22%
Growth Pattern Index   112.50%
GNP/Capita
Annual Increase 67–90   2.94%

Energy Total
  Billion Kec   52.131
Energy per Capita Kec   5,236

Kec per $ of GNP   2.29
Growth Ratio GNP/Kec   2.19

Electric Capacity Mw   8,693
Generation Billion Kwhr   29.590
Kilowatt Hours per Capita   2,972
Kwhr per $ of GNP   1.34

Economic Density
  GNP $/Sq Km   613,000

BERMUDA

	1970	1975	1980	1985	1990	1995	2000	2005	2010	2015	2020
Population 1967 Population	1.055	1.140	1.225	1.310	1.390	1.465	1.540	1.605	1.670	1.730	1.790
Population Millions	0.053	0.057	0.061	0.066	0.070	0.073	0.077	0.080	0.084	0.087	0.090
GNP / Capita 1967 $	2,835	3,258	3,705	4,170	4,680	5,260	5,900	6,540	7,310	8,080	8,980
GNP Billion $ 1967	0.150	0.185	0.227	0.273	0.325	0.385	0.454	0.525	0.610	0.699	0.804
Yearly Increase GNP		4.4%	4.1%	3.7%	3.5%	3.4%	3.2%	3.1%	3.0%	2.9%	2.8%

Map	North & Caribbean America
Capital	Hamilton
One U S $ =	.4183 Pound
Area-Total	53 Sq Km
Area-Arable	2 Sq Km
Population	52,000
Population Density	953 per Sq Km
Population Rate of Increase	1.80%
1967 GNP per Capita	2,410 US $

Hospital Beds	11.1 per 1000
Daily Newspapers	228 per 1000
Telephones	26,436
Television Sets	13,000
Tourist Receipt US $	63,000,000
Passenger Cars	9,800
Growth Pattern Index GNP/Capita	93.75%
Annual Increase 67-90	2.94%

Energy Total Billion Kec	0.128
Energy per Capita Kec	2,560
Kec per $ of GNP	1.56
Growth Ratio GNP/Kec	0.371
Electric Capacity Kw	69,600
Generation Billion Kwhr	0.190
Kilowatt Hours per Capita	3,799
Kwhr per $ of GNP	1.44
Economic Density GNP $/Sq Km	2,190,000

203

BOLIVIA

	1970	1975	1980	1985	1990	1995	2000	2005	2010	2015	2020
Population 1967 Population	1.043	1.110	1.170	1.235	1.300	1.350	1.400	1.445	1.490	1.530	1.570
Population Millions	4.760	5.060	5.340	5.640	5.930	6.160	6.380	6.600	6.800	6.980	7.160
GNP Capita 1967 $	174.5	216.5	265.0	324.0	395.5	485.0	606.5	702.0	847.0	1,035	1,200
GNP Billion $ 1967	0.830	1.098	1.412	1.825	2.340	2.990	3.865	4.640	5.750	7.210	8.600
Yearly Increase GNP	3.3%	3.1%	3.0%	2.9%	2.8%	2.6%	2.5%	2.3%	2.2%	2.1%	

Map	South America	
Capital	La Paz	
One U S $ =	11.88 Boliviano	
Area-Total	1,098,580 Sq Km	
Area-Arable	30,910 Sq Km	
Population	4,804,000	
Population Density	3.47 per Sq Km	
Birth-Death Rate %	4.40-2.00	
Population Rate of Increase	1.40%	
1967 GNP per Capita	189 US $	

H L Students	414 per 100000	
Hospital Beds	2.2 per 1000	
Daily Newspapers	23 per 1000	
Telephones	32,300	
Passenger Cars	14,500	
Steel Consumption	8 Kg/Cap	
Investment Ratio	19%	
Growth Pattern Index	81.25%	
GNP/Capita Annual Increase 67-90	3.25%	

Energy Total Billion Kec		0.968
Energy per Capita Kec		207
Kec per $ of GNP		1.23
Growth Ratio GNP/Kec		0.685
Electric Capacity Mw		222
Generation Billion Kwhr		0.672
Kilowatt Hours per Capita		143
Kwhr per $ of GNP		0.83
Economic Density GNP $/Sq Km		655

204

BRAZIL

	1967	1970	1975	1980	1985	1990	1995	2000	2005	2010	2015	2020
Population 1967 Population	1.000	1.094	1.239	1.399	1.550	1.710	1.870	2.025	2.164	2.310	2.460	2.600
Population Millions	85.7	93.7	106.0	119.8	132.8	146.4	160.1	173.1	185.8	197.9	210.6	222.5
GNP Capita 1967 $	309	339	470	622	816	1056	1368	1720	2140	2640	3135	3610
GNP Billion $ 1967	26.8	32.9	50	741	108.5	155	219	310.5	395	523.5	660	802
Yearly Increase GNP		8.8%	8.2%	7.7%	7.3%	6.8%	6.4%	6.0%	5.7%	5.2%	4.9%	

Map	South America
Capital	Brasilia
One U S $ =	4.560 Cruzeiro
Area-Total	8,511,965 Sq Km
Area-Arable	297,600 Sq Km
Population	90,840,000
Population Density	10.19 per Sq Km
Birth-Death Rate %	3.90-1.10
Population Rate of Increase	2.93%
1967 GNP per Capita	309 US $

H L Students	251 per 100000
Hospital Beds	3.5 per 1000
Daily Newspapers	36 per 1000
Telephones	1,560,701
Television Sets	6,000,000
Tourist Receipt US $	21,000,000
Passenger Cars	1,537,000
Steel Consumption	55 Kg/Cap
Investment Ratio	15%
Growth Pattern Index	118.75%
GNP/Capita Annual Increase 67-90	5.50%

Energy Total Billion Kec	39.735
Energy per Capita Kec	450
Kec per $ of GNP	1.27
Growth Ratio GNP/Kec	0.675
Electric Capacity Mw	8,555
Generation Billion Kwhr	38.181
Kilowatt Hours per Capita	432
Kwhr per $ of GNP	1.29
Economic Density GNP $/Sq Km	3,150

205

BRUNEI

	1970	1975	1980	1985	1990	1995	2000	2005	2010	2015	2020
Population 1967 Population	1.090	1.325	1.555	1.785	2.015	2.240	2.465	2.685	2.905	3.120	3.330
Population Millions	0.118	0.143	0.168	0.198	0.218	0.242	0.267	0.290	0.314	0.337	0.360
GNP/Capita 1967 $	871	957	1,075	1,182	1,288	1,401	1,528	1,660	1,800	1,944	2,090
GNP Billion $ 1967	0.103	0.137	0.181	0.228	0.280	0.340	0.406	0.491	0.565	0.650	0.753

Yearly Increase GNP	6.2%	5.2%	4.5%	4.5%	3.8%	3.5%	3.3%	3.1%	2.95%	2.8%

Map	Asia & Middle East						Energy Total Billion Kec	0.282
Capital	Brunei		Hospital Beds	3.9 per 1000		Energy per Capita Kec	2,519
One U S $ =	3.08 Dollar		Daily Newspapers	71 per 1000			
			Telephones	2,681		Kec per $ of GNP	2.88
Area-Total	5,765 Sq Km					Growth Ratio GNP/Kec	0.600
Area-Arable	660 Sq Km		Passenger Cars	7,000		Electric Capacity Kw	34,800
Population	116,000					Generation Billion Kwhr	0.104
Population Density	19 per Sq Km		Growth Pattern Index			Kilowatt Hours per Capita	928
			GNP/Capita	56.25%		Kwhr per $ of GNP	1.16
Population Rate of Increase	3.70%		Annual Increase 67-90	2.10%		Economic Density GNP $/Sq Km	14,920
1967 GNP per Capita	800 US $						

BULGARIA

	1967	1970	1975	1980	1985	1990	1995	2000	2005	2010	2015	2020
Population 1967 Population	1.000	1.021	1.060	1.094	1.128	1.165	1.192	1.220	1.245	1.265	1.285	1.308
Population Millions	8.31	8.51	8.83	9.11	9.38	9.70	9.94	10.15	10.33	10.51	10.70	10.88
GNP Capita 1967 $	690	815	1,073	1,410	1,807	2,260	2,805	3,390	4,000	4,750	5,505	6,340
GNP Billion $ 1967	5.74	6.94	9.50	12.82	16.92	21.91	27.88	34.41	41.32	50.00	59.00	68.98
Yearly Increase GNP		6.5%	6.2%	5.7%	5.3%	4.9%	4.3%	3.7%	3.5%	3.3%	3.1%	

Map	Europe	
Capital	Sofia	
One U S $ =	2.00 Lev	
Area-Total	110,912 Sq Km	
Area-Arable	45,580 Sq Km	
Population Density	8,436,000 75 per Sq Km	
Birth-Death Rate %	1.69-0.86	
Population Rate of Increase	0.81%	
1967 GNP per Capita	690 US $	

H L Students	1,103 per 100000
Hospital Beds	9.1 per 1000
Daily Newspapers	195 per 1000
Telephones	378,152
Television Sets	621,000
Passenger Cars	251
Investment Ratio	34%
Growth Pattern Index	181.25%
GNP/Capita Annual Increase 67-90	5.25%

Energy Total Billion Kec	27.765
Energy per Capita Kec	3,317
Kec per $ of GNP	4.43
Growth Ratio GNP/Kec	0.658
Electric Capacity Mw	3,462
Generation Billion Kwhr	15.764
Kilowatt Hours per Capita	1,883
Kwhr per $ of GNP	2.40
Economic Density GNP $/Sq Km	51,800

BURMA

	1970	1975	1980	1985	1990	1995	2000	2005	2010	2015	2020
Population 1967 Population	1.060	1.165	1.268	1.370	1.470	1.560	1.650	1.740	1.820	1.900	1.970
Population Millions	27.25	30.10	32.70	35.40	38.00	40.30	42.60	44.90	47.00	49.10	50.90
GNP 1967 $ Capita	74.1	83.8	94.7	106.8	119.0	132.5	147.6	164.7	182.6	201.8	222.4
GNP Billion $ 1967	2.020	2.520	3.095	3.780	4.525	5.350	6.280	7.410	8.580	9.900	11.330
Yearly Increase GNP		4.5%	4.3%	4.1%	3.7%	3.5%	3.3%	3.1%	3.0%	2.9%	2.7%

Map	Asia & Middle East	H L Students	127 per 100000
Capital	Rangoon	Hospital Beds	0.8 per 1000
One U S $ =	4.758 Kyat	Daily Newspapers	70 per 1000
		Telephones	22,080
Area-Total	678,033 Sq Km		
Area-Arable	160,870 Sq Km		
Population	26,980,000	Passenger Cars	28,900
Population Density	38 per Sq Km	Steel Consumption	3 Kg/Cap
Population Rate of Increase	2.10%	Growth Pattern Index GNP/Capita Annual Increase 67-90	37.50% 2.32%
1967 GNP per Capita	70 US $		

Energy Total Billion Kec	1.519
Energy per Capita Kec	57
Kec per $ of GNP	0.73
Growth Ratio GNP/Kec	0.478
Electric Capacity Mw	260
Generation Billion Kwhr	0.553
Kilowatt Hours per Capita	20
Kwhr per $ of GNP	0.33
Economic Density GNP $/Sq Km	2,675

BURUNDI

	1970	1975	1980	1985	1990	1995	2000	2005	2010	2015	2020
Population 1967 Population Population Millions	1.060 3.540	1.155 3.860	1.250 4.175	1.345 4.495	1.440 4.810	1.530 5.110	1.615 5.400	1.695 5.660	1.770 5.915	1.840 6.150	1.910 6.380
GNP/Capita 1967 $	53.0	60.0	75.0	82.2	89.2	100.0	111.0	118.0	125.0	132.0	146.5
GNP Billion $ 1967	0.188	0.232	0.313	0.369	0.430	0.511	0.600	0.667	0.740	0.810	0.935

Yearly Increase GNP	4.4%	3.8%	3.3%	3.1%	2.9%	2.7%	2.4%	2.2%	1.8%	1.6%

Map	Africa
Capital	Bujumbura
One U S $ =	87.50 Franc
Area-Total	27,834 Sq Km
Area-Arable	10,080 Sq Km
Population	3,475,000
Population Density	125 per Sq Km
Birth-Death Rate %	4.60-2.60
Population Rate of Increase	2.00%
1967 GNP per Capita	50 US $

H L Students Hospital Beds				8 per 100000 1.1 per 1000					
Telephones					3,200				
Passenger Cars					3,200				
Growth Pattern Index GNP/Capita Annual Increase 67-90					18.75% 2.55%				

Energy Total Billion Kec	0.031
Energy per Capita Kec	8
Kec per $ of GNP	0.14
Electric Capacity Kw	5,200
Generation Billion Kwhr	0.017
Kilowatt Hours per Capita	4
Kwhr per $ of GNP	0.08
Economic Density GNP $/Sq Km	6,000

CAMBODIA

	1967	1970	1975	1980	1985	1990	1995	2000	2005	2010	2015	2020
Population / 1967 Population	1.000	1.070	1.190	1.310	1.430	1.550	1.670	1.780	1.890	1.990	2.090	2.185
Population Millions	6.42	6.94	7.64	8.41	9.18	9.95	10.72	11.43	12.13	12.78	13.42	14.03
GNP/Capita 1967 $	150.5	173	217	272	335	399	502	508	752	902	1,088	1,305
GNP Billion $ 1967	0.966	1.200	1.658	2.285	3.073	3.980	5.580	6.950	9.120	11.500	14.600	18.300
Yearly Increase GNP		6.7%	6.6%	6.1%	5.5%	5.3%	5.1%	4.9%	4.8%	4.7%	4.6%	

Map	Asia & Middle East
Capital	Phnom Penh
One U S $ =	55.54 Riel
Area-Total	181,035 Sq Km
Area-Arable	29,840 Sq Km
Population	6,701,000
Population Density	35 per Sq Km
Birth-Death Rate %	5.0-2.0
Population Rate of Increase	2.40%
1967 GNP per Capita	148 US $

H L Students	139 per 100000
Hospital Beds	0.8 per 1000
Telephones	7,315
Television Sets	7,000
Passenger Cars	23,100
Growth Pattern Index GNP/Capita	75%
Annual Increase 67-90	4.35%

Energy Total Billion Kec	0.333
Energy per Capita Kec	50
Kec per $ of GNP	0.35
Growth Ratio GNP/Kec	0.634
Electric Capacity Mw	75
Generation Billion Kwhr	0.128
Kilowatt Hours per Capita	19
Kwhr per $ of GNP	0.10
Economic Density GNP $/Sq Km	5,250

CAMEROUN

	1970	1975	1980	1985	1990	1995	2000	2005	2010	2015	2020
Population 1967 Population	1.065	1.175	1.285	1.390	1.495	1.595	1.690	1.785	1.875	1.960	2.040
Population Millions	5.83	6.43	7.04	7.60	8.18	8.73	9.25	9.76	10.27	1.72	11.17
GNP/Capita 1967 $	154.5	173.2	192.0	214.6	237.6	263.6	292.0	322.0	356.0	394.0	433.0
GNP Billion $ 1967	0.900	1.113	1.350	1.632	1.942	2.300	2.700	3.144	3.620	4.230	4.840
Yearly Increase GNP	4.3%	4.0%	3.8%	3.6%	3.4%	3.2%	3.1%	2.9%	2.8%	2.7%	

Map	Africa	H L Students	34 per 100000
Capital	Yaounde	Hospital Beds	2.1 per 1000
One U S $ =	277.71 CFA Franc	Daily Newspapers	4 per 1000
		Telephones	5,000
Area-Total	475,442 Sq Km		
Area-Arable	43,000 Sq Km	Passenger Cars	26,900
Population	5,680,000		
Population Density	11.50 per Sq Km	Investment Ratio	14%
Birth-Death Rate %	5.0 - 2.6	Growth Pattern Index	37.50%
Population Rate of Increase	2.20%	GNP/Capita	
		Annual Increase 67-90	2.20%
1967 GNP per Capita	145 US $		

Energy Total Billion Kec	0.462
Energy per Capita Kec	83
Kec per $ of GNP	0.53
Growth Ratio GNP/Kec	0.412
Electric Capacity Mw	170
Generation Billion Kwhr	1.006
Kilowatt Hours per Capita	180
Kwhr per $ of GNP	1.25
Economic Density GNP $/Sq Km	1,665

211

CANADA

	1967	1970	1975	1980	1985	1990	1995	2000	2005	2010	2015	2020
Population / 1967 Population	1.000	1.050	1.135	1.215	1.289	1.370	1.440	1.510	1.574	1.638	1.695	1.740
Population Millions	20.44	21.50	23.24	24.88	26.40	28.04	29.50	30.95	32.24	33.55	34.70	35.60
GNP Capita 1967 $	2,805	3,060	3,490	3,982	4,545	5,140	5,785	6,460	7,190	7,915	8,730	9,575
GNP Billion $ 1967	57.1	65.9	81.2	99.5	119.8	144.0	170.5	200.0	231.8	265.5	303.0	340.0
Yearly Increase GNP		4.3%	4.1%	3.8%	3.7%	3.4%	3.2%	3.0%	2.7%	2.6%	2.3%	

Map   North & Caribbean America
Capital   Ottawa
One U S $ =   1.0259 Dollar

Area-Total   9,976,139 Sq Km
Area-Arable   434,040 Sq Km

Population   21,089,000
Population Density 2.05 per Sq Km

Birth-Death Rate %   1.7710.74
Population Rate of Increase   1.72%

1967 GNP per Capita   2,805 US $

H L Students   2,201 per 100000
Hospital Beds   11.1 per 1000
Daily Newspapers   212 per 1000
Telephones   8,821,000

Television Sets   6,100,000
Tourist Receipt US $ 918,000,000
Passenger Cars   6,159,600
Steel Consumption   489 Kg/Cap

Investment Ratio   24%
Growth Pattern Index   112.50%
GNP/Capita
Annual Increase 67-90   2.68%

Energy Total   176.164
  Billion Kec
Energy per Capita Kec   8,480

Kec per $ of GNP   2,880
Growth Ratio GNP/Kec   1.07

Electric Capacity Mw   35,933
Generation Billion Kwhr   176.841
Kilowatt Hours per Capita   8,513
Kwhr per $ of GNP   2.89

Economic Density   5,700
  GNP $/Sq Km

212

CENTRAL AFRICAN REPUBLIC

	1970	1975	1980	1985	1990	1995	2000	2005	2010	2015	2020
Population 1967 Population	1.070	1.200	1.330	1.460	1.580	1.700	1.820	1.940	2.050	2.155	2.260
Population Millions	1.560	1.750	1.940	2.127	2.304	2.480	2.655	2.830	2.990	3.140	3.296
GNP Capita 1967 $	125.2	133.8	144.0	154.5	164.8	175.0	187.0	199.0	211.0	224.5	235.0
GNP Billion $ 1967	0.196	0.234	0.279	0.329	0.380	0.433	0.496	0.563	0.632	0.705	0.775
Yearly Increase GNP	3.6%	3.5%	3.3%	3.0%	2.8%	2.7%	2.5%	2.3%	2.1%	1.9%	

Map	Africa
Capital	Bangui
One U S $ =	277.71 CFA Franc
Area-Total	622,984 Sq Km
Area-Arable	59,000 Sq Km
Population	1,518,000
Population Density	2.34 per Sq Km
Birth-Death Rate %	4.8-2.5
Population Rate of Increase	2.50%
1967 GNP per Capita	120 US $

Hospital Beds	1.8 per 1000
Daily Newspapers	0.6 per 1000
Telephones	2,800
Passenger Cars	4,300
Growth Pattern Index	
GNP/Capita	18.75%
Annual Increase 67-90	1.40%

Energy Total Billion Kec	0.054
Energy per Capita Kec	36
Kec per $ of GNP	0.29
Growth Ratio GNP/Kec	0.468
Electric Capacity Kw	12,800
Generation Billion Kwhr	0.034
Kilowatt Hours per Capita	22
Kwhr per $ of GNP	0.16
Economic Density GNP $/Sq Km	281

213

CEYLON

	1970	1975	1980	1985	1990	1995	2000	2005	2010	2015	2020
Population 1967 Population	1.075	1.200	1.320	1.435	1.550	1.660	1.770	1.880	1.985	2.085	2.180
Population Millions	12.58	14.03	15.44	16.20	18.13	19.42	20.70	22.00	23.21	24.40	25.50
GNP/Capita 1967 $	177	220	274	340	419	512	630	767	942	1,120	1,370
GNP Billion $ 1967	2.22	3.08	4.23	5.71	7.60	9.95	13.02	16.88	21.88	27.35	34.90
Yearly Increase GNP	6.8%	6.5%	6.2%	5.9%	5.5%	5.5%	5.4%	5.4%	5.2%	5.0%	

Map	Asia & Middle East	H L Students	141 per 100000
Capital	Colombo	Hospital Beds	3.1 per 1000
One U S $ =	5.958 Rupee	Daily Newspapers	44 per 1000
		Telephones	57,598
Area-Total	65,610 Sq Km		
Area-Arable	19,800 Sq Km		
Population	12,240,000	Passenger Cars	84,700
Population Density	178 per Sq Km	Steel Consumption	10 Kg/Cap
Birth-Death Rate %	3.2-0.8	Investment Ratio	19%
Population Rate of Increase	2.40%	Growth Pattern Index GNP/Capita	81.25%
		Annual Increase 67-90	4.45%
1967 GNP per Capita	152 US $		

Energy Total Billion Kec	1.368
Energy per Capita Kec	114
Kec per $ of GNP	0.73
Growth Ratio GNP/Kec	0.570
Electric Capacity Mw	217
Generation Billion Kwhr	0.650
Kilowatt Hours per Capita	54
Kwhr per $ of GNP	0.32
Economic Density GNP $/Sq Km	27,000

CHAD

	1970	1975	1980	1985	1990	1995	2000	2005	2010	2015	2020
Population / 1967 Population	1.075	1.240	1.405	1.570	1.735	1.900	2.060	2.210	2.360	2.510	2.650
Population Millions	3.665	4.230	4.795	5.355	5.915	6.480	7.025	7.540	8.050	8.560	9.040
GNP/Capita 1967 $	78.8	94.2	100.3	128.7	148.8	170.5	194.5	220.5	249.0	280.0	314.5
GNP Billion $ 1967	0.289	0.398	0.480	0.688	0.880	1.108	1.365	1.665	2.005	2.400	2.840
Yearly Increase GNP	6.6%	6.0%	5.5%	5.1%	4.7%	4.3%	4.0%	3.8%	3.6%	3.4%

Map	Africa
Capital	Fort-Lamy
One U S $ =	277.71 CFA Franc
Area-Total	1,284,000 Sq Km
Area-Arable	70,000 Sq Km
Population Density	2.66 per Sq Km
Population	3,510,000
Birth-Death Rate %	4.5-2.3
Population Rate of Increase	3.00%
1967 GNP per Capita	70 US $

Hospital Beds	1.1 per 1000
Daily Newspapers	0.4 per 1000
Telephones	3,953
Passenger Cars	3,700
Growth Pattern Index	
GNP/Capita	37.50%
Annual Increase 67-90	3.35%

Energy Total Billion Kec	0.061
Energy per Capita Kec	17
Kec per $ of GNP	0.23
Growth Ratio GNP/Kec	0.586
Generation Billion Kwhr	0.031
Kilowatt Hours per Capita	8
Kwhr per $ of GNP	0.10
Economic Density GNP $/Sq Km	185

215

CHILE

	1967	1970	1975	1980	1985	1990	1995	2000	2005	2010	2015	2020
Population 1967 Population	1.000	1.060	1.164	1.265	1.355	1.460	1.550	1.638	1.725	1.806	1.885	1.950
Population Millions	9.14	9.68	10.62	11.55	12.37	13.31	14.12	14.92	15.74	16.48	17.20	17.80
GNP Capita 1967 $	585	671	770	894	1,030	1,184	1,348	1,530	1,725	1,940	2,150	2,390
GNP Billion	5.34	6.50	8.20	10.32	12.75	15.78	19.05	22.91	27.00	31.55	36.80	42.55
Yearly Increase GNP		4.7%	4.5%	4.3%	4.0%	3.8%	3.7%	3.4%	3.4%	3.2%	3.1%	2.9%

Map	South America
Capital	Santiago
One U S $ =	13.60 Escudo
Area-Total	756,945 Sq Km
Area-Arable	45,110 Sq Km
Population	9,566,000
Population Density	11.9 per Sq Km
Birth-Death Rate %	3.40-1.10
Population Rate of Increase	2.50%
1967 GNP per Capita	585 US $

H L Students	625 per 100000
Hospital Beds	4.0 per 1000
Daily Newspapers	118 per 1000
Telephones	312,042
Television Sets	400,000
Passenger Cars	130,200
Steel Consumption	68 Kg/Cap
Investment Ratio	17%
Growth Pattern Index	68.75%
GNP/Capita Annual Increase 67-90	3.10%

Energy Total Billion Kec	10.764
Energy per Capita Kec	1,151
Kec per $ of GNP	1.99
Growth Ratio GNP/Kec	0.587
Electric Capacity Mw	1,720
Generation Billion Kwhr	6.918
Kilowatt Hours per Capita	739
Kwhr per $ of GNP	1.29
Economic Density GNP $/Sq Km	6,970

CHINA-MAINLAND

	1967	1970	1975	1980	1985	1990	1995	2000	2005	2010	2015	2020
Population 1967 Population	1.000	1.040	1.110	1.180	1.250	1.320	1.380	1.440	1.490	1.540	1.585	1.630
Population Millions	720	749	800	850	900	950	993	1,037	1,072	1,108	1,140	1,172
GNP Capita 1967 $	89.0	101.0	126.0	157.5	190.3	234.5	282.0	350.0	422.5	504.0	605.0	706.0
GNP Billion $ 1967	64.3	75.7	100.9	134.0	171.0	222.5	280.0	363.0	452.0	558.0	690.0	827.0
Yearly Increase GNP		5.9%	5.8%	5.6%	5.4%	5.3%	5.2%	4.5%	4.4%	4.3%	3.7%	

Map	Asia & Middle East	H L Students	122 per 100000
Capital	Peking	Daily Newspapers	19 per 1000
One U S $ =	2.00 Yuan		
Area-Total	9,561,000 Sq Km		
Area-Arable	1,093,540 Sq Km		
Population	740,000,000	Steel Consumption	21 Kg/Cap
Population Density	75 per Sq Km		
Birth-Death Rate %	3.4-1.5	Growth Pattern Index	87.50%
Population Rate of Increase	1.50%	GNP/Capita Annual Increase 67-90	4.30%
1967 GNP per Capita	80 US $	Economic Density GNP $/Sq Km	6,730

217

CHINA-TAIWAN

	1967	1970	1975	1980	1985	1990	1995	2000	2005	2010	2015	2020
Population 1967 Population	1.000	1.110	1.270	1.452	1.640	1.820	2.010	2.200	2.370	2.548	2.724	2.900
Population Millions	13.15	14.60	16.70	19.11	21.59	23.95	26.42	28.90	31.20	33.50	35.79	38.15
GNP Capita 1967 $	274	321	416	542	692	873	1,098	1,330	1,618	1,920	2,265	2,640
GNP Billion $ 1967	3.61	4.69	6.95	10.37	14.90	20.88	29.10	38.43	50.50	64.40	81.00	100.70
Yearly Increase GNP		8.2%	7.9%	7.5%	6.9%	6.8%	5.7%	5.6%	5.0%	4.7%	4.5%	

Map	Asia & Middle East
Capital	Taipei
One U S $ =	40.10 Dollar
Area-Total	35,691 Sq Km
Area-Arable	9,000 Sq Km
Population	13,800,000
Population Density	365 per Sq Km
Birth-Death Rate %	2.9-0.6
Population Rate of Increase	3.26%
1967 GNP per Capita	274 US $

H L Students	1,054 per 100000
Hospital Beds	1.0 per 1000
Daily Newspapers	64 per 1000
Telephones	280,192
Television Sets	193,000
Tourist Receipt US $	65,000,000
Passenger Cars	30,700
Steel Consumption	80 Kg/Cap
Investment Ratio	26%
Growth Pattern Index	118.75%
GNP/Capita	
Annual Increase 67-90	5 13%

Energy Total Billion Kec	10,984
Energy per Capita Kec	815
Kec per $ of GNP	2.64
Growth Ratio GNP/Kec	1.090
Electric Capacity Mw	2,062
Generation Billion Kwhr	10,036
Kilowatt Hours per Capita	745
Kwhr per $ of GNP	2.48
Economic Density GNP $/Sq Km	100,500

COLOMBIA

	1967	1970	1975	1980	1985	1990	1995	2000	2005	2010	2015	2020
Population 1967 Population	1.000	1.100	1.249	1.414	1.579	1.745	1.912	2.080	2.228	2.382	2.540	2.690
Population Millions	19.19	21.10	23.95	27.10	30.25	33.50	36.65	39.92	42.80	45.70	43.74	51.60
GNP Capita 1967 $	313	339	396	456.5	526	603	700	804	923	1,055	1,200	1,360
GNP Billion $ 1967	6.01	7.15	9.50	12.38	15.92	20.20	29.69	32.05	39.45	48.20	53.60	70.20
Yearly Increase GNP		5.8%	5.4%	5.1%	4.9%	4.7%	4.5%	4.2%	4.1%	4.0%	3.7%	

Map	South America	H L Students	268 per 100000
Capital	Bogota	Hospital Beds	2.4 per 1000
One U S $ =	18.58 Peso	Daily Newspapers	53 per 1000
		Telephones	817,423
Area-Total	1,138,914 Sq Km	Television Sets	500,000
Area-Arable	50,470 Sq Km	Tourist Receipt US $	43,000,000
Population	20,463,000	Passenger Cars	141,100
Population Density	17 per Sq Km	Steel Consumption	28 Kg/Cap
Birth-Death Rate %	4.40-1.10	Investment Ratio	22%
Population Rate of Increase	3.19%	Growth Pattern Index	37.50%
		GNP/Capita Annual Increase 67-90	2.90%
1967 GNP per Capita	313 US $		

Energy Total Billion Kec	11,423
Energy per Capita Kec	576
Kec per $ of GNP	1.80
Growth Ratio GNP/Kec	0.727
Electric Capacity Mw	2,368
Generation Billion Kwhr	7.000
Kilowatt Hours per Capita	353
Kwhr per $ of GNP	1.05
Economic Density GNP $/Sq Km	5,280

219

CONGO-BRAZZAVILLE

	1970	1975	1980	1985	1990	1995	2000	2005	2010	2015	2020
Population / 1967 Population	1.040	1.110	1.180	1.250	1.320	1.380	1.440	1.490	1.540	1.585	1.630
Population Millions	0.895	0.947	1.015	1.075	1.135	1.188	1.240	1.282	1.325	1.363	1.402
GNP/Capita 1967 $	226	285	352	439	549	675	831	1,016	1,234	1,504	1,798
GNP Billion $ 1967	0.202	0.269	0.357	0.473	0.624	0.803	1.030	1.305	1.635	2.050	2.525
Yearly Increase GNP	6.0%	5.8%	5.7%	5.6%	5.3%	5.1%	4.8%	4.6%	4.4%	4.2%	

Map	Africa
Capital	Brazzaville
One US $ =	277.71 CFA Franc
Area—Total	342,000 Sq Km
Area—Arable	6,300 Sq Km
Population Density	2.52 per Sq Km
Population	880,000
Birth-Death Rate %	4.1-2.4
Population Rate of Increase	1.50%
1967 GNP per Capita	190 US $

H L Students	129 per 100000
Hospital Beds	5.9 per 1000
Daily Newspapers	1.3 per 1000
Telephones	9,287
Television Sets	500
Growth Pattern Index	
GNP/Capita	87.50%
Annual Increase 67-90	4.70%

Energy Total Billion Kec	0.178
Energy per Capita Kec	205
Growth Ratio GNP/Kec	0.60
Electric Capacity Mw	22
Generation Billion Kwhr	0.055
Kilowatt Hours per Capita	63
Economic Density GNP $/Sq Km	477

CONGO-KINSHASA

	1970	1975	1980	1985	1990	1995	2000	2005	2010	2015	2020
Population / 1967 Population	1.060	1.165	1.268	1.370	1.470	1.560	1.650	1.740	1.820	1.900	1.970
Population Millions	17.42	19.08	20.70	22.43	24.05	25.55	27.00	28.50	29.80	31.10	32.25
GNP/Capita 1967 $	96.7	100.7	121.0	133.5	148.8	164.2	181.5	201.5	222.0	245.0	286.0
GNP Billion $ 1967	1.685	1.920	2.550	2.995	3.675	4.180	4.900	5.740	6.620	7.620	9.230
Yearly Increase GNP	5.4%	5.0%	4.6%	4.1%	3.6%	3.2%	3.0%	2.9%	2.8%	2.7%	

Map	Africa	
Capital	Kinshasa	
One US $ =	0.50 Zaire	
Area-Total	2,345,409 Sq Km	
Area-Arable	72,000 Sq Km	
Population	17,100,000	
Population Density	6.97 per Sq Km	
Birth-Death Rate %	4.3-2.0	
Population Rate of Increase	2.10%	
1967 GNP per Capita	90 US $	

H L Students	36 per 100000	
Hospital Beds	3.7 per 1000	
Telephones	23,919	
Television Sets	10,200	
Passenger Cars	46,100	
Steel Consumption	5 Kg/Cap	
Investment Ratio	21%	
Growth Pattern Index	37.50%	
GNP/Capita Annual Increase 67-90	2.20%	

Energy Total Billion Kec	1.426	
Energy per Capita Kec	85	
Kec per $ of GNP	0.87	
Growth Ratio GNP/Kec	0.725	
Generation Billion Kwhr	2.599	
Kilowatt Hours per Capita	155	
Kwhr per $ of GNP	1.68	
Economic Density GNP $/Sq Km	627	

221

COSTA RICA

	1970	1975	1980	1985	1990	1995	2000	2005	2010	2015	2020
Population 1967 Population	1.090	1.295	1.500	1.705	1.910	2.115	2.320	2.525	2.725	2.925	3.120
Population Millions	1.740	2.065	2.495	2.720	3.045	3.375	3.700	4.030	4.350	4.665	4.975
GNP Capita 1967 $	462	538	630	740	845	987	1,130	1,325	1,508	1,740	1,975
GNP Billion $ 1967	0.805	1.112	1.570	2.015	2.575	3.322	4.180	5.350	6.550	8.130	9.820
Yearly Increase GNP	7.3%	7.0%	6.6%	6.0%	5.4%	5.0%	4.7%	4.4%	4.2%	3.8%	

Map	North & Caribbean America	H L Students	487 per 100000
Capital	San Jose	Hospital Beds	3.5 per 1000
One U S $ =	6.62 Colon	Daily Newspapers	60 per 1000
		Telephones	50,093
Area-Total	50,700 Sq Km		
Area-Arable	6,220 Sq Km	Television Sets	75,000
Population	1,695,000	Passenger Cars	33,700
Population Density	31 per Sq Km		
Birth-Death Rate %	4.5-0.8	Investment Ratio	24%
Population Rate of Increase	3.50%	Growth Pattern Index	62.50%
		GNP/Capita Annual Increase 67-90	3.05%
1967 GNP per Capita	425 US $		

Energy Total Billion Kec	0.529
Energy per Capita Kec	323
Kec per $ of GNP	0.77
Growth Ratio GNP/Kec	0.556
Electric Capacity Mw	237
Generation Billion Kwhr	0.833
Kilowatt Hours per Capita	509
Kwhr per $ of GNP	1.11
Economic Density GNP $/Sq Km	13,200

CUBA

	1970	1975	1980	1985	1990	1995	2000	2005	2010	2015	2020
Population 1967 Population	1.070	1.183	1.295	1.415	1.535	1.630	1.740	1.835	1.935	2.020	2.110
Population Millions	8.59	9.50	10.40	11.38	12.33	13.10	13.90	14.70	15.50	16.22	16.92
GNP Capita 1967 $	348	380	412	447	486	527	568	613	664	712	766
GNP Billion $ 1967	2.99	3.61	4.29	5.09	6.00	6.91	7.90	9.02	10.28	11.54	12.95
Yearly Increase GNP	3.9%	3.7%	3.5%	3.2%	2.9%	2.7%	2.6%	2.5%	2.4%	2.3%	

Map North & Caribbean America	H L Students	470 per 100000	
Capital Havana	Hospital Beds	5.9 per 1000	
One U S $ = 1 Peso	Daily Newspapers	88 per 1000	
	Telephones	242,000	
Area-Total 114,524 Sq Km	Television Sets	575,000	
Area-Arable 20,440 Sq Km			
Population 8,250,000			
Population Density 69 per Sq Km	Steel Consumption	34 Kg/Cap	
Birth-Death Rate % 2.8-0.8	Growth Pattern Index	37.50%	
Population Rate of Increase 2.30%	GNP/Capita		
	Annual Increase 67-90	1.70%	
1967 GNP per Capita 330 US $			

Energy Total Billion Kec	8.281
Energy per Capita Kec	1,025
Kec per $ of GNP	3.14
Growth Ratio GNP/Kec	0.540
Electric Capacity Mw	1,410
Generation Billion Kwhr	4.780
Kilowatt Hours per Capita	592
Kwhr per $ of GNP	1.46
Economic Density GNP $/Sq Km	23,150

CYPRUS

	1970	1975	1980	1985	1990	1995	2000	2005	2010	2015	2020
Population 1967 Population	1.030	1.075	1.120	1.160	1.200	1.235	1.270	1.300	1.330	1.360	1.390
Population Millions	0.642	0.660	0.688	0.712	0.736	0.758	0.780	0.797	0.816	0.835	0.853
GNP Capita 1967 $	869	1,083	1,360	1,680	2,060	2,465	2,930	3,440	3,940	4,610	5,200
GNP Billion $ 1967	0.558	0.715	0.936	1.196	1.515	1.869	2.280	2.740	3.215	3.850	4.430
Yearly Increase GNP	5.7%	5.5%	5.1%	4.7%	4.3%	4.0%	3.7%	3.3%	3.0%	2.8%	

Map	Europe	H L Students	55 per 100000
Capital	Nicosia	Hospital Beds	4.8 per 1000
One U S $ =	.4167 Pound	Daily Newspapers	103 per 1000
		Telephones	33,396
Area-Total	9,251 Sq Km	Television Sets	32,000
Area-Arable	4,320 Sq Km	Tourist Receipt US $	14,000,000
		Passenger Cars	42,400
Population	630,000		
Population Density	66 per Sq Km	Investment Ratio	22%
		Growth Pattern Index	106.25%
Birth-Death Rate %	2.5-0.7	GNP/Capita	
Population Rate of Increase	1.00%	Annual Increase 67-90	4.45%
1967 GNP per Capita	750 US $		

Energy Total Billion Kec	0.805
Energy per Capita Kec	1,294
Kec per $ of GNP	1.40
Growth Ratio GNP/Kec	0.625
Electric Capacity Mw	175
Generation Billion Kwhr	0.510
Kilowatt Hours per Capita	819
Kwhr per $ of GNP	1.04
Economic Density GNP $/Sq Km	49,800

224

CZECHOSLOVAKIA

	1967	1970	1975	1980	1985	1990	1995	2000	2005	2010	2015	2020
Population 1967 Population	1.000	1.020	1.050	1.078	1.105	1.138	1.158	1.180	1.200	1.215	1.230	1.248
Population Millions	14.31	14.61	15.02	15.42	15.82	16.29	16.60	16.90	17.20	17.40	17.60	17.78
GNP Capita 1967 $	1,110	1,215	1,400	1,610	1,842	2,130	2,415	2,740	3,090	3,370	3,880	4,310
GNP Billion $ 1967	15.90	17.78	21.05	24.85	29.15	34.00	40.85	46.40	53.10	60.45	68.50	76.60
Yearly Increase GNP		3.5%	3.4%	3.3%	3.1%	3.0%	2.9%	2.7%	2.6%	2.5%	2.3%	

Map	Europe
Capital	Prague
One U S $ =	15.28 Koruna
Area-Total	127,869 Sq Km
Area-Arable	53,530 Sq Km
Population	14,418,000
Population Density	112 per Sq Km
Birth-Death Rate %	1.49-1.07
Population Rate of Increase	0.68%
1967 GNP per Capita	1,110 US $

H L Students	961 per 100000
Hospital Beds	12.5 per 1000
Daily Newspapers	283 per 1000
Telephones	1,789,373
Television Sets	2,712,000
Tourist Receipt US $	61,000,000
Passenger Cars	598,600
Steel Consumption	590 Kg/Cap
Investment Ratio	23%
Growth Pattern Index	112.50%
GNP/Capita Annual Increase 67-90	2.83%

Energy Total Billion Kec	82.954
Energy per Capita Kec	5,775
Kec per $ of GNP	4.95
Growth Ratio GNP/Kec	1.010
Electric Capacity Mw	10,071
Generation Billion Kwhr	43,607
Kilowatt Hours per Capita	3,036
Kwhr per $ of GNP	2.54
Economic Density GNP $/Sq Km	124,500

225

DAHOMEY

	1970	1975	1980	1985	1990	1995	2000	2005	2010	2015	2020
Population 1967 Population	1.085	1.240	1.395	1.550	1.705	1.855	2.005	2.155	2.300	2.440	2.575
Population Millions	2.720	3.105	3.496	3.884	4.270	4.650	5.030	5.400	5.760	6.110	6.450
GNP Capita 1967 $	82.3	84.2	91.0	95.3	99.5	103.5	106.2	114.5	121.3	125.5	131.0
GNP Billion $ 1967	0.224	0.262	0.318	0.370	0.425	0.482	0.535	0.618	0.698	0.767	0.845
Yearly Increase GNP	4.3%	3.8%	3.0%	2.8%	2.7%	2.6%	2.5%	2.4%	2.2%	2.0%	

Map	Africa	
Capital	Porto Novo	
One U S $ =	277.71 CFA Franc	
Area-Total	112,622 Sq Km	
Area-Arable	15,460 Sq Km	
Population	2,640,000	
Population Density	22 per Sq Km	
Birth-Death Rate %	5.4-2.6	
Population Rate of Increase	2.90%	
1967 GNP per Capita	80 US $	

H L Students	5 per 100000	
Hospital Beds	1.1 per 1000	
Daily Newspapers	0.3 per 1000	
Telephones	4,800	
Passenger Cars	9,900	
Growth Pattern Index		
GNP/Capita	12.50%	
Annual Increase 67-90	1.00%	

Energy Total Billion Kec	0.078	
Energy per Capita Kec	30	
Kec per $ of GNP	0.16	
Generation Billion Kwhr	0.025	
Kilowatt Hours per Capita	9	
Kwhr per $ of GNP	0.11	
Economic Density GNP $/Sq Km	1,778	

DENMARK

	1967	1970	1975	1980	1985	1990	1995	2000	2005	2010	2015	2020
Population / 1967 Population	1.000	1.020	1.060	1.090	1.125	1.160	1.186	1.210	1.230	1.250	1.270	1.290
Population Millions	4.839	4.930	5.125	5.270	5.430	5.605	5.730	5.850	5.950	6.045	6.140	6.240
GNP Capita 1967 $	2,497	2,760	3,320	3,940	4,650	5,370	6,210	7,110	8,170	9,350	10,500	11,780
GNP Billion $ 1967	12.08	13.60	17.00	20.75	25.22	30.10	35.60	41.60	48.60	56.50	64.50	73.40
Yearly Increase GNP		4.6%	4.3%	4.0%	3.6%	3.4%	3.2%	3.1%	2.9%	2.6%	2.5%	

Map	Europe	
Capital	Copenhagen	
One U S $ =	7.507 Krone	
Area-Total	43,069 Sq Km	
Area-Arable	27,090 Sq Km	
Population	4,910,000	
Population Density	112 per Sq Km	
Birth-Death Rate %	1.68-0.97	
Population Rate of Increase	0.78%	
1967 GNP per Capita	2,497 US $	

H L Students	1,203 per 100000	
Hospital Beds	9.1 per 1000	
Daily Newspapers	356 per 1000	
Telephones	1,516,802	
Television Sets	1,210,000	
Passenger Cars	954,700	
Steel Consumption	339 Kg/Cap	
Investment Ratio	21%	
Growth Pattern Index	125%	
GNP/Capita Annual Increase 67-90	3.40%	

Energy Total Billion Kec	22.843	
Energy per Capita Kec	4,690	
Kec per $ of GNP	1.71	
Growth Ratio GNP/Kec	0.912	
Electric Capacity Mw	3,920	
Generation Billion Kwhr	11,834	
Kilowatt Hours per Capita	2,429	
Kwhr per $ of GNP	0.89	
Economic Density GNP $/Sq Km	280,000	

227

DOMINICAN REPUBLIC

	1970	1975	1980	1985	1990	1995	2000	2005	2010	2015	2020
Population 1967 Population	1.110	1.280	1.500	1.720	1.940	2.160	2.380	2.600	2.810	3.020	3.230
Population Millions	4.43	5.14	5.98	6.86	7.74	8.62	9.49	10.38	11.20	12.07	12.89
GNP Capita 1967 $	291.0	322.0	354.5	391.8	432.0	476.0	522.0	574.0	629.0	689.0	758.0
GNP Billion $ 1967	1.290	1.655	2.118	2.685	3.340	4.100	4.950	5.960	7.050	8.320	9.780

Yearly Increase GNP	5.1%	5.0%	4.7%	4.4%	4.2%	3.9%	3.7%	3.4%	3.3%	3.2%

Map	North & Caribbean America		
Capital	Santo Domingo	H L Students	256 per 100000
One U S $ =	1 Peso	Hospital Beds	2.9 per 1000
		Daily Newspapers	26 per 1000
Area-Total	48,734 Sq Km	Telephones	35,735
Area-Arable	10,670 Sq Km	Television Sets	75,000
		Tourist Receipt US $	10,000,000
Population	4,174,000	Passenger Cars	33,300
Population Density	80 per Sq Km		
		Investment Ratio	14%
Birth-Death Rate %	4.8-1.5	Growth Pattern Index	37.50%
Population Rate of Increase	3.60%	GNP/Capita Annual Increase 67-90	2.00%
1967 GNP per Capita	275 US $		

Energy Total Billion Kec	0.841
Energy per Capita Kec	208
Kec per $ of GNP	6.44
Growth Ratio GNP/Kec	0.375
Electric Capacity Kw	192,600
Generation Billion Kwhr	0.699
Kilowatt Hours per Capita	173
Kwhr per $ of GNP	0.66
Economic Density GNP $/Sq Km	21,700

ECUADOR

	1970	1975	1980	1985	1990	1995	2000	2005	2010	2015	2020
Population 1967 Population	1.100	1.280	1.480	1.680	1.875	2.070	2.265	2.460	2.650	2.840	3.030
Population Millions	6.06	7.05	8.15	9.26	10.32	11.40	12.50	13.55	14.60	15.65	16.70
GNP 1967 $ Capita	244.5	267	291	318	347	379.5	413	457	512	546	596
GNP Billion $ 1967	1.480	1,880	2.365	2.940	3.585	4.330	5.170	6.200	7.480	8.550	9.950
Yearly Increase GNP	4.9%	4.7%	4.4%	4.1%	3.9%	3.7%	3.5%	3.4%	3.3%	3.1%	

Map	South America	H L Students	356 per 100000	Energy Total
Capital	Quito	Hospital Beds	2.3 per 1000	Billion Kec 1.492
One U S $ =	18.18 Sucre	Daily Newspapers	44 per 1000	Energy per Capita Kec 261
		Telephones	88,000	
Area-Total	283,561 Sq Km			Kec per $ of GNP 0.950
Area-Arable	25,960 Sq Km	Television Sets	65,000	Growth Ratio GNP/Kec 0.457
		Tourist Receipt US $	8,000,000	
Population	5,890,000	Passenger Cars	22,000	Electric Capacity Mw 290
Population Density	19 per Sq Km			Generation Billion Kwhr 0.850
				Kilowatt Hours per Capita 149
Birth-Death Rate %	4.7-1.3	Investment Ratio	12	Kwhr per $ of GNP 0.59
Population Rate of Increase	3.40%	Growth Pattern Index	37.50%	
		GNP/Capita		Economic Density
		Annual Increase 67-90	1.80%	GNP $/Sq Km 4,480
1967 GNP per Capita	231 US $			

229

EL SALVADOR

	1970	1975	1980	1985	1990	1995	2000	2005	2010	2015	2020
Population 1967 Population	1.110	1.300	1.505	1.716	1.935	2.155	2.380	2.600	2.815	3.015	3.250
Population Millions	3.500	4.100	4.730	5.400	6.120	6.780	7.500	8.200	8.850	9.500	10.250
GNP Capita 1967 $	310	366	428	507	585	690	803	940	1,088	1,252	1,450
GNP Billion $ 1967	1.085	1.500	2.030	2.735	3.580	4.680	6.020	7.700	9.620	11.900	14.850
Yearly Increase GNP	6.7%	6.2%	5.9%	5.5%	5.3%	5.1%	4.8%	4.6%	4.4%	4.3%

Map. North & Caribbean America	
Capital San Salvador	
One U S $ = 2.50 Colon	
Area-Total 21,393 Sq Km	
Area-Arable 6,480 per Sq Km	
Population 3,390,000	
Population Density 147 per Sq Km	
Birth-Death Rate % 4.8-1.3	
Population Rate of Increase 3.60%	
1967 GNP per Capita 280 US $	

H L Students	214 per 100000
Hospital Beds	2.2 per 1000
Daily Newspapers	51 per 1000
Telephones	36,842
Television Sets	35,000
Passenger Cars	31,000
Investment Ratio	11%
Growth Pattern Index	62.50%
GNP/Capita Annual Increase 67-90	3.25%

Energy Total Billion Kec	0.653
Energy per Capita Kec	199
Kec per $ of GNP	0.607
Growth Ratio GNP/Kec	0.493
Electric Capacity Mw	171
Generation Billion Kwhr	0.582
Kilowatt Hours per Capita	178
Kwhr per $ of GNP	0.59
Economic Density GNP $/Sq Km	4,120

230

ETHIOPIA

	1970	1975	1980	1985	1990	1995	2000	2005	2010	2015	2020
Population 1967 Population	1.060	1.150	1.240	1.330	1.420	1.500	1.580	1.650	1.720	1.790	1.850
Population Millions	25.15	27.28	29.40	31.55	33.65	35.56	37.45	39.15	40.80	42.45	43.90
GNP Capita 1967 $	95.0	128.3	165.0	208.2	258.6	316.3	391.2	479.0	577.5	702.0	847.0
GNP Billion $ 1967	2.39	3.50	4.85	6.57	8.71	11.25	14.64	18.75	23.55	29.80	37.20
Yearly Increase GNP		7.9%	6.8%	6.2%	5.8%	5.5%	5.3%	5.1%	4.9%	4.7%	4.5%

Map	Africa
Capital	Addis Ababa
One U S $ =	2.50 Dollar
Area-Total	1,221,900 Sq Km
Area-Arable	125,250 Sq Km
Population	24,769,000
Population Density	19 per Sq Km
Population Rate of Increase	1.90%
1967 GNP per Capita	77 US $

H L Students	17 per 100000
Hospital Beds	0.4 per 1000
Daily Newspapers	2 per 1000
Telephones	36,034
Television Sets	6,000
Investment Ratio	14%
Growth Pattern Index	78.75%
GNP/Capita Annual Increase 67-90	5.37%

Energy Total Billion Kec	0.543
Energy per Capita Kec	22
Kec per $ of GNP	0.234
Growth Ratio GNP/Kec	0.738
Generation Billion Kwhr	0.361
Kilowatt Hours per Capita	14
Kwhr per $ of GNP	0.17
Economic Density GNP $/Sq Km	1,490

231

FINLAND

	1967	1970	1975	1980	1985	1990	1995	2000	2005	2010	2015	2020
Population 1967 Population	1.000	1.020	1.058	1.090	1.120	1.158	1.180	1.210	1.232	1.250	1.268	1.290
Population Millions	4.666	4.760	4.940	5.099	5.230	5.410	5.510	5.650	5.760	5.840	5.920	6.020
GNP Capita 1967 $	1,874	2,150	2,640	3,140	3,760	4,475	5,215	6,040	6,980	8,025	9,175	10,400
GNP Billion $ 1967	8.74	10.24	13.04	15.99	19.65	24.13	28.89	34.10	40.20	46.80	54.30	62.60
Yearly Increase GNP		4.9%	4.6%	4.4%	4.2%	3.6%	3.5%	3.3%	3.1%	3.0%	2.9%	

Map	Europe	H L Students	1,110 per 100000	Energy Total Billion Kec	15,655
Capital	Helsinki	Hospital Beds	11.1 per 1000	Energy per Capita Kec	3,339
One U S $ =	4.20 Mark	Telephones	1,009,336		
Area-Total	337,009 Sq Km	Television Sets	927,000	Kec per $ of GNP	1.61
Area-Arable	27,610 Sq Km			Growth Ratio GNP/Kec	0.652
Population	4,703,000	Passenger Cars	580,700	Electric Capacity Mw	4,635
Population Density	13.80 per Sq Km	Steel Consumption	286 Kg/Cap	Generation Billion Kwhr	18,103
				Kilowatt Hours per Capita	3,861
Birth-Death Rate %	1.60-0.96	Investment Ratio	26%	Kwhr per $ of GNP	1.92
Population Rate of Increase	0.77%	Growth Pattern Index	125%		
		GNP/Capita	3.85%	Economic Density	25,900
1967 GNP per Capita	1,874 US $	Annual Increase 67-90		GNP $/Sq Km	

FRANCE

	1967	1970	1975	1980	1985	1990	1995	2000	2005	2010	2015	2020
Population / 1967 Population	1.000	1.040	1.095	1.140	1.200	1.255	1.300	1.343	1.380	1.413	1.450	1.484
Population Millions	49.55	51.55	54.20	56.55	59.50	62.30	64.50	66.60	68.40	70.10	71.90	73.60
GNP/Capita 1967 $	2,340	2,520	3,000	3,455	3,990	4,555	5,205	5,905	6,680	7,560	8,450	9,475
GNP Billion $ 1967	116.0	129.0	163.0	194.9	237.5	283.0	335.0	392.5	457.0	529.9	607.5	697.0
Yearly Increase GNP		4.7%	4.4%	4.0%	3.6%	3.4%	3.2%	3.1%	3.0%	2.9%	2.8%	

Map	Europe
Capital	Paris
One U S $ =	5.519 Franc
Area-Total	547,026 Sq Km
Area-Arable	198,160 Sq Km
Population Density	50,320,000 / 91 per Sq Km
Birth-Death Rate %	1.68-1.10
Population Rate of Increase	1.22%
1967 GNP per Capita	2,340 US $

H L Students	1,239 per 100000
Hospital Beds	8.4 per 1000
Daily Newspapers	251 per 1000
Telephones	7,503,479
Television Sets	7,916,000
Tourist Receipt US $	954,000,000
Passenger Cars	11,500,000
Steel Consumption	359 Kg/Cap
Investment Ratio	27%
Growth Pattern Index	100%
GNP/Capita Annual Increase 67-90	2.94%

Energy Total Billion Kec	163.986
Energy per Capita Kec	3,282
Kec per $ of GNP	1.32
Growth Ratio GNP/Kec	1.060
Electric Capacity Mw	34,133
Generation Billion Kwhr	119,404
Kilowatt Hours per Capita	2,389
Kwhr per $ of GNP	0.98
Economic Density GNP $/Sq Km	212,000

233

FRENCH OCEANIA

	1970	1975	1980	1985	1990	1995	2000	2005	2010	2015	2020
Population 1967 Population	1.080	1.230	1.380	1.530	1.670	1.820	1.960	2.095	2.230	2.360	2.490
Population Millions	0.105	0.119	0.134	0.148	0.162	0.177	0.190	0.203	0.216	0.229	0.242
GNP/Capita 1967 $	1,592	2,105	2,795	3,640	4,480	5,460	6,430	7,640	8,850	10,230	11,800
GNP Billion $ 1967	0.167	0.251	0.374	0.540	0.726	0.965	1.223	1.550	1.910	2.340	2.850
Yearly Increase GNP	8.5%	8.3%	7.6%	6.1%	5.9%	4.9%	4.9%	4.2%	4.1%	4.0%	

Map	Oceania	Hospital Beds	8.4 per 1000	Energy per Capita Kec	1,051
Capital	Papeete	Telephones	5,403	Kec per $ of GNP	0.51
One U S $ =	41.6 CFP Franc			Growth Ratio GNP/Kec	0.381
Area-Total	4,000 Sq Km	Passenger Cars	12,100	Generation Billion Kwhr	0.045
Area-Arable	640 Sq Km			Kilowatt Hours per Capita	449
Population	105,000	Growth Pattern Index	125%	Kwhr per $ of GNP	0.28
Population Density	24 per Sq Km	GNP/Capita		Economic Density	
Population Rate of Increase	2.80%	Annual Increase 67-90	5.36%	GNP $/Sq Km	32,500
1967 GNP per Capita	1,340 US $				

GABON

	1970	1975	1980	1985	1990	1995	2000	2005	2010	2015	2020
Population 1967 Population	1.024	1.060	1.096	1.132	1.166	1.196	1.220	1.240	1.260	1.280	1.298
Population Millions	0.485	0.501	0.518	0.536	0.551	0.566	0.577	0.586	0.596	0.606	0.614
GNP 1967 $ Capita	497	670	890	1,180	1,525	1,942	2,485	3,110	3,850	4,630	5,550
GNP Billion $ 1967	0.241	0.337	0.462	0.632	0.840	1.100	1.433	1.822	2.295	2.805	3.412
Yearly Increase GNP	7.0%	6.5%	6.4%	5.9%	5.5%	5.4%	4.9%	4.7%	4.1%	3.7%	

Map	Africa	H L Students	22 per 100000
Capital	Libreville	Hospital Beds	10.0 per 1000
One U S $ =	277.71 CFA Franc	Telephones	4,300
Area-Total	267,667 Sq Km	Television Sets	1,000
Area-Arable	1,270 Sq Km	Passenger Cars	6,300
Population	485,000		
Population Density	1.77 per Sq Km	Growth Pattern Index	
Birth-Death Rate %	3.5-2.5	GNP/Capita	118.75%
Population Rate of Increase	0.80%	Annual Increase 67-90	5.75%
1967 GNP per Capita	418 US $		

Energy Total Billion Kec	0.212
Energy per Capita Kec	442
Kec per $ of GNP	0.866
Growth Ratio GNP/Kec	0.672
Electric Capacity Kw	25,000
Generation Billion Kwhr	0.074
Kilowatt Hours per Capita	154
Kwhr per $ of GNP	0.28
Economic Density GNP $/Sq Km	745

EAST GERMANY

	1967	1970	1975	1980	1985	1990	1995	2000	2005	2010	2015	2020
Population 1967 Population	1	1	1	1	1	1	1	1	1	1	1	1
Population Millions	17.08	17.08	17.08	17.08	17.08	17.08	17.08	17.08	17.08	17.08	17.08	17.08
GNP Capita 1967 $	1,300	1,428	1,710	2,044	2,365	2,740	3,180	3,650	4,170	4,720	5,385	6,030
GNP Billion $ 1967	22.20	24.40	29.20	35.05	40.40	46.85	54.30	62.40	71.25	80.60	91.90	103.00
Yearly Increase GNP		3.6%	3.5%	3.3%	3.1%	3.0%	2.8%	2.7%	2.5%	2.4%	2.3%	

Map	Europe
Capital	Berlin (Soviet Sector)
One U S $ =	4.20 DDR Mark
Area-Total	107,901 Sq Km
Area-Arable	49,850 Sq Km
Population	17,096,000
Population Density	148 per Sq Km
Birth-Death Rate %	1.43-1.43
Population Rate of Increase	0.00%
1967 GNP per Capita	1,300 US $

H L Students	437 per 100000
Hospital Beds	12.5 per 1000
Daily Newspapers	445 per 1000
Telephones	1,896,151
Television Sets	4,173,000
Passenger Cars	920,200
Steel Consumption	437 Kg/Cap
Investment Ratio	20%
Growth Pattern Index	131.25%
GNP/Capita Annual Increase 67-90	3.30%

Energy Total Billion Kec	92.041
Energy per Capita Kec	5,387
Kec per $ of GNP Growth Ratio GNP/Kec	
Electric Capacity Mw	11,673
Generation Billion Kwhr	63,309
Kilowatt Hours per Capita	3,705
Kwhr per $ of GNP	2.68
Economic Density GNP $/Sq Km	206,000

236

WEST GERMANY

	1967	1970	1975	1980	1985	1990	1995	2000	2005	2010	2015	2020
Population 1967 Population	1.000	1.034	1.089	1.132	1.189	1.240	1.280	1.320	1.352	1.382	1.417	1.445
Population Millions	57.70	59.70	62.80	65.40	68.60	71.60	73.90	76.20	78.10	79.80	81.70	83.30
GNP Capita 1967 $	2,085	2,335	2,805	3,358	3,980	4,678	5,400	6,245	7,190	8,210	9,335	10,520
GNP Billion $ 1967	120.7	139.0	175.8	219.5	273.0	334.5	398.5	475.5	561.0	654.0	762.0	877.5
Yearly Increase GNP		4.8%		4.5%	4.3%	4.1%	3.8%	3.6%	3.3%	3.1%	2.9%	2.8%

Map	Europe	H L Students	695 per 100000
Capital	Berlin	Hospital Beds	11.1 per 1000
One U S $ =	3.63 Deutsche Mark	Daily Newspapers	328 per 1000
		Telephones	11,248,979
Area-Total	247,973 Sq Km	Television Sets	14,958,000
Area-Arable	81,790 Sq Km	Tourist Receipt US $	906,000,000
Population	60,842,000	Passenger Cars	11,322,400
Population Density	233 per Sq Km	Steel Consumption	579 Kg/Cap
Birth-Death Rate %	1.97-1.19	Investment Ratio	25%
Population Rate of		Growth Pattern Index	131.25%
Increase	1.14%	GNP/Capita	
		Annual Increase 67-90	3.60%
1967 GNP per Capita	2,085 US $		

Energy Total Billion Kec	269.793
Energy per Capita Kec	4,484
Kec per $ of GNP	2.01
Growth Ratio GNP/Kec	2.000
Electric Capacity Mw	47,054
Generation Billion Kwhr	210.325
Kilowatt Hours per Capita	3,495
Kwhr per $ of GNP	1.53
Economic Density GNP $/Sq Km	420,000

GHANA

	1967	1970	1975	1980	1985	1990	1995	2000	2005	2010	2015	2020
Population 1967 Population	1.000	1.080	1.220	1.360	1.500	1.640	1.780	1.910	2.040	2.165	2.290	2.410
Population Millions	8.14	8.79	9.93	11.08	12.21	13.34	14.48	15.54	16.60	17.62	18.62	19.60
GNP Capita 1967 $	308	323	345	368	397	420	451	482	517	548	587	629
GNP Billion $ 1967	2.05	2.83	3.42	4.07	4.85	5.61	6.54	7.49	8.59	9.64	10.91	12.31
Yearly Increase GNP	3.8%		3.6%	3.5%	3.2%	3.1%	2.9%	2.8%	2.6%	2.5%	2.3%	

Map	Africa
Capital	Accra
One U S $ =	1.0204 New Cedi
Area-Total	238,537 Sq Km
Area-Arable	28,350 Sq Km
Population	8,600,000
Population Density	34 per Sq Km
Birth-Death Rate %	4.7-2.0
Population Rate of Increase	2.70%
1967 GNP per Capita	252 US $

H L Students	59 per 100000
Hospital Beds	1.3 per 1000
Daily Newspapers	36 per 1000
Telephones	35,950
Television Sets	6,000
Passenger Cars	32,200
Steel Consumption	4 Kg/Cap
Investment Ratio	11%
Growth Pattern Index	37.50%
GNP/Capita Annual Increase 67-90	2.25%

Energy Total Billion Kec	1.058
Energy per Capita Kec	128
Kec per $ of GNP	0.425
Growth Ratio GNP/Kec	0.577
Electric Capacity Mw	631
Generation Billion Kwhr	2.589
Kilowatt Hours per Capita	309
Kwhr per $ of GNP	0.76
Economic Density GNP $/Sq Km	8,600

GREECE

	1967	1970	1975	1980	1985	1990	1995	2000	2005	2010	2015	2020
Population 1967 Population	1.000	1.021	1.056	1.086	1.121	1.155	1.178	1.202	1.222	1.239	1.260	1.280
Population Millions	8.72	8.91	9.21	9.50	9.79	10.08	10.25	10.49	10.64	10.83	11.00	11.16
GNP Capita 1967 $	808	925	1,215	1,552	1,990	2,488	3,055	3,700	4,430	5,250	6,150	7,110
GNP Billion $ 1967	7.04	8.24	11.19	14.72	19.46	25.08	31.24	38.80	47.20	56.90	67.70	79.40
Yearly Increase GNP		6.3%	6.0%	5.7%	5.2%	4.5%	4.3%	4.0%	3.8%	3.5%	3.2%	

Map	Europe
Capital	Athens
One U S $ =	30 Drachma
Area -Total	131,944 Sq Km
Area -Arable	38,510 Sq Km
Population Density	8,835,000
Population Density	66 per Sq Km
Birth-Death Rate %	1.8210.83
Population Rate of Increase	0.75%
1967 GNP per Capita	808 US $

H L Students	750 per 100000
Hospital Beds	5.9 per 1000
Telephones	761,550
Television Sets	7,000
Tourist Receipt US $	120,000,000
Passenger Cars	169,100
Steel Consumption	94 Kg/Cap
Investment Ratio	27%
Growth Pattern Index	118.75%
GNP/Capita	
Annual Increase 67-90	4.98%

Energy Total Billion Kec	8.959
Energy per Capita Kec	1,017
Kec per $ of GNP	1.07
Growth Ratio GNP/Kec	0.723
Electric Capacity Mw	1,715
Generation Billion Kwhr	7.360
Kilowatt Hours per Capita	836
Kwhr per $ of GNP	0.97
Economic Density GNP $/Sq Km	53,300

239

GUADELOUPE

	1970	1975	1980	1985	1990	1995	2000	2005	2010	2015	2020
Population 1967 Population	1.065	1.180	1.295	1.410	1.520	1.630	1.730	1.830	1.930	2.020	2.110
Population Millions	0.980	1.087	1.192	1.298	1.399	1.500	1.592	1.674	1.776	1.858	1.940
GNP Capita 1967 $	503	559	624	693	770	852	942	1,044	1,136	1,272	1,397
GNP Billion $ 1967	0.493	0.608	0.744	0.899	1.076	1.278	1.500	1.748	2.015	2.365	2.710
Yearly Increase GNP	4.3%	4.0%	3.8%	3.6%	3.5%	3.3%	3.1%	2.9%	2.8%	2.7%	

Map North & Caribbean America	H L Students 55 per 100000
Capital Basse-Terre	Hospital Beds 10.0 per 1000
One U S $ = 5.55 Franc	Daily Newspapers 9 per 1000
	Telephones 9,662
Area-Total 1,779 Sq Km	
Area-Arable 490 Sq Km	Television Sets 5,000
Population 323,000	
Population Density 180 per Sq Km	
Birth-Death Rate % 3.2-0.8	Growth Pattern Index 43.75%
Population Rate of Increase 2.30%	GNP/Capita Annual Increase 67-90 2.18%
1967 GNP per Capita 470 US $	

Energy Total Billion Kec	0.113
Energy per Capita Kec	355
Kec per $ of GNP	0.88
Growth Ratio GNP/Kec	0.340
Generation Billion Kwhr	0.072
Kilowatt Hours per Capita	226
Kwhr per $ of GNP	0.42
Economic Density GNP $/Sq Km	84,400

GUAM

	1970	1975	1980	1985	1990	1995	2000	2005	2010	2015	2020
Population 1967 Population	1.150	1.460	1.790	2.170	2.550	2.990	3.430	3.890	4.320	4.750	5.170
Population Millions	0.106	0.134	0.165	0.200	0.235	0.275	0.316	0.358	0.398	0.437	0.476
GNP Capita 1967 $	1,740	1,985	2,230	2,510	2,830	3,160	3,540	3,920	4,350	4,820	5,300
GNP Billion $ 1967	0.184	0.267	0.367	0.502	0.663	0.870	1.140	1.402	1.728	2.100	2.510
Yearly Increase GNP	7.7%	6.5%	6.5%	5.7%	5.6%	5.5%	4.2%	4.2%	4.0%	3.8%	

Map	Oceania	
Capital	Agana	
One U S $ =	1 Dollar	
Area-Total	549 Sq Km	
Area-Arable	120 Sq Km	
Population	102,000	
Population Density	171 per Sq Km	
Population Rate of Increase	5.10%	
1967 GNP per Capita	1,620 US $	

H L Students		
Hospital Beds		1,736 per 100000
Daily Newspapers		2.6 per 1000
Telephones		120 per 1000
		33,000
Television Sets		40,000
Passenger Cars		20,300
Growth Pattern Index		56.25%
GNP/Capita		
Annual Increase 67-90		2.45%

Energy Total Billion Kec	0.100
Energy per Capita Kec	1,004
Kec per $ of GNP	0.69
Growth Ratio GNP/Kec	0.609
Electric Capacity Kw	90,000
Generation Billion Kwhr	0.597
Kilowatt Hours per Capita	5,962
Kwhr per $ of GNP	3.48
Economic Density GNP $/Sq Km	276,500

GUATEMALA

	1967	1970	1975	1980	1985	1990	1995	2000	2005	2010	2015	2020
Population 1967 Population	1.000	1.105	1.255	1.430	1.600	1.765	1.940	2.105	2.270	2.430	2.590	2.750
Population Millions	4.18	5.22	5.92	6.75	7.55	8.33	9.15	9.93	10.72	11.48	12.22	12.98
GNP Capita 1967 $	300	333	381	444	513	591	679	776	890	1,018	1,161	1,329
GNP Billion $ 1967	1.417	1.738	2.225	3.000	3.865	4.910	6.200	7.700	9.550	11.680	14.200	17.210
Yearly Increase GNP		5.8%	5.5%	5.2%	4.9%	4.8%	4.5%	4.3%	4.1%	4.0%	3.8%	

Map	North & Caribbean America
Capital	Guatemala City
One U S $ =	1 Quetzal
Area-Total	108,889 Sq Km
Area-Arable	14,980 Sq Km
Population Density	43 per Sq Km
	5,014,000
Birth-Death Rate %	4.6-1.6
Population Rate of Increase	3.10%
1967 GNP per Capita	300 US $
H L Students	197 per 100000
Hospital Beds	3.1 per 1000
Daily Newspapers	38 per 1000
Telephones	36,165
Television Sets	65,000
Tourist Receipt US $	7,000,000
Steel Consumption	20 Kg/Cap
Investment Ratio	14%
Growth Pattern Index	56.25%
GNP/Capita Annual Increase 67-90	3.00%
Energy Total Billion Kec	1.167
Energy per Capita Kec	239
Kec per $ of GNP	0.72
Growth Ratio GNP/Kec	0.693
Electric Capacity Kw	149,600
Generation Billion Kwhr	0.610
Kilowatt Hours per Capita	125
Kwhr per $ of GNP	0.37
Economic Density GNP $/Sq Km	12,980

GUINEA

	1970	1975	1980	1985	1990	1995	2000	2005	2010	2015	2020
Population 1967 Population	1.080	1.220	1.360	1.500	1.640	1.780	1.910	2.040	2.165	2.290	2.410
Population Millions	3.995	4.515	5.030	5.550	6.060	6.580	7.070	7.550	8.010	8.470	8.910
GNP Capita 1967 $	100.2	118.8	138.2	162.5	189.3	218.5	253.5	292.5	339.0	390.0	446.0
GNP Billion $ 1967	0.400	0.536	0.695	0.902	1.147	1.440	1.790	2.210	2.715	3.305	3.970
Yearly Increase GNP	6.0%	5.7%	5.3%	4.9%	4.6%	4.4%	4.3%	4.2%	4.0%	3.8%	

Map	Africa
Capital	Conakry
One U S $ =	277.71 Franc
Area-Total	245,857 Sq Km
Area-Arable	1,140 Sq Km
Population	3,890,000
Population Density	15.1 per Sq Km
Birth-Death Rate %	4.9 – 2.6
Population Rate of Increase	2.70%
1967 GNP per Capita	90 US $

H L Students	11 per 100000
Hospital Beds	1.9 per 1000
Daily Newspapers	4 per 1000
Telephones	6,600
Passenger Cars	7,600
Steel Consumption	2 Kg/Cap
Investment Ratio	23%
Growth Pattern Index	56.25%
GNP/Capita Annual Increase 67-90	3.30%

Energy Total Billion Kec	0.372
Energy per Capita Kec	97
Kec per $ of GNP	1.08
Growth Ratio GNP/Kec	0.568
Electric Capacity Kw	19,500
Generation Billion Kwhr	0.225
Kilowatt Hours per Capita	59
Kwhr per $ of GNP	0.62
Economic Density GNP $/Sq Km	1,360

243

GUYANA

	1967	1970	1975	1980	1985	1990	1995	2000	2005	2010	2015	2020
Population 1967 Population	1.000	1.080	1.220	1.360	1.500	1.640	1.780	1.910	2.040	2.165	2.290	2.410
Population Millions	0.680	0.734	0.829	0.924	1.020	1.115	1.210	1.300	1.388	1.472	1.558	1.640
GNP/Capita 1967 $	324	368	447	538	642	765	900	1,043	1,205	1,382	1,570	
GNP Billion $ 1967	0.220	0.270	0.370	0.497	0.655	0.854	1.089	1.263	1.672	2.038	2.430	3.425
Yearly Increase GNP	6.5%		6.0%	5.7%	5.4%	5.0%	4.9%	4.5%	4.0%	3.6%	3.5%	

Map	South America	
Capital	Georgetown	
One U S $ =	2 Dollar	
Area-Total	214,969 Sq Km	
Area-Arable	1,950 Sq Km	
Population	742,000	
Population Density	3.16 per Sq Km	
Birth-Death Rate %	4.0-1.0	
Population Rate of Increase	2.70%	
1967 GNP per Capita	387 US $	

H L Students	84 per 100000	
Hospital Beds	4.8 per 1000	
Daily Newspapers	191 per 1000	
Telephones	12,815	
Passenger Cars	14,200	
Investment Ratio	23%	
Growth Pattern Index	87.50%	
GNP/Capita Annual Increase 67-90	3.85%	

Energy Total Billion Kec		0.647
Energy per Capita Kec		899
Kec per $ of GNP		2.66
Growth Ratio GNP/Kec		0.688
Electric Capacity Kw		92,100
Generation Billion Kwhr		0.287
Kilowatt Hours per Capita		399
Kwhr per $ of GNP		0.91
Economic Density GNP $/Sq Km		1,225

HAÏTI

	1970	1975	1980	1985	1990	1995	2000	2005	2010	2015	2020
Population 1967 Population	1.060	1.155	1.250	1.345	1.440	1.530	1.615	1.695	1.770	1.840	1.910
Population Millions	4.855	5.290	5.720	6.160	6.595	7.010	7.390	7.760	8.100	8.420	8.740
GNP Capita 1967 $	86.6	90.0	95.0	99.7	105.0	110.2	115.3	120.8	126.0	131.1	136.5
GNP Billion $ 1967	0.420	0.476	0.544	0.614	0.702	0.773	0.853	0.937	1.020	1.103	1.190
Yearly Increase GNP	2.9%	2.7%	2.4%	2.2%	2.0%	1.9%	1.8%	1.7%	1.6%	1.5%	

Map North & Caribbean America	H L Students 34 per 100000
Capital Port-au-Prince	Hospital Beds 0.7 per 1000
One U S $ = 5 Gourde	Daily Newspapers 5 per 1000
	Telephones
Area-Total 27,750 Sq Km	Television Sets 11,000
Area-Arable 3,700 Sq Km	Tourist Receipt US $ 2,000,000
Population 4,768,000	Passenger Cars 7,300
Population Density 165 per Sq Km	Steel Consumption 2 Kg/Cap
Birth-Death Rate % 4.5-2.0	
Population Rate of Increase 2.00%	Growth Pattern Index 6.25%
1967 GNP per Capita 84 US $	

Energy Total Billion Kec	0.146
Energy per Capita Kec	31
Kec per $ of GNP	0.38
Electric Capacity Kw	40,800
Generation Billion Kwhr	0.115
Kilowatt Hours per Capita	24
Kwhr per $ of GNP	0.20
Economic Density GNP $/Sq Km	13,880

245

HONDURAS

	1970	1975	1980	1985	1990	1995	2000	2005	2010	2015	2020
Population 1967 Population	1.100	1.280	1.480	1.680	1.875	2.070	2.265	2.460	2.650	2.840	3.030
Population Millions	2.690	3.135	3.520	4.110	4.590	5.060	5.545	6.020	6.490	6.950	7.410
GNP Capita 1967 $	252	280	316	351	394	431	495	550	618	690	768
GNP Billion $ 1967	0.676	0.877	1.110	1.442	1.810	2.175	2.745	3.310	4.020	4.780	5.690
Yearly Increase GNP	5.4%	4.8%	5.4%	4.6%	3.7%	4.8%	3.9%	4.0%	3.6%	3.6%	

Map North & Caribbean America	H L Students	133 per 100000	Energy Total
Capital Tegucigalpa	Hospital Beds	1.8 per 1000	Billion Kec 0.524
One U S $ = 2 Lempira	Daily Newspapers	17 per 1000	Energy per Capita Kec 216
	Telephones	11,150	
Area-Total 112,088 Sq Km			Kec per $ of GNP 0.70
Area-Arable 8,230 Sq Km	Television Sets	11,000	Growth Ratio GNP/Kec 0.625
Population 2,495,000	Passenger Cars	12,000	Electric Capacity Mw 91
Population Density 22 per Sq Km	Steel Consumption	10 Kg/Cap	Generation Billion Kwhr 0.280
			Kilowatt Hours per Capita 116
Birth-Death Rate % 4.9-1.6	Investment Ratio	19%	Kwhr per $ of GNP 0.39
Population Rate of	Growth Pattern Index	37.50%	
Increase 3.40%	GNP/Capita		Economic Density
	Annual Increase 67-90	2.25%	GNP $/Sq Km 5,070
1967 GNP per Capita 236 US $			

246

HONG KONG

	1970	1975	1980	1985	1990	1995	2000	2005	2010	2015	2020
Population 1967 Population											
Population Millions	1.080	1.260	1.440	1.620	1.800	1.980	2.160	2.330	2.500	2.670	2.840
	4.14	4.79	5.52	6.21	6.90	7.60	8.28	8.93	9.59	10.24	10.90
GNP Capita 1967 $	733	974	1,210	1,560	1,965	2,460	2,965	3,550	4,220	4,950	5,770
GNP Billion $ 1967	3.04	4.67	6.68	9.70	13.55	18.70	24.55	31.70	40.50	50.70	62.80
Yearly Increase GNP	9.0%	8.4%	7.7%	6.9%	6.2%	5.6%	5.2%	4.9%	4.6%	4.4%	

Map	Asia & Middle East
Capital	Victoria
One U S $ =	6 Dollar
Area-Total	1,034 Sq Km
Area-Arable	130 Sq Km
Population	3,990,000
Population Density	3,708 per Sq Km
Brith-Death Rate %	2.1-0.5
Population Rate of Increase	3.20%
1967 GNP per Capita	620 US $

H L Students	293 per 100000
Hospital Beds	3.7 per 1000
Daily Newspapers	493 per 1000
Telephones	426,540
Television Sets	164,000
Tourist Receipt US $	160,000,000
Passenger Cars	73,000
Steel Consumption	119 Kg/Cap
Growth Pattern Index GNP/Capita	118.75%
Annual Increase 67-90	5.10%

Energy Total Billion Kec	2.991
Energy per Capita Kec	761
Kec per $ of GNP	1.28
Growth Ratio GNP/Kec	0.766
Electric Capacity Mw	1,054
Generation Billion Kwhr	3,948
Kilowatt Hours per Capita	1,005
Kwhr per $ of GNP	2.74
Economic Density GNP $/Sq Km	229,000

247

HUNGARY

	1967	1970	1975	1980	1985	1990	1995	2000	2005	2010	2015	2020
Population 1967 Population	1.000	1.005	1.030	1.045	1.063	1.080	1.091	1.102	1.112	1.122	1.132	1.142
Population Millions	10.22	10.37	10.54	10.68	10.87	11.05	11.14	11.28	11.36	11.46	11.58	11.69
GNP/Capita 1967 $	900	1,048	1,300	1,600	1,915	2,278	2,695	3,160	3,700	4,340	4,990	5,760
GNP Billion $ 1967	9.20	10.72	13.70	17.08	20.80	25.19	30.88	35.60	42.10	49.70	57.70	67.40

Yearly Increase GNP	5.0%	4.5%	4.0%	3.8%	3.6%	3.5%	3.4%	3.3%	3.2%	3.1%

Map	Europe	H L Students	513 per 100000
Capital	Budapest	Hospital Beds	7.7 per 1000
One U S $ =	11.74 Forint	Daily Newspapers	205 per 1000
		Telephones	684,389
Area-Total	93,030 Sq Km		
Area-Arable	56,130 Sq Km	Television Sets	1,397,000
		Tourist Receipt US $	48,000,000
Population	10,295,000	Passenger Cars	163,600
Population Density	110 per Sq Km	Steel Consumption	307 Kg/Cap
Birth-Death Rate %	1.51-1.12	Investment Ratio	27%
Population Rate of Increase	0.40%	Growth Pattern Index	137.50%
		GNP/Capita Annual Increase 67-90	4.10%
1967 GNP per Capita	900 US $		

Energy Total Billion Kec	28.889
Energy per Capita Kec	2,816
Kec per $ of GNP	2.96
Growth Ratio GNP/Kec	0.687
Electric Capacity Mw	2,601
Generation Billion Kwhr	15.764
Kilowatt Hours per Capita	1,501
Kwhr per $ of GNP	1.56
Economic Density GNP $/Sq Km	99,000

248

ICELAND

	1967	1970	1975	1980	1985	1990	1995	2000	2005	2010	2015	2020
Population 1967 Population	1.000	1.055	1.140	1.225	1.310	1.390	1.465	1.540	1.605	1.670	1.730	1.790
Population Millions	199.0	210.0	227.0	244.0	260.5	276.5	291.6	306.4	319.5	332.5	344.4	356.0
GNP Capita 1967 $	2,780	3,060	3,545	4,070	4,660	5,300	6,000	6,760	7,640	8,580	9,600	10,690
GNP Billion $ 1967	0.541	0.643	0.850	0.994	1.213	1.411	1.748	2.066	2.436	2.850	3.305	3.805

Yearly Increase GNP	5.7%	4.3%	4.1%	3.9%	3.6%	3.4%	3.3%	3.3%	3.2%	3.0%	2.8%

Map	Europe		H L Students	614 per 100000		Energy Total	
Capital	Reykjavik		Hospital Beds	11.1 per 1000		Billion Kec	0.842
One U S $ =	88 Krona		Daily Newspapers	435 per 1000		Energy per Capita Kec	4,188
			Telephones	66,267			
Area-Total	103,000 Sq Km					Kec per $ of GNP	1.39
Area-Arable	10 Sq Km		Television Sets	24,000		Growth Ratio GNP/Kec	1.30
			Tourist Receipt US $	3,000,000			
Population	203,000		Passenger Cars	37,500		Electric Capacity Mw	193
Population Density	1.93 per Sq Km		Steel Consumption	164 Kg/Cap		Generation Billion Kwhr	0.729
						Kilowatt Hours per Capita	3,626
Birth-Death Rate %	2.09-0.69		Investment Ratio	33%		Kwhr per $ of GNP	1.30
Population Rate of Increase	1.80%		Growth Pattern Index	130%			
			GNP/Capita			Economic Density	
1967 GNP per Capita	2,720 US $		Annual Increase 67-90	2.86%		GNP $/Sq Km	5,250

INDIA

	1967	1970	1975	1980	1985	1990	1995	2000	2005	2010	2015	2020
Population 1967 Population	1.000	1.080	1.199	1.324	1.450	1.573	1.692	1.806	1.920	2.030	2.140	2.239
Population Millions	511	552	612.5	676	741	804	864	922	981	1,036	1,094	1,145
GNP Capita 1967 $	90.0	99.5	115.8	136.2	159.5	186.5	217.5	255.0	297.5	353.5	404.0	470.0
GNP Billion $ 1967	45.9	54.9	70.9	92.2	118.2	149.5	187.8	235.0	292.0	356.0	442.0	539.0
Yearly Increase GNP		5.2%	5.1%	5.0%	4.8%	4.6%	4.5%	4.4%	4.3%	4.2%	4.0%	

Map	Asia & Middle East	H L Students	225 per 100000	Energy Total Billion Kec	96,378
Capital	New Delhi	Hospital Beds	0.6 per 1000	Energy per Capita Kec	183
One U S $ =	7.553 Rupee	Daily Newspapers	13 per 1000		
		Telephones	1,057,193	Kec per $ of GNP	1.95
Area-Total	3,268,090 Sq Km	Television Sets	8,000	Growth Ratio GNP/Kec	0.685
Area-Arable	1,637,200 Sq Km	Tourist Receipt US $	35,000,000		
Population	536,983,000	Passenger Cars	505,200	Electric Capacity Mw	14,314
Population Density	156 per Sq Km	Steel Consumption	11 Kg/Cap	Generation Billion Kwhr	48,000
				Kilowatt Hours per Capita	91
Birth-Death Rate %	4.2-1.7	Growth Pattern Index		Kwhr per $ of GNP	0.91
Population Rate of Increase	2.48%	GNP/Capita Annual Increase 67-90	62.50% 3.25%	Economic Density GNP $/Sq Km	14,050
1967 GNP per Capita	90 US $				

INDONESIA

	1967	1970	1975	1980	1985	1990	1995	2000	2005	2010	2015	2020
Population 1967 Population	1.000	1.070	1.126	1.305	1.415	1.535	1.640	1.750	1.850	1.949	2.045	2.132
Population Millions	110.1	117.8	131.0	143.4	155.8	169.0	180.5	192.5	203.8	214.5	225.0	234.5
GNP Capita 1967 $	104	110	121	131	145	161	178	196	218	240	265	292
GNP Billion $ 1967	11.48	12.94	15.88	18.80	22.60	27.20	32.15	37.75	44.40	51.50	59.60	68.60
Yearly Increase GNP	4.1%		3.9%	3.8%	3.7%	3.6%	3.4%	3.3%	3.3%	3.1%	3.0%	2.8%

Map	Oceania	H L Students	175 per 100000
Capital	Djakarta	Hospital Beds	0.7 per 1000
One US $ =	378 Rupiah	Daily Newspapers	7 per 1000
		Telephones	181,377
Area-Total	1,491,564 Sq Km	Television Sets	72,000
Area-Arable	126,970 Sq Km	Tourist Receipt US $	2,000,000
Population	116,000,000	Passenger Cars	505,200
Population Density	74 per Sq Km	Steel Consumption	2 Kg/Cap
Birth-Death Rate %	4.9-2.1	Investment Ratio	9%
Population Rate of Increase	2.34%	Growth Pattern Index	37.50%
		GNP/Capita Annual Increase 67-90	1.93%
1967 GNP per Capita	104 US $		

Energy Total Billion Kec	11.234
Energy per Capita Kec	99
Kec per $ of GNP	0.93
Growth Ratio GNP/Kec	0.405
Generation Billion Kwhr	2.080
Kilowatt Hours per Capita	18
Kwhr per $ of GNP	0.17
Economic Density GNP $/Sq Km	7,700

IRAN

	1967	1970	1975	1980	1985	1990	1995	2000	2005	2010	2015	2020
Population 1967 Population	1.000	1.090	1.230	1.382	1.530	1.682	1.832	1.980	2.110	2.390	2.390	2.520
Population Millions	26.28	28.66	32.39	36.40	40.25	44.40	48.25	52.10	55.50	59.25	62.90	66.25
GNP Capita 1967 $	283	340	451	600	774	998	1,262	1,590	1,985	2,420	2,885	3,425
GNP Billion $ 1967	7.45	9.76	14.58	21.84	31.15	44.30	60.90	82.95	109.0	143.2	181.2	226.5
Yearly Increase GNP		8.4%	8.2%	7.4%	7.3%	6.6%	6.3%	5.6%	5.2%	4.8%		4.6%

Map	Asia & Middle East	H L Students	149 per 100000
Capital	Tehran	Hospital Beds	1.0 per 1000
One U S $ =	75.75 Rial	Daily Newspapers	15 per 1000
		Telephones	250,300
Area-Total	1,648,000 Sq Km		
Area-Arable	115,930 Sq Km	Television Sets	200,000
		Tourist Receipt US $	42,000,000
Population	27,892,000	Passenger Cars	180,400
Population Density	16 per Sq Km	Steel Consumption	63 Kg/Cap
Birth-Death Rate %	4.8-1.8	Investment Ratio	19%
Population Rate of		Growth Pattern Index	118.75%
Increase	2.84%	GNP/Capita	
		Annual Increase 67-90	5.60%
1967 GNP per Capita	283 US $		

Energy Total Billion Kec	12.920
Energy per Capita Kec	478
Kec per $ of GNP	1.590
Growth Ratio GNP/Kec	0.971
Electric Capacity Mw	1,089
Generation Billion kwhr	5.008
Kilowatt Hours per Capita	185
Economic Density GNP $/Sq Km	4,520

252

IRAQ

	1970	1975	1980	1985	1990	1995	2000	2005	2010	2015	2020
Population 1967 Population	1.080	1.230	1.380	1.530	1.670	1.820	1.960	2.095	2.230	2.360	2.490
Population Millions	9.11	10.40	11.65	12.92	14.10	15.37	16.53	17.70	18.82	19.92	21.03
GNP Capita 1967 $	264	328	405	505	623	754	905	1,075	1,250	1,472	1,675
GNP Billion $ 1967	2.41	3.41	4.72	6.53	8.78	11.60	14.97	19.00	23.55	29.35	35.25
Yearly Increase GNP	7.2%	6.8%	6.4%	6.0%	5.6%	5.2%	4.8%	4.4%	4.0%	3.7%

Map	Asia & Middle East	H L Students	419 per 100000
Capital	Baghdad	Hospital Beds	1.9 per 1000
One U S $ =	.3571 Dinar	Daily Newspapers	12 per 1000
		Telephones	113,388
Area-Total	434,924 Sq Km	Television Sets	175,000
Area-Arable	74,960 Sq Km	Tourist Receipt US $	47,000,000
		Passenger Cars	61,500
Population	9,350,000	Steel Consumption	50 Kg/Cap
Population Density	19 per Sq Km		
Birth-Death Rate %	4.8-1.5	Growth Pattern Index	93.75%
Population Rate of Increase	2.80%	GNP/Capita Annual Increase 67-90	4.40%
1967 GNP per Capita	230 US $		

Energy Total Billion Kec	5.560
Energy per Capita Kec	644
Kec per $ of GNP	2.66
Growth Ratio GNP/Kec	0.641
Generation Billion Kwhr	2.325
Kilowatt Hours per Capita	269
Kwhr per $ of GNP	0.73
Economic Density GNP $/Sq Km	4,470

253

IRELAND

	1967	1970	1975	1980	1985	1990	1995	2000	2005	2010	2015	2020
Population 1967 Population	1.000	1.010	1.020	1.033	1.050	1.060	1.070	1.076	1.085	1.090	1.096	1.105
Population Millions	2.899	2.925	2.958	2.989	3.045	3.075	3.100	3.120	3.145	3.160	3.180	3.200
GNP Capita 1967 $	1,067	1,195	1,419	1,602	1,934	2,220	2,546	2,900	3,280	3,725	4,060	4,410
GNP Billion $ 1967	3.09	3.50	4.20	4.97	5.89	6.83	7.90	9.06	10.30	11.77	12.88	14.10
Yearly Increase GNP		3.7%	3.6%	3.2%	3.0%	2.9%	2.7%	2.6%	2.5%	1.9%	1.8%	

Map	Europe
Capital	Dublin
One U S $ =	.4183 Pound
Area-Total	70,283 Sq Km
Area-Arable	11,940 Sq Km
Population Density	2,921,000
	41 per Sq Km
Birth-Death Rate %	2.09-1.13
Population Rate of Increase	0.30%
1967 GNP per Capita	1,067 US $

H L Students	799 per 100000
Hospital Beds	14.3 per 1000
Daily Newspapers	242 per 1000
Telephones	274,134
Television Sets	441,000
Passenger Cars	340,900
Steel Consumption	107 Kg/Cap
Investment Ratio	21%
Growth Pattern Index	100%
GNP/Capita	
Annual Increase 67-90	3.25%

Energy Total Billion Kec	8.344
Energy per Capita Kec	2,867
Kec per $ of GNP	2.47
Growth Ratio GNP/Kec	0.389
Electric Capacity Mw	1,292
Generation Billion Kwhr	4,980
Kilowatt Hours per Capita	1,711
Kwhr per $ of GNP	1.52
Economic Density GNP $/Sq Km	42,800

254

ISRAEL

	1967	1970	1975	1980	1985	1990	1995	2000	2005	2010	2015	2020
Population 1967 Population	1.000	1.113	1.272	1.460	1.643	1.824	2.012	2.196	2.375	2.552	2.730	2.908
Population Millions	2.67	2.97	3.40	3.09	4.38	4.86	5.36	5.85	6.33	6.80	7.24	7.76
GNP Capita 1967 $	1,490	1,888	2,320	2,790	3,305	3,850	4,450	5,150	5,890	6,750	7,695	8,740
GNP Billion $ 1967	3.98	5.64	7.87	10.86	14.44	18.70	23.84	30.10	37.25	45.90	55.95	67.80
Yearly Increase GNP		6.9%	6.6%	5.8%	5.3%	5.0%	4.7%	4.5%	4.3%	4.0%	3.9%	

Map	Asia & Middle East
Capital	*Jerusalem
One U S $ =	3.50 Pound
Area-Total	20,700 Sq Km
Area-Arable	4,110 Sq Km
Population	2,822,000
Population Density	129 per Sq Km
Birth-Death Rate %	2.610.7
Population Rate of Increase	3.27%
1967 GNP per Capita	1,490 US $

H L Students	1,488 per 100000
Hospital Beds	8.4 per 1000
Daily Newspapers	188 per 1000
Telephones	419,118
Television Sets	30,000
Tourist Receipt US $	97,000,000
Passenger Cars	112,600
Steel Consumption	270 Kg/Cap
Investment Ratio	21%
Growth Pattern Index	112.50%
GNP/Capita	
Annual Increase 67-90	4.18%

Energy Total Billion Kec	5.530
Energy per Capita Kec	2,014
Kec per $ of GNP	1.52
Growth Ratio GNP/Kec	0.690
Electric Capacity Mw	1,012
Generation Billion Kwhr	5.506
Kilowatt Hours per Capita	2,005
Kwhr per $ of GNP	1.31
Economic Density GNP $/Sq Km	192,500

*NOT RECOGNISED BY MOST COUNTRIES

ITALY

	1967	1970	1975	1980	1985	1990	1995	2000	2005	2010	2015	2020
Population 1967 Population	1.000	1.020	1.054	1.083	1.119	1.151	1.174	1.198	1.217	1.232	1.252	1.272
Population Millions	52.35	53.40	55.20	56.70	58.50	60.25	61.45	62.60	63.60	64.50	65.55	66.50
GNP Capita 1967 $	1,279	1,460	1,815	2,220	2,660	3,160	3,730	4,350	5,050	5,775	6,620	7,520
GNP Billion $ 1967	67.0	78.0	100.0	125.8	155.7	190.5	229.0	272.2	321.0	372.2	433.5	500.0
Yearly Increase GNP		5.1%	4.7%	4.3%	4.1%	3.7%	3.5%	3.3%	3.2%	3.1%		2.9%

Map	Europe
Capital	Rome
One U S $ =	629.10 Lira
Area-Total	301,225 Sq Km
Area-Arable	151,950 Sq Km
Population	53,170,000
Population Density	174 per Sq Km
Birth-Death Rate %	1.76-1.01
Population Rate of Increase	0.74%
1967 GNP per Capita	1,279 US $

H L Students	715 per 100000
Hospital Beds	10.0 per 1000
Daily Newspapers	112 per 1000
Telephones	7,752,024
Television Sets	8,099,000
Tourist Receipt US $	1,476,000,000
Passenger Cars	8,178,500
Steel Consumption	325 Kg/Cap
Investment Ratio	19%
Growth Pattern Index	118.75%
GNP/Capita Annual Increase 67-90	3.98%

Energy Total Billion Kec	116.883
Energy per Capita Kec	2,215
Kec per $ of GNP	1.67
Growth Ratio GNP/Kec	0.528
Electric Capacity Mw	30,264
Generation Billion Kwhr	106.127
Kilowatt Hours per Capita	2,011
Kwhr per $ of GNP	1.48
Economic Density GNP $/Sq Km	222,500

IVORY COAST

	1970	1975	1980	1985	1990	1995	2000	2005	2010	2015	2020
Population 1967 Population	1.165	1.500	1.860	2.280	2.700	3.160	3.640	4.120	4.580	5.040	5.490
Population Millions	4.67	6.02	7.46	9.15	10.84	12.70	14.62	16.55	18.40	20.24	22.05
GNP Capita 1967 $	340	523	783	1,163	1,670	2,385	3,250	4,350	5,680	7,270	8,950
GNP Billion $ 1967	1.59	3.15	5.83	10.63	18.12	30.30	47.50	71.90	104.50	147.00	192.72
Yearly Increase GNP	14.6%	13.3%	12.8%	11.2%	10.7%	9.7%	8.7%	7.8%	6.9%	6.0%	

Map	Africa
Capital	Abidjan
One U S $ =	277.71 CFA Franc
Area-Total	322,463 Sq Km
Area-Arable	88,590 Sq Km
Population	4,195,000
Population Density	12.45 per Sq Km
Birth-Death Rate %	5.0-2.5
Population Rate of Increase	2.80%
1967 GNP per Capita	263 US $

H L Students	66 per 100000
Hospital Beds	2.0 per 1000
Daily Newspapers	3 per 1000
Telephones	24,390
Television Sets	7,000
Passenger Cars	40,600
Investment Ratio	19%
Growth Pattern Index	156.25%
GNP/Capita Annual Increase 67-90	8.35%

Energy Total Billion Kec	0.687
Energy per Capita Kec	167
Kec per $ of GNP	0.57
Growth Ratio GNP/Kec	0.808
Generation Billion Kwhr	0.372
Kilowatt Hours per Capita	90
Kwhr per $ of GNP	0.30
Economic Density GNP $/Sq Km	3,260

JAMAICA

	1967	1970	1975	1980	1985	1990	1995	2000	2005	2010	2015	2020
Population / 1967 Population	1.000	1.060	1.155	1.250	1.345	1.440	1.530	1.615	1.695	1.770	1.840	1.910
Population Millions	1.876	1.988	2.165	2.344	2.524	2.702	2.872	3.030	3.180	3.320	3.452	3.584
GNP/Capita 1967 $	533	578	680	787	910	1,055	1,205	1,369	1,559	1,742	1,962	2,185
GNP Billion $ 1967	0.996	1.148	1.470	1.848	2.295	2.855	3.460	4.140	4.950	5.790	6.790	7.840
Yearly Increase GNP		5.1%	4.6%	4.4%	4.2%	3.9%	3.6%	3.4%	3.2%	3.0%	2.9%	

Map	North & Caribbean America	H L Students	119 per 100000
Capital	Kingston	Hospital Beds	3.5 per 1000
One U S $ =	.8383 Dollar	Daily Newspapers	71 per 1000
		Telephones	61,012
Area-Total	10,962 Sq Km		
Area-Arable	2,410 Sq Km	Television Sets	56,000
		Tourist Receipt US $	80,000,000
Population	1,959,000	Passenger Cars	60,000
Population Density	171 per Sq Km		
		Investment Ratio	29%
Birth-Death Rate %	3.9-0.8	Growth Pattern Index	68.75%
Population Rate of Increase	2.00%	GNP/Capita Annual Increase 67-90	8.35%
1967 GNP per Capita	531 US $		

Energy Total Billion Kec	1.913
Energy per Capita Kec	999
Kec per $ of GNP	1.79
Growth Ratio GNP/Kec	0.359
Generation Billion Kwhr	1.068
Kilowatt Hours per Capita	558
Kwhr per $ of GNP	0.97
Economic Density GNP $/Sq Km	90,500

JAPAN

	1967	1970	1975	1980	1985	1990	1995	2000	2005	2010	2015	2020
Population 1967 Population	1.000	1.030	1.072	1.112	1.156	1.200	1.234	1.264	1.292	1.314	1.343	1.365
Population Millions	99.9	102.8	107.0	111.0	115.4	119.8	123.2	126.1	129.0	131.2	134.0	136.3
GNP Capita 1967 $	1,155	1,375	1,920	2,540	3,285	4,205	5,260	6,540	7,980	9,600	11,380	13,300
GNP Billion $ 1967	115.2	141.2	205.5	281.5	379.5	503.8	648.0	825.0	1,028	1,259	1,524	1,812
Yearly Increase GNP		7.8%	6.5%	6.1%	5.8%	5.1%	4.9%	4.5%	4.1%	3.9%	3.5%	

Map	Asia & Middle East
Capital	Tokyo
One U S $ =	358.7 Yen
Area-Total	369,765 Sq Km
Area-Arable	56,840 Sq Km
Population	102,322,000
Population Density	270 per Sq Km
Birth-Death Rate %	1.9-0.7
Population Rate of Increase	0.96%
1967 GNP per Capita	1,155 US $

H L Students	1,398 per 100000
Hospital Beds	11.1 per 1000
Daily Newspapers	492 per 1000
Telephones	17,330,791
Television Sets	21,027,000
Tourist Receipt US $	126,000,000
Passenger Cars	5,209,000
Steel Consumption	494 Kg/Cap
Investment Ratio	39%
Growth Pattern Index	187.50%
GNP/Capita	
Annual Increase 67-90	5.75%

Energy Total Billion Kec	254.247
Energy per Capita Kec	2,515
Kec per $ of GNP	1.98
Growth Ratio GNP/Kec	0.875
Electric Capacity Mw	52,650
Generation Billion Kwhr	265.074
Kilowatt Hours per Capita	2,622
Kwhr per $ of GNP	2.05
Economic Density GNP $/Sq Km	312,000

JORDAN

	1970	1975	1980	1985	1990	1995	2000	2005	2010	2015	2020
Population 1967 Population	1.080	1.220	1.360	1.500	1.640	1.780	1.910	2.040	2.165	2.290	2.410
Population Millions	2.200	2.482	2.770	3.050	3.340	3.620	3.890	4.150	4.410	4.660	4.900
GNP ──── 1967 $ Capita	315	416	545	715	917	1,175	1,508	1,860	2,315	2,838	3,420
GNP Billion $ 1967	0.684	1.035	1.510	2.175	3.055	4.250	5.850	7.615	10.200	13.200	16.730
Yearly Increase GNP	9.7%	7.8%	7.6%	7.0%	6.8%	6.5%	6.1%	5.8%	5.3%	4.8%	

Map	Asia & Middle East	H L Students	168 per 100000
Capital	Amman	Hospital Beds	1.7 per 1000
One US $ =	.3571 Dinar	Daily Newspapers	12 per 1000
		Telephones	34,500
Area-Total	97,740 Sq Km		
Area-Arable	11,400 Sq Km	Television Sets	17,000
		Tourist Receipt US $	13,000,000
Population	2,160,000	Passenger Cars	20,400
Population Density	21 per Sq Km		
Birth-Death Rate %	4.7-1.6	Investment Ratio	19%
Population Rate of Increase	2.70%	Growth Pattern Index	112.50%
		GNP/Capita Annual Increase 67-90	5.45%
1967 GNP per Capita	268 US $		

Energy Total Billion Kec	0.588		
Energy per Capita Kec	279		
Kec per $ of GNP	0.99		
Growth Ratio GNP/Kec	0.765		
Generation Billion Kwhr	0.156		
Kilowatt Hours per Capita	74		
Kwhr per $ of GNP	0.27		
Economic Density GNP $/Sq Km	5,600		

KENYA

	1970	1975	1980	1985	1990	1995	2000	2005	2010	2015	2020
Population 1967 Population	1.085	1.240	1.395	1.550	1.705	1.855	2.005	2.155	2.300	2.440	2.575
Population Millions	10.78	12.32	13.85	15.40	16.93	18.42	19.96	21.40	22.85	24.24	25.54
GNP Capita 1967 $	124.0	138.0	152.0	168.2	187.0	205.5	227.5	248.0	274.0	301.0	329.0
GNP Billion $ 1967	1.338	1.700	2.105	2.590	3.165	3.782	4.530	5.300	6.250	7.300	8.400
Yearly Increase GNP	4.9%	4.5%	4.3%	4.1%	3.8%	3.6%	3.4%	3.2%	3.0%	2.8%	

Map	Africa	H L Students	49 per 100000
Capital	Nairobi	Hospital Beds	1.4 per 1000
One U S $ =	7.143 Shilling	Daily Newspapers	9 per 1000
		Telephones	65,445
Area-Total	582,6644 Sq Km	Television Sets	15,000
Area-Arable	16,700 Sq Km	Tourist Receipt US $	46,000,000
		Passenger Cars	80,600
Population	10,506,000		
Population Density	17 per Sq Km	Investment Ratio	21%
Birth-Death Rate %	5.0-2.0	Growth Pattern Index	37.50%
Population Rate of Increase	2.90%	GNP/Capita Annual Increase 67-90	2.05%
1967 GNP per Capita	117 US $		

Energy Total Billion Kec	1.479
Energy per Capita Kec	144
Kec per $ of GNP	1.23
Growth Ratio GNP/Kec	0.789
Electric Capacity Mw	153
Generation Billion Kwhr	0.626
Kilowatt Hours per Capita	61
Kwhr per $ of GNP	0.50
Economic Density GNP $/Sq Km	1,978

KOREA - NORTH

	1967	1970	1975	1980	1985	1990	1995	2000	2005	2010	2015	2020
Population 1967 Population	1.000	1.070	1.205	1.340	1.475	1.610	1.740	1.870	1.990	2.110	2.225	2.335
Population Millions	12.70	13.60	15.30	17.02	18.73	20.45	22.10	23.75	25.26	26.80	28.26	29.65
GNP/Capita 1967 $	230	260.5	325.5	401	492	605	739	903	1,090	1,303	1,563	1,822
GNP Billion $ 1967	2.83	3.54	4.97	6.83	9.20	12.38	16.32	21.60	27.55	34.90	44.20	54.00
Yearly Increase GNP		7.0%	6.6%	6.3%	6.1%	5.7%	5.6%	5.1%	4.8%	4.6%	4.5%	

Map: Asia & Middle East
Capital: Pyongyang
One U S $ = 1.20 Won

Area-Total: 120,538 Sq Km
Area-Arable: 18,940 Sq Km

Population: 13,300,000
Population Density: 105 per Sq Km

Birth-Death Rate %: 3.9-1.1
Population Rate of Increase: 2.60%

1967 GNP per Capita: 230 US $

Steel Consumption: 109 Kg/Cap

Growth Pattern Index
GNP/Capita: 87.50%
Annual Increase 67-90: 4.25%

Economic Density
GNP $/Sq Km: 23,500

KOREA REPUBLIC

	1970	1975	1980	1985	1990	1995	2000	2005	2010	2015	2020
Population 1967 Population	1.092	1.236	1.394	1.548	1.705	1.860	2.018	2.154	2.298	2.442	2.580
Population Millions	32.50	36.79	41.49	46.00	50.65	55.30	59.99	64.07	68.40	72.75	76.70
GNP Capita 1967 $	197.5	281	381	524	698	907	1,145	1,430	1,745	2,085	2,490
GNP Billion $ 1967	6.42	10.32	15.77	24.10	35.40	50.15	68.70	91.60	111.93	151.15	190.80
Yearly Increase GNP	9.3%	8.3%	8.1%	7.3%	6.8%	6.5%	5.7%	5.5%	4.9%	4.2%	

Map	Asia & Middle East
Capital	Seoul
One U S $ =	312 Won
Area-Total	98,477 Sq Km
Area-Arable	23,190 Sq Km
Population	31,130,000
Population Density	302 per Sq Km
Birth-Death Rate %	3.6-1.1
Population Rate of Increase	2.91%
1967 GNP per Capita	162 US $

H L Students	574 per 100000
Hospital Beds	0.8 per 1000
Daily Newspapers	75 per 1000
Telephones	489,912
Television Sets	95,000
Tourist Receipt US $	17,000,000
Passenger Cars	33,100
Steel Consumption	29 Kg/Cap
Investment Ratio	27%
Growth Pattern Index	143.75%
GNP/Capita Annual Increase 67-90	6.53%

Energy Total Billion Kec	17.643
Energy per Capita Kec	579
Kec per $ of GNP	3.50
Growth Ratio GNP/Kec	0.640
Electric Capacity Mw	1,453
Generation Billion Kwhr	6.400
Kilowatt Hours per Capita	210
Kwhr per $ of GNP	0.35
Economic Density GNP $/Sq Km	48,700

263

KUWAIT

	1970	1975	1980	1985	1990	1995	2000	2005	2010	2015	2020
Population 1967 Population	1.170	1.520	1.900	2.350	2.850	3.350	3.850	4.330	4.810	5.280	5.740
Population Millions	0.609	0.790	0.988	1.222	1.481	1.740	2.000	2.250	2.500	2.745	2.980
GNP/Capita 1967 $	3,755	4,135	4,590	5,070	5,560	6,150	6,730	7,370	8,010	8,750	9,430
GNP Billion $ 1967	2.28	3.27	4.54	6.20	8.24	10.71	13.46	16.58	20.00	24.00	28.12
Yearly Increase GNP		7.4%	6.9%	6.4%	5.8%	5.2%	4.7%	4.2%	3.8%	3.5%	3.2%

Map	Asia & Middle East	H L Students	170 per 100000	Energy Total Billion Kec	6.429
Capital	Kuwait	Hospital Beds	6.7 per 1000	Energy per Capita Kec	11,905
One US $ =	0.3571 Dinar	Daily Newspapers	52 per 1000		
		Telephones	51,168	Kec per $ of GNP	1.89
Area-Total	16,000 Sq Km			Growth Ratio GNP/Kec	0.782
Area-Arable	3 Sq Km	Televison Sets	100,000		
Population	570,000	Passenger Cars	92,500	Generation Billion Kwhr	1.970
Population Density	33 per Sq Km	Steel Consumption	363 Kg/Cap	Kilowatt Hours per Capita	5,500
				Kwhr per $ of GNP	0.80
Birth-Death Rate %	4.7-0.6	Investment Ratio	26%		
Population Rate of Increase	9.40%	Growth Pattern Index	81.25%	Economic Density GNP $/Sq Km	114,200
		GNP/Capita Annual Increase 67-90	2.00%		
1967 GNP per Capita	3,530 US $				

LAOS

	1970	1975	1980	1985	1990	1995	2000	2005	2010	2015	2020
Population 1967 Population	1.070	1.200	1.330	1.460	1.580	1.700	1.820	1.940	2.050	2.155	2.260
Population Millions	2.960	3.120	3.680	4.040	4.370	4.700	5.040	5.360	5.670	5.955	6.250
GNP Capita 1967 $	94.0	106.3	123.4	138.0	156.0	173.8	194.8	212.0	235.0	261.0	290.5
GNP Billion $ 1967	0.278	0.332	0.453	0.568	0.682	0.817	0.982	1.137	1.330	1.554	1.814
Yearly Increase GNP	6.7%	6.4%	5.7%	5.0%	4.3%	3.7%	3.4%	3.2%	3.1%	3.0%	

Map	Asia & Middle East	
Capital	Vientiane	
One U S $ =	240 Kip	
Area-Total	236,800 Sq Km	
Area-Arable	8,000 Sq Km	
Population Density	11.58 per Sq Km	
Birth-Death Rate %	4.2-1.7	
Population Rate of Increase	2.50%	
1967 GNP per Capita	90 US $	

H L Students	13 per 100000	
Daily Newspapers	3 per 1000	
Telephones	2,454	
Passenger Cars	10,600	
Steel Consumption	2 Kg/Cap	
Growth Pattern Index	37.50%	
GNP/Capita Annual Increase 67-90	2.45%	

Energy Total Billion Kec		0.084
Energy per Capita Kec		29
Kec per $ of GNP		0.48
Growth Ratio GNP/Kec		0.366
Generation Billion Kwhr		0.033
Kilowatt Hours per Capita		11
Kwhr per $ of GNP		0.12
Economic Density GNP $/Sq Km		1,050

265

LEBANON

	1970	1975	1980	1985	1990	1995	2000	2005	2010	2015	2020
Population 1967 Population	1.070	1.210	1.345	1.480	1.610	1.740	1.860	1.985	2.105	2.220	2.330
Population Millions	2.700	3.050	3.390	3.730	4.060	4.380	4.680	5.000	5.300	5.590	5.870
GNP Capita 1967 $	576	681	796	923	1,078	1,258	1,440	1,665	1,894	2,145	2,425
GNP Billion $ 1967	1.550	2.075	2.695	3.440	4.375	5.520	6.745	8.330	10.050	11.980	14.220
Yearly Increase GNP	6.0%	5.5%	5.0%	4.9%	4.7%	4.5%	4.2%	3.8%	3.6%	3.5%	

Map	Asia & Middle East	H L Students	1,156 per 100000
Capital	Beirut	Hospital Beds	4.0 per 1000
One U S $ =	3.27 Pound	Telephones	150,370
Area-Total	10,400 Sq Km	Television Sets	375,000
Area-Arable	3,160 Sq Km	Tourist Receipt US $	110,000,000
Population		Passenger Cars	123,900
Population Density	242 per Sq Km	Steel Consumption	104 Kg/Cap
		Investment Ratio	19%
Population Rate of Increase	2.60%	Growth Pattern Index GNP/Capita	68.75%
		Annual Increase 67-90	3.20%
1967 GNP per Capita	520 US $		

Energy Total Billion Kec	1.739
Energy per Capita Kec	673
Kec per $ of GNP	1.225
Growth Ratio GNP/Kec	0.555
Electric Capacity Mw	374
Generation Billion Kwhr	1.036
Kilowatt Hours per Capita	401
Kwhr per $ of GNP	0.69
Economic Density GNP $/Sq Km	127,000

LIBERIA

	1970	1975	1980	1985	1990	1995	2000	2005	2010	2015	2020
Population 1967 Population	1.050	1.130	1.210	1.290	1.370	1.435	1.500	1.560	1.620	1.680	1.730
Population Millions	1.165	1.253	1.342	1.431	1.521	1.592	1.665	1.732	1.798	1.866	1.920
GNP Capita 1967 $	265	336	424	600	661	820	1,010	1,235	1,480	1,800	2,130
GNP Billion $ 1967	0.308	0.421	0.562	0.806	1.005	1.308	1.680	2.140	2.660	3.358	4.090
Yearly Increase GNP	6.4%	5.9%	5.7%	5.5%	5.3%	5.1%	4.9%	4.6%	4.3%	4.0%	

Map	Africa	
Capital	Monrovia	
One U S $ =	1 Dollar	
Area-Total	111,369 Sq Km	
Area-Arable	38,500 Sq Km	
Population	1,150,000	
Population Density 9.97	per Sq Km	
Birth-Death Rate %	4.4-2.5	
Population Rate of Increase	1.70%	
1967 GNP per Capita	230 US $	

H L Students	113 per 100000
Hospital Beds	2.0 per 1000
Daily Newspapers	9 per 1000
Telephones	3,600
Television Sets	4,000
Passenger Cars	13,400
Steel Consumption	17 Kg/Cap
Growth Pattern Index GNP/Capita	93.75%
Annual Increase 67-90	4.68%

Energy Total Billion Kec	0.324
Energy per Capita Kec	286
Kec per $ of GNP	1.38
Growth Ratio GNP/Kec	0.468
Electric Capacity Kw	152,100
Generation Billion Kwhr	0.573
Kilowatt Hours per Capita	507
Kwhr per $ of GNP	1.52
Economic Density GNP $/Sq Km	2,300

LIBYA

	1967	1970	1975	1980	1985	1990	1995	2000	2005	2010	2015	2020
Population 1967 Population	1.000	1.090	1.325	1.555	1.785	2.015	2.240	2.465	2.685	2.905	3.120	3.330
Population Millions	1.738	1.895	2.300	2.700	3.100	3.505	3.895	4.290	4.665	5.050	5.420	5.790
GNP Capita 1967 $	1,073	1,411	2,170	2,750	3,385	4,180	5,150	6,230	7,380	8,760	10,250	11,740
GNP Billion $ 1967	1.87	2.68	5.00	7.42	10.43	14.65	20.08	26.75	34.40	44.20	55.60	68.10
Yearly Increase GNP		13.5%	8.3%	7.1%	7.0%	6.5%	5.9%	5.1%	5.1%	5.1%	4.7%	4.1%

Map	Africa
Capital	Tripoli & Behghazi
One U S $ =	.3571 Pound
Area-Total	1,759,540 Sq Km
Area-Arable	25,110 Sq Km
Population	1,869,000
Population Density	0.99 per Sq Km
Population Rate of Increase	3.70%
1967 GNP per Capita	1,073 US $

H L Students	132 per 100000
Hospital Beds	3.3 per 1000
Daily Newspapers	20 per 1000
Telephones	31,700
Tourist Receipt US $	15,000,000
Passenger Cars	77,300
Steel Consumption	305 Kg/Cap
Investment Ratio	31%
Growth Pattern Index	187.50%
GNP/Capita Annual Increase	6.04%

Energy Total Billion Kec	0.890
Energy per Capita Kec	493
Kec per $ of GNP	0.444
Growth Ratio GNP/Kec	0.790
Electric Capacity Kw	168,500
Generation Billion Kwhr	0.274
Kilowatt Hours per Capita	151
Kwhr per $ of GNP	0.11
Economic Density GNP £/Sq Km	1,058

MADAGASCAR

	1970	1975	1980	1985	1990	1995	2000	2005	2010	2015	2020
Population 1967 Population	1.070	1.190	1.310	1.430	1.550	1.670	1.780	1.890	1.990	2.090	2.185
Population Millions	6.80	7.56	8.32	9.08	9.84	10.62	11.32	12.01	12.65	13.30	13.90
GNP 1967 $ Capita	122.2	132.3	144.6	158.0	171.0	186.3	202.0	217.8	236.0	254.5	277.0
GNP Billion $ 1967	0.832	1.000	1.205	1.434	1.682	1.978	2.286	2.615	2.985	3.380	3.850
Yearly Increase GNP	4.0%	3.8%	3.5%	3.3%	3.1%	2.9%	2.7%	2.6%	2.5%	2.4%	

Map	Africa	H L Students	52 per 100000
Capital	Tananarive	Hospital Beds	2.8 per 1000
One U S $ =	277.71 Franc	Daily Newspapers	8 per 1000
		Telephones	23,993
Area-Total	587,041 Sq Km		
Area-Arable	28,560 Sq Km	Passenger Cars	41,600
Population	6,643,000	Steel Consumption	9 Kg/Cap
Population Density	10.82 per Sq Km		
Birth-Death Rate %	4.6-2.2	Investment Ratio	11%
Population Rate of Increase	2.40%	Growth Pattern Index GNP/Capita	28.13%
		Annual Increase 67-90	1.70%
1967 GNP per Capita	116 US $		

Energy Total Billion Kec	0.392
Energy per Capita Kec	60
Kec per $ of GNP	0.49
Growth Ratio GNP/Kec	0.388
Generation Billion Kwhr	0.195
Kilowatt Hours per Capita	29
Kwhr per $ of GNP	0.24
Economic Density GNP $/Sq Km	1,242

269

MALAWI

	1970	1975	1980	1985	1990	1995	2000	2005	2010	2015	2020
Population 1967 Population	1.070	1.190	1.310	1.430	1.550	1.670	1.780	1.890	1.990	2.090	2.185
Population Millions	4.425	4.920	5.415	5.910	6.405	6.900	7.360	7.815	8.230	8.640	9.040
GNP / Capita 1967 $	59.5	74.4	93.0	115.0	141.5	174.6	210.3	257.5	312.0	377.0	457.0
GNP Billion $ 1967	0.263	0.366	0.503	0.680	0.908	1.202	1.547	2.010	2.568	3.255	4.130
Yearly Increase GNP	6.8%	6.5%	6.2%	5.9%	5.7%	5.6%	5.4%	5.0%	4.9%	4.8%	

Map	Africa
Capital	Zomba
One U S $ =	0.4167 Pound
Area-Total	117,800 Sq Km
Area-Arable	29,270 Sq Km
Population Density	4,398,000
	35 per Sq Km
Population Rate of Increase	2.40%
1967 GNP per Capita	51 US $

H L Students	16 per 100000
Hospital Beds	1.3 per 1000
Telephones	10,174
Passenger Cars	8,800
Steel Consumption	1 Kg/Cap
Investment Ratio	16%
Growth Pattern Index	75.00%
GNP/Capita	
Annual Increase 67-90	4.50%

Energy Total Billion Kec	0.174
Energy per Capita Kec	40
Kec per $ of GNP	0.940
Growth Ratio GNP/Kec	0.500
Electric Capacity Kw	49,100
Generation Billion Kwhr	0.117
Kilowatt Hours per Capita	27
Kwhr per $ of GNP	0.47
Economic Density GNP $/Sq Km	1,780

MALAYSIA

	1970	1975	1980	1985	1990	1995	2000	2005	2010	2015	2020
Population 1967 Population	1.105	1.255	1.430	1.600	1.770	1.940	2.110	2.270	2.430	2.590	2.750
Population Millions	11.10	12.62	14.40	16.10	17.80	19.52	21.25	22.85	24.50	26.15	27.70
GNP Capita 1967 $	375	450	536	639	765	917	1,080	1,262	1,500	1,735	2,010
GNP Billion $ 1967	4.16	5.66	7.74	10.29	13.60	17.92	22.95	28.82	36.75	45.40	55.70
Yearly Increase GNP	6.3%	6.1%	5.9%	5.7%	5.6%	5.2%	4.9%	4.6%	4.3%	4.2%	

Map	Asia & Middle East
Capital	Kuala Lumpur
One U S $ =	3.09 Dollar
Area—Total	201,301 Sq Km
Area—Arable	26,240 Sq Km
Population	10,583,000
Population Density	7.42 per Sq Km
Birth-Death Rate %	3.5-0.8
Population Rate of Increase	3.10%
1967 GNP per Capita	335 US $

H L Students	184 per 100000
Daily Newspapers	75 per 1000
Telephones	156,354
Television Sets	121,000
Tourist Receipt US $	15,000,000
Steel Consumption	45 Kg/Cap
Growth Pattern Index GNP/Capita	75%
Annual Increase 67-90	3.65%

Kec per $ of GNP	1.27
Growth Ratio GNP/Kec	0.660
Kilowatt Hours per Capita	332
Kwhr per $ of GNP	0.92
Economic Density GNP $/Sq Km	16,750

271

MALI

	1970	1975	1980	1985	1990	1995	2000	2005	2010	2015	2020
Population 1967 Population	1.060	1.165	1.268	1.370	1.470	1.560	1.650	1.740	1.820	1.900	1.970
Population Millions	4.975	5.470	5.950	6.435	6.900	7.325	7.750	8.165	8.540	8.920	9.250
GNP 1967 $ Capita	89.0	104.5	120.0	138.2	158.0	178.2	203.5	227.0	264.5	285.5	320.0
GNP Billion $ 1967	0.443	0.572	0.713	0.890	1.090	1.303	1.578	1.852	2.260	2.645	2.960
Yearly Increase GNP	5.2%	4.8%	4.5%	4.1%	3.7%	3.5%	3.4%	3.3%	3.2%	3.1%	

Map	Africa	Hospital Beds	0.8 per 1000
Capital	Bamako	Daily Newspapers	0.5 per 1000
One U S $ =	555.42 Franc	Telephones	7,800
Area-Total	1,240,000 Sq Km		
Area-Arable	72,000 Sq Km		
Population	4,881,000	Passenger Cars	4,800
Population Density	3.79 per Sq Km		
Birth-Death Rate %	5.0-2.5	Growth Pattern Index	37.50%
Population Rate of Increase	2.10%	GNP/Capita Annual Increase 67-90	3.00%
1967 GNP per Capita	80 US $		

Energy Total Billion Kec	0.104
Energy per Capita Kec	21
Kec per $ of GNP	0.28
Growth Ratio GNP/Kec	0.655
Generation Billion Kwhr	0.035
Kilowatt Hours per Capita	7
Kwhr per $ of GNP	0.09
Economic Density GNP $/Sq Km	303

MALTA

	1970	1975	1980	1985	1990	1995	2000	2005	2010	2015	2020
Population 1967 Population	1	1	1	1	1	1	1	1	1	1	1
Population Millions	0.319	0.319	0.319	0.319	0.319	0.319	0.319	0.319	0.319	0.319	0.319
GNP Capita 1967 $	689	876	1,138	1,423	1,782	2,202	2,695	3,220	3,820	4,460	5,140
GNP Billion $ 1967	0.219	0.280	0.363	0.454	0.569	0.704	0.860	1.050	1.215	1.420	1.635
Yearly Increase GNP	5.0%	5.4%	4.5%	4.5%	4.3%	4.0%	4.0%	3.2%	3.0%	2.8%	

Map	Europe	
Capital	Valletta	
One U S $ =	.4167 Pound	
Area-Total	316 Sq Km	
Area-Arable	160 Sq Km	
Population	323,000	
Population Density	1,800 per Sq Km	
Birth-Death Rate %	1.61-0.90	
Population Rate of Increase	0.40%	
1967 GNP per Capita	587 US $	

H L Students	399 per 100000	
Hospital Beds	10.0 per 1000	
Telephones	33,092	
Television Sets	37,000	
Tourist Receipt US $	19,000,000	
Passenger Cars	31,500	
Investment Ratio	30%	
Growth Pattern Index	112.50%	
GNP/Capita Annual Increase 67-90	4.95%	

Energy Total Billion Kec	0.313	
Energy per Capita Kec	979	
Kec per $ of GNP	1.34	
Growth Ratio GNP/Kec	0.563	
Electric Capacity Mw	55	
Generation Billion Kwhr	0.219	
Kilowatt Hours per Capita	686	
Kwhr per $ of GNP	1.06	
Economic Density GNP $/Sq Km	592,000	

MARTINIQUE

	1970	1975	1980	1985	1990	1995	2000	2005	2010	2015	2020
Population 1967 Population	1.060	1.165	1.268	1.370	1.470	1.560	1.650	1.740	1.820	1.900	1.970
Population Millions	0.350	0.384	0.419	0.452	0.485	0.515	0.545	0.575	0.601	0.627	0.650
GNP/Capita 1967 $	0,597	0,713	0,850	0,996	1,168	1,352	1,578	1,700	1,880	2,440	2,810
GNP Billion $ 1967	0.209	0.274	0.356	0.450	0.567	0.697	0.860	0.977	1.130	1.530	1.825
Yearly Increase GNP		5.6%	5.3%	4.9%	4.7%	4.5%	4.3%	4.1%	3.9%	3.7%	3.6%

Map	North & Caribbean America
Capital	Fort de France
One U S $ =	5.55 Franc
Area-Total	1,102 Sq Km
Area-Arable	320 Sq Km
Population	332,000
Population Density	299 per Sq Km
Birth-Death Rate %	3.0-0.7
Population Rate of Increase	2.10%
1967 GNP per Capita	540 US $

H L Students	405 per 100000
Hospital Beds	8.4 per 1000
Daily Newspapers	67 per 1000
Telephones	14,130
Television Sets	6,000
Passenger Cars	25,200
Growth Pattern Index	68.75%
GNP/Capita Annual Increase 67-90	3.40%

Energy Total Billion Kec	0.127
Energy per Capita Kec	390
Kec per $ of GNP	0.81
Growth Ratio GNP/Kec	0.583
Generation Billion Kwhr	0.072
Kilowatt Hours per Capita	222
Kwhr per $ of GNP	0.35
Economic Density GNP $/Sq Km	162,500

274

MAURITANIA

	1970	1975	1980	1985	1990	1995	2000	2005	2010	2015	2000
Population 1967 Population	1.060	1.150	1.240	1.330	1.420	1.500	1.580	1.650	1.720	1.790	1.850
Population Millions	1.176	1.276	1.376	1.476	1.575	1.664	1.753	1.831	1.908	1.986	2.054
GNP Capita 1967 $	180	250	355	485	666	910	1,220	1,615	2,165	2,840	3,660
GNP Billion $ 1967	0.212	0.319	0.475	0.705	1.048	1.515	2.135	3.010	4.120	5.640	7.510
Yearly Increase GNP		8.8%	8.7%	8.4%	8.1%	7.6%	7.4%	7.1%	6.7%	6.4%	6.0%

Map	Africa	Hospital Beds	0.3 per 1000
Capital	Nouakchott		
One U S $ =	277.71 CFA Franc		
Area–Total	1,030,700 Sq Km		
Area–Arable	2,630 Sq Km		
Population	1,140,000	Passenger Cars	3,700
Population Density	1.06 per Sq Km		
Birth–Death Rate %	4.5–2.5	Growth Pattern Index	118.75%
Population Rate of Increase	1.90%	GNP/Capita Annual Increase 67-90	8.70%
1967 GNP per Capita	147 US $		

Energy Total Billion Kec	0.067
Energy per Capita Kec	60
Kec per $ of GNP	0.36
Growth Ratio GNP/Kec	0.691
Electric Capacity Mw	25
Generation Billion Kwhr	0.044
Kilowatt Hours per Capita	39
Kwhr per $ of GNP	0.23
Economic Density GNP $/Sq Km	157

MAURITIUS

	1970	1975	1980	1985	1990	1995	2000	2005	2010	2015	2020
Population 1967 Population	1.070	1.205	1.340	1.475	1.610	1.740	1.870	1.990	2.110	2.225	2.335
Population Millions	0.829	0.933	1.038	1.142	1.246	1.347	1.448	1.540	1.632	1.722	1.808
GNP Capita 1967 $	270	273.5	282.5	292	310	319	332	343	355.5	365	379
GNP Billion $ 1967	0.224	0.255	0.293	0.334	0.386	0.428	0.481	0.528	0.580	0.628	0.688
Yearly Increase GNP	2.9%	2.8%	2.6%	2.5%	2.4%	2.3%	2.1%	2.0%	1.9%	1.8%	

Map	Africa
Capital	Port Louis
One U S $ =	5.26 Rupee
Area-Total	2,045 Sq Km
Area-Arable	1,040 Sq Km
Population	799,000
Population Density	389 per Sq Km
Birth-Death Rate %	3.1-0.9
Population Rate of Increase	2.60%
1967 GNP per Capita	257 US $

H L Students	23 per 100000
Hospital Beds	4.0 per 1000
Daily Newspapers	96 per 1000
Telephones	15,966
Television Sets	13,000
Tourist Receipt US $	3,000,000
Passenger Cars	12,300
Investment Ratio	15%
Growth Pattern Index	12.50%
GNP/Capita Annual Increase 67-90	0.80%

Energy Total Billion Kec	0.142
Energy per Capita Kec	180
Kec per $ of GNP	0.55
Growth Ratio GNP/Kec	0.667
Electric Capacity Kw	101,400
Generation Billion Kwhr	0.203
Kilowatt Hours per Capita	257
Kwhr per $ of GNP	1.08
Economic Density GNP $/Sq Km	97,500

MEXICO

	1967	1970	1975	1980	1985	1990	1995	2000	2005	2010	2015	2020
Population 1967 Population	1.000	1.120	1.340	1.575	1.820	2.070	2.310	2.540	2.820	3.075	3.340	3.620
Population Millions	45.7	51.2	61.5	71.9	83.0	94.5	105.4	116.2	128.8	140.0	152.6	165.2
GNP Capita 1967 $	528	595	710	849	993	1,175	1,362	1,570	1,798	2,030	2,295	2,570
GNP Billion $ 1967	24.1	30.4	43.6	60.9	82.5	111.0	143.8	183.0	231.5	284.5	350.5	425.0
Yearly Increase GNP		7.4%	6.9%	6.3%	6.1%	5.3%	4.9%	4.8%	4.5%	4.3%	3.9%	

Map North & Caribbean America	
Capital Mexico City	
One U S $ = 12.49 Peso	
Area-Total 1,972,546 Sq Km	
Area-Arable 238,170 Sq Km	
Population 48,933,000	
Population Density 23 per Sq Km	
Birth-Death Rate % 4.4-1.0	
Population Rate of Increase 3.93%	
1967 GNP per Capita 528 US $	

H L Students	338 per 100000
Hospital Beds	2.0 per 1000
Daily Newspapers	116 per 1000
Telephones	1,174,885
Television Sets	2,150,000
Tourist Receipt US $	1,137,000,000
Passenger Cars	1,000,000
Steel Consumption	75 Kg/Cap
Investment Ratio	18%
Growth Pattern Index	81.25%
GNP/Capita Annual Increase 67-90	3.53%

Energy Total Billion Kec	50.300
Energy per Capita Kec	1,064
Kec per $ of GNP	2.04
Growth Ratio GNP/Kec	0.660
Electric Capacity Mw	5,969
Generation Billion Kwhr	22.872
Kilowatt Hours per Capita	483
Kwhr per $ of GNP	0.88
Economic Density GNP $/Sq Km	12.220

MONGOLIA

	1967	1970	1975	1980	1985	1990	1995	2000	2005	2010	2015	2020
Population 1967 Population	1.000	1.075	1.240	1.405	1.570	1.735	1.900	2.060	2.210	2.360	2.510	2.650
Population Millions	1.170	1.258	1.450	1.643	1.836	2.030	2.223	2.408	2.585	2.760	2.933	3.100
GNP Capita 1967 $	410	465	581	715	877	1,080	1,320	1,610	1,945	2,322	2,790	3,250
GNP Billion $ 1967	0.480	0.585	0.843	1.178	1.612	2.190	2.940	3.845	5.030	6.420	8.200	10.080
Yearly Increase GNP		7.6%	6.9%	6.5%	6.3%	6.0%	5.7%	5.3%	5.0%	4.8%	4.2%	

Map	Asia & Middle East
Capital	Ulan Bator
One U S $ =	4 Tugrik
Area-Total	1,565,000 Sq Km
Area-Arable	35,000 Sq Km
Population	1,240,000
Population Density	0.74 per Sq Km
Birth-Death Rate %	4.0–1.0
Population Rate of Increase	3.06%
1967 GNP per Capita	410 US $

H L Students	755 per 100000
Hospital Beds	9.1 per 1000
Daily Newspapers	16 per 1000
Telephones	16,220
Growth Pattern Index	87.50%
GNP/Capita Annual Increase 67-90	4.25%
Kec per $ of GNP	3.84
Kwhr per $ of GNP	1.07
Economic Density GNP $/Sq Km	306

278

MOROCCO

	1970	1975	1980	1985	1990	1995	2000	2005	2010	2015	2020
Population 1967 Population	1.080	1.230	1.380	1.530	1.670	1.820	1.960	2.095	2.230	2.360	2.490
Population Millions	15.28	17.40	19.52	21.64	23.60	25.75	27.75	29.60	31.55	33.40	35.20
GNP Capita 1967 $	207	234	270	305	345	394	443	502	564	642	723
GNP Billion $ 1967	3.17	4.07	5.28	6.60	8.14	10.12	12.29	14.83	17.80	21.45	25.60
Yearly Increase GNP	5.1%	5.4%	4.5%	4.3%	4.2%	4.1%	3.9%	3.8%	3.8%	3.6%	

Map	Africa	H L Students	64 per 100000
Capital	Rabat	Hospital Beds	1.5 per 1000
One U S $ =	5.06 Dirham	Daily Newspapers	14 per 1000
		Telephones	160,326
Area-Total	445,050 Sq Km	Television Sets	100,000
Area-Arable	79,000 Sq Km	Tourist Receipt US $	84,000,000
Population	15,050,000	Passenger Cars	189,500
Population Density	32 per Sq Km	Steel Consumption	18 Kg/Cap
Birth-Death Rate %	4.6-1.5	Investment Ratio	18%
Population Rate of Increase	2.80%	Growth Pattern Index GNP/Capita	50%
		Annual Increase 67-90	2.6%
1967 GNP per Capita	191 US $		

Energy Total Billion Kec	2.638
Energy per Capita Kec	180
Kec per $ of GNP	0.93
Growth Ratio GNP/Kec	0.707
Electric Capacity Mw	494
Generation Billion Kwhr	1.543
Kilowatt Hours per Capita	105
Kwhr per $ of GNP	0.53
Economic Density GNP $/Sq Km	6,080

MOZAMBIQUE

	1970	1975	1980	1985	1990	1995	2000	2005	2010	2015	2020
Population 1967 Population	1.035	1.090	1.140	1.200	1.250	1.300	1.340	1.380	1.410	1.440	1.470
Population Millions	7.38	7.75	8.12	8.55	8.90	9.26	9.55	9.84	10.05	10.27	10.48
GNP Capita 1967 $	207	259	322	398	490	600	740	900	1,100	1,320	1,635
GNP Billion $ 1967	1.53	2.01	2.65	3.41	4.37	5.55	7.07	8.85	11.05	13.58	17.12
Yearly Increase GNP	6.0%	5.5%	5.3%	5.1%	4.9%	4.8%	4.6%	4.4%	4.2%	4.0%	

Map	Africa	
Capital	Lourenso Marques	
One US $ =	28.71 Escudo	
Area-Total	783,030 Sq Km	
Area-Arable	26,490 Sq Km	
Population	7,376,000	
Population Density	9.12 per Sq Km	
Population Rate of Increase	1.20%	
1967 GNP per Capita	180 US $	

	1975	1990	1995
H L Students		10 per 100000	
Hospital Beds		1.9 per 1000	
Daily Newspapers		7 per 1000	
Telephones			22,636
Steel Consumption			9 Kg/Cap
Growth Pattern Index GNP/Capita			81.25%
Annual Increase 67-90			4.42%

		2020
Energy Total Billion Kec		1.109
Energy per Capita Kec		152
Kec per $ of GNP		0.628
Growth Ratio GNP/Kec		0.595
Generation Billion Kwhr		0.390
Kilowatt Hours per Capita		53
Kwhr per $ of GNP		0.27
Economic Density GNP $/Sq Km		1,635

MUSCAT & OMAN

	1970	1975	1980	1985	1990	1995	2000	2005	2010	2015	2020
Population 1967 Population	1	1	1	1	1	1	1	1	1	1	1
Population Millions	0.565	0.565	0.565	0.565	0.565	0.565	0.565	0.565	0.565	0.565	0.565
GNP Capita 1967 $	213	334	518	837	1,170	1,720	2,540	3,680	5,030	6,970	9,450
GNP Billion $ 1967	0.121	0.189	0.293	0.473	0.660	0.970	1.433	2.075	2.840	3.930	5.330
Yearly Increase GNP	9.3%	9.2%	8.8%	8.5%	8.2%	7.9%	7.5%	7.0%	6.6%	6.3%

Map   Asia & Middle East
Capital   Muscat
One US $ =   0.4183 Riyal
Area-Total   212,379 Sq Km
Population   565,000
Population Density 2.66 per Sq Km
Population Rate of Increase   0.00%
1967 GNP per Capita   150 US $

Hospital Beds   0.4 per 1000

Growth Pattern Index
GNP/Capita   150%
Annual Increase 67-90   9.30%

Energy Total
Billion Kec   0.024
Energy per Capita Kec   42

Growth Ratio GNP/Kec   0.652

Economic Density
GNP $/Sq Km   382

281

NEPAL

	1970	1975	1980	1985	1990	1995	2000	2005	2010	2015	2020
Population 1967 Population	1.060	1.150	1.240	1.330	1.420	1.500	1.580	1.650	1.720	1.790	1.850
Population Millions	11.08	12.02	12.96	13.90	14.85	15.68	16.52	17.25	17.98	18.72	19.36
GNP 1967 $ Capita	113.3	133.6	158.6	185.8	215.4	247.0	283.2	320.8	360.5	408.0	456.0
GNP Billion $ 1967	1.256	1.606	2.055	2.584	3.200	3.874	4.680	5.535	6.480	7.640	8.820
Yearly Increase GNP	5.0%	4.8%	4.6%	4.4%	4.0%	3.6%	3.4%	3.2%	3.0%	2.9%	

Map	Asia & Middle East
Capital	Kathmandu
One US $ =	10.125 Rupee
Area-Total	140,797 Sq Km
Area-Arable	22,660 Sq Km
Population	10,845,000
Population Density	75 per Sq Km
Birth-Death Rate %	4.1-2.1
Population Rate of Increase	1.90%
1967 GNP per Capita	102 US $

H L Students	100.2 per 100000
Hospital Beds	0.2 per 1000
Daily Newspapers	3 per 1000
Telephones	5,400
Tourist Receipt US $	800,000
Passenger Cars	4,000
Growth Pattern Index GNP/Capita	31.25%
Annual Increase 67-90	3.30%

Energy Total Billion Kec	0.112
Energy per Capita Kec	10
Kec per $ of GNP	0.088
Growth Ratio GNP/Kec	0.322
Electric Capacity Kw	37,700
Generation Billion Kwhr	0.055
Kilowatt Hours per Capita	5
Kwhr per $ of GNP	0.03
Economic Density GNP $/Sq Km	7,600

282

NETHERLANDS

	1970	1975	1980	1985	1990	1995	2000	2005	2010	2015	2020
Population 1967 Population	1.040	1.103	1.159	1.223	1.284	1.333	1.380	1.425	1.462	1.503	1.542
Population Millions	13.12	13.91	14.62	15.43	16.18	16.80	17.38	17.95	18.43	18.94	19.42
GNP Capita 1967 $	2,000	2,340	2,730	3,130	3,580	4,060	4,625	5,310	5,950	6,740	7,460
GNP Billion $ 1967	26.24	32.60	39.95	48.35	57.90	68.25	80.50	95.40	109.60	125.50	144.80
Yearly Increase GNP	4.4%	4.1%	3.9%	3.6%	3.5%	3.3%	3.1%	2.8%	2.7%	2.6%	

Map	Europe
Capital	*Amsterdam
One U S $ =	3.601 Guilder
Area-Total	33,612 Sq Km
Area-Arable	9,130 Sq Km
Population	12,873,000
Population Density	375 per Sq Km
Birth-Death Rate %	1.86-0.82
Population Rate of Increase	1.34%
1967 GNP per Capita	1,804 US $
*Seat of Government:	The Hague

H L Students	1,445 per 100000
Hospital Beds	5.3 per 1000
Daily Newspapers	301 per 1000
Telephones	2,912,384
Television Sets	2,658,000
Tourist Receipt US $	342,000,000
Passenger Cars	1,950,000
Steel Consumption	347 Kg/Cap
Investment Ratio	29%
Growth Pattern Index	106.25%
GNP/Capita Annual Increase 67-90	3.00%

Energy Total Billion Kec	52.549
Energy per Capita Kec	4,116
Kec per $ of GNP	2.08
Growth Ratio GNP/Kec	0.897
Electric Capacity Mw	9,296
Generation Billion Kwhr	33.345
Kilowatt Hours per Capita	2,616
Kwhr per $ of GNP	1.31
Economic Density GNP $/Sq Km	687,000

NEW CALEDONIA

	1970	1975	1980	1985	1990	1995	2000	2005	2010	2015	2020
Population 1967 Population	1.080	1.220	1.360	1.500	1.640	1.780	1.910	2.040	2.165	2.290	2.410
Population Millions	0.102	0.115	0.128	0.141	0.154	0.167	0.180	0.192	0.204	0.215	0.227
GNP Capita 1967 $	1,742	1,945	2,156	2,405	2,654	2,945	3,255	3,610	3,960	4,310	4,730
GNP Billion $ 1967	0.177	0.223	0.276	0.339	0.409	0.493	0.585	0.693	0.806	0.928	1.075
Yearly Increase GNP	4.8%	4.5%	4.2%	3.9%	3.7%	3.5%	3.3%	3.1%	2.8%	2.7%	

Map	Oceania					
Capital	Noumea	H L Students	66 per 100000	Energy Total Billion Kec	0.815
One U S $ =	552 Franc	Hospital Beds	14.3 per 1000	Energy per Capita Kec	8,491
		Daily Newspapers	43 per 1000		
Area-Total	19,000 Sq Km	Telephones	6,573	Kec per $ of GNP	4.82
Area-Arable	800 Sq Km			Growth Ratio GNP/Kec	0.530
Population	98,000			Generation Billion Kwhr	0.643
Population Density 4.95 per Sq Km				Kilowatt Hours per Capita	6,697
		Growth Pattern Index	93.75%	Kwhr per $ of GNP	4.43
Population Rate of Increase	2.70%	GNP/Capita		Economic Density	
		Annual Increase 67-90	2.18%	GNP $/Sq Km	8,000
1967 GNP per Capita	1,620 US $				

NEW ZEALAND

	1967	1970	1975	1980	1985	1990	1995	2000	2005	2010	2015	2020
Population 1967 Population	1.000	1.060	1.155	1.248	1.346	1.442	1.524	1.607	1.687	1.764	1.836	1.900
Population Millions	2.73	2.89	3.15	3.40	3.67	3.93	4.16	4.39	4.61	4.81	5.00	5.18
GNP Capita 1967 $	2,000	2,335	2,710	3,085	3,490	3,920	4,390	4,890	5,390	6,010	6,650	7,280
GNP Billion $ 1967	5.45	6.74	8.54	10.49	12.79	15.34	18.24	21.40	24.80	28.90	33.25	37.62
Yearly Increase GNP		4.8%	4.2%	4.0%	3.7%	3.5%	3.2%	3.1%	3.0%	2.8%	2.5%

Map	Oceania
Capital	Wellington
One U S $ =	.8969 Dollar
Area-Total	268,675 Sq Km
Area-Arable	7,820 Sq Km
Population	2,770,000
Population Density	10.15 per Sq Km
Birth-Death Rate %	2.26-0.89
Population Rate of Increase	1.99%
1967 GNP per Capita	2,000 US $

H L Students	1,743 per 100000
Hospital Beds	10.0 per 1000
Daily Newspapers	373 per 1000
Telephones	1,155,465
Television Sets	604,000
Tourist Receipt US $	22,000,000
Passenger Cars	829,900
Steel Consumption	276 Kg/Cap
Investment Ratio	23%
Growth Pattern Index	87.50%
GNP/Capita Annual Increase 67-90	2.97%

Energy Total Billion Kec	7.368
Energy per Capita Kec	2,678
Kec per $ of GNP	1.30
Growth Ratio GNP/Kec	0.825
Electric Capacity Mw	3,138
Generation Billion Kwhr	12.295
Kilowatt Hours per Capita	4,469
Kwhr per $ of GNP	2.15
Economic Density GNP $/Sq Km	20,300

NICARAGUA

	1967	1970	1975	1980	1985	1990	1995	2000	2005	2010	2015	2020
Population / 1967 Population	1.000	1.100	1.280	1.480	1.680	1.875	2.070	2.265	2.460	2.650	2.840	3.030
Population Millions	1.783	1.960	2.280	2.640	2.995	3.340	3.690	4.040	4.385	4.720	5.060	5.400
GNP / Capita $ 1967	359	397	474	567	675	805	953	1,112	1,310	1,522	1,772	2,050
GNP Billion $ 1967	0.641	0.778	1.080	1.095	2.020	2.690	3.518	4.500	5.745	7.190	8.960	11.080

Yearly Increase GNP	6.8%	6.7%	6.2%	5.9%	5.5%	5.1%	5.0%	4.6%	4.5%	4.3%

Map	North & Caribbean America
Capital	Managua
One U S $ =	7.026 Cordoba
Area-Total	130,000 Sq Km
Area-Arable	8,730 Sq Km
Population	1,915,000
Population Density	13.70 per Sq Km
Birth-Death Rate %	4.7-1.6
Population Rate of Increase	3.40%
1967 GNP per Capita	359 US $
H L Students	236 per 100000
Hospital Beds	2.4 per 1000
Daily Newspapers	49 per 1000
Telephones	23,484
Television Sets	35,000
Investment Ratio	18%
Growth Pattern Index	68.75%
GNP/Capita Annual Increase 67-90	3.60%
Energy Total Billion Kec	0.642
Energy per Capita Kec	348
Kec per $ of GNP	0.755
Growth Ratio GNP/Kec	0.578
Electric Capacity Kw	156,600
Generation Billion Kwhr	0.484
Kilowatt Hours per Capita	262
Kwhr per $ of GNP	0.65
Economic Density GNP $/Sq Km	492

286

NIGER

	1970	1975	1980	1985	1990	1995	2000	2005	2010	2015	2020
Population 1967 Population	1.075	1.240	1.405	1.570	1.735	1.900	2.060	2.210	2.360	2.510	2.650
Population Millions	3.820	4.410	4.985	5.580	6.160	6.750	7.320	7.850	8.380	8.900	9.410
GNP Capita 1967 $	79.7	98.0	120.4	143.5	169.8	200.0	232.5	269.8	312.0	359.5	412.0
GNP Billion $ 1967	0.304	0.432	0.600	0.801	1.044	1.350	1.700	2.115	2.610	3.200	3.877
Yearly Increase GNP	7.2%	6.5%	5.9%	5.4%	5.0%	4.7%	4.5%	4.3%	4.1%	3.9%	

Map	Africa	
Capital	Niamey	
One U S $ =	277.71 CFA Franc	
Area-Total	1,267,000 Sq Km	
Area-Arable	115,010 Sq Km	
Population	3,909,000	
Population Density	2.80 per Sq Km	
Birth-Death Rate %	5.2–2.5	
Population Rate of Increase	3.00%	
1967 GNP per Capita	70 US $	

Hospital Beds	7.2 per 1000	
Daily Newspapers	0.4 per 1000	
Telephones		3,172
Growth Pattern Index		43.75%
GNP/Capita		
Annual Increase 67–90		3.95%

Energy Total Billion Kec		0.057
Energy per Capita Kec		14
Kec per $ of GNP		0.19
Growth Ratio GNP/Kec		0.370
Generation Billion Kwhr		0.028
Kilowatt Hours per Capita		7
Kwhr per $ of GNP		0.09
Economic Density GNP $/Sq Km		196

NIGERIA

	1967	1970	1975	1980	1985	1990	1995	2000	2005	2010	2015	2020
Population 1967 Population	1.000	1.070	1.184	1.299	1.418	1.529	1.635	1.738	1.840	1.940	2.033	2.120
Population Millions	61.5	65.7	72.6	79.8	87.1	93.9	100.3	106.6	112.9	119.0	124.5	130.1
GNP Capita 1967 $	80.0	87.5	102.2	119.0	138.0	159.0	184.5	212.4	241.0	280.0	318.0	362.0
GNP Billion $ 1967	4.92	5.74	7.42	9.50	12.01	14.92	18.50	22.65	27.20	33.35	39.60	47.20
Yearly Increase GNP		5.2%	5.1%	4.8%	4.4%	4.3%	4.1%	3.7%	3.6%	3.5%	3.4%	

Map	Africa	H L Students	13 per 100000	Energy Total Billion Kec	1.745
Capital	Lagos	Hospital Beds	0.5 per 1000	Energy per Capita Kec	27
One U S $ =	.3571 Pound	Daily Newspapers	7 per 1000		
		Telephones	75,900	Kec per $ of GNP	0.39
Area-Total	923,773 Sq Km			Growth Ratio GNP/Kec	0.760
Area-Arable	217,950 Sq Km	Television Sets	38,000		
		Tourist Receipt US $	3,000,000	Electric Capacity Mw	485
Population	63,870,000	Passenger Cars	63,000	Generation Billion Kwhr	1.105
Population Density	67 per Sq Km	Steel Consumption	5 Kg/Cap	Kilowatt Hours per Capita	17
				Kwhr per $ of GNP	0.23
Birth-Death Rate %	5.0-2.5	Growth Pattern Index	50%		
Population Rate of Increase	2.32%	GNP/Capita Annual Increase 67-90	3.05%	Economic Density GNP $/Sq Km	5,330
1967 GNP per Capita	80 US $				

NORWAY

	1967	1970	1975	1980	1985	1990	1995	2000	2005	2010	2015	2020
Population 1967 Population	1.000	1.021	1.060	1.092	1.125	1.162	1.190	1.218	1.240	1.260	1.280	1.302
Population Millions	3.784	3.872	4.016	4.141	4.260	4.405	4.510	4.610	4.700	4.770	4.850	4.940
GNP Capita 1967 $	2,199	2,440	2,885	3,370	3,885	4,460	5,140	5,890	6,710	7,600	8,550	9,660
GNP Billion $ 1967	8.32	9.45	11.53	13.93	16.58	19.64	23.20	27.18	31.59	36.25	41.50	47.60
Yearly Increase GNP		4.0%	3.9%	3.5%	3.4%	3.3%	3.2%	3.0%	2.8%	2.7%	2.6%	

Map	Europe
Capital	Oslo
One U S $ =	7.14 Krone
Area-Total	324,219 Sq Km
Area-Arable	8,430 Sq Km
Population	3,851,000
Population Density	11.65 per Sq Km
Birth-Death Rate %	1.76-0.97
Population Rate of Increase	0.80%
1967 GNP per Capita	2,199 US $

H L Students	588 per 100000
Hospital Beds	9.1 per 1000
Daily Newspapers	383 per 1000
Telephones	1,036,027
Television Sets	739,000
Passenger Cars	619,000
Steel Consumption	371 Kg/Cap
Investment Ratio	27%
Growth Pattern Index	112.50%
GNP/Capita Annual Increase 67-90	3.10%

Energy Total Billion Kec	16.214
Energy per Capita Kec	4,245
Kec per $ of GNP	1.80
Growth Ratio GNP/Kec	0.760
Electric Capacity Mw	12,030
Generation Billion Kwhr	56.707
Kilowatt Hours per Capita	14,847
Kwhr per $ of GNP	6.18
Economic Density GNP $/Sq Km	25,700

PAKISTAN

	1970	1975	1980	1985	1990	1995	2000	2005	2010	2015	2020
Population / 1967 Population	1.067	1.169	1.269	1.375	1.479	1.570	1.660	1.751	1.839	1.917	1.990
Population Millions	114.5	125.3	136.1	147.5	158.7	168.5	178.2	188.0	197.2	205.6	213.8
GNP Capita 1967 $	142	170	202	240	282	328	406	474	546	629	731
GNP Billion $ 1967	16.25	21.30	27.50	35.40	44.60	55.30	72.50	89.00	107.50	129.00	156.00
Yearly Increase GNP	5.0%	4.7%	4.6%	4.4%	4.0%	3.9%	3.8%	3.5%	3.4%	3.3%	

Map	Asia & Middle East	H L Students	278 per 100000	Energy Total
Capital	Islamabad	Hospital Beds	0.3 per 1000	Billion Kec	10.611
One U S $ =	4.781 Rupee	Daily Newspapers	18 per 1000	Energy per Capita Kec	87
		Telephones	176,807		
Area-Total	946,716 Sq Km	Television Sets	32,000	Kec per $ of GNP	0.71
Area-Arable	282,140 Sq Km	Tourist Receipt US $	6,000,000	Growth Ratio GNP/Kec	0.568
Population	126,000,000	Passenger Cars	139,400	Electric Capacity Mw	1,731
Population Density	113 per Sq Km	Steel Consumption	8 Kg/Cap	Generation Billion Kwhr	6.500
				Kilowatt Hours per Capita	53
Birth-Death Rate %	5.0-1.8	Investment Ratio	16%	Kwhr per $ of GNP	1.19
Population Rate of Increase	2.13%	Growth Pattern Index	62.50%		
		GNP/Capita		Economic Density	
		Annual Increase 67-90	3.45%	GNP $/Sq Km	14,650
1967 GNP per Capita	129 US $				

PANAMA

	1967	1970	1975	1980	1985	1990	1995	2000	2005	2010	2015	2020
Population 1967 Population	1.000	1.095	1.285	1.475	1.660	1.845	.030	2.215	2.395	2.575	2.755	2.930
Population Millions	1.329	1.458	1.710	1.962	2.204	2.455	2.700	2.945	3.185	3.425	3.660	3.925
GNP Capita 1967 $	581	666	836	1,034	1,265	1,530	1,816	2,140	2,505	2,880	3,315	3,770
GNP Billion $ 1967	0.773	0.971	1.429	2.030	2.785	3.760	4.905	6.310	7.960	9.860	12.100	13.320
Yearly Increase GNP		8.1%	7.3%	6.5%	6.2%	5.5%	5.1%	4.7%	4.4%	4.2%	4.0%	

Map	North & Caribbean America	H L Students	697 per 100000
Capital	Panama City	Hospital Beds	3.3 per 1000
One U S $ =	1 Balboa	Daily Newspapers	81 per 1000
		Telephones	58,608
Area-Total	75,650 Sq Km		
Area-Arable	5,640 Sq Km	Television Sets	108,000
Population	1,417,000	Passenger Cars	40,400
Population Density	18 per Sq Km	Steel Consumption	36 Kg/Cap
Birth-Death Rate %	4.2-1.0	Investment Ratio	23%
Population Rate of Increase	3.30%	Growth Pattern Index	106.25%
		GNP/Capita Annual Increase 67-90	4.25%
1967 GNP per Capita	581 US $		

Energy Total Billion Kec	1.790
Energy per Capita Kec	1,304
Kec per $ of GNP	2.15
Growth Ratio GNP/Kec	0.405
Electric Capacity Kw	128,900
Generation Billion Kwhr	0.663
Kilowatt Hours per Capita	483
Kwhr per $ of GNP	0.70
Economic Density GNP $/Sq Km	10,150

291

PANAMA CANAL ZONE

	1970	1975	1980	1985	1990	1995	2000	2005	2010	2015	2020
Population 1967 Population	1.140	1.400	1.680	2.000	2.330	2.690	3.050	3.400	3.745	4.130	4.450
Population Millions	0.066	0.081	0.098	0.116	0.135	0.156	0.177	0.197	0.218	0.240	0.258
GNP Capita 1967 $	1,850	2,065	2,345	2,630	2,930	3,260	3,590	3,960	4,380	4,850	5,350
GNP Billion $ 1967	0.122	0.168	0.229	0.305	0.397	0.509	0.635	0.780	0.955	1.162	1.455

Yearly Increase GNP	6.6%	6.3%	5.9%	5.4%	4.9%	4.5%	4.2%	4.1%	4.0%	3.9%

Map North & Caribbean America	H L Students	2,293 per 100000	Energy Total Billion Kec	0.322
One U S $ = 1 Dollar	Hospital Beds	16.7 per 1000	Energy per Capita Kec	5,747
Area-Total 1,432 Sq Km	Telephones	10,619	Kec per $ of GNP	2.72
Area-Arable 10 Sq Km			Growth Ratio GNP/Kec	0.380
Population 62,000	Passenger Cars	17,800	Electric Capacity Kw	110,600
Population Density 39 per Sq Km			Generation Billion Kwhr	0.599
			Kilowatt Hours per Capita	10,696
Population Rate of Increase 4.60%	Growth Pattern Index GNP/Capita	87.50%	Kwhr per $ of GNP	6.95
1967 GNP per Capita 1,720 US $	Annual Increase 67-90	2.35%	Economic Density GNP $/Sq Km	69,900

PARAGUAY

	1970	1975	1980	1985	1990	1995	2000	2005	2010	2015	2020
Population 1967 Population	1.090	1.260	1.430	1.600	1.770	1.940	2.110	2.270	2.430	2.590	2.750
Population Millions	2.355	2.720	3.090	3.460	3.825	4.190	4.560	4.900	5.250	5.600	5.945
GNP 1967 $ Capita	241.8	273.5	305.0	342.4	385.0	428.0	480.0	536.0	603.0	676.0	755.0
GNP Billion $ 1967	0.568	0.744	0.943	1.185	1.472	1.793	2.188	2.620	3.164	3.780	4.480
Yearly Increase GNP	5.5%		4.9%	4.7%	4.4%	4.2%	4.1%	3.9%	3.7%	3.6%	3.4%

Map	South America	H L Students	290 per 100000	
Capital	Asuncion	Hospital Beds	2.0 per 1000	
One U S $ =	126.00 Guarani			
Area-Total	406,752 Sq Km	Telephones	19,128	
Area-Arable	9,470 Sq Km	Television Sets	15,000	
Population	2,315,000	Passenger Cars	6,900	
Population Density	5.33 per Sq Km	Steel Consumption	6 Kg/Cap	
Birth-Death Rate %	4.50-1.20	Investment Ratio	15%	
Population Rate of Increase	3.10%	Growth Pattern Index GNP/Capita	43.75%	
		Annual Increase 67-90	2.4%	
1967 GNP per Capita	224 US $			

Energy Total Billion Kec	0.316
Energy per Capita Kec	141
Kec per $ of GNP	0.57
Growth Ratio GNP/Kec	0.360
Electric Capacity Kw	108,400
Generation Billion Kwhr	0.179
Kilowatt Hours per Capita	80
Kwhr per $ of GNP	0.42
Economic Density GNP $/Sq Km	1,192

293

PERU

	1967	1970	1975	1980	1985	1990	1995	2000	2005	2010	2015	2020
Population 1967 Population	1.000	1.088	1.228	1.380	1.525	1.678	1.826	1.970	2.100	2.238	2.378	2.505
Population Millions	12.39	13.49	15.20	17.09	18.89	20.78	22.60	24.39	26.00	27.68	29.40	31.01
GNP Capita 1967 $	283	308.5	357	411	471	549	639	725	824	936	1,065	1,200
GNP Billion $ 1967	3.51	4.16	5.43	7.03	8.90	11.39	14.42	17.68	21.41	25.92	31.30	37.20
Yearly Increase GNP		5.5%	5.3%	5.2%	5.1%	4.8%	4.2%	4.0%	3.9%	3.8%	3.5%	

Map	South America
Capital	Lima
One U S $ =	3.90 Sol
Area-Total	1,285,216 Sq Km
Area-Arable	26,250 Sq Km
Population Density	13,172,000 9.63 per Sq Km
Birth-Death Rate %	4.40-1.20
Population Rate of Increase	3.06%
1967 GNP per Capita	283 US $

H L Students	674 per 100000
Hospital Beds	2.4 per 1000
Daily Newspapers	47 per 1000
Telephones	165,121
Television Sets	300,000
Tourist Receipt US $	22,000,000
Steel Consumption	21 Kg/Cap
Investment Ratio	19%
Growth Pattern Index	62.50%
GNP/Capita Annual Increase 67-90	2.95%

Energy Total Billion Kec	8.086
Energy per Capita Kec	633
Kec per $ of GNP	2.19
Growth Ratio GNP/Kec	0.401
Electric Capacity Mw	1,629
Generation Billion Kwhr	4.880
Kilowatt Hours per Capita	382
Kwhr per $ of GNP	0.61
Economic Density GNP $/Sq Km	2,730

PHILIPPINES

	1967	1970	1975	1980	1985	1990	1995	2000	2005	2010	2015	2020
Population 1967 Population	1.000	1.120	1.276	1.468	1.660	1.850	2.042	2.240	2.422	2.606	2.788	2.970
Population Millions	34.66	38.81	44.15	50.90	57.55	64.15	70.85	77.60	84.00	90.40	96.60	103.00
GNP/Capita 1967 $	278	303.5	352.5	408.5	471	542.5	616	711	814.5	930.5	1,060	1,225
GNP Billion $ 1967	9.64	11.78	15.58	20.75	27.12	34.85	43.60	55.15	68.35	84.15	102.20	126.30
Yearly Increase GNP		5.7%	5.6%	5.4%	5.1%	4.6%	4.5%	4.4%	4.2%	4.1%	4.0%	

Map	Asia & Middle East
Capital	Quezon City
One U S $ =	6.25 Peso
Area-Total	300,000 Sq Km
Area-Arable	85,460 Sq Km
Population	37,178,000
Population Density	116 per Sq Km
Population Rate of Increase	3.34%
1967 GNP per Capita	278 US $

H L Students	1,605 per 100000
Hospital Beds	1.4 per 1000
Daily Newspapers	27 per 1000
Telephones	241,496
Television Sets	190,000
Tourist Receipt US $	48,000,000
Passenger Cars	232,700
Steel Consumption	30 Kg/Cap
Investment Ratio	23%
Growth Pattern Index	56.25%
GNP/Capita Annual Increase 67-90	2.95%

Energy Total Billion Kec	8.912
Energy per Capita Kec	248
Kec per $ of GNP	0.86
Growth Ratio GNP/Kec	0.493
Generation Billion Kwhr	7.000
Kilowatt Hours per Capita	195
Kwhr per $ of GNP	1.45
Economic Density GNP $/Sq Km	31,200

295

POLAND

	1967	1970	1975	1980	1985	1990	1995	2000	2005	2010	2015	2020
Population 1967 Population	1.000	1.032	1.090	1.140	1.188	1.244	1.284	1.328	1.356	1.400	1.430	1.465
Population Millions	31.94	32.98	34.82	36.41	37.95	39.78	41.02	42.40	43.60	44.70	45.70	46.80
GNP Capita 1967 $	780	878	1,070	1,282	1,511	1,800	2,100	2,450	2,800	3,220	3,690	4,195
GNP Billion $ 1967	24.9	29.0	37.3	46.7	57.4	71.5	86.1	103.9	122.1	143.9	168.8	196.2
Yearly Increase GNP		5.1%	4.6%	4.2%	4.0%	3.8%	3.6%	3.4%	3.3%	3.2%	3.0%	

Map	Europe
Capital	Warsaw
One U S $ =	24-40 Zloty
Area-Total	312,520 Sq Km
Area-Arable	154,940 Sq Km
Population	32,555,000
Population Density	102 per Sq Km
Birth-Death Rate %	1.62-0.76
Population Rate of Increase	1.17%
1967 GNP per Capita	780 US $

H L Students	904 per 100000
Hospital Beds	7.7 per 1000
Daily Newspapers	199 per 1000
Telephones	1,650,896
Television Sets	3,389,000
Tourist Receipt US $	18,000,000
Passenger Cars	373,900
Steel Consumption	323 Kg/Cap
Investment Ratio	27%
Growth Pattern Index	131.25%
GNP/Capita	
Annual Increase 67-90	3.7%

Energy Total Billion Kec	123.666
Energy per Capita Kec	3,828
Kec per $ of GNP	4.68
Growth Ratio GNP/Kec	1.700
Electric Capacity Mw	11,591
Generation Billion Kwhr	55.844
Kilowatt Hours per Capita	1,728
Kwhr per $ of GNP	2.07
Economic Density GNP $/Sq Km	79,800

296

PORTUGAL

	1967	1970	1975	1980	1985	1990	1995	2000	2005	2010	2015	2020
Population 1967 Population	1.000	1.022	1.062	1.099	1.131	1.170	1.200	1.230	1.255	1.276	1.298	1.320
Population Millions	9.38	9.62	9.96	10.29	10.61	10.98	11.26	11.53	11.77	11.99	12.17	12.38
GNP/Capita 1967 $	493	595	803	1,050	1,372	1,785	2,278	2,884	3,555	4,290	5,140	6,110
GNP Billion $ 1967	4.62	5.72	8.00	10.79	14.58	19.61	25.61	33.30	41.85	51.40	62.50	75.60
Yearly Increase GNP		6.9%		6.5%	6.2%	6.0%	5.5%	5.3%	4.7%	4.2%	4.0%	3.9%

Map	Europe	H L Students	412 per 100000
Capital	Lisbon	Hospital Beds	5.9 per 1000
One U S $ =	28.81 Escudo	Daily Newspapers	71 per 1000
		Telephones	653,407
Area-Total	91,971 Sq Km	Television Sets	277,000
Area-Arable	43,700 Sq Km	Tourist Receipt US $	214,000,000
Population	9,560,000		
Population Density	103 per Sq Km	Steel Consumption	61 Kg/Cap
Birth-Death Rate %	2.05-1.00	Investment Ratio	19%
Population Rate of Increase	0.84%	Growth Pattern Index	125%
		GNP/Capita Annual Increase 67-90	5.73%
1967 GNP per Capita	493 US $		

Energy Total Billion Kec	5.122
Energy per Capita Kec	541
Kec per $ of GNP	1.14
Growth Ratio GNP/Kec	1.000
Electric Capacity Mw	2,030
Generation Billion Kwhr	6.281
Kilowatt Hours per Capita	663
Kwhr per $ of GNP	0.60
Economic Density GNP $/Sq Km	50,400

PORTUGUESE GUINEA

	1970	1975	1980	1985	1990	1995	2000	2005	2010	2015	2020
Population 1967 Population	1.005	1.015	1.024	1.033	1.041	1.048	1.055	1.060	1.065	1.070	1.075
Population Millions	0.531	0.536	0.541	0.546	0.550	0.554	0.557	0.560	0.563	0.565	0.567
GNP/Capita 1967 $	255	345	462	618	815	1,072	1,415	1,833	2,380	3,040	3,940
GNP Billion $ 1967	0.135	0.185	0.250	0.338	0.448	0.593	0.788	1.026	0.335	1.730	2.235
Yearly Increase GNP	6.5%	6.3%	6.1%	5.9%	5.7%	5.6%	5.5%	5.4%	5.3%	5.2%	

Map	Africa
Capital	Bissau
One U S $ =	28.81 Escudo
Area-Total	36,125 Sq Km
Area-Arable	2,630 Sq Km
Population Density	14.70 per Sq Km
Population	530,000
Population Rate of Increase	0.20%
1967 GNP per Capita	210 US $

Hospital Beds	1.6 per 1000
Daily Newspapers	4 per 1000
Telephones	1,517
Growth Pattern Index GNP/Capita	106.25%
Annual Increase 67-90	6.05%

Energy Total Billion Kec	0.031
Energy per Capita Kec	59
Kec per $ of GNP	0.27
Growth Ratio GNP/Kec	0.506
Electric Capacity Kw	5,600
Generation Billion Kwhr	0.009
Kilowatt Hours per Capita	17
Kwhr per $ of GNP	0.07
Economic Density GNP $/Sq Km	44,200

298

PUERTO RICO

	1967	1970	1975	1980	1985	1990	1995	2000	2005	2010	2015	2020
Population 1967 Population	1.000	1.050	1.135	1.215	1.289	1.370	1.440	1.510	1.574	1.638	1.695	1.748
Population Millions	2.695	2.830	3.059	3.268	3.470	3.696	3.880	4.065	4.245	4.410	4.565	4.700
GNP Capita 1967 $	1,387	1,578	1,935	2,340	2,805	3,315	3,900	4,515	5,2	5,980	6,850	7,800
GNP Billion $ 1967	3.74	4.47	5.93	7.65	9.74	12.22	15.12	18.38	22.50	26.35	31.30	36.65
Yearly Increase GNP		5.8%	5.2%	4.9%	4.6%	4.4%	4.0%	3.8%	3.6%	3.5%	3.2%	

Map	North & Caribbean America	H L Students	1,771 per 100000
Capital	San Juan	Hospital Beds	4.6 per 1000
One U S $ =	1 Dollar	Daily Newspapers	102 per 1000
		Telephones	248,415
Area-Total	8,897 Sq Km		
Area-Arable	2,440 Sq Km	Television Sets	470,000
		Tourist Receipt US $	202,000,000
Population	2,754,000	Passenger Cars	383,300
Population Density	303 per Sq Km		
		Investment Ratio	31%
Birth-Death Rate %	2.5-0.6	Growth Pattern Index	118.75%
Population Rate of Increase	1.72%	GNP/Capita	
		Annual Increase 67-90	3.85%
1967 GNP per Capita	1,387 US $		

Energy Total Billion Kec	7.385
Energy per Capita Kec	2,712
Kec per $ of GNP	1.71
Growth Ratio GNP/Kec	0.525
Generation Billion Kwhr	6.182
Kilowatt Hours per Capita	2,270
Kwhr per $ of GNP	1,10
Economic Density GNP $/Sq Km	421,000

299

QATAR

	1970	1975	1980	1985	1990	1995	2000	2005	2010	2015	2020
Population 1967 Population	1.170	1.520	1.900	2.350	2.850	3.350	3.850	4.330	4.810	5.280	5.740
Population Millions	0.088	0.114	0.143	0.176	0.224	0.251	0.289	0.325	0.361	0.396	0.430
GNP/Capita 1967 $	4,040	5,440	6,260	6,740	7,200	7,710	8,240	8,830	9,240	9,950	10,450
GNP Billion $ 1967	0.355	0.621	0.881	1.190	1.570	1.934	2.380	2.865	3.370	3.940	4.500
Yearly Increase GNP		11.7%	7.3%	6.2%	5.2%	4.6%	4.1%	3.7%	3.3%	3.0%	2.6%

Map	Asia & Middle East		
Capital	Doha	Hospital Beds	7.7 per 1000
One U S $ =	4.75 Riyal	Telephones	8,237
Area-Total	22,014 Sq Km		
		Energy Total Billion Kec	0.115
		Energy per Capita Kec	1,443
Population Population Density	100,000 3.4 per Sq Km	Kec per $ of GNP Growth Ratio GNP/Kec	0.42 0.774
		Generation Billion Kwhr	0.074
		Kilowatt Hours per Capita	924
Population Rate of Increase	6.90%	Growth Pattern Index GNP/Capita Annual Increase 67-90	162.50% 3.50%
		Kwhr per $ of GNP	0.30
1967 GNP per Capita	3,250 US $	Economic Density GNP $/Sq Km	11,080

REUNION

	1970	1975	1980	1985	1990	1995	2000	2005	2010	2015	2020
Population 1967 Population	1.085	1.240	1.395	1.550	1.705	1.855	2.005	2.155	2.300	2.440	2.575
Population Millions	0.449	0.513	0.577	0.641	0.706	0.768	0.830	0.891	0.952	1.010	1.063
GNP 1967 $ Capita	672	928	1,271	1,695	2,050	2,740	3,560	4,630	5,850	7,320	8,950
GNP Billion $ 1967	0.302	0.476	0.733	1.085	1.445	2.100	2.955	4.103	5.560	7.380	9.520
Yearly Increase GNP	9.6%	9.1%	8.2%	7.8%	7.4%	7.0%	6.6%	6.2%	5.8%	5.2%	

Map	Africa
Capital	St. Denis
One U S $ =	277 CFA Franc
Area-Total	2,510 Sq Km
Area-Arable	620 Sq Km
Population Density	436,000
	165 per Sq Km
Birth-Death Rate %	3.7-2.4
Population Rate of Increase	2.90%
1967 GNP per Capita	560 US $

H L Students	90 per 100000
Hospital Beds	6.7 per 1000
Daily Newspapers	66 per 1000
Telephones	12,431
Television Sets	14,000
Passenger Cars	22,300
Investment Ratio	24%
Growth Pattern Index	125%
GNP/Capita Annual Increase 67-90	5.75%

Energy Total Billion Kec	0.086
Energy per Capita Kec	201
Kec per $ of GNP	0.45
Growth Ratio GNP/Kec	0.654
Generation Billion Kwhr	0.092
Kilowatt Hours per Capita	215
Kwhr per $ of GNP	0.36
Economic Density GNP $/Sq Km	92,500

301

ROMANIA

	1967	1970	1975	1980	1985	1990	1995	2000	2005	2010	2015	2020
Population 1967 Population	1.000	1.020	1.054	1.084	1.112	1.149	1.170	1.198	1.219	1.235	1.252	1.274
Population Millions	19.29	19.68	20.32	20.91	21.44	22.13	22.53	23.10	23.47	23.80	24.18	24.57
GNP Capita 1967 $	720	883	1,208	1,610	2,050	2,635	3,320	4,110	5,005	6,040	7,185	8,350
GNP Billion $ 1967	13.87	17.38	24.96	33.62	43.95	58.60	74.80	95.00	117.60	143.60	173.40	205.00
Yearly Increase GNP		7.5%	6.1%	5.5%	5.3%	5.0%	4.9%	4.4%	4.1%	3.8%	3.4%	

Map	Europe
Capital	Bucharest
One U S $ =	12-18 Leu
Area-Total	237,500 Sq Km
Area-Arable	105,600 Sq Km
Population	20,010,000
Population Density	81 per Sq Km
Birth-Death Rate %	2.63-0.96
Population Rate of Increase	0.73%
1967 GNP per Capita	720 US $

H L Students	734 per 100000
Hospital Beds	7.7 per 1000
Daily Newspapers	158 per 1000
Telephones	568,588
Television Sets	1,115,000
Steel Consumption	212 Kg/Cap
Growth Pattern Index GNP/Capita	187.50%
Annual Increase 67-90	5.75%

Energy Total Billion Kec	47.062
Energy per Capita Kec	2,386
Kec per $ of GNP	3.16
Growth Ratio GNP/Kec	1.100
Electric Capacity Mw	5,611
Generation Billion Kwhr	25.605
Kilowatt Hours per Capita	1,298
Kwhr per $ of GNP	1.64
Economic Density GNP $/Sq Km	58,400

RUANDA

	1970	1975	1980	1985	1990	1995	2000	2005	2010	2015	2020
Population 1967 Population	1.105	1.255	1.430	1.600	1.765	1.940	2.105	2.270	2.430	2.590	2.750
Population Millions	3.660	4.150	4.730	5.395	5.840	6.420	6.965	7.510	8.040	8.560	9.100
GNP Capita 1967 $	68.2	84.3	103.0	126.0	151.5	176.5	206.5	240.0	276.0	315.0	360.0
GNP Billion $ 1967	0.249	0.350	0.487	0.678	0.885	1.133	1.437	1.800	2.220	2.700	3.280
Yearly Increase GNP	7.1%	6.8%	6.2%	5.5%	5.1%	4.8%	4.5%	4.2%	3.9%	3.8%

Map	Africa	H L Students	7 per 100000
Capital	Kigali	Hospital Beds	1.3 per 1000
One U S $ =	100 Franc	Telephones	1,389
Area-Total	26,338 Sq Km		
Area-Arable	9,950 Sq Km	Passenger Cars	2,900
Population	3,500,000	Steel Consumption	1 Kg/Cap
Population Density	126 per Sq Km		
Birth-Death Rate %	5.2-2.2	Growth Pattern Index	37.50%
Population Rate of Increase	3.10%	GNP/Capita Annual Increase 67-90	4.10%
1967 GNP per Capita	60 US $		

Energy Total Billion Kec	0.035
Energy per Capita Kec	10
Kec per $ of GNP	0.13
Growth Ratio GNP/Kec	0.410
Generation Billion Kwhr	0.069
Kilowatt Hours per Capita	20
Kwhr per $ of GNP	0.28
Economic Density GNP $/Sq Km	7,530

RYUKYU ISLANDS

	1970	1975	1980	1985	1990	1995	2000	2005	2010	2015	2020
Population 1967 Population	1.040	1.100	1.155	1.215	1.270	1.320	1.370	1.410	1.450	1.485	1.520
Population Millions	0.994	1.051	1.103	1.161	1.213	1.262	1.310	1.348	1.386	1.420	1.452
GNP Capita 1967 $	651	924	1,285	1,760	2,239	3,045	3,885	4,930	6,030	7,250	8,620
GNP Billion $ 1967	0.647	0.972	1.418	2.045	2.695	3.660	5.080	6.650	8.360	10.300	12.500
Yearly Increase GNP	8.5%	8.1%	7.6%	6.9%	6.3%	5.9%	5.5%	4.7%	4.3%	4.0%	

Map Asia & Middle East	
Capital Naha City (Okinawa)	
One U S $ = 1 Dollar	
Area-Total 2,196 Sq Km	
Area-Arable 510 Sq Km	
Population Density 982,000 / 435 per Sq Km	
Birth-Death Rate % 2.2-0.5	
Population Rate of Increase 1.30%	
1967 GNP per Capita 540 US $	

H L Students	736 per 100000
Hospital Beds	3.5 per 1000
Daily Newspapers	269 per 1000
Telephones	54,762
Passenger Cars	38,300
Growth Pattern Index	143.75%
GNP/Capita Annual Increase 67-90	6.35%
Energy Total Billion Kec	0.513
Energy per Capita Kec	531
Kec per $ of GNP	0.95
Growth Ratio GNP/Kec	0.812
Electric Capacity Kw	287,200
Generation Billion Kwhr	1,211
Kilowatt Hours per Capita	1,254
Kwhr per $ of GNP	2.14
Economic Density GNP $/Sq Km	235,000

SAUDI ARABIA

	1970	1975	1980	1985	1990	1995	2000	2005	2010	2015	2020
Population 1967 Population	1.050	1.130	1.210	1.290	1.370	1.435	1.500	1.560	1.620	1.680	1.730
Population Millions	7.34	7.90	8.46	9.02	9.57	10.03	10.49	10.91	11.33	11.76	12.10
GNP 1967 $ Capita	422	573	795	1,070	1,372	1,790	2,190	2,965	3,640	4,300	5,130
GNP Billion $ 1967	3.02	4.53	6.73	9.65	13.12	17.95	22.95	32.50	41.30	50.60	62.10
Yearly Increase GNP	8.5%	8.3%	7.5%	7.0%	6.5%	5.9%	5.4%	4.9%	4.5%	4.1%	

Map Asia & Middle East	H L Students 28 per 100000
Capital Riyadh	Hospital Beds 0.9 per 1000
One U S $ = 4.50 Riyal	Daily Newspapers 7 per 1000
	Telephones 44,250
Area-Total 2,149,690 Sq Km	Television Sets 40,000
Area-Arable 4,620 Sq Km	
Population 7,230,000	Steel Consumption 41 Kg/Cap
Population Density 3.24 per Sq Km	
Population Rate of	Growth Pattern Index 131.25%
Increase 1.70%	GNP/Capita
	Annual Increase 67-90 6.10%
1967 GNP per Capita 350 US $	

Energy Total	
Billion Kec	3.622
Energy per Capita Kec	510
Kec per $ of GNP	1.25
Growth Ratio GNP/Kec	0.745
Electric Capacity Kw	173,100
Generation Billion Kwhr	0.850
Kilowatt Hours per Capita	119
Kwhr per $ of GNP	0.33
Economic Density	
GNP $/Sq Km	1,090

SENEGAL

	1970	1975	1980	1985	1990	1995	2000	2005	2010	2015	2020
Population 1967 Population	1.070	1.190	1.310	1.430	1.550	1.670	1.780	1.890	1.990	2.090	2.185
Population Millions	3.925	4.370	4.805	5.250	5.690	6.130	6.530	6.940	7.305	7.675	8.025
GNP/Capita 1967 $	231	256	282.5	310	344	380	418	462	508	558	605
GNP Billion $ 1967	0.907	1.118	1.357	1.628	1.958	2.330	2.735	3.205	3.715	4.280	4.860
Yearly Increase GNP	5.5%	4.8%	4.3%	3.9%	3.6%	3.4%	3.2%	3.0%	2.8%	2.6%	

Map	Africa	H L Students	94 per 100000
Capital	Dakar	Hospital Beds	1.4 per 1000
One U S $ =	277.71 CFA Franc	Daily Newspapers	5 per 1000
		Telephones	26,244
Area-Total	196,192 Sq Km		
Area-Arable	57,220 Sq Km	Television Sets	1,200
Population	3,780,000		
Population Density	19 per Sq Km		
Birth-Death Rate %	4.6-2.2	Growth Pattern Index	37.50%
Population Rate of Increase	2.40%	GNP/Capita Annual Increase 67-90	2.10%
1967 GNP per Capita	214 US $		

Energy Total Billion Kec	0.541
Energy per Capita Kec	146
Kec per $ of GNP	0.645
Growth Ratio GNP/Kec	0.407
Electric Capacity Mw	95
Generation Billion Kwhr	0.287
Kilowatt Hours per Capita	77
Kwhr per $ of GNP	0.34
Economic Density GNP $/Sq Km	3,970

SIERRA LEONE

	1970	1975	1980	1985	1990	1995	2000	2005	2010	2015	2020
Population 1967 Population	1.040	1.100	1.155	1.215	1.270	1.320	1.370	1.410	1.450	1.485	1.520
Population Millions	2.536	2.684	2.820	2.964	3.100	3.220	3.340	3.440	3.540	3.620	3.705
GNP 1967 $ Capita	157	189	226	267	317	374	441	514	601	697	811
GNP Billion $ 1967	0.397	0.508	0.638	0.791	0.982	1.202	1.472	1.768	2.125	2.524	3.005
Yearly Increase GNP	5.0%	4.6%	4.4%	4.3%	4.2%	4.1%	4.0%	3.9%	3.7%	3.5%	

Map	Africa	H L Students	34 per 100000
Capital	Freetown	Hospital Beds	0.8 per 1000
One U S $ =	.8333 Leone	Daily Newspapers	5 per 1000
		Telephones	7,000
Area-Total	71,740 Sq Km		
Area-Arable	36,640 Sq Km	Television Sets	3,000
Population	2,512,000		
Population Density	34 per Sq Km	Passenger Cars	16,000
Birth-Death Rate %	4.4-2.2	Growth Pattern Index	56.25%
Population Rate of Increase	1.30%	GNP/Capita Annual Increase 67-90	3.60%
1967 GNP per Capita	140 US $		

Energy Total Billion Kec	0.151
Energy per Capita Kec	61
Kec per $ of GNP	0.30
Growth Ratio GNP/Kec	0.476
Generation Billion Kwhr	0.144
Kilowatt Hours per Capita	58
Kwhr per $ of GNP	0.36
Economic Density GNP $/Sq Km	4,770

SINGAPORE

	1970	1975	1980	1985	1990	1995	2000	2005	2010	2015	2020
Population 1967 Population	1.070	1.205	1.340	1.475	1.610	1.740	1.870	1.990	2.110	2.225	2.335
Population Millions	2.090	2.355	2.620	2.885	3.146	3.404	3.655	3.890	4.125	4.350	4.565
GNP 1967 $ Capita	770	1,013	1,318	1,680	2,145	2,685	3,340	4,050	4,810	5,670	6,880
GNP Billion $ 1967	1.61	2.39	3.45	4.85	6.75	9.15	12.20	15.75	19.85	24.60	31.35
Yearly Increase GNP	8.3%		7.6%	7.0%	6.6%	6.3%	5.9%	5.3%	4.7%	4.3%	4.0%

Map	Asia & Middle East	Energy Total	1.364
Capital	Singapore	Billion Kec	
One US $ =	3.09 Dollar	Energy per Capita Kec	685
Area-Total	582 Sq Km	Kec per $ of GNP	0.99
Area-Arable	130 Sq Km	Growth Ratio GNP/Kec	0.715
Population	2,017,000	Electric Capacity Mw	464
Population Density	3,366 per Sq Km	Generation Billion Kwhr	1.639
		Kilowatt Hours per Capita	824
Birth-Death Rate %	2.5-0.6	Kwhr per $ of GNP	1.13
Population Rate of Increase	2.60%	Economic Density GNP $/Sq Km	2,165,000
1967 GNP per Capita	646 US $		

H L Students	665 per 100000	
Hospital Beds	3.6 per 1000	
Daily Newspapers	325 per 1000	
Telephones		119,184
Television Sets		108,000
Tourist Receipt US $		49,000,000
Passenger Cars		126,500
Growth Pattern Index		118.75%
GNP/Capita Annual Increase 67-90		5.33%

SOMALIA

	1970	1975	1980	1985	1990	1995	2000	2005	2010	2015	2020
Population 1967 Population	1.120	1.350	1.590	1.860	2.120	2.400	2.680	2.950	3.220	3.480	3.730
Population Millions	2.980	3.590	4.230	4.950	5.640	6.385	7.130	7.850	8.560	9.250	9.915
GNP Capita 1967 $	51.0	53.5	55.0	57.0	60.2	62.6	65.1	67.5	70.0	72.8	75.4
GNP Billion $ 1967	0.152	0.192	0.232	0.282	0.339	0.399	0.464	0.530	0.599	0.674	0.747
Yearly Increase GNP	4.8%	4.4%	4.0%	3.7%	3.3%	3.0%	2.7%	2.5%	2.3%	2.1%	

Map	Africa	H L Students	2 per 100000
Capital	Mogadiscio	Hospital Beds	1.8 per 1000
One U S $ =	7.143 Shilling	Daily Newspapers	2 per 1000
		Telephones	4,800
Area-Total	637,657 Sq Km		
Area-Arable	9,570 Sq Km		
Population	2,730,000	Passenger Cars	8,200
Population Density	4.17 per Sq Km		
Population Rate of Increase	4.10%	Growth Pattern Index GNP/Capita	9.38%
		Annual Increase 67-90	0.80%
1967 GNP per Capita	50 US $		

Energy Total Billion Kec	0.075
Energy per Capita Kec	27
Kec per $ of GNP	0.46
Growth Ratio GNP/Kec	0.234
Electric Capacity Kw	6,200
Generation Billion Kwhr	0.016
Kilowatt Hours per Capita	5
Kwhr per $ of GNP	0.10
Economic Density GNP $/Sq Km	209

SOUTH AFRICA

	1967	1970	1975	1980	1985	1990	1995	2000	2005	2010	2015	2020
Population 1967 Population	1.000	1.080	1.210	1.348	1.478	1.615	1.748	1.872	1.990	2.130	2.230	2.340
Population Millions	21.18	22.83	25.60	28.50	31.24	34.20	36.99	39.60	42.09	45.00	47.20	49.50
GNP Capita 1967 $	619	695	852	1,014	1,200	1,392	1,609	1,843	2,128	2,430	2,775	3,150
GNP Billion $ 1967	13.09	15.88	21.80	28.90	37.50	47.80	59.40	72.10	89.75	109.20	132.00	155.90
Yearly Increase GNP		6.5%	5.8%	5.3%	5.0%	4.4%	4.2%	4.1%	4.0%	3.9%	3.8%	

Map	Africa	H L Students	360 per 100000
Capital	Capetown	Hospital Beds	5.3 per 1000
One U S $ =	.7180 Rand	Daily Newspapers	57 per 1000
		Telephones	1,397,725
Area-Total	1,221,037 Sq Km		
Area-Arable	120,580 Sq Km	Tourist Receipt US $	77,000,000
		Passenger Cars	1,405,000
Population	19,618,000	Steel Consumption	189 Kg/Cap
Population Density	15 per Sq Km		
		Investment Ratio	23%
Birth-Death Rate %	4.0-1.6	Growth Pattern Index	112.50%
Population Rate of Increase	2.62%	GNP/Capita Annual Increase 67-90	3.60%
1967 GNP per Capita	619 US $		

Energy Total Billion Kec	59.033
Energy per Capita Kec	2,721
Kec per $ of GNP	4.35
Growth Ratio GNP/Kec	1.878
Generation Billion Kwhr	43.485
Kilowatt Hours per Capita	2,005
Kwhr per $ of GNP	3.06
Economic Density GNP $/Sq Km	10,800

SOUTHERN RHODESIA

	1967	1970	1975	1980	1985	1990	1995	2000	2005	2010	2015	2020
Population 1967 Population	1.000	1.080	1.260	1.440	1.620	1.800	1.980	2.160	2.330	2.500	2.670	2.840
Population Millions	4.53	4.90	5.71	6.55	7.34	8.15	8.98	9.79	10.50	11.33	12.10	12.89
GNP Capita 1967 $	233	248	269	296	324	352	386	423	461	500	541	588
GNP Billion $ 1967	1.053	1.212	1.592	1.930	2.375	2.860	3.460	4.140	4.840	5.670	6.550	7.580
Yearly Increase GNP	5.7%	5.2%	4.6%	3.9%	3.7%	3.5%	3.4%	3.2%	3.0%	2.9%	2.8%	

Map	Africa	H L Students	19 per 100000
Capital	Salisbury	Hospital Beds	3.3 per 1000
One U S $ =	0.3571 Pound	Daily Newspapers	15 per 1000
		Telephones	125,844
Area-Total	389,361 Sq Km	Television Sets	45,000
Population	5,090,000	Passenger Cars	108,800
Population Density	11.62 per Sq Km	Steel Consumption	31 Kg/Cap
Birth-Death Rate %	4.8-1.4	Investment Ratio	21%
Population Rate of Increase	3.20%	GNP/Capita Annual Increase 67-90	1.80%
1967 GNP per Capita	233 US $		

Energy Total Billion Kec	2.766
Energy per Capita Kec	559
Kec per $ of GNP	2.10
Generation Billion Kwhr	2.898
Kilowatt Hours per Capita	586
Kwhr per $ of GNP	2.32
Economic Density GNP $/Sq Km	2,700

311

SPAIN

	1967	1970	1975	1980	1985	1990	1995	2000	2005	2010	2015	2020
Population 1967 Population	1.000	1.027	1.067	1.100	1.145	1.180	1.210	1.240	1.265	1.290	1.310	1.335
Population Millions	32.14	33.00	34.45	35.70	36.85	37.80	39.00	39.90	40.95	41.80	42.59	43.29
GNP Capita 1967 $	822	969	1,290	1,637	2,078	2,595	3,170	3,810	4,550	5,350	6,290	7,240
GNP Billion $ 1967	26.4	32.0	44.5	58.4	76.5	98.2	123.5	151.9	186.5	224.0	268.0	314.5
Yearly Increase GNP		6.8%	5.9%	5.5%	5.2%	4.7%	4.5%	4.2%	3.7%	3.6%	3.2%	

Map	Europe	H L Students	491 per 100000
Capital	Madrid	Hospital Beds	5.0 per 1000
One U S $ =	69.73 Peseta	Daily Newspapers	175 per 1000
		Telephones	3,702,244
Area-Total	504,750 Sq Km	Television Sets	5,300,000
Area-Arable	204,820 Sq Km	Tourist Receipt US $	1,213,000,000
Population	32,949,000	Passenger Cars	1,577,200
Population Density	64 per Sq Km	Steel Consumption	188 Kg/Cap
Birth-Death Rate %	2.05-0.87	Investment Ratio	22%
Population Rate of Increase	0.88%	Growth Pattern Index GNP/Capita	131.25%
		Annual Increase 67-90	5.10%
1967 GNP per Capita	822 US $		

Energy Total Billion Kec	43,035
Energy per Capita Kec	1,312
Kec per $ of GNP	1.54
Growth Ratio GNP/Kec	0.931
Electric Capacity Mw	14,910
Generation Billion Kwhr	44,099
Kilowatt Hours per Capita	1,345
Kwhr per $ of GNP	1.50
Economic Density GNP $/Sq Km	52,300

SUDAN

	1967	1970	1975	1980	1985	1990	1995	2000	2005	2010	2015	2020
Population 1967 Population	1.000	1.085	1.240	1.395	1.550	1.705	1.855	2.005	2.155	2.300	2.440	2.575
Population Millions	14.36	15.68	17.80	20.00	22.24	24.45	26.60	28.80	30.90	33.00	35.00	36.95
GNP 1967 $ Capita	90.5	120.0	130.5	143.5	146.5	170.0	183.0	198.0	223.0	235.0	253.0	274.5
GNP Billion $ 1967	1.290	1.880	2.320	2.870	3.680	4.170	4.870	5.730	6.900	8.700	8.850	11.180
Yearly Increase GNP		4.3%	4.1%	3.9%	3.7%	3.5%	3.3%	3.0%	2.9%	2.7%	2.5%	

Map	Africa	H L Students	62 per 100000
Capital	Khartoum	Hospital Beds	1.0 per 1000
One U S $ =	.3482 Pound		
		Telephones	45,086
Area-Total	2,505,813 Sq Km		
Area-Arable	71,000 Sq Km	Television Sets	15,000
		Tourist Receipt US $	1,000,000
Population	15,186,000	Passenger Cars	27,400
Population Density	5.73 per Sq Km	Steel Consumption	6 Kg/Cap
Birth-Death Rate %	5.2-1.8	Growth Pattern Index	31.25%
Population Rate of Increase	2.90%	GNP/Capita Annual Increase 67-90	2.82%
1967 GNP per Capita	90 US $		

Energy Total Billion Kec	1.321
Energy per Capita Kec	89
Kec per $ of GNP	0.96
Growth Ratio GNP/Kec	0.329
Electric Capacity Kw	97,400
Generation Billion Kwhr	0.334
Kilowatt Hours per Capita	22
Kwhr per $ of GNP	0.24
Economic Density GNP $/Sq Km	514

SURINAM

	1970	1975	1980	1985	1990	1995	2000	2005	2010	2015	2020
Population 1967 Population	1.060	1.155	1.250	1.345	1.440	1.530	1.615	1.695	1.770	1.840	1.910
Population Millions	0.435	0.473	0.512	0.551	0.590	0.637	0.662	0.695	0.726	0.754	0.783
GNP/Capita 1967 $	432	563	716	896	1,098	1,314	1,573	1,875	2,214	2,608	3,038
GNP Billion $ 1967	0.188	0.266	0.366	0.493	0.649	0.837	1.040	1.303	1.605	1.966	2.375
Yearly Increase GNP	7.2%		6.6%	6.1%	5.6%	5.2%	4.8%	4.5%	4.2%	4.1%	3.9%

Map	South America	H L Students	206 per 100000
Capital	Paramaribo	Hospital Beds	5.3 per 1000
One U S $ =	1.87 Guilder	Daily Newspapers	49 per 1000
		Telephones	9,600
Area-Total	163,265 Sq Km		
Area-Arable	450 Sq Km	Television Sets	300
Population	398,000		
Population Density	2.22 per Sq Km	Passenger Cars	10,900
Population Rate of Increase	3.50%	Growth Pattern Index GNP/Capita Annual Increase 67-90	143.75% 4.90%
1967 GNP per Capita	363 US $		

Energy Total Billion Kec	0.780
Energy per Capita Kec	2,081
Kec per $ of GNP	5.33
Growth Ratio GNP/Kec	0.725
Generation Billion Kwhr	1.076
Kilowatt Hours per Capita	2,869
Kwhr per $ of GNP	6.41
Economic Density GNP $/Sq Km	913

SWEDEN

	1967	1970	1975	1980	1985	1990	1995	2000	2005	2010	2015	2020
Population 1967 Population	1.000	1.020	1.060	1.090	1.115	1.145	1.170	1.192	1.210	1.225	1.245	1.270
Population Millions	7.87	8.03	8.29	8.59	8.78	8.97	9.12	9.30	9.53	9.64	9.82	10.00
GNP 1967 $ Capita	3,041	3,360	3,980	4,510	5,210	5,965	6,800	7,740	8,840	9,930	11,120	12,400
GNP Billion $ 1967	23.93	26.98	32.92	38.78	45.80	53.50	62.00	72.50	84.25	95.60	109.20	124.00
Yearly Increase GNP		4.0%	3.8%	3.5%	3.4%	3.3%	3.2%	3.0%	2.8%	2.7%	2.6%	

Map	Europe	Energy Total	42,439
Capital	Stockholm	Billion Kec	
One U S $ =	5.188 Krona	Energy per Capita Kec	5,359
Area-Total	449,793 Sq Km	Kec per $ of GNP	1.58
Area-Arable	30,310 Sq Km	Growth Ratio GNP/Kec	0.966
Population	7,978,000	Electric Capacity Mw	13,731
Population Density	17 per Sq Km	Generation Billion Kwhr	58,039
		Kilowatt Hours per Capita	7,730
Birth-Death Rate %	1.43–1.04	Kwhr per $ of GNP	2.22
Population Rate of Increase	0.71%	Economic Density GNP $/Sq Km	53,300
1967 GNP per Capita	3,041 US $		

H L Students	1,250 per 100000
Hospital Beds	14.3 per 1000
Daily Newspapers	518 per 1000
Telephones	3,934,694
Television Sets	2,345,000
Passenger Cars	2,072,000
Steel Consumption	623 Kg/Cap
Investment Ratio	24%
Growth Pattern Index	112.50%
GNP/Capita Annual Increase 67–90	3.00%

SWITZERLAND

	1967	1970	1975	1980	1985	1990	1995	2000	2005	2010	2015	2020
Population 1967 Population	1.000	1.050	1.150	1.240	1.325	1.415	1.490	1.517	1.640	1.715	1.770	1.840
Population Millions	6.07	6.37	6.91	7.43	8.00	8.58	9.05	9.52	9.98	10.39	10.79	11.15
GNP/Capita 1967 $	2,595	2,820	3,240	3,650	4,050	4,510	5,055	5,550	6,155	6,770	7,440	8,105
GNP Billion $ 1967	15.75	17.95	22.38	27.10	32.40	38.60	45.60	52.90	61.40	70.30	80.10	90.40
Yearly Increase GNP		4.5%	3.9%	3.6%	3.5%	3.4%	3.2%	3.0%	2.7%	2.6%	2.5%	

Map	Europe
Capital	Bern
One US $ =	4.304 Franc
Area-Total	41,288 Sq Km
Area-Arable	4,040 Sq Km
Population	6,230,000
Population Density	147 per Sq Km
Birth-Death Rate %	1.71-0.93
Population Rate of Increase	1.88%
1967 GNP per Capita	2,595 US $

H L Students	593 per 100000
Hospital Beds	11.1 per 1000
Daily Newspapers	368 per 1000
Telephones	2,685,800
Television Sets	1,011,000
Tourist Receipt US $	694,000,000
Passenger Cars	1,180,500
Steel Consumption	357 Kg/Cap
Investment Ratio	26%
Growth Pattern Index	75.00%
GNP/Capita Annual Increase 67-90	2.44%

Energy Total Billion Kec	18.583
Energy Per Capita Kec	3,012
Kec per $ of GNP	1.07
Growth Ratio GNP/Kec	0.685
Electric Capacity Mw	9,500
Generation Billion Kwhr	25.210
Kilowatt Hours per Capita	4,087
Kwhr per $ of GNP	1.55
Economic Density GNP $/Sq Km	381,000

316

SYRIA

	1970	1975	1980	1985	1990	1995	2000	2005	2010	2015	2020
Population 1967 Population	1.080	1.240	1.395	1.550	1.705	1.855	2.005	2.155	2.300	2.440	2.575
Population Millions	6.02	6.92	7.78	8.65	9.75	10.35	11.20	12.01	12.80	13.60	14.34
GNP 1967 $ Capita	348.5	406	468	537	621	708	824	944	1,080	1,212	1,396
GNP Billion $ 1967	2.10	2.81	3.64	4.64	6.05	7.33	9.23	11.35	13.84	16.48	20.00
Yearly Increase GNP	6.0%	5.6%	5.4%	5.2%	5.0%	4.6%	4.2%	4.0%	3.8%	3.6%	

Map	Asia & Middle East	
Capital	Damascus	
One U S $ =	4.32 Pound	
Area-Total	185,180 Sq Km	
Area-Arable	58,610 Sq Km	
Population Density	5,866,000 30 per Sq Km	
Birth-Death Rate %	4.7-1.5	
Population Rate of Increase	2.90%	
1967 GNP per Capita	234 US $	

H L Students		
Hospital Beds	593 per 100000	
Daily Newspapers	1.1 per 1000	
Telephones	15 per 1000	96,613
Television Sets		70,000
Passenger Cars		29,000
Steel Consumption		32 Kg/Cap
Investment Ratio		18%
Growth Pattern Index		62.50%
GNP/Capita Annual Increase 67-90		4.30%

Energy Total Billion Kec		2.475
Energy per Capita Kec		434
Kec per $ of GNP		1.68
Growth Ratio GNP/Kec		0.595
Electric Capacity Mw		216
Generation Billion Kwhr		0.773
Kilowatt Hours per Capita		135
Kwhr per $ of GNP		0.52
Economic Density GNP $/Sq Km		7,020

TANZANIA

	1970	1975	1980	1985	1990	1995	2000	2005	2010	2015	2020
Population 1967 Population	1.070	1.200	1.330	1.460	1.580	1.700	1.820	1.940	2.050	2.155	2.260
Population Millions	13.03	14.61	16.20	17.79	19.25	20.70	22.17	23.61	24.98	26.23	27.55
GNP Capita 1967 $	80.3	93.2	108.0	125.5	144.0	164.7	189.5	215.0	245.0	280.0	317.0
GNP Billion $ 1967	1.045	1.362	1.750	2.234	2.770	3.410	4.200	5.070	6.120	7.350	8.710
Yearly Increase GNP	4.1%	4.0%	3.5%	3.4%	3.3%	3.2%	3.1%	3.0%	3.0%	2.8%	

Map	Africa	H L Students	9 per 100000
Capital	Dar es Salaam	Daily Newspapers	3 per 1000
One U S $ =	7.143 Shilling	Telephones	29,348
Area-Total	939,702 Sq Km		
Area-Arable	117,020 Sq Km		
Population	12,926,000		
Population Density	12.97 per Sq Km		
Birth-Death Rate %	4.7-2.2	Growth Pattern Index	50%
Population Rate of Increase	2.50%	GNP/Capita Annual Increase 67-90	2.60%
1967 GNP per Capita	80 US $		

Energy Total Billion Kec	0.654
Energy Per Capita Kec	53
Kec per $ of GNP	0.875
Growth Ratio GNP/Kec	0.400
Generation Billion Kwhr	0.299
Kilowatt Hours per Capita	24
Kwhr per $ of GNP	0.30
Economic Density GNP $/Sq Km	1,034

318

THAILAND

	1967	1970	1975	1980	1985	1990	1995	2000	2005	2010	2015	2020
Population 1967 Population	1.000	1.100	1.250	1.420	1.585	1.754	1.922	2.092	2.242	2.400	2.563	2.712
Population Millions	32.68	35.98	40.84	46.40	51.85	57.30	62.80	68.40	73.49	78.50	83.70	88.60
GNP Capita 1967 $	155	178.4	221.5	280	348	435	535	662	811	995	1,212	1,462
GNP Billion $ 1967	5.07	6.42	9.03	12.99	18.05	24.95	33.50	45.30	59.55	78.10	101.50	129.90
Yearly Increase GNP	7.0%		6.9%	6.8%	6.7%	6.4%	6.2%	5.6%	5.5%	5.4%	5.1%	

Map	Asia & Middle East	H L Students	102 per 100000
Capital	Bangkok	Hospital Beds	0.9 per 1000
One U S $ =	21.00 Baht	Daily Newspapers	22 per 1000
		Telephones	114,419
Area-Total	514,000 Sq Km	Television Sets	210,000
Area-Arable	114,150 Sq Km	Tourist Receipt US $	58,000,000
Population	34,738,000	Passenger Cars	129,500
Population Density	64 per Sq Km	Steel Consumption	23 Kg/Cap
Birth-Death Rate %	4.6-1.3	Investment Ratio	25%
Population Rate of Increase	3.06%	Growth Pattern Index GNP/Capita	87.50%
		Annual Increase 67-90	4.55%
1967 GNP per Capita	155 US $		

Energy Total Billion Kec	6,873
Energy per Capita Kec	203
Kec per $ of GNP	1.12
Growth Ratio GNP/Kec	0.389
Generation Billion Kwhr	3,137
Kilowatt Hours per Capita	93
Kwhr per $ of GNP	0.45
Economic Density GNP $/Sq Km	9,850

TOGO

	1970	1975	1980	1985	1990	1995	2000	2005	2010	2015	2020
Population 1967 Population	1.070	1.205	1.340	1.475	1.610	1.740	1.870	1.990	2.110	2.225	2.335
Population Millions	1.845	2.080	2.310	2.544	2.775	2.980	3.225	3.434	3.640	3.840	4.025
GNP / Capita 1967 $	156	180.2	210	242.5	282	325.5	368	424	490	563	637
GNP Billion $ 1967	0.288	0.375	0.485	0.617	0.782	0.968	1.188	1.452	1.778	2.160	2.580

Yearly Increase GNP	5.4%	5.2%	4.9%	4.6%	4.4%	4.2%	4.0%	3.9%	3.8%	3.6%

Map	Africa
Capital	Lome
One U S $ =	277.71 CRA Franc
Area-Total	56,000 Sq Km
Area-Arable	21,600 Sq Km
Population	1,815,000
Population Density	31 per Sq Km
Birth-Death Rate	5.0-2.4
Population Rate of Increase	2.60%
1967 GNP per Capita	140 US $

H L Students	5 per 100000
Hospital Beds	1.4 per 1000
Daily Newspapers	6 per 1000
Telephones	2,800
Passenger Cars	5,800
Steel Consumption	6 Kg/Cap
Growth Pattern Index GNP/Capita	50%
Annual Increase 67-90	3.10%

Energy Total Billion Kec	0.095
Energy per Capita Kec	53
Kec per $ of GNP	0.40
Electric Capacity Kw	22,400
Generation Billion Kwhr	0.056
Kilowatt Hours per Capita	31
Kwhr per $ of GNP	0.19
Economic Density GNP $/Sq Km	4,230

TRINIDAD & TOBAGO

	1970	1975	1980	1985	1990	1995	2000	2005	2010	2015	2020
Population 1967 Population	1.080	1.220	1.360	1.500	1.640	1.780	1.910	2.040	2.165	2.290	2.410
Population Millions	1.090	1.231	1.372	1.515	1.656	1.798	1.929	2.060	2.184	1.315	2.435
GNP/Capita 1967 $	0.866	1,022	1,167	1,356	1,560	1,783	2,044	2,322	2,640	2,975	3,345
GNP Billion $ 1967	0.945	1.260	1.600	2.055	2.584	3.205	3.946	4.790	5.770	6.910	8.150
Yearly Increase GNP	5.9%	5.5%	5.1%	4.8%	4.4%	4.2%	4.0%	3.8%	3.6%	3.3%	

Map	North & Caribbean America	H L Students	107 per 100000
Capital	Port of Spain	Hospital Beds	4.4 per 1000
One U S $ =	2 Dollar	Daily Newspapers	102 per 1000
		Telephones	49,030
Area-Total	5,128 Sq Km	Television Sets	41,000
Area-Arable	1,390 Sq Km	Tourist Receipt US $	22,000,000
Population	1,040,000	Passenger Cars	67,600
Population Density	197 per Sq Km		
Birth-Death Rate %	3.0-0.8	Investment Ratio	20%
Population Rate of Increase	2.70%	Growth Pattern Index GNP/Capita	112.50%
		Annual Increase 67-90	3.00%
1967 GNP per Capita	783 US $		

Energy Total Billion Kec	4,310
Energy per Capita Kec	4,221
Kec per $ of GNP	5.39
Growth Ratio GNP/Kec	0.476
Electric Capacity Mw	253
Generation Billion Kwhr	1.139
Kwhr per $ of GNP	1,115
Economic Density GNP $/Sq Km	15,400

321

TRUCIAL OMAN

	1970	1975	1980	1985	1990	1995	2000	2005	2010	2015	2020
Population 1967 Population	1.170	1.520	1.900	2.350	2.850	3.350	3.850	4.330	4.810	5.280	5.740
Population Millions	0.211	0.274	0.342	0.423	0.513	0.603	0.693	0.780	0.866	0.950	1.033
GNP/Capita 1967 $	1,415	2,215	2,760	3,315	4,090	4,940	5,890	7,050	8,320	9,700	11,220
GNP Billion $ 1967	0.298	0.606	0.945	1.400	2.095	2.970	4.065	5.500	7.200	9.210	11.600
Yearly Increase GNP	9.5%		9.3%		8.5%	8.0%	7.3%	6.7%	6.2%	5.5%	5.0%	4.7%

Map: Asia & Middle East
Sheikdoms & Capitals: Abu Dhabi-Dubai-Sharjah-Ajman-Umm al Qaiwain-Ras al Khaimah-Fujairah
One U S $ = 0.47 Abu Dhabi Dinar
4.75 Dubai Riyal
Area-Total 83,600 Sq Km
Population 135,000
Population Density 2.15 per Sq Km
Population Rate of Increase 9.10%
1967 GNP per Capita 1,050 US $

Growth Pattern Index
GNP/Capita 187.50%
Annual Increase 67-90 6.06%

Energy Total Billion Kec 0.123
Energy per Capita Kec 924
Kec per $ of GNP 0.33

Economic Density
GNP $/Sq Km 2,260

TUNISIA

	1967	1970	1975	1980	1985	1990	1995	2000	2005	2010	2015	2020
Population 1967 Population	1.000	1.065	1.180	1.295	1.410	1.520	1.630	1.730	1.830	1.90	2.020	2.110
Population Millions	4.560	4.855	5.380	5.900	6.425	6.930	7.435	7.880	8.340	8.800	9.210	9.625
GNP Capita 1967 $	214	252.4	295	366	448	549	667.5	814	980	1,171	1,400	1,650
GNP Billion $ 1967	0.91	1.23	1.59	2.16	2.87	3.80	4.96	6.40	8.18	10.30	12.89	16.15
Yearly Increase GNP		6.5%	6.3%	6.0%	5.8%	5.5%	5.3%	5.0%	4.7%	4.6%	4.5%	

Map	Africa
Capital	Tunis
One U S $ =	.525 Dinar
Area-Total	164,150 Sq Km
Area-Arable	45,100 Sq Km
Population Density	5,027,000 28 per Sq Km
Birth-Death Rate %	4.5-1.6
Population Rate of Increase	2.30%
1967 GNP per Capita	214 US $

H L Students	161 per 100000
Hospital Beds	2.6 per 1000
Daily Newspapers	22 per 1000
Telephones	61,923
Television Sets	37,000
Tourist Receipt US $	45,000,000
Passenger Cars	60,600
Steel Consumption	11 Kg/Cap
Investment Ratio	21%
Growth Pattern Index	81.25%
GNP/Capita Annual Increase 67-90	4.15%

Energy Total Billion Kec	1.099
Energy per Capita Kec	235
Kec per $ of GNP	1.090
Growth Ratio GNP/Kec	0.650
Electric Capacity Mw	262
Generation Billion Kwhr	0.678
Kilowatt Hours per Capita	145
Kwhr per $ of GNP	0.63
Economic Density GNP $/Sq Km	5,800

323

TURKEY

	1967	1970	1975	1980	1985	1990	1995	2000	2005	2010	2015	2020
Population 1967 Population	1.000	1.098	1.201	1.334	1.458	1.590	1.715	1.834	1.945	2.055	2.168	2.270
Population Millions	32.72	35.25	39.30	43.65	47.70	52.00	56.10	60.00	63.65	67.20	71.00	74.25
GNP Capita 1967 $	353	400	507	640	799	988	1,219	1,488	1,778	2,150	2,545	2,980
GNP Billion $ 1967	11.54	14.10	19.91	27.95	38.10	51.45	68.40	89.40	113.10	144.50	182.00	221.50

Yearly Increase GNP	7.1%	7.0%	6.3%	6.2%	5.8%	5.5%	5.2%	5.0%	4.7%	4.0%

Map	Europe	H L Students	384 per 100000
Capital	Ankara	Hospital Beds	1.8 per 1000
One U S $ =	9.08 Lira	Daily Newspapers	45 per 1000
		Telephones	450,485
Area-Total	780,576 Sq Km		
Area-Arable	266,010 Sq Km	Television Sets	6,500
		Tourist Receipt US $	13,000,000
Population	34,375,000	Passenger Cars	112,600
Population Density	42 per Sq Km	Steel Consumption	26 Kg/Cap
Birth-Death Rate %	4.3-1.6	Investment Ratio	18%
Population Rate of Increase	2.53%	Growth Pattern Index GNP/Capita	93.75%
		Annual Increase 67-90	4.55%
1967 GNP per Capita	353 US $		

Energy Total Billion Kec	15.120
Energy per Capita Kec	450
Kec per $ of GNP	1.19
Growth Ratio GNP/Kec	0.523
Electric Capacity Mw	1,973
Generation Billion Kwhr	6.886
Kilowatt Hours per Capita	205
Kwhr per $ of GNP	0.54
Economic Density GNP $/Sq Km	14,800

U A R E G Y P T

	1967	1970	1975	1980	1985	1990	1995	2000	2005	2010	2015	2020
Population / 1967 Population	1.000	1.078	1.201	1.334	1.458	1.590	1.715	1.834	1.945	2.055	2.168	2.270
Population Millions	30.91	33.30	37.18	41.25	45.06	49.10	53.05	56.70	60.10	63.50	67.10	70.25
GNP/Capita	160.0	213.5	246.0	282.5	324.5	371.0	425.0	485.0	553.0	629.0	715.0	812.0
GNP Billion $ 1967	4.95	7.11	9.15	11.64	14.60	18.19	22.55	27.50	33.20	39.90	47.95	57.00
Yearly Increase GNP		5.2%		4.9%	4.6%	4.5%	4.4%	4.0%	3.8%	3.7%	3.6%	3.5%

Map	Africa
Capital	Cairo
One U S $ =	.4348 Pound
Area-Total	1,001,449 Sq Km
Area-Arable	28,010 Sq Km
Population Density	31 per Sq Km
Birth-Death Rate %	4.3-1.5
Population Rate of Increase	2.53%
1967 GNP per Capita	160 US $

H L Students	565 per 100000
Hospital Beds	2.2 per 1000
Telephones	365,000
Television Sets	418,000
Passenger Cars	115,900
Steel Consumption	21 Kg/Cap
Investment Ratio	14%
Growth Pattern Index	56.25%
GNP/Capita Annual Increase 67-90	3.65%

Energy Total Billion Kec	9.540
Energy per Capita Kec	301
Kec per $ of GNP	1.66
Growth Ratio GNP/Kec	0.598
Electric Capacity Mw	2,725
Generation Billion Kwhr	6.735
Kilowatt Hours per Capita	212
Kwhr per $ of GNP	1.27
Economic Density GNP $/Sq Km	4,940

325

UGANDA

	1970	1975	1980	1985	1990	1995	2000	2005	2010	2015	2020
Population 1967 Population	1.070	1.200	1.330	1.460	1.580	1.700	1.820	1.940	2.050	2.155	2.260
Population Millions	8.56	9.52	10.55	11.58	12.53	13.49	14.42	15.40	16.28	17.10	17.92
GNP 1967 $ Capita	97.0	116.3	137.3	163.5	190.8	224.5	264.7	305.0	369.0	417.0	482.0
GNP Billion $ 1967	0.830	1.108	1.448	1.894	2.387	3.030	3.820	4.680	6.000	7.120	8.630
Yearly Increase GNP	9.2%	7.1%	6.2%	6.0%	5.9%	5.4%	5.2%	4.8%	4.5%	4.4%	

Map	Africa	
Capital	Kampala	
One U S $ =	7.143 Shilling	
Area-Total	236,037 Sq Km	
Area-Arable	48,880 Sq Km	
Population	9,500,000	
Population Density	34 per Sq Km	
Birth-Death Rate %	4.3-1.8	
Population Rate of Increase	2.50%	
1967 GNP per Capita	95 US $	

H L Students	23 per 100000
Hospital Beds	1.1 per 1000
Daily Newspapers	6 per 1000
Telephones	25,874
Television Sets	9,000
Tourist Receipt US $	12,000,000
Passenger Cars	32,800
Growth Pattern Index GNP/Capita	56.25%
Annual Increase 67-90	3.10%

Energy Total Billion Kec	0.504
Energy per Capita Kec	61
Kec per $ of GNP	0.55
Growth Ratio GNP/Kec	0.483
Generation Billion Kwhr	0.541
Kilowatt Hours per Capita	66
Kwhr per $ of GNP	0.65
Economic Density GNP $/Sq Km	3,180

UNITED KINGDOM

	1967	1970	1975	1980	1985	1990	1995	2000	2005	2010	2015	2020
Population 1967 Population	1.000	1.020	1.052	1.080	1.110	1.144	1.166	1.190	1.210	1.228	1.245	1.265
Population Millions	55.07	56.25	58.00	59.50	61.10	63.05	64.25	65.50	66.60	67.60	68.60	69.60
GNP Capita 1967 $	1,975	2,165	2,520	2,908	3,340	3,820	4,370	4,985	5,610	6,315	7,100	7,850
GNP Billion $ 1967	108.7	121.8	146.2	173.1	204.1	240.9	280.5	326.1	374.0	427.1	487.1	546.3

Yearly Increase GNP	3.7%	3.5%	3.3%	3.2%	3.1%	3.0%	2.8%	2.6%	2.4%	2.3%

Map	Europe
Capital	London
One U S $ =	.4183 Pound
Area-Total	244,030 Sq Km
Area-Arable	73,820 Sq Km
Population	55,534,000
Population Density	226 per Sq Km
Birth-Death Rate %	1.71-1.19
Population Rate of Increase	0.71%
1967 GNP per Capita	1,975 US $

H L Students	716 per 100000
Hospital Beds	10.0 per 1000
Daily Newspapers	488 per 1000
Telephones	12,799,000
Television Sets	15,419,000
Tourist Receipt US $	677,000,000
Passenger Cars	10,949,000
Steel Consumption	422 Kg/Cap
Investment Ratio	18%
Growth Pattern Index	112.50%
GNP/Capita Annual Increase 67-90	2.94%

Energy Total Billion Kec	277.270
Energy per Capita Kec	5,004
Kec per $ of GNP	2.57
Growth Ratio GNP/Kec	1.575
Electric Capacity Mw	59,628
Generation Billion Kwhr	223.972
Kilowatt Hours per Capita	4,042
Kwhr per $ of GNP	1.92
Economic Density GNP $/Sq Km	445,000

327

UNITED STATES

	1970	1975	1980	1985	1990	1995	2000	2005	2010	2015	2020
Population 1967 Population	1.040	1.113	1.185	1.248	1.310	1.370	1.428	1.478	1.525	1.569	1.620
Population Millions	207.0	222.0	236.0	249.0	261.5	273.5	285.0	294.8	303.8	313.0	322.5
GNP/Capita 1967 $	4,340	4,990	5,740	6,560	7,400	8,250	9,250	10,280	11,350	12,380	13,500
GNP Billion $ 1967	899.0	1,109	1,352	1,640	1,930	2,260	2,635	3,030	3,440	3,865	4,360
Yearly Increase GNP	4.3%		4.1%		3.9%	3.3%	3.2%	3.1%	2.8%	2.5%	2.4%	2.3%

Map   North & Caribbean America
Capital   Washington

Area-Total   9,363,353 Sq Km
Area-Arable 1,764,400 Sq Km

Population   203,216,000
Population Density   21 per Sq Km

Birth-Death Rate   1.7610.96
Population Rate of
  Increase   1.47%

1967 GNP per Capita   4,040 US $

H L Students   3,471 per 100000
Hospital Beds   8.4 per 1000
Daily Newspapers   309 per 1000
Telephones   109,255,000

Television Sets   82,200,000
Tourist Receipt US $ 1,770,000,000
Passenger Cars   81,281,300
Steel Consumption   685 Kg/Cap

Investment Ratio   18%
Growth Pattern Index   125%
GNP/Capita
Annual Increase 67-90   2.70%

Energy Total
  Billion Kec   2,078.156
Energy per Capita Kec   10,331

Kec per $ of GNP   2.44
Growth Ratio GNP/Kec   1.044

Electric Capacity Mw   310,125
Generation Billion Kwhr   1,434.908
Kilowatt Hours per Capita   7,133
Kwhr per $ of GNP   1,64

Economic Density
  GNP $/Sq Km   85,800

U S VIRGIN ISLANDS

	1967	1970	1975	1980	1985	1990	1995	2000	2005	2010	2015	2020
Population 1967 Population	1.000	1.170	1.520	1.900	2.350	2.850	3.350	3.850	4.330	4.810	5.280	
Population Millions	0.056	0.068	0.085	0.106	0.132	0.160	0.188	0.216	0.243	0.270	0.296	0.322
GNP Capita 1967 $	2,380	2,670	3,240	3,900	4,600	5,450	6,350	7,540	8,500	9,730	10,950	12,250
GNP Billion $ 1967	0.105	0.175	0.276	0.415	0.606	0.870	1.192	1.625	2.066	2.614	3.240	3.940
Yearly Increase GNP	10.7	9.5%	8.5%	7.7%	7.2%	6.7%	6.0%	5.0%	4.6%	4.3%	4.0%	

Map North & Caribbean America	H L Students 2,380 per 100000
Capital Charlotte Amalie (St Th)	Hospital Beds 4.4 per 1000
One U S $ = 1 Dollar	Daily Newspapers 112 per 1000
	Telephones 14,984
Area-Total 344 Sq Km	
Area-Arable 60 Sq Km	Television Sets 16,000
Population 56,000	
Population Density 163 per Sq Km	
	Growth Pattern Index
Population Rate of	GNP/Capita 131.25%
Increase 8.20%	Annual Increase 67-90 3.68%
1967 GNP per Capita 2,380 US $	

Energy Total Billion Kec	0.390
Energy per Capita Kec	6,718
Kec per $ of GNP	2.28
Growth Ratio GNP/Kec	0.375
Electric Capacity Kw	99,300
Generation Billion Kwhr	0.258
Kilowatt Hours per Capita	4,448
Kwhr per $ of GNP	1.16
Economic Density GNP $/Sq Km	306,000

329

USSR

	1967	1970	1975	1980	1985	1990	1995	2000	2005	2010	2015	2020
Population 1967 Population	1.000	1.042	1.105	1.169	1.230	1.302	1.354	1.407	1.452	1.498	1.540	1.580
Population Millions	235.5	245.0	260.0	274.7	289.9	306.0	318.5	330.8	342.0	352.5	363.0	372.0
GNP Capita 1967 $	970	1,130	1,458	1,838	2,265	2,760	3,365	3,975	4,650	5,390	6,165	7,050
GNP Billion $ 1967	228.0	272.0	379.5	505.5	656.0	845.0	1,072	1,315	1,590	1,900	2,235	2,620
Yearly Increase GNP		6.9%	5.9%	5.3%	5.2%	4.9%	4.2%	3.8%	3.6%	3.3%	3.2%	

Map	Europe	H L Students	1,830 per 100000
Capital	Moscow	Hospital Beds	10.0 per 1000
One U S $ =	0.90 Ruble	Daily Newspapers	305 per 1000
		Telephones	10,800,000
Area-Total	22,402,200 Sq Km		
Area-Arable	2,243,000 Sq Km	Television Sets	26,800,000
Population	240,571,000		
Population Density	10.50 per Sq Km	Steel Consumption	428 Kg/Cap
Birth-Death Rate %	1.79-0.77	Investment Ratio	27%
Population Rate of Increase	1.42%	Growth Pattern Index GNP/Capita	168.75%
		Annual Increase 67-90	4.62%
1967 GNP per Capita	970 US $		

Energy Total Billion Kec	965.215
Energy per Capita Kec	4,058
Kec per $ of GNP	4.08
Growth Ratio GNP/Kec	1.318
Electric Capacity Mw	142,504
Generation Billion Kwhr	636.191
Kilowatt Hours per Capita	2,675
Kwhr per $ of GNP	2.57
Economic Density GNP $/Sq Km	10,180

UPPER VOLTA

	1970	1975	1980	1985	1990	1995	2000	2005	2010	2015	2020
Population 1967 Population	1.065	1.175	1.285	1.390	1.495	1.595	1.690	1.785	1.875	1.960	2.040
Population Millions	5.390	5.945	6.500	7.030	7.560	8.060	8.550	9.025	9.480	9.915	10.310
GNP Capita 1967 $	54.1	61.8	70.5	80.0	89.2	105.0	113.8	127.3	140.8	177.5	193.0
GNP Billion $ 1967	0.292	0.368	0.458	0.562	0.675	0.846	0.971	1.150	1.362	1.760	1.990
Yearly Increase GNP	4.7%	4.5%	4.2%	3.8%	3.7%	3.6%	3.5%	3.3%	3.0%	2.5%	

Map	Africa	H L Students	1.1 per 100000
Capital	Ouagadougou	Hospital Beds	0.4 per 1000
One U S $ =	277.71 CFA Franc	Telephones	2,999
Area-Total	274,200 Sq Km	Television Sets	5,000
Area-Arable	96,640 Sq Km	Passenger Cars	5,200
Population	5,278,000		
Population Density	18 per Sq Km	Growth Pattern Index	25.00%
Birth-Death Rate %	4.9-2.8	GNP/Capita	
Population Rate of Increase	2.20%	Annual Increase 67-90	2.55%
1967 GNP per Capita	50 US $		

Energy Total	0.052
Billion Kec	
Energy per Capita Kec	10
Kec per $ of GNP	0.22
Growth Ratio GNP/Kec	0.438
Electric Capacity Kw	10,600
Generation Billion Kwhr	0.023
Kilowatt Hours per Capita	4
Kwhr per $ of GNP	0.08
Economic Density	
GNP $/Sq Km	924

331

URUGUAY

	1967	1970	1975	1980	1985	1990	1995	2000	2005	2010	2015	2020
Population 1967 Population	1.000	1.040	1.100	1.155	1.215	1.270	1.320	1.370	1.410	1.450	1.485	1.520
Population Millions	2.783	2.995	3.032	3.215	3.385	3.540	3.675	3.815	3.925	4.035	4.130	4.230
GNP 1967 $ Capita	577	592	630	670	728	768	804	835	875	935	1,000	1,104
GNP Billion $ 1967	1.608	1.772	1.910	2.155	2.460	2.715	2.950	3.180	3.430	3.770	4.130	4.660
Yearly Increase GNP		2.6%	2.4%	2.3%	1.9%	1.7%	1.6%	1.5%	1.4%	1.3%	1.2%	

Map	South America	H L Students	629 per 100000
Capital	Montevideo	Hospital Beds	4.8 per 1000
One U S $ =	250.00 Peso	Daily Newspapers	314 per 1000
		Telephones	205,174
Area-Total	186,926 Sq Km		
Area-Arable	19,570 Sq Km	Television Sets	215,000
Population	2,852,000	Passenger Cars	142,000
Population Density	14.92 per Sq Km	Steel Consumption	10 Kg/Cap
Birth-Death Rate %	2.40-0.90	Investment Ratio	12%
Population Rate of		Growth Pattern Index	25%
Increase	1.30%	GNP/Capita	
		Annual Increase 67-90	1.25%
1967 GNP per Capita	577 US $		

Energy Total Billion Kec	2.230
Energy per Capita Kec	791
Kec per $ of GNP	1.56
Growth Ratio GNP/Kec	0.450
Generation Billion Kwhr	1.825
Kilowatt Hours per Capita	647
Kwhr per $ of GNP	1.28
Economic Density GNP $/Sq Km	8,200

VENEZUELA

	1967	1970	1975	1980	1985	1990	1995	2000	2005	2010	2015	2020
Population 1967 Population	1.000	1.125	1.285	1.486	1.687	1.882	2.085	2.295	2.489	2.682	2.870	3.070
Population Millions	9.35	10.52	12.04	13.90	15.78	17.62	19.51	21.48	23.30	25.12	26.85	28.71
GNP 1967 $ Capita	911	991	1,115	1,250	1,395	1,560	1,728	1,906	2,085	2,290	2,510	2,740
GNP Billion $ 1967	8.54	10.42	13.61	16.99	22.05	27.02	33.60	40.20	48.15	57.40	67.50	78.60
Yearly Increase GNP		5.5%	5.0%	4.8%	4.5%	4.1%	4.0%	3.5%	3.4%	3.2%	3.1%	

Map	South America	H L Students	629 per 100000
Capital	Caracas	Hospital Beds	3.2 per 1000
One U S $ =	4.50 Bolivar	Daily Newspapers	62 per 1000
		Telephones	345,704
Area-Total	912,050 Sq Km		
Area-Arable	52,140 Sq Km	Television Sets	700,000
Population	10,035,000	Passenger Cars	482,000
Population Density	10.27 per Sq Km	Steel Consumption	147 Kg/Cap
Birth-Death Rate %	4.60–1.00	Investment Ratio	25%
Population Rate of Increase	3.44%	Growth Pattern Index GNP/Capita	68.75%
		Annual Increase 67-90	2.35%
1967 GNP per Capita	911 US $		

Energy Total Billion Kec	24,636
Energy per Capita Kec	2,543
Kec per $ of GNP	2.44
Growth Ratio GNP/Kec	0.765
Electric Capacity Mw	2,740
Generation Billion Kwhr	10,814
Kilowatt Hours per Capita	1,116
Kwhr per $ of GNP	1.11
Economic Density GNP $/Sq Km	9,380

333

VIETNAM - NORTH

	1967	1970	1975	1980	1985	1990	1995	2000	2005	2010	2015	2020
Population 1967 Population	1.000	1.080	1.260	1.440	1.620	1.800	1.980	2.160	2.330	2.500	2.670	2.840
Population Millions	20.10	21.80	25.45	29.10	32.56	36.40	40.00	43.60	47.05	50.50	53.95	57.40
GNP Capita 1967 $	100.0	113.3	141.7	174.0	214.0	263.5	323.0	393.0	475.0	566.0	680.0	793.0
GNP Billion $ 1967	2.01	2.47	3.60	5.07	6.96	9.58	12.82	17.12	22.40	28.55	36.60	41.50
Yearly Increase GNP		7.7%	7.1%	7.1%	6.5%	6.3%	6.0%	5.9%	5.5%	5.0%	4.8%	2.5%

Map: Asia & Middle East
Capital: Hanoi
One U S $ = 2.94 Dong

Area-Total: 158,750 Sq Km
Area-Arable: 20,180 Sq Km

Population: 21,340,000
Population Density: 127 per Sq Km

Population Rate of Increase: 3.20%

1967 GNP per Capita: 100 US $

H L Students   29 per 100000

Steel Consumption   4 Kg/Cap

GNP/Capita
Annual Increase 67-90   4.25%

Economic Density
GNP $/Sq Km   12,650

VIETNAM - SOUTH

	1970	1975	1980	1985	1990	1995	2000	2005	2010	2015	2020
Population 1967 Population	1.080	1.220	1.360	1.500	1.640	1.780	1.910	2.040	2.165	2.290	2.410
Population Millions	18.33	20.75	23.10	25.50	27.55	30.25	32.40	34.60	36.80	38.95	41.00
GNP Capita 1967 $	162.6	184.0	226.0	275.4	336.0	408.0	498.0	595.0	707.0	839.0	994.0
GNP Billion $ 1967	2.98	3.82	5.23	7.02	9.26	12.34	16.18	20.58	26.00	32.65	40.75
Yearly Increase GNP	6.5%	6.3%	6.0%	5.6%	5.4%	5.2%	4.9%	4.8%	4.6%	4.3%	

Map	Asia & Middle East	H L Students	200 per 100000
Capital	Saigon	Hospital Beds	1.7 per 1000
One U S $ =	117.50 Piastre	Daily Newspapers	70 per 1000
		Telephones	30,964
Area-Total	173,809 Sq Km		
Area-Arable	28,370 Sq Km	Tourist Receipt US $	2,000,000
Population	17,867,000	Passenger Cars	34,100
Population Density	98 per Sq Km	Steel Consumption	12 Kg/Cap
Population Rate of Increase	2.70%	Growth Pattern Index GNP/Capita Annual Increase 67-90	81.25% 3.75%
1967 GNP per Capita	144 US $		

Energy Total Billion Kec	5.653
Energy per Capita Kec	324
Kec per $ of GNP	2.05
Electric Capacity Mw	438
Generation Billion Kwhr	0.830
Kilowatt Hours per Capita	47
Kwhr per $ of GNP	0.30
Economic Density GNP $/Sq Km	14,050

335

WINDWARD ISLANDS

	1970	1975	1980	1985	1990	1995	2000	2005	2010	2015	2020
Population 1967 Population	1.060	1.165	1.268	1.370	1.470	1.560	1.650	1.740	1.820	1.900	1.970
Population Millions	0.399	0.435	0.474	0.512	0.549	0.572	0.616	0.650	0.680	0.710	0.735
GNP Capita 1967 $	241	304	390	478	598	745	920	1,125	1,388	1,710	2,090
GNP Billion $ 1967	0.095	0.132	0.185	0.244	0.328	0.425	0.566	0.730	0.943	1.210	1.540
Yearly Increase GNP	7.2%	6.9%	6.5%	6.0%	5.8%	5.5%	5.3%	5.2%	5.1%	5.0%	

Map	North & Caribbean America
Capital	Dominica: Poseau
	Grenada: St. George
	St. Lucia: Castries
One U S $ =	1.98 Dollar
Area-Total	2,071 Sq Km
Population Density	388,000
Population Density	179 per Sq Km
Population Rate of Increase	2.20%
1967 GNP per Capita	212 US $

Telephones	6,563
Growth Pattern Index GNP/Capita	87.50%
Annual Increase	4.60%

Energy Total Billion Kec	0.8
Energy per Capita Kec	200
Generation Billion Kwhr	0.035
Kilowatt Hours per Capita	93
Economic Density GNP $/Sq Km	38,100

336

YEMEN

	1970	1975	1980	1985	1990	1995	2000	2005	2010	2015	2020
Population 1967 Population	1.065	1.175	1.285	1.390	1.495	1.595	1.690	1.785	1.875	1.960	2.040
Population Millions	5.680	6.265	6.850	7.410	7.975	8.500	9.000	9.510	9.990	10.440	10.865
GNP Capita 1967 $	79.4	97.1	118.1	142.1	169.5	198.0	232.5	268.0	307.0	350.0	396.0
GNP Billion $ 1967	0.443	0.609	0.810	1.054	1.350	1.685	2.090	2.550	3.070	3.660	4.300
Yearly Increase GNP	6.5%	5.9%	5.4%	5.0%	4.6%	4.3%	4.1%	3.8%	3.6%	3.4%	

Map	Asia & Middle East	Hospital Beds	0.4 per 1000
Capital	San'a		
One US $ =	1.071 Rial		
Area-Total	195,000 Sq Km		
Population Population Density	5,000,000 26 per Sq Km		
Population Rate of Increase	2.20%	Growth Pattern Index GNP/Capita Annual Increase 67-90	37.50% 3.90%
1967 GNP per Capita	70 US $		

Energy Total Billion Kec	0.067
Energy per Capita Kec	13
Kec per $ of GNP	0.13
Growth Ratio BNP/Kec	0.653
Generation Billion Kwhr	0.017
Kilowatt Hours per Capita	3
Kwhr per $ of GNP	0.04
Economic Density GNP $/Sq Km	19,150

YUGOSLAVIA

	1967	1970	1975	1980	1985	1990	1995	2000	2005	2010	2015	2020
Population 1967 Population	1.000	1.030	1.070	1.110	1.149	1.191	1.221	1.265	1.285	1.310	1.330	1.355
Population Millions	19.75	20.28	21.15	21.91	22.68	23.49	24.10	24.80	25.40	25.85	26.25	26.78
GNP Capita 1967 $	530	638	865	1,138	1,491	1,882	2,322	2,830	3,375	4,050	4,825	5,650
GNP Billion $ 1967	10.5	13.1	18.4	24.9	33.8	44.3	56.1	70.3	87.0	104.8	126.8	151.1
Yearly Increase GNP		7.0%	6.7%	6.3%	5.5%	4.8%	4.6%	4.4%	4.1%	3.9%	3.6%	

Map	Europe
Capital	Belgrade
One U S $ =	12.5 Dinar
Area-Total	255,804 Sq Km
Area-Arable	82,460 Sq Km
Population	20,351,000
Population Density	78 per Sq Km
Birth-Death Rate	1.89-0.86
Population Rate of Increase	0.93%
1967 GNP per Capita	530 US $

H L Students	1,057 per 100000
Hospital Beds	5.9 per 1000
Daily Newspapers	83 per 1000
Telephones	549,019
Television Sets	1,281,313
Tourist Receipt US $	1,299,000
Passenger Cars	439,900
Steel Consumption	130 Kg/Cap
Investment Ratio	38%
Growth Pattern Index	143.75%
GNP/Capita Annual Increase 67-90	5.65%

Energy Total Billion Kec	25.112
Energy per Capita Kec	1,247
Kec per $ of GNP	2.22
Growth Ratio GNP/Kec	0.971
Electric Capacity Mw	4,700
Generation Billion Kwhr	20.235
Kilowatt Hours per Capita	1,038
Kwhr per $ of GNP	1.81
Economic Density GNP $Sq Km	41,000

338

ZAMBIA

	1970	1975	1980	1985	1990	1995	2000	2005	2010	2015	2020
Population 1967 Population	1.075	1.240	1.405	1.570	1.735	1.900	2.060	2.210	2.360	2.510	2.650
Population Millions	4.245	4.895	5.550	6.200	6.850	7.500	8.140	8.735	9.320	9.910	10.475
GNP Capita 1967 $	375.5	543	786	1,085	1,446	1,900	2,480	3,100	3,850	4,700	5,690
GNP Billion $ 1967	1.59	2.66	4.36	6.73	9.90	14.25	20.19	27.00	35.84	46.60	59.60
Yearly Increase GNP	10.8%	10.3%	9.1%	8.0%	7.6%	7.2%	6.6%	6.0%	5.4%	5.0%	

Map	Africa	
Capital	Lusaka	
One U S $ =	.7143 Kwacha	
Area-Total	752,614 Sq Km	
Area-Arable	48,000 Sq Km	
Population	4,208,000	
Population Density	5.25 per Sq Km	
Birth-Death %	5.1-2.0	
Population Rate of Increase	3.00%	
1967 GNP per Capita	298 US $	

H L Students	23 per 100000
Hospital Beds	2.6 per 1000
Daily Newspapers	9 per 1000
Telephones	47,735
Television Sets	17,000
Tourist Receipt US $	7,000,000
Passenger Cars	48,200
Steel Consumption	10 Kg/Cap
Investment Ratio	35%
Growth Pattern Index	162.50%
GNP/Capita Annual Increase 67-90	7.15%

Energy Total Billion Kec	2.259
Energy per Capita Kec	553
Kec per $ of GNP	1.94
Growth Ratio GNP/Kec	0.783
Generation Billion Kwhr	3.413
Kilowatt Hours per Capita	836
Kwhr per $ of GNP	2.75
Economic Density GNP $/Sq Km	1,555

	AMERICAN SAMOA	BHUTAN	BOTSWANA
Map	Asia & Middle East	Asia & Middle East	Africa
Capital	Pago Pago (Tutuila Is.)	Thimbu	Gaberones
One US $ =	1 Dollar	7.553 Rupee	.7143 Rand
Area-Total	197 Sq Km	47,000 Sq Km	600,372 Sq Km
Area-Arable	80 Sq Km	—	4,280 Sq Km
Population	32,000	825,000	629,000
Population Density	146 per Sq Km	16 per Sq Km	0.98 per Sq Km
Population Rate of Increase	5.40%	2.00%	3.00%
1967 GNP per Capita	490 US $	60 US $	90 US $
H L Students	200 per 100000		
Hospital Beds	7.2 per 1000		2.5 per 1000
Daily Newspapers	65 per 1000		
Telephones	2,100 (In Pago Pago)		2,966
Television Sets	1,000		
Passenger Cars			2,200
Energy Total Billion Kec	0.073		
Energy per Capita Kec	2,370		
Kec per $ of GNP	7.92		
Electric Capacity Kw	11,000		
Generation Billion Kwhr	0.034		
Kilowatt Hours per Capita	1,096		
Kwhr per $ of GNP	2.18		
Economic Density GNP $/Sq Km	71,000	1,000	88

340

	BRITISH HONDURAS	**BRITISH SOLOMON ISL**	**CAPE VERDE ISLANDS**
Map	North & Caribbean Amer	Oceania	Africa
Capital	Belize City	Honiara	Praia
One US $ =	1.67 Dollar	.8964 Dollar	28.4 Escudo
Area-Total	22,965 Sq Km	29,785 Sq Km	4,033 Sq Km
Area-Arable	470 Sq Km	1,450 Sq Km	300 Sq Km
Population	120,000	150,000	250,000
Population Density	4.94 per Sq Km	4.92 per Sq Km	58 per Sq Km
Population Rate of Increase	3.10%	2.00%	2.40%
1967 GNP per Capita	360 US $	180 US $	110 US $
H L Students	103 per 100000		
Hospital Beds	5.0 per 1000	5.9 per 1000	2.0 per 1000
Daily Newspapers	55 per 1000		
Telephones	2,111		
Passenger Cars	3,000		
Energy Total Billion Kec	0.058	0.015	0.024
Energy per Capita Kec	504	131	97
Kec per $ of GNP	1.34	0.63	0.94
Electric Capacity Kw	6,000		3,000
Generation Billion Kwhr	0.016	0.008	0.009
Kilowatt Hours per Capita	137	54	36
Kwhr per $ of GNP	0.36	0.26	0.14
Economic Density GNP $/Sq Km	1,780	10	6,500

	CEUTA & MELILLA	CHANNEL ISLANDS	COMORO ISLANDS
Map	Africa	Europe	Africa
Capital	Ceuta Melilla	St Helier– St Peter Port	Moroni
One US $ =	69.73 Peseta	0.4183 Pound	277 CFA Franc
Area-Total	31 Sq Km	195 Sq Km	2,171 Sq Km
Area-Arable		60 Sq Km	900 Sq Km
Population	163,000	117,000	270,000
Population Density	5,200 per Sq Km	595 per Sq Km	115 per Sq Km
Population Rate of Increase	0.90%	0.80%	3.70%
1967 GNP per Capita	280 US $	980 US $	110 US $
Hospital Beds		10.0 per 1000	2.3 per 1000
Growth Pattern Index		87.50%	
GNP/Capita Annual Increase 67-90		3.50%	
Energy Total Billion Kec			0.009
Energy per Capita Kec			34
Kec per $ of GNP			0.32
Electric Capacity Kw	17,500		
Economic Density GNP $/Sq Km	1,454,500	585,000	12,700

	EQUATORIAL GUINEA	FAEROE ISLANDS	FIJI ISLANDS
Map	Africa	Europe	Oceania
Capital	Santa Isabel	Thorshavn	Suva
One US $ =	70 Peseta	7.507 Krone	0.83 Dollar
Area-Total	28,051 Sq Km	1,399 Sq Km	18,272 Sq Km
Area-Arable	2,210 Sq Km	30 Sq Km	2,250 Sq Km
Population	286,000	38,000	519,000
Population Density	9.87 per Sq Km	27 per Sq Km	27 per Sq Km
Population Rate of Increase	1.80%	1.60%	3.20%
1967 GNP per Capita	240 US $	1,710 US $	290 US $
Hospital Beds	5.9 per 1000	6.7 per 1000	3.1 per 1000
Daily Newspapers	4 per 1000		20 per 1000
Telephones			14,507
Passenger Cars			2,300
Energy Total Billion Kec	0.045	0.096	0.174
Energy per Capita Kec	161	2,539	345
Kec per $ of GNP	0.66	1.37	1.15
Generation Billion Kwhr	0.015	0.063	0.132
Kilowatt Hours per Capita	53	1,657	261
Kwhr per $ of GNP	0.19	0.92	0.84
Economic Density GNP $/Sq Km	2,390	46,400	767

	FRENCH GUYANA	**FR TER AFAR & ISSAS**	**GAMBIA**
Map	South America	Africa	Africa
Capital	Cayenne	Djibouti	Bathurst
One US $ =	5.519 Franc	242 Franc	0.4167 Pound
Area-Total	91,000 Sq Km	22,000 Sq Km	11,295 Sq Km
Area-Arable	20 Sq Km	10 Sq Km	2,000 Sq Km
Population	40,000	85,000	357,000
Population Density	0.42 per Sq Km	3.77 per Sq Km	30 per Sq Km
Birth-Death Rate %			3.9-2.1
Population Rate of Increase	2.00%	1.50%	2.00%
1967 GNP per Capita	790 US $	580 US $	90 US $
Hospital Beds	14.3 per 1000	10.0 per 1000	1.5 per 1000
Daily Newspapers	34 per 1000		5 per 1000
Telephones	2,990		1,494
Passenger Cars		7,000	
Energy Total Billion Kec	0.042	0.057	0.018
Energy per Capita Kec	916	705	51
Kec per $ of GNP	1.10	1.55	0.49
Generation Billion Kwhr	0.016	0.034	0.012
Kilowatt Hours per Capita	347	419	34
Kwhr per $ of GNP	0.50	0.55	0.36
Economic Density GNP $/Sq Km	303	2,180	2,740

	GIBRALTAR	GILBERT & ELLICE ISL	GREENLAND
Map	Europe	Oceania	Europe
Capital	Gibraltar	Tarawa	Godthaab
One US $ =	0.4183 Pound	0.8964 Dollar	7.507 Krone
Area-Total	6 Sq Km	886 Sq Km	2,175,600 Sq Km
Area-Arable		410 Sq Km	
Population	27,000	54,000	47,000
Population Density	4,161 per Sq Km	62 per Sq Km	0.02 per Sq Km
Population Rate of Increase	0.60%	2.60%	3.90%
1967 GNP per Capita	610 US $	380 US $	760 US $
Hospital Beds	9.1 per 1000	9.1 per 1000	16.7 per 1000
Daily Newspapers	120 per 1000		
Telephones	5,444		1,952
Television Sets	6,000		
Energy Total Billion Kec	0.039	0.015	0.250
Energy per Capita Kec	1,559	277	5,566
Kec per $ of GNP	2.36	0.57	5.53
Generation Billion Kwhr	0.039		0.063
Kilowatt Hours per Capita	1,559		1,399
Kwhr per $ of GNP	2.49		1.74
Economic Density GNP $/Sq Km	2,500,000	23,600	16

	IFNI	**ISLE OF MAN**	**LEEWARD ISLANDS**
Map	Africa	Europe	N & C America
Capital	Ifni	Douglas	St. John's
One US $ =	5.06 Dirham	0.4183 Pound	1.98 Dollar
Area-Total	1,500 Sq Km	588 Sq Km	907 Sq Km
Area-Arable		230 Sq Km	
Population	56,000	50,000	143,000
Population Density	35 per Sq Km	85 per Sq Km	154 per Sq Km
Population Rate of Increase	1.40%	0.60%	0.90%
1967 GNP per Capita	150 US $	1,250 US $	243 US $
Hospital Beds	3.7 per 1000	14.3 per 1000	
Telephones			1,405
Television Sets			3,500
Energy Total Billion Kec			0.177
Energy per Capita Kec			1,246
Kec per $ of GNP			424
Electric Capacity Kw	1,100		
Generation Billion Kwhr			0.046
Kilowatt Hours per Capita			323
Kwhr per $ of GNP			1.28
Economic Density GNP $/Sq Km	5,340	103,000	37,700

	LESOTHO	MACAU	MALDIVE ISLANDS
Map	Africa	Asia & Middle East	Asia & Middle East
Capital	Maseru	Macao	Male
One US $ =	.7143 Rand	14.5 Pataca	5.952 Rupee
Area-Total	30,355 Sq Km	16 Sq Km	298 Sq Km
Area-Arable	3,530 Sq Km		
Population	930,000	260,000	108,000
Population Density	29 per Sq Km	16,750 per Sq Km	348 per Sq Km
Birth-Death Rate %	4.0-2.3		
Population Rate of Increase	2.90%	6.80%	1.80%
1967 GNP per Capita	60 US $	240 US $	80 US $
H L Students	34 per 100000		
Hospital Beds	1.9 per 1000	4.0 per 1000	0.2 per 1000
Daily Newspapers		114 per 1000	
Telephones	1,844	5,319	
Energy Total Billion Kec		0.080	
Energy per Capita Kec		309	
Kec per $ of GNP		1.18	
Electric Capacity Kw		17,500	
Generation Billion Kwhr		0.046	
Kilowatt Hours per Capita		176	
Kwhr per $ of GNP		0.61	
Economic Density GNP $/Sq Km	1.740	4,000,000	26,850

	NETHERLANDS ANTILLES	**NEW HEBRIDES**	**PAPUA & NEW GUINEA**
Map	N & C America	Oceania	Oceania
Capital	Willemstad	Vila	Port Moresby
One US $ =	1.8 Guilder	0.8964 Dollar 89.64 CFP Franc	0.8973 Dollar
Area-Total	961 Sq Km	14,763 Sq Km	461,691 Sq Km
Area-Arable	50 Sq Km	700 Sq Km	
Population	218,000	80,000	2,303,000
Population Density	220 per Sq Km	5.22 per Sq Km	4.88 per Sq Km
Population Rate of Increase	1.40%	2.20%	2.50%
1967 GNP per Capita	1,180 US $	280 US $	200 US $
Hospital Beds	8.4 per 1000	10.0 per 1000	
Daily Newspapers	138 per 1000		
Telephones	24,920		16,312
Passenger Cars	29,100	1,200	
Investment Ratio	15%		
GNP/Capita Annual Increase 67-90	0.50%		4.00%
Energy Total Billion Kec	3.805	0.031	0.269
Energy per Capita Kec	17,460	399	116
Kec per $ of GNP	18.55	1.27	0.49
Electric Capacity Kw		3,600	
Generation Billion Kwhr	1.215	0.008	0.130
Kilowatt Hours per Capita	5,651	102	55
Kwhr per $ of GNP	4.80	0.24	0.25
Economic Density GNP $/Sq Km	260,000	1,950	980

348

	PORTUGUESE TIMOR	**SAO TOME & PRINCIPE**	**SEYCHELLES ISLANDS**
Map	Oceania	Africa	Africa
Capital	Dili	Sao Tome	Victoria
One US $ =	28.8 Escudo	28.8 Escudo	5.5 Rupee
Area-Total	14,925 Sq Km	964 Sq Km	376 Sq Km
Area-Arable		300 Sq Km	170 Sq Km
Population	590,000	66,000	51,000
Population Density	38 per Sq Km	62 per Sq Km	130 per Sq Km
Population Rate of Increase	1.50%	0.20%	2.20%
1967 GNP per Capita	80 US $	280 US $	60 US $
H L Students			94 per 100000
Hospital Beds	1.5 per 1000	33.3 per 1000	7.2 per 1000
Daily Newspapers			48 per 1000
Passenger Cars		34,300	1,000
Energy Total Billion Kec		0.008	0.012
Energy per Capita Kec		121	239
Kec per $ of GNP		0.36	3.05
Electric Capacity Kw		4,300	1,700
Generation Billion Kwhr		0.006	
Kilowatt Hours per Capita		93	
Kwhr per $ of GNP		0.40	
Economic Density GNP $/Sq Km	3,060	18,000	8,000

349

	SIKKIM	SOUTHERN YEMEN	SPANISH SAHARA
Map	Asia & Middle East	Asia & Middle East	Africa
Capital	Gangtok	Aden	El Aaiun
One US $ =	7.553 Rupee	.4182 Donar	69.73 Peseta
Area-Total	7,107 Sq Km	287,683 Sq Km	266,000 Sq Km
Area-Arable		2,520 Sq Km	2 Sq Km
Population	191,000	1,220,000	48,000
Population Density	26 per Sq Km	4.07 per Sq Km	0.17 per Sq Km
Population Rate of Increase	1.90%	2.30%	2.30%
1967 GNP per Capita	60 US $	130 US $	210 US $
Hospital Beds		1.0 per 1000	5.0 per 1000
Telephones		9,110	
Television Sets		20,000	
Passenger Cars		9,000	2,200
Growth Pattern Index		12.50%	
GNP/Capita Annual Increase 67-90		1.40%	
Energy Total Billion Kec		0.512	
Energy per Capita Kec		428	
Kec per $ of GNP		15.60	
Electric Capacity Kw		82,700	3,430
Generation Billion Kwhr		0.178	
Kilowatt Hours per Capita		148	
Kwhr per $ of GNP		7.01	
Economic Density GNP $/Sq Km	1,568	526	37

	SWAZILAND	TONGA	TRUST TER. PACIFIC ISL.
Map	Africa	Oceania	Oceania
Capital	Mbabane	Nuku' alofa	Saipan
One US $ =	0.718 Rand	0.87 Dollar	1 Dollar
Area-Total Area-Arable	17,363 Sq Km 2,540 Sq Km	699 Sq Km 550 Sq Km	1,799 Sq Km
Population Population Density	410,000 22 per Sq Km	83,000 113 per Sq Km	95,000 52 per Sq Km
Population Rate of Increase	2.90%	3.30%	2.70%
1967 GNP per Capita	280 US $	310 US $	260 US $
H L Students Hospital Beds	18 per 100000 3.5 per 1000	2.9 per 1000	
Telephones	4,461	895	
Investment Ratio	22%		
GNP/Capita Annual Increase 67-90	5.90%		
Electric Capacity Kw		1,900	
Economic Density GNP $/Sq Km	6,220	34,280	13,500

	WEST IRIAN	**WESTERN SAMOA**
Map	Oceania	Oceania
Capital	Djajapura	Apia
One US $ =	378 Rupiah	0.7143 Tala
Area-Total Area-Arable	412,781 Sq Km	2,842 Sq Km 900 Sq Km
Population Population Density	815,000 2.12 per Sq Km	141,000 47 per Sq Km
Population Rate of Increase	2.60%	2.70%
1967 GNP per Capita	50 US $	130 US $
H L Students Hospital Beds		16 per 100000 4.2 per 1000
Telephones		1,800
Energy Total Billion Kec	0.052	0.014
Energy per Capita Kec	58	104
Kec per $ of GNP	1.24	0.73
Electric Capacity Kw		5,800
Generation Billion Kwhr	0.012	0.009
Kilowatt Hours per Capita	13	65
Kwhr per $ of GNP	0.28	0.45
Economic Density GNP $/Sq Km	107	704

CHAPTER THIRTEEN

Maps

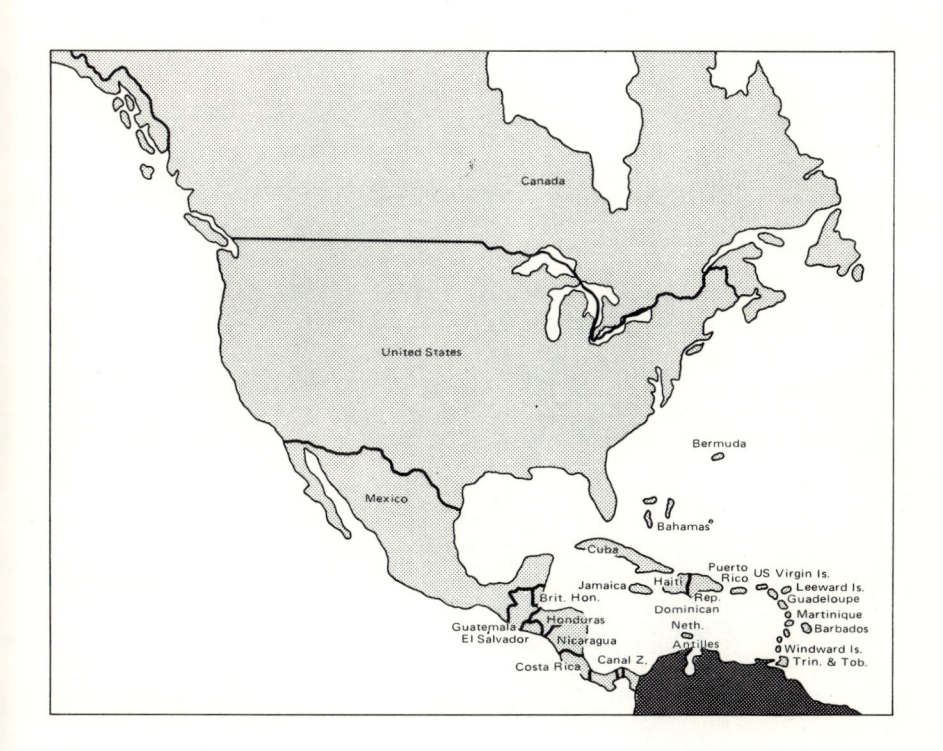

MAP II

MAP III

World Markets of Tomorrow

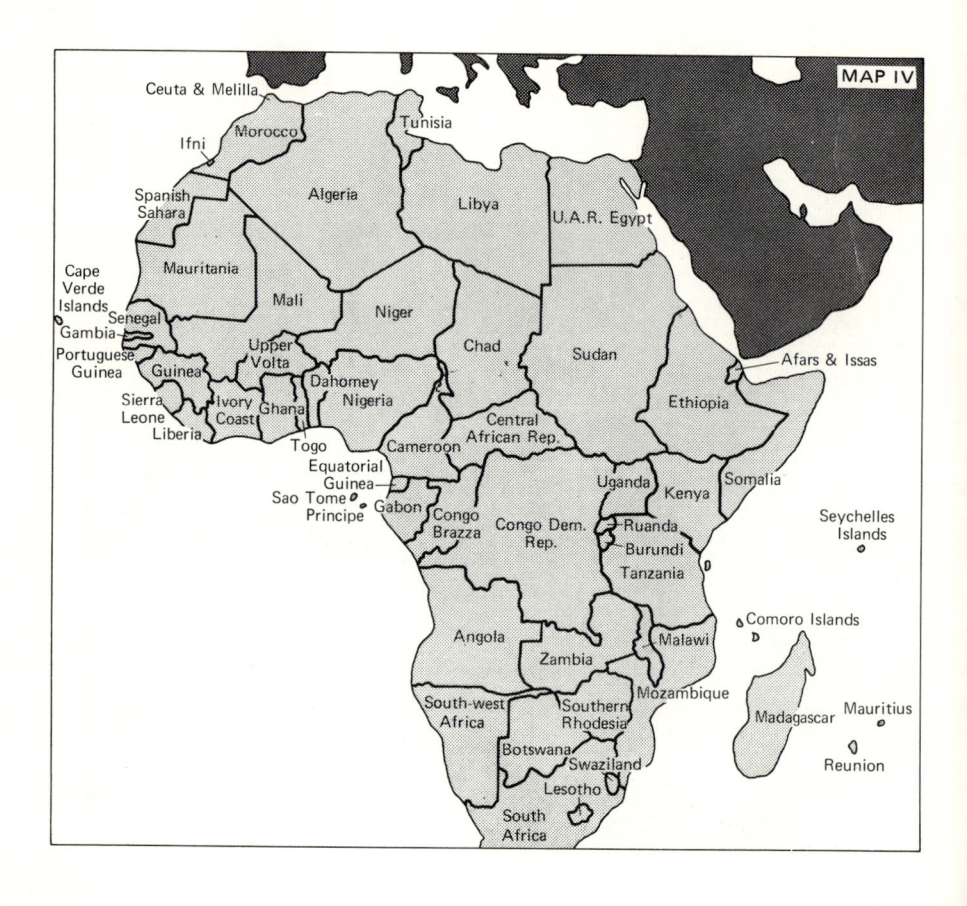

MAP IV

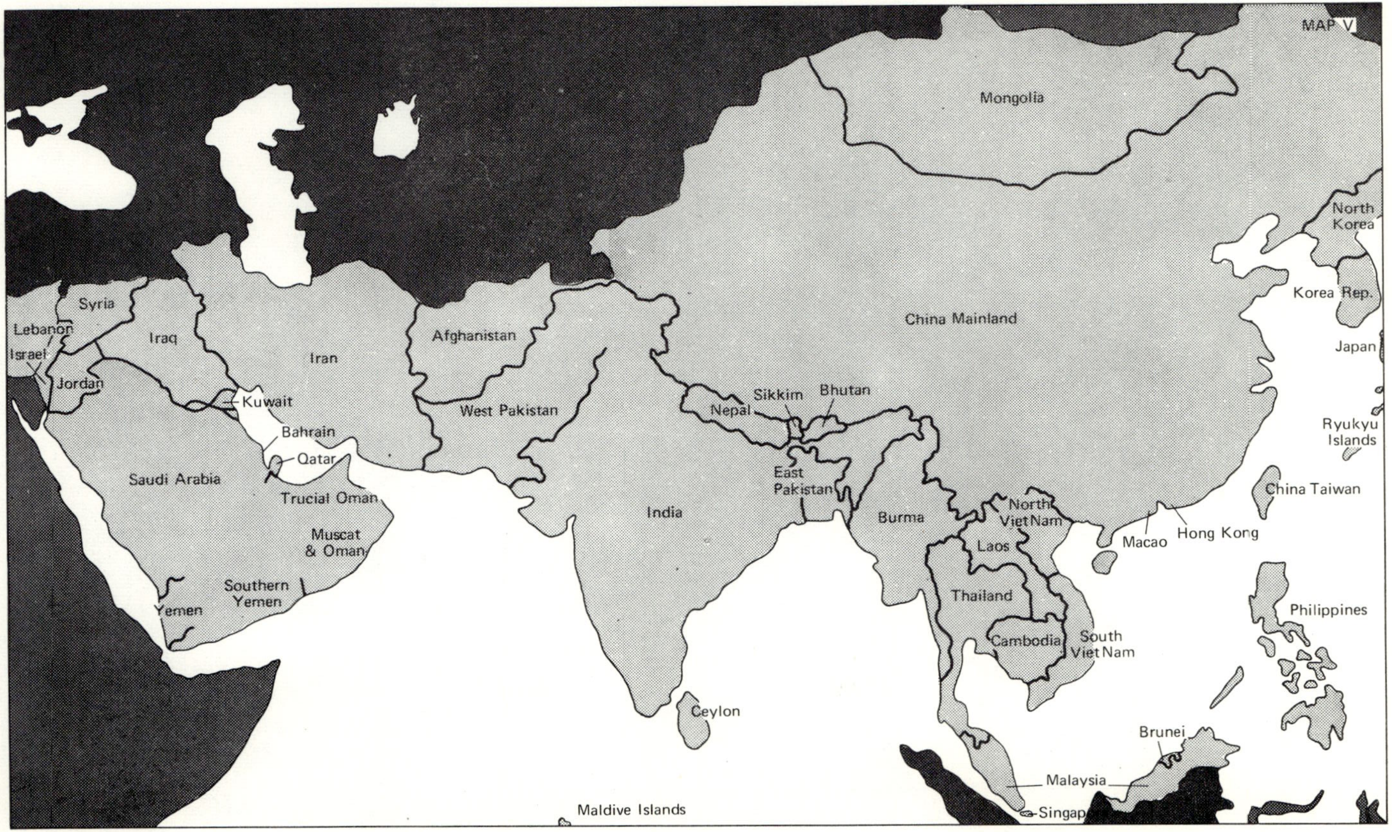
MAP V
Mongolia
China Mainland
North Korea
Korea Rep.
Japan
Ryukyu Islands
China Taiwan
Hong Kong
Macao
Philippines
Syria
Lebanon
Israel
Jordan
Iraq
Iran
Kuwait
Bahrain
Qatar
Saudi Arabia
Trucial Oman
Muscat & Oman
Southern Yemen
Yemen
Afghanistan
West Pakistan
Nepal
Sikkim
Bhutan
East Pakistan
India
Ceylon
Maldive Islands
Burma
North Viet Nam
Laos
Thailand
Cambodia
South Viet Nam
Brunei
Malaysia
Singap

World Markets of Tomorrow

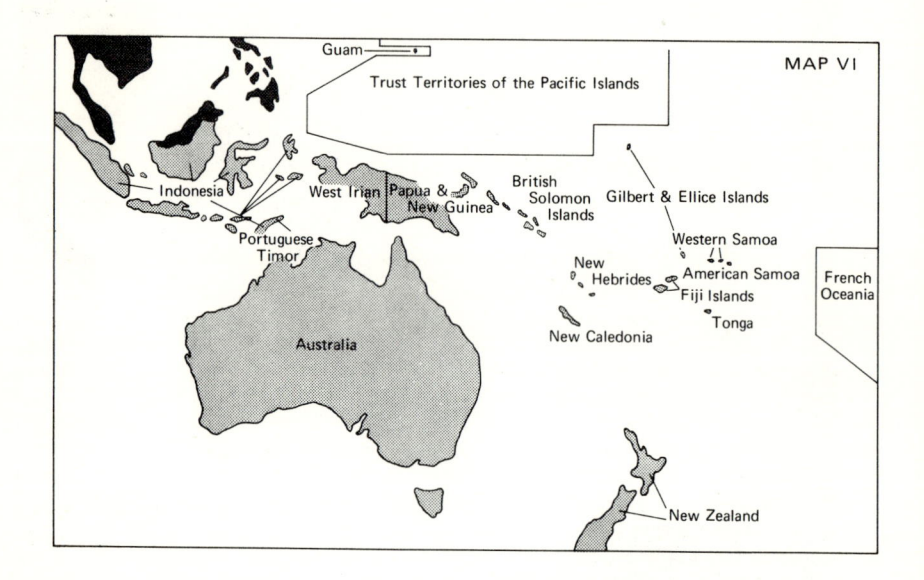

MAP VI

Guam
Trust Territories of the Pacific Islands
Indonesia
West Irian
Papua & New Guinea
Portuguese Timor
British Solomon Islands
Gilbert & Ellice Islands
Western Samoa
New Hebrides
American Samoa
Fiji Islands
New Caledonia
Tonga
French Oceania
Australia
New Zealand

CHAPTER FOURTEEN

Complementary Notes

USE OF SEMI-LOGARITHMIC AND LOG-LOG SCALE PAPER FOR CHARTS

Many of the readers are undoubtedly familiar with the semi-logarithmic (or proportional scale) of which considerable use is made throughout this volume, because it gives exactly the same accuracy over a wide range of figures.

Moreover, since, with such a scale, the slope of the curve gives a direct measure of the rate of growth, such charts have the advantage of providing a true image of fundamental trends.

It is easy to alarm a non-technical reader by showing him the growth of electric power in the United States portrayed with an arithmetic scale. The same growth plotted on a semi-logarithmic scale clearly shows that no environmental or economic nightmare is likely to develop.

When showing a relationship such as Number of Automobiles in Use *v.* Gross National Product, where both the horizontal scale and the vertical scale vary over a wide range, double logarithmic, also called log-log, scale is used.

The reader will not fail to note that, with either the semi-logarithmic or the log-log scale, there is no more crowding at the one end of the scale than at the other. It is indeed a most impartial way of giving equal representation to all countries.

USE OF EXCHANGE RATES TO DERIVE GNP 'PER CAPITA' IN US $ EQUIVALENTS (5)

The figures of GNP *per capita* in U.S. dollars have been converted from the national currency estimates on the basis of exchange rates.

It should be pointed out that the use of exchange rates for this purpose may result in some overstatement of differences in GNP among countries, especially as between those in the highest and lowest income categories. The reason for this lies primarily in the divergent price and product structures of different countries.

Exchange rates equate at best the prices of internationally traded goods and services, which in many countries form the large bulk of the total national product.

Specifically, the prices of agricultural products and of services in developing countries are in most cases considerable lower, relative to industrial prices, than in more developed countries.

Moreover, agricultural output generally accounts for the larger part of the overall national product in developing countries, while the opposite is true of developed countries. As a result, the internal purchasing power of the currency of a low income country will generally be greater than indicated by the exchange rate.

The use of exchange rates for converting national currency estimates into U.S. dollar equivalents is further complicated by the fact that the official par value rates do not always constitute equilibrium rates. Countries experiencing substantial inflations frequently maintain pegged exchange rates over long periods, so that a straight conversion on the basis of the overvalued rates would overstate both the absolute level of the GNP in terms of U.S. dollars and its increase over time.

Special problems arise with regard to the estimates for the centrally planned (socialist) economies. The national accounts for these countries are compiled originally in terms of 'net material product' and adjustments have to be made in order to derive approximate estimates of GNP.

There is also the problem of selecting an appropriate exchange rate for conversion of the national currency estimates into U.S. dollars, since the 'basic' rates maintained by these countries are frequently far removed from hypothetical 'equilibrium' rates.

Finally, the indications are that, in the absence of market conditions, the internal cost and price relationship in these countries are even more than usually out of line with international prices. Special caution needs to be exercised therefore, in using the figures for these countries.

GROSS DOMESTIC PRODUCT AND OTHER AGGREGATES AS RELATED TO GROSS NATIONAL PRODUCT

Consistent and reliable Gross National Product data at Market (current) Prices and at Constant Prices was available for most of the countries for which economic growth has been projected. For the Eastern European countries, only Gross Domestic Product data was available. For this aggregate as well as for others, the definitions are given here:

Gross National Product (GNP) = Gross Domestic Product (GDP) plus Net Factor Income from Abroad

GDP less indirect taxes net of subsidies = GDP at Factor Cost

GDP at Factor Cost less Depreciation = National Domestic Product (NDP) at Factor Cost

NDP plus Net Factor Income from abroad = National Income

GROSS DOMESTIC FIXED CAPITAL FORMATION

Gross Domestic Fixed Capital Formation is the sum of the expenditure incurred on:

1. *Fixed Capital Formation*, which consists of:

    Land, which is defined as including inland waters but as excluding building on sites. Land reclamation is included if it represents an addition to land availability.

    Dwellings, including expenditures on all permanent fixtures but excluding the value of the land before improvement.

Complementary Notes 361

Non-residential buildings (all buildings other than dwellings) includes: industrial buildings, warehouses, office buildings, stores, restaurants, hotels, farm buildings and buildings for religious, educational and similar purposes. Movable equipment which is not part of the structure is not included.

Other construction and works: New construction and major alterations and repairs. Permanent ways of railroads, subways, marine construction, piers and other harbor facilities, car parking facilities, airports, athletic fields, roads, streets and sewers, electricity transmission lines, gas mains and pipes and communication systems such as telephone and telegraph lines. Large expenditure by farmers for irrigation projects, flood control, forest clearance, land reclamation resulting from flood, should be included.

Transport equipment: Ships, motorcars and aircraft for commercial use, trucks and commercial vehicles, tractors for road haulage, vehicles used for public transport systems, railway and tramway rolling stock, carts and wagons.

Machinery and other equipment: All capital expenditures not included in the above groups. This includes power-generating machinery, agricultural machinery and implements, tractors (others than for road haulage), office machinery, mining, construction and other industrial machinery and equipment and instruments used by professional persons.

2. *Increase in Stocks*

The value of the physical change in raw materials, work in progress—other than work in progress on dwellings and non-residential buildings which is included in fixed capital formation—and finished goods which are held by enterprises and in government stockpiles.

The following tabulates explicitly the items included and those excluded:

ITEMS INCLUDED	ITEMS EXCLUDED
Value of purchases by Enterprises	Expenditure of a capital nature by general government for defence is treated as general government consumption expenditure
Own-account construction of fixed assets: Civilian construction and works machinery and equipment, by enterprises	
All expenses directly related to the acquisition of capital goods, such as: transportation and installation charges, fees for engineering, architectural, legal and other services	Expenditure by households on durable goods other than new dwellings is treated as private consumption expenditure
Expenditures on irrigation projects, flood control, forest clearance, land reclamation and improvements, etc.	Indirect expenditures related to the acquisition of capital goods, including flotation costs, commissions and other financing costs are regarded as current expenditure
Expenditures on repairs over and above what is needed to keep the capital goods in the state of continuous working condition	The value of newly discovered mineral deposits and other natural resources
Transfer costs involved in the purchase of used domestic assets, including transportation costs, legal fees, installation expenses	Normal repairs & maintenance are treated as current expenditures
Changes in work in progress on dwellings and non-residential buildings	

Agriculture and Fisheries, Mining & Quarrying, Manufacturing, Construction, Transportation, Storage and Communication, Wholesale and Retail Trade, Banking Institutions, Ownership of Dwellings, Public Administration and Services are the National Accounts Headings under which the United Nations compile Gross Fixed Capital Formation.

Bibliography

1. *United Nations Yearbook of National Accounts Statistics, 1969.* Vol. I: Individual Country Data, Vol. II: International Tables.
2. *United Nations Statistical Yearbook, 1969.*
3. *United Nations Monthly Bulletin of Statistics.*
4. United Nations Statistical Papers, series J1 through J13 (1964-1968), of World Energy Supplies.
5. *World Bank Atlas*, Population, Per Capita Product and Growth Rates, International Bank for Reconstruction and Development 1970.
6. World Economic Growth-Tasks for the 1970's. National Industrial Conference Board, Inc. for the International Industrial Conference, San Francisco, September 1969.
7. *The Year 2000*, Herman Kahn & Anthony Wiener, The MacMillan Co.
8. *The Sources of Growth in the United States*, Edward F. Denison, Committee for Economic Development, New York, 1962.
   Why Growth Rates Differ. Experience in Nine Western Countries, Edward F. Denison, The Brookings Institution, Washington, 1967.
9. 'Le Progres Technique—Une Illusion Comptable?' Francois Hetman, *Analyse & Prevision*, March 1970.
10. "Material Resources" Richard L. Meier, From *Mankind 2000*, Oslo Universitetsforlagst & London, Allen & Unwin.
11. 'Who is Aiding Whom?' Stuart H. Van Dyke, *Columbia Journal of World Business*, Vol. 2, March-April 1970.
12. *Overseas Development—The Coming Challenge*, R. B. M. King, Moorgate and Wall Street, Hill Samuel & Co. Ltd. Pages 73-84, Spring 1970.
13. 'Le Theme de l'Environnement', Bertrand de Jouvenel, *Analyse & Prevision*, September 1970.
14. 'Growth of Energy Consumption and National Income throughout the World', Fremont Felix, American Power Conference, Chicago, Illinois, April 15, 1964, and I.E.E.E. Spectrum, July 1964.
15. 'Analysis of Recorded Use and Growth of Energy and Electricity and Improved Methods of Forecasting Future Demands for All Countries of the World' Fremont Felix, World Power Conference Tokyo Sectional Meeting, 16-20 October 1966.
16. *UNESCO Statistical Year Book—1968.*
17. *FAO Production Year Book—1969.*
18. 'Turning junk and trash into a resource', *Business Week*, October 10 1970.
19. 'Background Notes on the Countries of the World', Bureau of Public Affairs, Department of State, Superintendent of Documents, U.S. Government Printing Office, Washington, D.C.
20. 'Annual Growth Rate on Downward Trend', Fremont Felix, *Electrical World*, July 6, 1970.
21. 'Energy Use: Basic to Economic Growth', Fremont Felix, *Electrical World* January 15, 1971.

22. 'Energy for Tomorrow', Wilfrid E. Johnson, Commissioner, United States Atomic Energy Commission, Keynote address before the Fifth Intersociety Conversion Energy Conference, Las Vegas, Nevada, September 22, 1970.
23. 'Civil Engineering—The Ideal Profession', Dr. Ellis L. Armstrong, Commissioner, Bureau of Reclamation, Department of the Interior, The Transit of Chi Epsilon, the National Civil Engineering Honorary, V41, N.Y.
24. 'Change and Development: The Great Task for Latin America', Dr. Paul Prebisch, Director of the Latin American Institute for Economic and Social Planning. April 23, 1970 meeting of the Board of Governors of the Inter-American Development Bank.
25. 'International Directory of Electricity Suppliers', *Electrical World*, McGraw-Hill Inc., New York, N.Y.
26. 'Is Overpopulation Really the Problem?' Herman P. Miller, Chief Population Division of the Bureau of the Census, *The Conference Board Record*, May 1970.
27. 'Extrapolation Without Reason', Gordon B. Carson, The Bent of Tau Beta Pi, December 1970.
28. *'A Report Towards Balanced Growth: Quantity with Quality'* Page 23-24. United States Government Printing Office, Washington, D.C. 20402.
29. 'Environmental Problems of Energy Production and Utilization', Item 4 of the Provisional Agenda: 22 February-5 March 1971, Committee on Natural Resources. United Nations Economic and Social Council.
30. '1984 . . . Plus One', George H. Brown, Director, Bureau of the Census, U.S. Department of Commerce, *The Conference Board Record*, December 1970.
31. 'Measuring Raw Material Needs to the Year 2000', George H. Blackett, President, The Institute for Interindustry Data, New York, N.Y. *The Conference Board Record*, January 1971.
32. 'The Determinants of Economic Growth', P. D. Henderson, *Economic Growth in Britain*, London 1966.
33. 'Industrialization, Employment and Urbanisation', Helen Hughes, *Finance and Development*, March 1971.
34. 'Nuclear Power: 1971', Remarks by James T. Ramey, Commissioner U.S. Atomic Energy Commission, San Francisco Electric Club, March 15, 1971.
35. 'Technology and Society—A Challenge to Private Enterprise', Congress Theme, XXIIIrd-Congress of the International Chamber of Commerce, Vienna, 17 April 1971.